S0-BAN-161

THE FATHERS
OF THE CHURCH

A NEW TRANSLATION

VOLUME 33

THE FATHERS
OF THE CHURCH

A NEW TRANSLATION

† ROY JOSEPH DEFERRARI
Editorial Director Emeritus

EDITORIAL BOARD

BERNARD M. PEEBLES
The Catholic University of America
Editorial Director

PAUL J. MORIN
The Catholic University of America
Managing Editor

ROBERT P. RUSSELL, O.S.A.
Villanova University

THOMAS P. HALTON
The Catholic University of America

†MARTIN R. P. McGUIRE
The Catholic University of America

WILLIAM R. TONGUE
The Catholic University of America

HERMIGILD DRESSLER, O.F.M.
The Catholic University of America

SR. M. JOSEPHINE BRENNAN, I.H.M.
Marywood College

REDMOND A. BURKE, C.S.V.
The Catholic University of America

Chrysotomus, Joannes, Saint,
= Patriarch of Constantinople,
d. 407.

SAINT JOHN CHRYSOSTOM

COMMENTARY ON SAINT JOHN THE APOSTLE AND EVANGELIST

Homilies 1-47

Translated by

SISTER THOMAS AQUINAS GOGGIN, S.C.H.

THE CATHOLIC UNIVERSITY OF AMERICA PRESS
Washington, D.C. 20017

MIDDLEBURY COLLEGE LIBRARY

BR
60
F3 C4   8/1974
         Eng
V. 1

NIHIL OBSTAT:

JOHN A. GOODWINE

Censor Librorum

IMPRIMATUR:

✠ FRANCIS CARDINAL SPELLMAN

Archbishop of New York

November 13, 1956

Copyright © 1957 by

THE CATHOLIC UNIVERSITY OF AMERICA PRESS, INC.

All rights reserved

Reprinted with corrections 1969

Library of Congress Catalog Card No.: 57-1545

S.B.N. 8132-0033-4

CONTENTS

INTRODUCTION

OHN OF CONSTANTINOPLE his contemporaries called the great Chrysostom and left it to a later day—though one not far removed from his own—to coin the epithet by which he is known to posterity.[1] Endowed with a gift of truly golden eloquence, St. John lived in a milieu peculiarly adapted to foster the development of such a talent, and he was not one to bury his. Like the Gospel prototype, he multiplied it many times over by prudent use. But as in the case of many a gifted man, the extent of his greatness was really appreciated only after his days had ended on a minor chord.

St. John Chrysostom's life is one of the most completely documented of the lives of the fourth-century Church Fathers. Biographical sources[2] include reliable witnesses close to his own time, and some information may, of course, be obtained

---

1 The first authentic mention is found in a Latin writer, Facundus of Hermiane, about 547, and several other instances survive, showing its use later in that century. Universal acceptance of the surname dates only from the eighth century. Cf. Baur, *S. Jean Chrysostome et ses oeuvres,* 58-60.

2 For an exhaustive summary of the biographical sources, cf. Baur, *Der heilige Johannes Chrysostomus und seine Zeit,* I xi-xxvii.

from his own works.[3] Probably the most important ancient biographical source is the *Dialogus de vita Chrysostomi* written shortly after St. John's death by Palladius, Bishop of Hellenopolis, in about 408. With Plato's *Phaedo* as model, the bishop used the device of an imaginary conversation between an anonymous Eastern bishop and Theodore, a deacon. As a personal friend of the subject of his biography and an eyewitness of the events related, Palladius was in a position to give a story valuable for its wealth of detail, though some allowance must be made for possible bias.

The *Ecclesiastical Histories* of Sozomen, Socrates, and Theodoret are also ancient biographical sources for St. John, ranking as such in the order named. They must, however, be used with caution. Other potential sources of biographical data merit only rapid mention, since their authors are hagiographers rather than historians. Critical biographers in modern times have thoroughly explored, and assessed by scientific historical methods, this mass of biographical evidence. Their appraisal results in a simple but tragic tale which in brief outline is as follows.

In Antioch in Syria between 344 and 347 a *magister militum Orientis,* Secundus by name, and his young wife Anthusa became the parents of their second child, John. Shortly thereafter, Secundus died, leaving Anthusa to carry on by herself the difficult task of rearing and educating their son.[4] Later in life, St. John acknowledged gratefully how much he owed to his mother's devoted care. Deeply religious herself, she saw to it that he received thorough instruction in piety. She sent him to the best secular schools available in Antioch, where he followed the program of studies customary at the time and

---

3 An impressive number of Mss. of his works is extant. Bardy gives a summary in *DTC* 18 (1924) 669-672; cf. Baur, *S. Jean . . .,* 28-32.
4 Their elder daughter died in her youth.

had very able teachers, among them the well-known Libanius. Throughout these formative years the boy seems to have shown himself co-operative and receptive.

Though he was brought up as a Christian, John was not baptized until about 369. Such deferment of baptism was the common custom during the second half of the fourth century, even among the very pious. Meletius, Bishop of Antioch, who baptized him, had an important influence on him at this period when his religious education, begun under Anthusa, was completed. The teaching of Meletius was supplemented by that of a remarkable man of learning, Diodorus, one of the directors of the religious school which the young John attended at this time.

Under his guidance John began to withdraw from the pursuit of classical and profane studies and to apply himself more and more to the study of Scripture,[5] living all the while an ascetic and religious life. It was Diodorus who founded the exegetical school of Antioch, which was less preoccupied with allegory than the school of Alexandria was, and more inclined to accept the literal or historical sense of Scripture. It is this spirit which inspired St. John Chrysostom in his commentaries on the Gospel of St. John as found in the *Homilies* in the present volume, and which adds greatly to the interest and efficacy of his exegesis. Unlike a fellow student, Theodore, later Bishop of Mopsuestia, who afterward fell into heresy,[6] St. John applied with prudence and moderation the principles taught by Diodorus.

After his baptism St. John entered one of the ascetic societies near Antioch, and several years later felt drawn to live the

---

5 Like other educated churchmen of the day—e.g., Basil, Jerome, Augustine—St. John Chrysostom concluded that for Christians the pursuit of pagan learning ought to be tolerated only in so far as it would prepare them to be able to defend and propagate their faith.

6 He became the father of the Nestorian heresy. Cf. Attwater, *St. John Chrysostom,* p. 16 note.

life of an anchorite in one of the caves near that city.[7] At the
end of two years, however, indiscretion in the matter of fasting and austerities so impaired his health that he was forced to
return to Antioch to recuperate his strength. There he once
more took up his duties as lector. It seems safe to suppose that
his earliest literary works were already completed by this time,
since nearly all of them deal with monastic and ascetic
subjects.[8]

The chronology of the early part of the Antiochene period of
his life is uncertain, but it was probably at about 381 that
Meletius made him deacon. His life up to this time had been
rather tranquil, for he was not as yet actively involved in the
turbulent warring of heretical factions. With the beginning of
his active ministry, however, he began to feel the pull of
the current.

Bishop Meletius died at Constantinople in 381, while presid-
ing over the Second Ecumenical Council, and the aged
Flavian succeeded to the see of Antioch. In 386 the latter
ordained John priest and from that year his importance to
the Church historian begins. As deacon he had been engaged
in assisting with liturgical functions, in caring for the sick and
the poor, and in the instruction of catechumens. His literary
labors did not cease; perhaps the most famous of his works,
The Priesthood, seems to have been composed at about
this time.

Flavian, because of his own advanced age, felt unable to
discharge his episcopal duty of instructing his flock by preaching. Hence he was glad to avail himself of the services of the
talented John. For the next twelve years the principal occupa-

---

7 In his treatise, *The Priesthood,* he tells of a strange episode wherein
at this time he escaped with difficulty having the episcopacy forced
on him. In writing this work St. John seems to have been influenced
by the *Apologia* of St. Gregory Nazianzen to such an extent that it is
doubtful whether all the details ought to be accepted literally.

8 These earliest compositions were written, by contrast with his later
productions which were, for the most part, oral.

tion of the latter was preaching. The historian Socrates says that he was the first to preach from the deacon's ambo rather than from the altar, so that he might be closer to his audience. Every Sunday found him here, and at certain seasons of the year, especially during Lent, he preached almost every day.

Occasionally, unusual events occurred to provide him with material for the display of passionate and dramatic eloquence. The most famous of these was the sedition of Antioch in 387 when indignation and discontent at the imposition of a special tax by Emperor Theodosius I flared up and resulted in mob violence and the crowd destroyed a number of statues of various members of the imperial family, including that of the emperor himself.

A period of trepidation and suspense followed. Lent passed slowly by while they awaited the return of Archbishop Flavian, who had gone to Constantinople, at great cost to himself, to intercede in behalf of his people. In the interval St. John Chrysostom delivered a series of twenty vigorous sermons, consoling, calming, admonishing—and ingeniously making use of the episode as a point of departure from which to develop the theme of repentance. When the bishop finally returned with the emperor's pardon, St. John's efforts had resulted not only in keeping his troubled flock in check, but also in giving a tremendous impetus to his own prestige. He seems, besides, to have become fully awakened to his own powers as an orator and the most fruitful period of his preaching followed.

It was during this time, about 390, that he delivered the series of eighty-eight homilies forming a commentary on the Gospel of St. John, forty-seven of which form the contents of this volume. It appears that the pastor was now more closely in rapport with his flock, and he seemed more at his ease. Starting with commentary on consecutive passages of the Scripture, he went on to give eloquent, yet practical, moral instruction. Besides the homilies on the fourth Gospel, he also delivered during this period ninety homilies on the Gospel of St. Matthew, thirty-two homilies on the Epistle to the Romans, and others.

The populace of Antioch became very much attached to their brilliant preacher, and in the ordinary course of events he would have succeeded Flavian as bishop. However, Nectarius, Bishop of Constantinople, died in 397, and intrigue was immediately active over the vacant see. After several months of both open and secret rivalry, Emperor Arcadius, at the suggestion of his minister Eutropius, summoned John of Antioch to Constantinople as a compromise candidate. He was brought from the scene of his labors by a ruse, and early in 398 was consecrated Bishop of Constantinople.

This metropolis, with its scarcely assimilated Western and Oriental elements, and saddled with a court noted for its luxury and intrigue, was a far cry from Antioch, however turbulent and confused the latter might at times have seemed. But St. John now had complete authority to effect reform where he saw fit. The courage and directness of his attack won him eventually the lasting enmity of those in high places. The clergy were especially antagonized when he stripped the episcopal residence of all the adjuncts of luxurious living, attacked the greed and selfishness of certain of their number, combated the dangerous abuse practiced by some clerics of keeping 'spiritual sisters' in their houses, contrary to the express prohibition of the Council of Nicaea, and so organized ecclesiastical charity as to preclude waste or misdirection of alms.

Though he could not preach as regularly or as often as in Antioch, he was able to continue to espouse the cause of the poor and to attack greed and selfishness where it existed among the wealthy. As in Antioch, he condemned the vanity and extravagance of women and the preoccupation of so many with vicious and degrading forms of entertainment. As a result, some of his flock, both rich and poor, felt a passionate devotion to their bishop, but many others viewed his efforts with ill-disguised hostility.

At first, he had only esteem and admiration from Empress Eudoxia. However, a series of incidents began which implicated him in events of the highest political importance. At the beginning of 399, Eutropius fell from favor and upon seeking sanctuary in a church—though he had himself tried to do away with immunity of ecclesiastical asylum—was saved for a time by the intervention of St. John. Then, mistrusting the power of this protection, he fled, was seized, exiled, and later put to death. Thereupon, the Bishop of Constantinople took occasion to deliver two powerful homilies on the 'vanity of vanities' and the power of the Church. By these he deeply wounded some of his hearers and inspired considerable hatred.

A second episode was his successful opposition to the overbearing demands of the Arian Goth, Gainas. His prudence and strength of character greatly added to his prestige, but also aroused feelings of jealousy and bitterness.

He also had the courage to admonish the empress for an act of injustice to a poor widow, so that he began to fall from favor in that quarter at a time when Eudoxia, because of the eclipse of Eutropius, was at the height of her power. The situation was aggravated when she was told that in a sermon against the vain extravagance of women the bishop was pointing the finger deliberately at her.

Ecclesiastical intrigue, fomented during his unavoidable absence from his see, then laid the groundwork for his final downfall. Through the machinations of Theophilus, Patriarch of Alexandria, St. John was first accused of a list of ridiculous allegations and then by the so-called Synod of the Oak was declared to be deposed.

He was to have been exiled, but the empress, fearful because of the angry threats of the populace and the occurrence of a sudden accident in her palace, gave orders for him to be recalled. Though somewhat hesitant, St. John returned, to the joy of many of his flock.

Several months later, because of a fancied slight, Eudoxia once again set in motion the machinery necessary to maneuver his deposition and exile. Arcadius signed a new decree of exile and on June 24, 404, St. John was once more placed under military escort and conducted to Cucusus in the furthest confines of Armenia, a rugged and lonely spot. His letters—some 238 of which are extant—to friends and others, picture vividly the discomforts of the journey and the hardships of the place.

Emperor Honorius and Pope Innocent I, on learning of the circumstances of his deposition, attempted to assemble a new synod, but their legates were thrown into prison and later sent home. The Pope thereupon broke off all communion with the patriarchs of Alexandria, Antioch, and Constantinople, the chief recalcitrants. St. John still had a large number of faithful friends and supporters and so it did not seem to his enemies that he was far enough away from Constantinople. Hence, during the summer of 407 his guards were directed to transfer him to Pithyus, near the Caucasus.

The exiled bishop was required to set out on the long and difficult journey in company with two guards who were told to proceed with all possible speed. They obeyed instructions to the letter, though it meant the greatest hardship for their captive. At length, toward the middle of September the little party arrived in the vicinity of Comana in Pontus, after a journey of some 400 miles, still at a great distance from their final destination. On the morning of September 14, though St. John was so fatigued as to be scarcely able to move, his custodians insisted on starting out with him, but after a brief interval he became very ill and they had to return to the martyrion where they had spent the previous night. There, after receiving Communion, he died.

The eighty-eight[9] homilies comprising the *Commentary on the Gospel of St. John* were preached at Antioch about 390. Internal evidence indicates that, as a rule, they were delivered in a church and in the early morning.[10] The term 'homily' is used to denote an informal discourse usually explaining or commenting on a passage of Scripture. The Homilies on the Gospel of St. John, follow a definite pattern, the outline of which may be quite readily discerned. Each homily begins with a brief, rather formal, and often quite stylized, introduction. This is followed by the explanation of or commentary upon one or more verses. Then comes a moral exhortation, usually centering around a single virtue (or its opposite vice), and often suggested by the text of the day. The conclusion is invariably a short prayer ending in a fervent doxology, made up of stereotyped phrases, though not always identical in each case.

Not only is a careful plan followed in the individual homily, but the group as a whole is unified. The preacher follows the sequence of the Gospel texts without deviation, except for frequent repetition of the texts of the day for the sake of emphasis. It also may be noted that these homilies have a distinctive feature in that they are more controversial in tone than those on the Gospel of St. Matthew, the Acts, or the Epistles of St. Paul. In his exegesis of texts that have been the object of heretical attack by Arians of various degrees of heterodoxy—especially the Anomeans—or others, he includes their arguments, placing them on the lips of an imaginary

---

9 This is the more commonly accepted number. But some editions follow the numeration of Morellus, who regards *Homily 1* as a mere introduction, since it is not based on any text of St. John's Gospel. In that case, *Homily 2* is called *Homily 1*, etc., and the last homily will therefore be number 87. However, the first homily has the same pattern as the others and is an integral part of the series, so it seems more logical to call it *Homily 1*. This numeration has been followed in the present translation.

10 Cf. Homily 23, p. 222; Homily 31, p. 310.

objector or heckler. Then he proceeds with summary skill to
refute them, often using the device of a dialogue.

St. John's method of exegesis followed that of the school
of Antioch where he pursued his Scriptural studies. At
Antioch, the literal or historical interpretation of Scripture
was favored in preference to the allegorical meaning as advocated by the school of Alexandria. The Antiochenes, without
ruthlessly proscribing allegory, gently relegated it to the
background and taught that the historic sense of the Scriptures
must not be lost sight of.

In the homilies the deep reverence which the saint felt for
Scripture is everywhere apparent and he frequently referred
to the care which all must exercise in its study. There is every
evidence that he himself was thoroughly acquainted with both
the Old and New Testaments. Numerous and apt quotations
abound, in particular from the Epistles of St. Paul, for whom
he seems to have felt the greatest regard. He forged weapons
against heretical teachings from his exegesis, but he was not
primarily the exegete and aimed to teach practical morality
rather than to spin out theoretical knowledge. He was quick
to point out such moral lessons as resulted from the text—to
such an extent as sometimes to disappoint the reader when, in
the very process of making exalted reflections by way of
commentary on a passage, he suddenly breaks off to develop
some rather trite and homely moral.

On the other hand, these exhortations regarding morals
provide a great deal of interesting information about fourth-
century life and times. We hear much of the rich and the
poor, the theatre, the games, the schools, the church, the
home, the family; in fact, there is scarcely a phase of human
living upon which he did not touch. In Homily 23 he declared
that he deliberately made his exhortations touch on such a
variety of topics for 'I fear that, if my words are concerned

about one thing only, I may, all unaware, be treating one illness while you are struggling with others.'

A large part of his audience, as a matter of fact, found its chief attraction, not in the refinements of doctrine and morals, but in impassioned flights of rhetoric. It delighted in all the subtleties and tricks, the gestures and intonations, the figures of sound and meaning which were part of the traditional stock in trade of the sophists who then had such great popular appeal as public speakers. St. John Chrysostom's eloquence is in striking contrast to theirs, for it owes its golden quality to the sincerity and depth of its meaning, expressed as it is in the crystalline clarity of language that betrays careful training in the principles of Atticism.

Nevertheless, however gifted as orator, St. John Chrysostom was pre-eminently the teacher, and not infrequently he made sage observations on methods of teaching.[11] He spoke of the advisability of imparting new knowledge a little at a time, which explained his very gradual unfolding of St. John's Gospel in the homilies.[12] He was clearly aware of the truth of the old principle: *'Repetitio mater studiorum,'* for he repeated the same texts many times in the same homily. Probably another motive for this was the desire to increase the familiarity of his listeners with Scripture and thus compensate for the lack of multiple copies and the prevailing lack of literacy.

Many of the homilies are lengthy, and would require more than an hour for delivery.[13] Even the shorter ones would seem long to a modern audience. His frequent comments on the inattentiveness or very evident boredom of his congregation seem to indicate that he did not always have before him

11 Cf. Homily 30, p. 293.
12 Cf. Homily 4, p. 43.
13 This is in marked contrast to St. Augustine.

the most eager and attentive of audiences.[14] In one instance he declared his intention of continuing to preach even if he should end with no listeners. At least he would be earning heavenly merit for himself by his fidelity to duty, a reward all the greater for the fact that he was receiving none of it in this life.[15]

Almost from the time of his death St. John Chrysostom was regarded by both East and West not only as an outstanding preacher and exegete, but as an authoritative voice in matters of faith. Strangely enough, both the orthodox and the heterodox have wished to claim him, beginning as early as Pelagius, only eight years after his death. Yet, in no case where he is cited can anything positive against the true faith be found, and at the Council of Chalcedon in 451 he was pronounced a Doctor of the Universal Church.

Certain passages referring to the Blessed Virgin have been a source of difficulty, since St. John at times implies in her regard human imperfections which, while not sinful, might seem to derogate from the perfection which is associated with her fullness of grace.[16] However, these passages must be interpreted in the light of the age in which they were written. It should not be surprising that, at a time when the divinity of the Son was seriously and widely held in question, there might be some obscurity, in the minds of even her devout clients, about the prerogatives of His Mother.[17] But in no instance does he impute to her anything more serious than the infir-

---

14 Christian towns in the fourth century were not divided into parishes, each with a separate group of clergy. Thus, St. John preached by turns in the different churches, and to all members of the community without distinction.

15 Cf. Homily 30, p. 295.

16 Cf. Homily 21 n. 12; also, John Henry Cardinal Newman, *Certain Difficulties Felt by Anglicans in Catholic Teaching* II 130-152, where the subject of St. John Chrysostom's references to our Lady are discussed in some detail.

17 Cf. Attwater, *op. cit.* 4

mities of human nature, and, much more frequently, he explicitly speaks in her praise.

An impressive list of translations of one or more of his works (made from the sixteenth to the twentieth centuries) into more than twenty languages has been compiled by Dom Baur.[18] The *Homilies on the Gospel of St. John* have been translated into English by G. T. Stupart in *A Library of the Fathers*, 2 pts. (Oxford 1848-1852). With a few additional notes, this translation was included in *A Select Library of the Nicene and Post-Nicene Fathers, Vol.* 14, ed. P. Schaff (New York 1890). The fact that this version was not fortified by a full knowledge of Catholicism curtails its usefulness in the case of a writer such as St. John. In the absence of an adequate critical edition, the text used hereunder is that given in the edition of the Benedictine Bernard de Montfaucon (Paris 1718-38) as reworked by Theobald Fix (Paris 1836-37).

Scriptural texts as quoted by St. John Chrysostom naturally differ somewhat from the Latin Vulgate; he was either using the Greek Septuagint and the Greek version of the New Testament or quoting from memory. In the present translation his Greek wording has been followed, but the effort has been made to use as far as possible the English of the Confraternity edition of the following: Genesis to Ruth inclusive, the Psalms, and the New Testament. For the remainder of the Old Testament the Challoner revision of the Rheims-Douay translation has been used wherever it corresponds to the Greek text of St. John Chrysostom.

Grateful acknowledgment is made of the generous assistance of Sister Mary Eileen, S.C.H., in her painstaking preparation of the typescript; and of the kind and always gracious services of Robert H. Haynes of the Widener Library of Harvard University.

---

18 Cf. Baur, *Der heilige* . . . I 139-222.

SELECT BIBLIOGRAPHY

Text:

St. John Chrysostom, *Opera Omnia* VIII, 2 Parts: *Commentarius in Sanctum Joannem Apostolum et Evangelistam*, ed. Bernard de Montfaucon (*ed. alt.* [T. Fix] Paris 1836-37). This re-edition of Montfaucon's text is reprinted in J. P. Migne, *Patrologia Graeca* 59 (Paris 1862). Cf. Paul W. Harkins, 'The Text Tradition of Chrysostom's Commentary on John,' *Theological Studies* 19 (1958) 405f.

Secondary Works:

T. E. Ameringer, O.F.M., *The Stylistic Influence of the Second Sophistic on the Panegyrical Sermons of St. John Chrysostom* (Washington 1921).

Donald Attwater, *St. John Chrysostom* (Milwaukee 1939).

Otto Bardenhewer, *Geschichte der altkirchlichen Literatur* (Freiburg i. B. 1912), III 324-365.

G. Bardy, 'Jean Chrysostome (Saint),' *DTC* 18 (1924) 660-690.

C. Baur, O.S.B., *S. Jean Chrysostome et ses oeuvres dans l'histoire littéraire* (Louvain 1907).

..................., *Der heilige Johannes Chrysostomus und seine Zeit*, 2 vols. (München 1929-1930).

A. Fliche et V. Martin, *Histoire de l'église depuis les origìnes jusqu'à nos jours* IV: *De la mort de Théodose a l'élection de Gregoire le Grand* (Paris 1937).

A. Merk, ed., *Novum Testamentum Graece et Latìne* (7th ed., Rome 1951).

Palladius, *Dialogue concerning the Life of Chrysostom*, trans. H. Moore (London 1921).

A. Puech, *St. Jean Chrysostome et les moeurs de son temps* (Paris 1891).

..................., *Saint Jean Chrysostome* (Paris 1900).

SAINT JOHN CHRYSOSTOM

COMMENTARY ON SAINT JOHN THE APOSTLE AND EVANGELIST

Homilies 1-47

Translated by

SISTER THOMAS AQUINAS GOGGIN, S.C.H., Ph.D.
Halifax, Nova Scotia

Homily 1

WHENEVER DEVOTEES of the pagan games learn that an outstanding athlete and winner of laurels has come from some place or other, they all flock to watch his efforts, observing his skill and all his strength. And you may see the entire audience of many thousands, all those present, straining the eyes of both body and mind in order not to miss anything of what is taking place.

So also, if some renowned musician should come for a visit, these same spectators again fill the theatre as before. Having put aside all immediate occupations, necessary and urgent though these often are, they go up and take their seats, and most eagerly listen to the songs and accompaniments, criticizing the harmony of both. Indeed, this is the practice of the majority of men. Further, some who are well versed in rhetoric behave in the same way with regard to sophists. For the latter also have shows and audiences, and applause, and clamor, and searching criticism of their words.[1]

Now, if both the spectators of athletes and the audiences of flute-players and sophists take their places with so much

---

1 Like other Fathers and Doctors of the early Church, St. John Chrysostom frequently mentions, and deplores, the attraction felt by his contemporaries for such forms of entertainment.

eagerness, how much attentiveness and eager interest you
ought rightly to display toward me, since it is not some flute-
player, nor even a sophist, who now comes forward to the
contest, but a man crying out from heaven and sending forth
a voice more sonorous than thunder. He has reached the whole
world, has taken possession of it and has filled it with his cry,
not by loudly lifting up his voice, but by uttering his words
with the aid of divine grace.

It is truly a wondrous thing that the sound, though so great,
is not harsh or discordant, but sweeter and more pleasing than
all musical harmony, and also more capable of soothing.
Besides all this, it is very holy, and most awful, and teeming
with such great mysteries, and productive of so many benefits,
that those who receive them with eagerness and preserve them
with care are no longer merely men. They do not even remain
upon the earth, but rise superior to everything belonging
to this life and change their state to that of the angels, so that
they dwell on earth as if in heaven.

It is the Son of Thunder,[2] the Beloved [disciple] of Christ,
the pillar of all the churches in the world, who now comes to
us. It is he who possesses the keys of heaven, who has drunk
the chalice of Christ, and has been baptized with His baptism,[3]
and who so confidently reclined on the breast of the Lord.[4] He
is not taking part in a play, or concealing his head by a mask
(for he will not discourse on topics suited to this). He is not
mounting the platform, or beating time on the stage floor
with his foot, nor is he decked out in golden raiment,[5] but he
enters clad in a garment of indescribable beauty. He appears
to us, having 'put on Christ,'[6] his beautiful 'feet shod with

---

2 Cf. Luke 9.54; Mark 3.17.
3 Cf. Mark 10.38,39.
4 Cf. John 13.23.
5 By contrast with the sophists of the day who made large use of
  artificial devices, such as exaggerated gestures, to compensate for the
  sterility of the topics on which they spoke.
6 Rom. 13.14; Gal. 3.27.

the readiness of the gospel of peace,'[7] wearing a girdle, not about his breast, but around his loins; a girdle, not fashioned of purple leather or coated with gold, but woven and composed of truth.

It is not as one playing a part that this man now appears to us, for there is no pretense in him, or make-believe, or legend, but with head uncovered he preaches the naked truth. He is not trying to persuade his listeners that he is something different from what he is, by means of his bearing, his glance, his voice. He does not need instruments such as the harp or lyre, or anything of the kind, to accompany his declaiming, but he effects everything by his speech alone, which is sweeter and produces a more beneficial sound than any harper or any music.

He has all heaven for his stage; for theatre, the world; for audience, all the angels, and also as many men as are already 'angels' or even desire to become so. For only these would have the ability to hear this harmony correctly, and to show it forth in their works, and to be the kind of listeners which the occasion demands. All the rest, like little children, listen without understanding what they hear, but are distracted by cakes and childish playthings. So also they who laugh, fare sumptuously, and live for wealth and power and sensuality, hear what is said, but give evidence of nothing great or noble in their works, because they have become completely preoccupied with brick-making and clay.[8]

The powers above stand by this Apostle, astounded at the beauty of his soul, and his understanding, and the bloom of his virtue, in consequence of which he attracted even Christ Himself and received the grace of the Spirit. Having prepared his soul as a golden-toned lyre, well-made and inlaid with precious stones, he brought it about that the Holy Spirit should send forth a great and sublime sound by its means.

---

7 Eph. 6.15.
8 I.e., worldly pursuits.

Accordingly, let us listen no longer as to the fisherman, the son of Zebedee, but as to the One who 'knows the deep things of God,'[9] I mean the Holy Spirit, as He strokes this lyre. In truth, he will speak nothing human to us, but will draw whatever he may say, from deep spiritual reserves, from those awesome mysteries which even the angels did not know, before they took place. They also have learned by the voice of John, along with us, and through us they have acquired knowledge of what we have learned. And another Apostle also has made this clear, saying: 'In order that the manifold wisdom of God may be made known to the principalities and powers through the Church.'[10] If, then, the principalities and powers and cherubim and seraphim have learned these things through the Church, it is evident that even they endeavored to listen very earnestly. Indeed, we have been honored not a little because the angels have learned in our company things which they did not know. (However, I postpone for awhile discussing the fact that they do learn through us.)

Let us, therefore, be very silent, and also of exemplary conduct, not only today, or on the day when we listen to a sermon, but throughout our whole life, inasmuch as at all times it is good to hearken to him. If we like to know what is going on in the palace: for example, what the king has said, what he has done, what he is planning about his subjects—even if oftentimes this information does not concern us—how much more desirable it is to hear what God has said, especially since all this does concern us. Now, this man will tell us about all these things accurately because he is a friend of the King Himself; nay, more, because he possesses Him speaking within himself and hears from Him everything which He hears from the Father. 'I have called you friends,' He says, 'because all

---

9 1 Cor. 2.10.
10 Eph. 3.10.

things which I have heard from my Father I have made known to you.'[11]

Accordingly, just as we should all hasten to assemble if we suddenly saw someone from on high bending down from the pinnacle of heaven and announcing that he was about to give out accurate information about the affairs of the place, let us now also react in this way because this man is indeed speaking to us from there. He is not of this world, as Christ Himself testifies: 'You are not of this world.'[12] And he has, speaking within him, the Paraclete who is present everywhere, who knows the things of God as clearly as the soul of man knows its own affairs: the Spirit of holiness, the righteous Spirit, who guides, leads by the hand to heaven, makes eyes new, gives the power to see the future as the present, and grants us power, even while in the flesh, to perceive heavenly things.

Let us, then, keep in readiness for Him great tranquility [of soul] throughout our life. Let no one who is lazy, drowsy, or impure enter this place and remain; nay, let us transport ourselves to heaven, since there he speaks these words to the citizens of heaven, and if we remain on earth, we derive no great profit thereby. For the words of John are nothing to those who do not wish to be set free from this swinish life, even as the things of earth are nothing to him.

Thunder truly arouses terror in our souls because it has an unexplained sound. The voice of this man, however, does not disturb any of the faithful, but even frees them from terror and confusion. It terrifies only demons and their slaves. That we may see how it confounds them, let us, therefore, keep silence, both exterior and interior, especially the latter. What advantage is there if the lips are silent while the soul is disturbed and greatly troubled? I am seeking that stillness which

11 John 15.15.
12 John 15.19.

is of the mind and of the soul, because it is the ear of the soul that I want. Then, let no desire of wealth disturb us, or love of fame, or despotism of anger, or the importunate crowd of the other passions. Indeed, unless the hearing is purified of them, it cannot perceive, as it ought, the sublimity of what is said, nor can it grasp, as it must, the awesome and ineffable character of these mysteries, and all the other virtues contained in these divine utterances. If one cannot learn a melody well on a flute or a lyre without giving the matter his complete attention, how will the hearer who sits down to listen to mystic words be able to comprehend them with a sluggish soul?

That is why Christ admonished us, saying: 'Do not give holy things to dogs nor cast pearls before swine.'[13] He called these words 'pearls'—although they are much more valuable than pearls—for we have nothing more precious than this substance. That is why He often used to compare their sweetness to honey, not because this was an adequate measure of their sweetness, but because among us there is no other thing sweeter than honey.

Further, in testimony to the fact that they do indeed greatly excel the nature of precious stones and sweetness of all honey, listen to the Prophet speaking of them and pointing out this superiority. They are, he says, 'desirable above gold and a very precious stone, and sweeter than honey and the honeycomb,'[14] but they are so only to those in sound health. Wherefore he added: 'For your servant keeps them.' And elsewhere again, after saying that they are sweet, he added: 'to my palate.' 'How sweet to my palate,' he says, 'are your promises.' And he goes on to insist on their excellence by the words: 'sweeter than honey and the honey-comb to my mouth,'[15] because he was in very sound health. Well, then, let us not on our part

---

13 Matt. 7.6.
14 Ps. 18.11,12.
15 Ps. 118.103.

approach these words in ill health, but let us receive nourishment from them, after having restored our souls to health.

Now, though I have spoken at such length by way of preamble, I have not yet come to the study of these texts[16] for the following reason: in order that each one, having put aside every kind of weakness, may enter into them as if he were entering into heaven, purged of anger and worldly cares and strivings, and free from all other passions. Otherwise, unless the soul has been thus purified, it is not possible to derive any great profit from them.

And let no one tell me that there is but a short time before our next service. It is possible, not in five days only, but in one moment of time, to change one's whole life. What, indeed, is worse than a robber and murderer? Is this not the worst form of wickedness? Nevertheless, [the good thief] won his way directly to the summit of virtue and went to paradise itself, without needing days, or a half day, but only one brief moment.[17]

Hence, it is possible to change suddenly and to become gold instead of clay. Since virtue and vice are not innate, change is easy because it is not inhibited by any compulsion. 'If you be willing and will hearken to me,' Scripture says, 'you shall eat the good things of the land.'[18] Do you perceive that there is need only of the will? Of the will—not merely that faculty which is the common possession of all men—but good will. To be sure, I know that all men even now wish to fly up to heaven, but it is necessary to bring that desire to fruition by one's works.

The merchant who wishes to grow rich does not rest content with having the desire in his mind, but he prepares a ship, and gathers a crew, and hires a pilot, and fits out the ship in all other respects, and borrows gold, and traverses the sea, and

16 I.e., of the Gospel of St. John.
17 Cf. Luke 23.39-43.
18 Isa. 1.19.

10   SAINT JOHN CHRYSOSTOM

goes off to a foreign land, and endures many dangers, and suffers all the other risks which they who sail the sea experience.

So we must bring our will to fruition by deeds. We also are sailing on a voyage, not from one land to another, but from earth to heaven. Therefore, let us prepare our reasoning power as a pilot fit to conduct us on high, and let us gather a crew obedient to it. Let us fit out a strong ship, of the kind that will not be submerged by the buffeting and discouragements of this life, nor raised up by the wind of false pretense, but will be sleek and swift. If we thus prepare the ship, thus the pilot and the crew, we shall sail with a favoring wind, and shall draw to ourselves the Son of God, the true Pilot. He will not permit our bark to be overwhelmed; even if countless winds blow, He will rebuke the winds and the sea and will bring about a great calm in place of the tempest.[19]

Well, then, prepare yourselves in this way and come to the next meeting; that is, if you desire at all earnestly to hear something of advantage and to store the words away in your souls. Let no one be 'the wayside,' no one 'the rocky ground,' no one 'full of thorns.'[20] Let us make ourselves fertile soil; I say this because we ourselves shall then cast the seeds with eagerness if we see the earth made ready for sowing. But if it is stony and hard, pardon us if we are not willing to labor in vain. If we refrain from sowing and begin to cut out the thorns, it would be sheer madness to cast seeds again into the uncultivated soil.

He who enjoys the advantage of listening to instruction of this sort will not partake of the Devil's table. 'For what has justice in common with iniquity?'[21] You have stood listening to John and learning the things of the Spirit through him; will you afterwards go away to listen to harlots saying shame-

---

19 Cf. Luke 8.24,25.
20 Matt. 13.4,5,7.
21 2 Cor. 6.14.

ful things and acting out more shameful ones, and to witness effeminate men being cuffed and cuffing one another? How will you be able to be properly purified if smeared with such filth as this?

But why is it necessary to describe in detail all the indecency found there? In truth, everything there is ridicule, everything is dishonor, everything is scurrility—both railings and gibes; everything is license, everything is corruption.

See, I warn and admonish all of you: Let no one who enjoys the bounty of this table corrupt his soul by those pernicious spectacles. All things said and done there are Satan's pomps. You who have been initiated know what promises you made to us; rather, what promises you made to Christ, for He Himself initiated you. You know what you said to Him, regarding the pomps of Satan, how you then renounced them, together with Satan and his angels, and promised not even to glance in their direction.[22] Accordingly, it is not a little to be feared that, if one should become reckless of these promises, he would render himself unworthy of these mysteries.

Do you not see how in royal palaces it is not they who have given offense, but they who have been held in honor, who are summoned to share the king's counsel and are ranked among the royal friends? A priest has come to us from heaven, sent by God Himself, to speak of certain fundamental truths, but you sit listening to mimes, neglecting to listen to what He wills, and the message He sends us. How many thunderbolts, how great divine visitations does not this behavior richly deserve? For, just as one must not partake of the table of demons, so one must neither take part in listening to demons nor approach with soiled apparel the shining table,[23] laden with such good things and prepared by God Himself.

Indeed, so great is its efficacy that it raises us up directly to heaven itself, if only we frequent it with proper dispositions.

---

22 The reference is to the promises made at baptism.
23 Here, apparently, the Scriptures.

It is not possible for one who perseveringly attunes himself to the words of God to remain fixed in his present weakness; he will of necessity acquire wings and fly aloft to the heavenly abode itself and become possessed of an infinite treasure-trove of blessings.

May all of us attain these by the grace and mercy of our Lord Jesus Christ, through whom and with whom glory be to the Father, together with the all-holy Spirit, now and always, and forever and ever. Amen.

Homily 2 (John 1.1)

'In the beginning was the Word.'

If John were about to address us and to tell us about his own affairs, it would be necessary to speak of his family, his native land, and his education. However, since not he, but God through his agency, is speaking to humanity, it seems to me to be superfluous and beside the point to inquire into these details.

Yet it really is not superfluous, but very necessary, to do so. When you learn who he was, and whence, and his parentage, and what sort of man, and after this you listen to his voice and all his teaching, then you will know truly that these utterances were not his, but belonged to the divine Power moving his soul.

Of what native land, then, was he? Of no native land, but of an inglorious village, of a place little esteemed, and producing nothing of value. Writers vilify Galilee, saying: 'Ask and see that no prophet has arisen out of Galilee.'[1] Even a true Israelite impugned it, saying: 'Can anything good come out of Nazareth?'[2] Yes, a native of this land, he did not even belong to a renowned village. Further, he was not even of a name well known there, but the son of a poor fisherman, so

---

1 John 7.52.
2 John 1.46.

poor that he also trained his sons to the same trade. Now, you all know that no workman will choose to make his son heir to his own trade unless extreme poverty force him, especially when the occupation is lowly. But none would be poorer nor lowlier than that of fisherman; none, further, more ignorant. However, even among such as these, some are greater, others less. But this Apostle of ours, even in this place, had the lower rank. He did not fish in the sea, but labored in a small lake. And while he was engaged there with his father and his brother James, and was mending torn nets (a circumstance which itself was a sign of extreme poverty), Christ called him.[3]

With regard to profane learning, we may gather also from these facts that he had none whatsoever. Besides, Luke bears witness to this, writing that he was not only of low estate, but also uneducated.[4] Naturally. As he was so poor, and did not frequent marketplaces, or meet prominent men, but had confined himself to fishing, and since whenever he did hold converse with anyone he was associated with hucksters of fish and cooks, how would he be any better than an animal or brute beast? How could he avoid imitating the dumbness of the very fish?

This fisherman, then, engaged about the lake with nets and fish, coming from Bethsaida of Galilee, son of a poor fisherman, poor even to extreme poverty, of low estate to the last degree of lowliness, learning letters neither before nor after becoming acquainted with Christ: let us see what he says and about what he discourses to us. Surely, it is about things in the fields? About those in the rivers? About the fish business? One would expect, no doubt, to hear these items of information from a fisherman.

However, fear not; we shall hear none of these, but heavenly things which no one ever before has learned. He

3 Cf. Matt. 4.21,22; Mark 1.19,20.
4 Cf. Acts 4.13.

comes to convey to us sublime teachings, and a virtuous way and philosophy of life, in a manner befitting one who draws his speech from the very treasures of the Spirit, and like one who has just now come from heaven itself. Further, it was not likely that even all in heaven knew these things, as I have just now said.

Tell me, are these the words of a fisherman? Of an accomplished orator? Of a sophist or a philosopher? Of someone educated in profane learning? Not at all. For it is not at all within the power of the human soul to utter [of itself] such teachings about that incorrupt and blessed Nature; about the powers closely associated with It; about immortality and everlasting life; about the nature of mortal bodies and of the immortal beings they will afterwards become; about punishment, about the future judgment, and about the accounts to be rendered: for words, for deeds, for thoughts, and for intentions. And [it is not within human power of itself] to know why man exists, why the world, and what man actually is, and what he seems to be, but is not; what vice is, and what virtue.

Some of this information the followers of Plato and Pythagoras have sought out. I mention these philosophers, because we ought not to recall the others at all, so ridiculous have they all become on this subject through their exaggeration. Some of the former, whom they more admired, and believed to be leaders of that science, are especially those who have composed and written something about politics and laws.[5] Nevertheless, in all respects these philosophers have been more shamefully ridiculous than children. They have wasted their whole life

---

5 Plato. The attitude manifested by St. John Chrysostom here is typical of that of the Church Fathers of the fourth and fifth centuries, who in general esteemed Plato as the most Christian of the pagan philosophers, though fully alert to the danger to the faith immanent both in the attractive doctrines of Plato and in their later development in Platonism. Like St. John, they were uncompromising in their round condemnation of such doctrines as he mentions here. Cf. R. Arnou, 'Platonisme des Pères,' DTC 12 (1929) 2258-2392.

in making women common to all, and upsetting the order of life itself, and corrupting the sanctity of marriage, and making other such ridiculous legislation.[6] And with regard to their teachings about the soul, they have omitted nothing at all that is excessively shameful, saying that the souls of men become flies and gnats, and shrubs,[7] declaring that God Himself is a soul, and making other such unseemly statements.

This is not the only thing worthy of blame, but the fickleness of their words as well. For, even as people are tossed this way and that in the Strait of Euripus, so they have never persevered in the same ideas, since they make all their statements from obscure and undependable reasoning.

But this fisherman of ours is not like that. He speaks all things with assurance and, as one founded on a rock, he never wavers. And as he has been deemed worthy to be in the very sanctuary and possesses the Lord of all speaking within him, he has felt no human influence. They, on the contrary, are like persons who have not been deemed worthy to enter the royal palace even in a dream, yet spend time outside in the market-place with other men, and from their own imagining conjure up what cannot be seen. Thus, [these philosophers] have strayed into gross error, since they have desired to speak about things unspeakable and, like the blind and the intoxicated, have knocked up against one another in their very wandering; not only against one another, but also against themselves, by everywhere and always changing their minds about the same matters.

But this unlettered man, this ordinary citizen, coming from Bethsaida, the son of Zebedee—even if the heathen ridicule, times without number, the coarseness of the names, I shall utter them nonetheless with more boldness. In the measure in which his nation appears barbarous to them and foreign to pagan education, so much the brighter do our claims

---

6 Cf. Plato, *Republic,* esp. 5.449D-466.
7 Empedocles; cf. Diogenes Laertius 8.2.

appear. The 'barbarian' and 'illiterate' utters such words as no man on earth has ever known, and not merely speaks them, but also convinces by them—though if the former alone were true it would still be a great marvel. But if, actually, in addition, he furnishes another proof greater than this, that his words are God-inspired, in the fact that all his hearers through all time believe, who will not marvel at the power dwelling within him? And this is so, because that is the greatest proof, as I have said, that he does not draw up his teaching from his own resources.

This 'barbarian,' then, by the writing of his Gospel has taken possession of the whole world. With his body he has gained control of the middle of Asia, where of old all those of Greek persuasion used to teach philosophy, and there he is fearful to the demons; shining in the midst of his enemies, dispersing their darkness, and destroying the stronghold of the demons. And by his soul he has withdrawn to that place which was suited to one who has done such things.

Indeed, he has blotted out and obliterated all the teachings of the pagans, while his become brighter day by day. From the time when both he and the other fishermen lived, the teachings of Pythagoras have fallen silent, as well as those of Plato, which at one time seemed authoritative—and many do not even know them by name. Yet, Plato was summoned to hold converse with rulers, they say, and had many followers, and sailed to Sicily.[8] And Pythagoras, having gained Magna Graecia, performed countless magic tricks there. To converse with cattle (they say that he actually did this) was nothing else than witchcraft. And a very clear conclusion follows from this: that he who conversed in this way with brute

---

8 Such information relevant to the ancient pagan philosophers, so casually imparted by St. John, shows that he was far from sharing in the ignorance in that regard which he notes as common in his day. Under Libanius and other teachers he had, of course, followed the usual program of higher studies which regularly included such knowledge.

beasts has in no way helped the human race, but even has done it the greatest harm.

Surely, the nature of man was more suited to the teaching of philosophy; nevertheless he conversed, they say, with eagles and oxen, by using witchcraft. He did not cause irrational nature to exercise the power of reason (since this is impossible for a man to do), but he deceived the ignorant by tricks. Refraining from teaching man anything useful, he taught that to eat beans was the same as to eat the heads of one's ancestors, and persuaded his followers that the soul of their teacher once was a shrub, then a maiden, then a fish.[9]

It is not unreasonable, is it, that all those teachings are extinct and completely obliterated? This is to be expected and is the logical result. But not so with the teachings of that ordinary and unlettered man; on the contrary, Syrians, and Egyptians, and Indians, and Persians, and Ethiopians and countless other nations, having translated to their language the teachings originating from him, barbarians though they are, have learned to study philosophy.

Not in vain, then, have I said that the whole world has become a theatre for him. He has not trumped up foolishness about the nature of brute beasts, to the neglect of his fellow human beings, a procedure which would be a mark of exceeding vanity and extreme foolishness. But, guiltless of this fault along with the rest, he strove for one single object: that the whole world might learn something that would be both useful to it and capable of conducting it from earth to heaven. Wherefore, he did not conceal his teaching in gloom and darkness, as did those others who veiled the evil contained in their teaching in the obscurity of what was said, as in a cloak; on the contrary, the teachings of John are clearer than sunbeams, and so they lie open to all the men in the world.

He did not teach as that other[10] did, bidding his disciples

---

9 This teaching comes down to us from Empedocles Fr. 117D.
10 Pythagoras; cf. Diogenes Laertius 8.1.

to be silent for five years, or to sit like senseless stones, nor did he deceitfully preach that everything consists in numbers. But having torn away all this satanic obscurity and perversion, he mingled so much simplicity with his words that all he said was clear, not only to men and scholars, but even to women and children. He believed that they were both true and useful for all his hearers, and all the years subsequent to him corroborate this. He has drawn the whole world after him and has rid our life of all bizarre show, once we have heard these words. Wherefore, we who listen to them prefer to part from our life rather than from the teachings he has given us.

From this, then, and from all other considerations, it is plain that no part of the teachings of this man is human, but divine and heavenly are the instructions which have come to us through this divine soul. We shall not see noise of words or pomposity of style, or careful ordering and artificial, foolish arrangement of nouns and verbs (for these things are far removed from all philosophy), but invincible and divine strength, irresistible power of authentic doctrines, and a wealth of good things without number.

Now, undue attention to style was such an excess, and worthy of mere sophists—not so much, even, of sophists, as of silly young men—that their philosopher himself[11] represents his teacher as very much ashamed of this art and saying to the jury that they will hear from him utterances made simply and extemporaneously, not adorned with elaborate expressions or decked out with artificially chosen nouns and verbs. 'It would not, of course, be befitting my age, gentlemen,' he says, 'for me to come in to you like a lad inventing speeches.'[12] Yet see how very ridiculous [Plato] is. That which he has represented his master as avoiding, on the ground that it is disgraceful, and unworthy of philosophy, and the work of striplings, this he himself has practiced most of all. Thus,

11 I.e., Plato.
12 Plato *Apol. Socr.* 1b.

they were altogether enslaved to vainglory, and nothing in Plato, except this, is out of the ordinary.[13]

And just as, if you should uncover those sepulchres which have been whitened outside, you would find them full of corruption and nauseous odors and rotting bones, so also, if you should strip the teachings of the philosopher of their stylistic adornment, you would observe them to be full of much disgusting matter, especially when he discusses the soul, since he both honors it and desecrates it immoderately. And this is the diabolic trick: never to observe due proportion, but to lead those caught by the strategy to blasphemy, by means of exaggerations in both directions. For at one time he says that the soul is of the substance of God, but, having thus raised it up inordinately and sacrilegiously, he wantonly affronts it with a different excess, bringing it into swine, asses, and animals even less esteemed than these.

But, enough of this; we have carried the discussion beyond due measure. If it were possible to learn something useful from this review, it would be necessary to spend even more time on it. But, if the object is only to observe how great unseemliness and absurdity these things possess, then we have carried on the discussion further than necessary. Wherefore, putting aside their fictions, let us take hold of our own teachings which have been brought down to us from above by the tongue of this fisherman, and which contain nothing merely human. Come, then, let us bring forth into the midst his own words, recalling now that which we urged at the beginning of our discourse so as to pay attention to his words with diligence.

What, then, does this Evangelist say at once, as he begins? 'In the beginning was the Word and the Word was with God.'

---

13 St. John admired Plato as a master of artistic prose. His scornful words here, however, are in keeping with the attitude of aloofness to pagan letters which he felt constrained to manifest officially. Cf. Homily 3 n. 1.

Do you see the great freedom and power of the words, how he speaks without equivocating or conjecturing, but declares everything openly? It is characteristic of a teacher not to be uncertain about what he says. If he who gives instruction to others needs another who is able to confirm his words, he should by rights join the ranks not of teachers, but of pupils.

And if someone should say: 'Why, omitting the First Cause, does he at once speak to us about the second?' we shall decline to speak of 'first' and 'second'; for the Divinity is superior to number and the sequence of time. Therefore, we have refrained from using these expressions, and we affirm that the Father is the Unbegotten, and the Son is begotten of the Father.

'Yes, of course,' he replies, 'but why does he pass over the Father and discuss the Son?'

Because He was known to all, if not as the Father, at least as God; but the Only-begotten was not known. Therefore with reason he hastened, right from the introduction, to bring knowledge of Him to those who did not know Him. Elsewhere he has not been silent about the Father, in the sections of his work appropriate to this discussion. And notice, I beg, his spiritual prudence. He knows that men pay greatest honor to the First Cause, that which has no beginning, and have esteemed It as God. For this reason he begins from that point first, and goes on to say that God is—and not, as Plato does, that He now is intellect or, at another time, soul. These statements fall far short of this divine and pure nature, which in truth has nothing in common with us, but is removed from participation in created things (I mean, does not share in their substance, but not that He does not share in their existence).

Because of this, then, he has called Him 'Word.' Since he intends to teach that this Word is the only-begotten Son of God, that no one may conceive the suspicion that His is a begetting subject to suffering, he anticipates this evil suspicion and removes it by applying to Him beforehand the appellation of 'the Word,' making it plain that the Son proceeds from the Father, and that this occurs effortlessly.

Do you see that, as I have said, he has not been silent about the Father in these words about the Son? And if these instances do not suffice to account for everything, do not wonder. Our discussion is about God, though we are unable to speak or think of Him worthily. Therefore, this [writer] nowhere uses the word 'substance' of Him—for it is not possible to say what God is in substance—but everywhere he reveals Him to us through His works.

Now, someone may notice that this Word a little further on is called 'Light,' and the 'Light' is called 'Life.' But not only for this reason did he so call Him[14]—though it was for this reason first—but secondly, because He would reveal to us truths belonging to His Father. 'For all things that I have heard from the Father,' He would say, 'I have made known to you.'[15] Moreover, he calls Him both 'Life' and 'Light,' for by this knowledge He has bestowed light upon us and, thence, life.[16]

Indeed, one appellation cannot at all suffice, nor two, nor three, nor even more, to teach the things of God. We must be satisfied to be able to come to the knowledge of Him, though dimly, through many names even. Now, John has not spoken of Him simply as 'Word,' but by the addition of the article distinguishes Him from the rest of things by this means, also. Do you see how it was not without reason I said that this Evangelist speaks to us from heaven? Notice how, right from the outset, having furnished the soul of his hearers with wings, he has led their understanding on high. Having set it higher than all sensible objects—above earth, above sea, above the sky—he conducts it also above the angels, and

14 Namely to reveal Him to us by His works.
15 John 15.15.
16 I.e., the life of grace.

higher than the Cherubim and Seraphim, and above the Thrones, and the Principalities, and the Powers, and finally persuades it to make its way beyond all creation.

What then? Having led us up to such a height, he will not be able, will he, to place limitations on us there? By no means; it is just as if someone should bring to the middle of the sea a man who has been standing by the seashore and gazing upon cities and beaches and harbors. He has indeed removed him from the objects upon which he was previously looking, but has not placed any bounds on his gaze, and has, rather, brought him to unbounded vision. So, also, the Evangelist, having brought us above creation, and having despatched us to the ages before it, projects our sight upward, not allowing it to reach any limit in the heights, since there is none.

The intellect, going up to 'the beginning,' seeks to know what sort of 'beginning' there was. Then, finding the 'was' always outstripping its imagination, the reason cannot come to a stop anywhere. But peering attentively ahead, and being unable to cease its flight anywhere, in weariness it turns back again below. The expression 'In the beginning was' is nothing else than, and must signify, everlasting existence and existence without end.

Do you recognize genuine philosophy and divine teachings here, not like those of the pagans who set time limits and say that some gods are older, some younger? There is nothing like this among us. For, if God exists, as, of course, He does exist, there is nothing prior to Him; if He is the Maker of all things, He Himself is first; if He is the Lord and Master of all things, all things, both creatures and ages, exist later than He.

I also wished to attack other questions, but perhaps our minds have become weary. Wherefore, after giving some counsels which may be of use to you for comprehending both the things that have been said and those that are still to be said, I shall bring this talk to an end.

What, then, are these things? I realize that many of you

have become listless because of the length of my sermon. This happens when the soul is sluggish because of its numerous temporal cares. It may be compared to the eye, which, when it is clear and radiant, is keen-sighted and would not easily grow remiss in distinguishing even the smallest objects. But when, because some evil humor has flowed down from the head or some dark vapor has come up from below, a kind of thick cloud forms before the pupil, this permits it to perceive nothing, not even somewhat large objects. This can also happen in the case of the soul. When it is pure and has no troublesome passion, it perceives exceedingly clearly whatever it ought to perceive; but when, made turbid by many passions, it utterly loses its virtue, it cannot easily be satisfied with spiritual things but quickly grows weary and falls back. Giving way to sleep and sloth, it takes no heed of the things pertaining to virtue and of the quite different life belonging to it, and does not approach it with any readiness.

That you may not suffer this affliction (for I shall not cease continually giving you these admonitions), strengthen your understanding that you may not hear the same warnings as those which the faithful among the Hebrews heard from Paul. He said that his sermon to them was long and difficult to explain, not because it was so by nature, but because, he said, 'You have grown dull of hearing.'[17] He who is sluggish and weak is by nature bored by a short sermon as much as by a long one, and thinks that things are difficult of comprehension, when they are clear and easily understood. However, let no one here be like this, but, having put aside all temporal concerns, let him listen to these teachings.

When a desire for wealth takes possession of the listener, a desire to listen cannot possess him at the same time, since the soul, being one, cannot be sufficient for many desires. The one desire corrupts the other, and the soul, thus divided, becomes weaker, until one desire prevails and monopolizes the

---

17 Heb. 5.11.

whole for itself. This can happen even in the case of children. When a man has one child only, he loves it exceedingly, but when he becomes the father of many children, the portions of his divided love are weaker. If this happens where the dominion and power of nature hold sway, and where the loved ones are closely akin, what should we say with regard to that desire and disposition which proceed from the will, and especially when such desires mutually repel one another? Indeed, the love of possessions is opposed to the love of listening [to divine teachings].

We are entering heaven when we enter here. I do not mean the place, but our dispositions, for it is possible for one who is actually on earth to stand in heaven, and to see the things there, and to hear words from there. Let no one, therefore, bring the things of earth into heaven; let no one here present be anxious about the affairs of his household. It is necessary to carry to the house and the marketplace the profits gained from this place, and to keep them, and not to burden this [church] with the troubles of the house and the marketplace. It is for this reason that we approach the chair of the teacher: that from there we may wash away from ourselves the defilement of wordly affairs. If we are going to suffer harm, even in this short time, from things said and done outside, it were better not to enter at all.

Let no one, therefore, be concerned while in church about affairs at home, but even while at home let him occupy himself with what was heard in church. Let these things be more precious to us than all others. The former concern the soul, while the latter concern the body; rather, the things discussed here concern both soul and body. Wherefore, let these things be our primary interest, and all the others be subordinate to them. These things belong both to the present life and to the life to come, but those belong to neither, unless they are directed according to the law placed over the former. Not only is it possible to learn from these what we shall be after this, and how we shall then live, but also how we shall manage our present life.

In truth, this house is a spiritual clinic, intended that we may there heal whatever wounds we have received outside; not that, after acquiring other wounds there also, we may depart in this condition. If, when the Holy Spirit speaks to us, we do not pay attention, not only shall we not be cleansed of former stains, but we shall receive others besides. Let us, then, approach with great eagerness the book which is being revealed to us. We shall not need much effort afterwards if we study the beginning and the foundation carefully; but, having put forth a little exertion at the start, we shall be then able to instruct others, also, according to St. Paul.[18] This Apostle is very exalted, and laden with abundant teachings, and he occupies himself with them rather than with other things.

Let us not, then, listen perfunctorily. The reason we are giving our interpretation a little at a time is that all things may become easily intelligible for you, and may not escape your memory. Let us fear, therefore, lest we ever become liable to the verdict which declares: 'If I had not come and spoken to them, they would have no sin.'[19] What greater benefit shall we enjoy than those who have not heard, if we go home carrying away nothing—even after listening—but only admiring what has been said?

Grant us, then, to sow our seed in good soil; grant this, that you may draw us to you the more. If one of you has thorns, let him cast the fire of the Spirit upon them. If another has a hard and obstinate heart, using the same fire let him make it soft and pliant. If someone by the wayside is trodden on by many distractions, let him go into more sheltered places and not lie exposed to those who wish to come in to plunder: in order that we may see your crops shooting forth

18 Cf. Rom. 15.14.
19 John 15.22.

leaves. I say this because if we conduct ourselves in this way and if we take part with great eagerness in the hearing of divine things, we shall get rid of all temporal cares, if not all at once, at least gradually.

Therefore, let us pay attention, in order that it may not be said of us that our ears are as 'of the deaf asp.'[20] How is this kind of listener any different from a wild beast? And how would he not be more irrational than any unreasoning creature if he does not pay attention when God speaks? For, if to be pleasing to God is to be truly human, he who does not wish to hear how he may accomplish this is nothing else than a wild beast. Therefore, consider how wicked it would be to make ourselves into wild beasts instead of men, when Christ desires to make us like angels instead of men.

Indeed, to be a slave to one's belly, and to be possessed by the desire for temporal things, and to be angry, to bite, to trample is the part, not of men, but of wild beasts. Yet, the wild beasts, each one of them, has, so to speak, a single passion, and that according to its nature. But the man who has cast aside the rule of reason, and who has broken off from the way of life according to God, gives himself up to every passion. No longer does he become merely a wild beast, but some multiform and fickle monster—who can plead no excuse because of his nature. For, all his wickedness proceeds from his will and his intellect.

However, may there never be cause to suspect these defects of the Church of Christ; for we are convinced that you possess the more noble qualities and those conducive to salvation. The more we are convinced of this, so much the more shall we not refrain from the least word of caution, so that, having arrived at the very peak of perfection, we may attain to the promised rewards.

May we all obtain these by the grace and mercy of our

---

20 Ps. 57.5.

Lord Jesus Christ, through whom and with whom glory be
to the Father, together with the Holy Spirit, forever and
ever. Amen.

Homily 3 (John 1.1)

At this point it is unnecessary to urge you to listen to me
attentively, so quickly have you made my [previous] exhortation fruitful by your actions. Your coming here, your attentive
posture, your crowding on one another—pushing together to
secure a closer position where my voice may be more clearly
heard—and your unwillingness to leave, though closely packed
together, until this spiritual theatre is dismissed, your clamor-
ous applause and all such things may be thought indicative
of the fervor in your soul and of your earnest desire to listen.
Therefore, it is actually unnecessary to urge you on in this
regard.

However, I must speak of another matter and admonish
you: to persevere in this fervor, and not only to show it here,
but also, when you are at home, I urge the husband to speak
of these things to his wife, the father to his child. I suggest, on
the one hand, that the first-mentioned tell their own [thoughts
on the subject] and then ask for those of the others, and in
this way all of you will contribute to this worthwhile feast.

Indeed, let no one tell me that it is unnecessary for us to
busy children with these matters. As a matter of fact, they
ought not only to be occupied with them, but to have their
whole interest in them. However, because of your weakness, I
do not insist on this, nor do I forbid them worldly study,[1] just

---

1 The traditional program of education in Greek and Roman antiquity,
embracing the study of grammar, poetry, rhetoric, and philosophy, had
as its texts and models the works of pagan authors for the most
part. The Churchmen of the early centuries recognized the value and
necessity of these studies as a preparation for the reading and understanding of the Scriptures and for the teaching of Christian doctrine.
It was the training in which they themselves had been schooled. At

as I do not remove you altogether from secular pursuits. But I demand that out of these seven days you consecrate one to the common Lord of us all. Truly, is it not strange that we require our slaves to serve us all the time, while we allot to God not even the smallest part of our leisure time, especially since all our service profits Him not at all (for God is in want of nothing) but, on the contrary, redounds to our benefit?

Further, when you bring the children to the theatre, you are not placing before them the sciences or anything of the kind; yet, if it is a question of getting them together for some spiritual profit, you call the affair a waste of time. Now, how can you fail to rouse God to anger, since you have leisure for all other things, and allot time for them, but think that to pursue the things of God is onerous and inopportune for your children?

Not so, brethren, not so. In fact, youth especially needs instruction. Since they are impressionable, they quickly take in what is said. Even as a symbol in wax, so is the thing heard imprinted in the understanding of the young. Besides, at that time their character begins to incline toward wickedness or virtue. Therefore, if someone lead them away from the very beginning and inception of evil, and guide them in the way of virtue, he will establish them there for the future, as if in a habitual and natural state. And they will not be disposed to change easily for the worse, since this habitual disposition influences them to accomplish good deeds. Thus they will become more deserving of respect in our eyes than

the same time, they were keenly aware of the potential danger to faith and morals in the detailed study of pagan philosophy and myths. Hence, they tolerated what St. John calls 'worldly study' only because there was no Christian substitute as yet available for the works of the pagan authors, and only in so far as it was necessary as a preparation for teachers and preachers and defenders of the faith. We often find them casting scornful aspersion on pagan letters in works in which the language, syntax, and allusions—even the style—strikingly betray their own intimate acquaintance with these same works. For a detailed discussion of the question, cf. H. Leclercq, 'Lettres Classiques,' *DACL* 8 (1929) 2885-2916.

aged men, and more useful in worldly affairs, showing forth in their youth the qualities of mature men.

It is not possible, as I have just said, for those who enjoy such instruction, and consort with such an Apostle, to depart without deriving some great and genuine benefit, whether it be man or woman or child who partakes of this banquet. If we tame wild beasts by training them by our words, how much more shall we bring men under control by this spiritual training, especially since there is great difference between the means employed and the object of the training in both cases. We have not such ferocity as animals have, since theirs is a product of their nature; ours, of our will. And the power of the word is not the same, for the word used on animals proceeds from the human intellect, while the other proceeds from the power of the Spirit and His grace.

Accordingly, let him who despairs of himself reflect on tame animals and never will he be thus cast down. Let him come often to this place of healing. Let him listen to the laws of the Spirit continually and, on returning home, let him engrave on his mind what he has heard, and thus he will live in good hope and complete security, as he perceives his improvement by experience. When the Devil sees the law of God written on a soul and the heart become His writing-tablets, he will not come back again. Indeed, wherever the divine writing is —not engraved on a bronze pillar, but impressed by the Holy Spirit on the mind that loves God and is bright with an abundance of grace—he will not be able to look directly at it, but will turn his back far away from us. Nothing is so fearful to him, and to the thoughts inspired by him, as the mind which thinks of divine things and the soul which is bathed always in this fountain of grace. And no detail of this life, however annoying, will be able to trouble such a soul, nor will anything be able to puff it up or exalt it, even if it be auspicious; but amid such turbulence and distress it will enjoy great tranquility.

Now, it is not the nature of things that causes disturbance to rise within us, but the weakness of our minds. If the cause of our trouble lies in the things that happen to us, all men must be disturbed by them. We all sail the same sea, and it would be impossible not to be affected by the waves and the spray. But, if there are some who have stood aloof from the storm and the raging sea, it is plain that events do not make the storm; it is the condition of our minds that does so. Therefore, if we so dispose them that they will endure all things with equanimity, we shall not experience a storm, or even a swelling wave, but there will always be a bright calm.

I truly do not know how I have been brought to begin with this exhortation, since I planned to say none of these things. Pardon, then, my garrulity. And do so because I fear—and I fear very much—lest this eager attention of yours toward me may become somewhat weakened. If I were optimistic about it I should not have spoken these words to you now, for it would be adequate to make everything easy for me.

However, it is now time to return to the discussion before us today so that you may not approach the contest already weary. Contests lie before us against the enemies of truth, against men who are contriving every scheme to destroy the glory of the Son of God—or, rather, their own. His, in truth, remains forever, just as it is, lessened in no way by the tongue of blasphemy, but as they strive to humble Him whom they say they worship they fill their countenances with dishonor and their souls with chastening.

What, then, do they say as I speak these words? That the words 'In the beginning was the Word' do not simply mean eternity because such a predication was also made both of heaven and of earth. O great shamelessness and impiety! I speak to you about God, and you bring up to me the earth and the men sprung from the earth? Well, in that case, since Christ is called the Son of God, and also God, man, too, who is called the son of God, must be God. For Scripture says: 'I have said, ye are all gods and sons of the Most High.'[2] Will you strive with the Only-begotten about sonship and will you say that He has nothing more than you in this regard?

'By no means' is the answer. Yet, you do this, even though you do not say it in word. How? Because you say that He, like you, has shared in the adoption of sons by grace; for by maintaining that He is not Son of God by nature, you declare that He is one not otherwise than by grace.

Let us also examine the proofs which they bring up to us. 'In the beginning,' Scripture says, 'God created heaven and earth. And the earth was waste and void.'[3] And 'There was a man of Ramathaimsophim.'[4] These are the arguments which they think are strong. And they are strong, but strong to point out the correctness of the teachings we hold, and weaker than all others in proving their blasphemy. What, I ask, has 'was' in common with 'created'? And what, 'God' with 'man'? Why do you ningle the non-miscible and confuse the unconfused, and make above below. In this context, it is not only 'was' which indicates eternity, but also the words 'In the beginning was' and 'The Word was.'

Therefore, even as the word 'being,' when it is said of a man, means only the present time, but when said about God means eternity, so also 'was,' when predicated of our nature, indicates past time to us—and that time limited—but when predicated of God indicates eternity. It was sufficient, therefore, for a man who heard 'earth' and 'man' to read into them nothing more than what it was fitting to think of created nature. That which 'becomes,' whatever it may be, has come into being in time or in the ages before; but the Son of God is before not only time, but all previous ages, since He is their Creator and Maker. For the Apostle says: 'Through whom He made even the ages.'[5]

2 Ps. 81.6.
3 Gen. 1.1,2.
4 1 Kings 1.1.
5 Heb. 1.2.

Now, a maker exists before any of his works. But, since some men are so lacking in sense as, even after this, to conjure up some exaggerated idea about creatures, he anticipates the attitude of his hearer by using the expressions 'created' and 'There was a man,' and thus cuts short all shameless argument. Everything that has been created, both heaven and earth, has been created in time and has a beginning in time, and no one of these things is timeless, because it has been made. So that, when you give a hearing to [the argument] 'He created the earth' and 'There was a man,' you are vainly playing the fool by pondering senseless foolishness.

I might go on to mention another exaggeration. What is it? That even if a statement was made about the earth: 'In the beginning was the earth,' and about man: 'In the beginning was man,' not even thus ought we to conjure up some idea about them greater than those we now know. The appellation of 'earth' and of 'man'—whatever may be predicated of them—by a foregone conclusion do not allow the mind to conjure up something greater about them than what we now know; just as 'the Word,' also, even if but little has been said about Him, does not permit of anything disparaging or base being thought of Him. And the case is similar when he goes on to say of the earth: 'The earth was waste and void.'[6] Once he had said that He created it and had thus placed on it its proper limitation, he uttered the following statements confidently, knowing that no one would be so foolish as to conceive the notion that the earth is without beginning and was not made. The words 'earth' and 'created' are sufficient to persuade even the very stupid that the earth is not everlasting nor uncreated, but is one of the creatures made in time.

Besides this, the term 'was,' predicated of the earth and of man, is not indicative of absolute existence, but, with regard to man, it indicates his being from a certain place; with regard to earth, its being of a certain quality. He did not say simply:

6 Gen. 1.1.

'The earth was,' and then fall silent, but showed what its condition was, even after it had been created: for example, that 'it was waste and void,' still covered by the waters and in confusion.

With regard to Elcana, also, he did not say merely: 'There was a man,' but added also whence he was, namely, 'of Ramathaimsophim.' But with regard to 'the Word,' not so. I am ashamed to be assessing this matter by those examples. If we find fault with those who do this with regard to men, when there is a great difference in the standing of those so measured, even though in truth their substance is one, how is it not extreme madness to begin such a discussion where the difference both in nature and in all other respects is so infinite? May He who is blasphemed by them be propitious to us. We have not invented the necessity of such discussion; they who are making war on their own salvation have furnished it.

What, then, do I say? That the first 'was,' with regard to the Word, makes plain His being eternal, for, 'In the beginning,' he says, 'was the Word.' And the second 'was' makes it plain with whom He was. Since it is especially characteristic of God to be eternal and without beginning, John gave first place to this point. Then, lest anyone on hearing: 'He was in the beginning' might also say that He was unbegotten, he at once relieved the difficulty by saying: 'He was with God,' before declaring what He was. And lest anyone might think that the Word Himself was simply a word uttered, or else merely conceived in the mind, he removed this difficulty by the addition of the article, as I have said before, and also by this second phrase. He did not say: 'He was in God,' but: 'He was with God,' making clear to us His eternity as to person. And then he went on to reveal this more clearly by adding that this Word also 'was God.'

'But still created,' someone objects. Well, then, what prevented John from saying it that way: 'In the beginning God created the Word?' In speaking of the earth, at least, Moses did not say: 'In the beginning was the earth,' but: 'He created it'; and then, 'it was.' What, then, prevented John also from saying: 'In the beginning God created the Word'? If Moses, in speaking of the earth, feared lest anyone might say that it was uncreated, much more should John have been afraid [to say what he did] about the Son if He were indeed created. The universe, in truth, since it is visible, proclaims its Maker by this very fact. 'The heavens,' Scripture says, 'show forth the glory of God.'[7] but the Son is invisible and exceedingly and infinitely transcends the created universe. If, then, where we did not need either teaching or instruction to learn that the universe is created, the Prophet nevertheless sets this fact down clearly, even ahead of the rest, much greater would be the necessity for John to state this about the Son if He really were created.

'Yes, indeed,' you will say, 'but Peter says clearly and unmistakably that He was.'

'Where and when?'

'When, in addressing the Jews, he said: "God made Him Lord and Christ." '[8]

But why did you not add the text which follows: 'This Jesus whom you crucified'? Or are you ignorant that some of the words are said of His pure nature [as God], others of His incarnate nature? If this is not so, but you interpret all absolutely as referring to the Godhead, you will also conclude that God can suffer; but, if He cannot suffer, He was not created. If blood flowed forth from the Deity Itself and Its ineffable nature, and if It were pierced and cut by nails, instead of Christ's flesh, in the crucifixion, your fallacy would therefore be reasonable. But, if not even the Devil himself would utter this blasphemy, why do you yourself pretend not to recognize an error which is so unpardonable and one which not even the demons have used as an argument? Besides, the words 'Lord' and 'Christ' are not used of His essence but of

7 Ps. 18.1.
8. Acts 2.36.

His rank; the one refers to His power, the other to His anointing.

What, then, would you say of the Son of God? Even if He were a creature as you maintain, this contention would have no place, for He was not first created and then chosen out by God, nor does He have a merely transitory sovereignty, but one that is His by nature and essence. For, when asked whether He was a king, He said: 'For this was I born.'[9] Peter speaks the above words as of One who has had hands of anointing laid upon Him. His statement refers entirely to the humanity [of Christ].

And why do you wonder if Peter says this? Paul, addressing the Athenians, calls Him 'man' only, in the following words: 'A man whom he has appointed, and whom he has guaranteed to all by raising him from the dead.'[10] He says nothing about the form of God or that He is 'equal to God,'[11] or that He is 'the brightness of His glory'[12]—and rightly so. By no means was it the time for these words; it was enough at this time for them to admit that He was man and that He rose from the dead. Christ, also, had acted in this way. And Paul, having learned from His example, composed his instructions after this fashion.

Indeed, Christ did not reveal His Godhead to us all at once. At first, He was thought to be the Prophet and the Christ, but merely man; later, it appeared from His deeds and words what He was. It was for this reason that Peter, also, used this method of approach in the beginning; and I say this for this was the first sermon he addressed to the Jews. Inasmuch as they were not then able to understand clearly about His Godhead, he therefore treated of matters pertaining to His humanity, in order that their hearing, having been exercised by these ideas, might become prepared for the rest of his teaching.

Moreover, if someone should be willing to peruse the entire

9 John 18.37.
10 Acts 17.31.
11 Phil. 2.7.
12 Heb. 1.3.

discourse mentioned above, he will find what I say very clear. He calls Him 'man' both in actual fact and by the words by which he speaks of His suffering and resurrection, and His generation in the flesh. When Paul says: 'Who was born to him, according to the flesh, of the offspring of David,'[13] he teaches us nothing else but that the expression 'He made' was accepted with reference to His humanity, as we also maintain. The Son of Thunder, on the contrary, is now speaking to us about ineffable and ageless Existence. Wherefore, omitting the expression 'He created,' he has declared: 'He was.' However, if He were actually a creature, he would have been obliged to make this clear in particular.

Indeed, Paul feared that some foolish person might get the idea that the Son is greater that the Father and will have Him who begot Him subject to Him, and this is the reason why, in writing to the Corinthians, he said: 'But when he says all things are subject to him, undoubtedly he is excepted who has subjected all things to him,[14] Yet, who could possibly get the idea that the Father will ever be subject to the Son in common with all other things? If, nevertheless, Paul feared these unreasonable suspicions and said: 'He is excepted who has subjected all things to him,' much more ought John to have feared, if the Son of God were a creature, that someone might think He was unbegotten, and he ought to have clarified this teaching first of all.

But now, since He was in truth begotten, with reason neither John nor anyone else—whether Apostle or Prophet—said that He was a creature. And the Only-begotten Himself would not have omitted to mention this if He were one. He who said such lowly things of Himself, through His humility, would not have kept silence in regard to this. In truth, I think it not unreasonable to suppose that He was silent with respect to greatness that He in fact did possess, rather than that He

13 Rom. 1.3.
14 1 Cor. 15.27,28.

omitted to mention any actual lack of greatness and failed to teach that He did not possess it. In the former case there was a good reason for silence in the fact that he wished to teach men to be humble, and therefore was silent with regard to the greatness of His personal characteristics; in the latter case, you would have no just excuse to mention for silence.

Indeed, for what reason would He remain silent if He were a creature, with regard to His being created, since He omitted to mention many of His real attributes? So, He who for the sake of teaching humility often spoke of lowly things and those not advantageous to Himself, if He were actually a creature, would much more certainly not have failed to say so. Indeed, do you not see Him doing and saying everything so that no one may suppose Him to be unbegotten, uttering things unbecoming His dignity and His essence, and descending to the lowly state of Prophet? The words: 'As I hear, I judge,' and 'He has given me commandment what I should say and what I should declare,'[15] and so many others are but those of a prophet.

If, then, because He desired to prevent the suspicion [that He is unbegotten] He did not scorn to speak such humble words, much more would He have said such things, if He were a creature, in order that no one might think that He was not— for example: 'Do not think that I am begotten of the Father; I have been created, not begotten, nor am I of His substance.' As a matter of fact, He did exactly the opposite. He spoke such words as forced even those who did not wish it, even against their will, to admit the opposite idea—for instance: 'I am in the Father and the Father in me'; and 'Have I been so long a time with you, and you have not known me? Philip, he who sees me sees also the Father';[16] and 'That all men may honor the Son even as they honor the Father'; 'As the Father raises the dead and gives them life, even so the Son also gives

15 John 5.30; 12.49.
16 John 14.11,9.

life to whom he will'; 'My Father works even until now, and
I work.'[17] 'Even as the Father knows me and I know the
Father.'[18] 'I and the Father are one.'[19] And everywhere, by
putting 'as' and 'so' and 'being one with the Father,' He made
clear His complete equality with Him.

His own power, on the other hand, He proved both by these
words and by many more besides, as when He said: 'Peace,
be still'; 'I will, be thou made clean'; 'Thou deaf and dumb
spirit, I command thee, go out of him';[20] and: 'You have heard
that it was said to the ancients, "Thou shalt not kill"; but I
say to you that everyone who is angry with his brother shall
be liable to judgment.'[21] And He laid down many other
similar precepts and worked miracles sufficient to prove His
power; rather, the least part of them is adequate to convince
and persuade those not altogether senseless.

But vainglory is a powerful thing to make the understanding of those caught by it blind to the most evident truths
and to persuade them to contend with those who confess the
truth. It even incites to pretended ignorance and strife still
others who know the truth very well and have been persuaded
of it. This happened to the Jews, since it was not through
ignorance that they denied the Son of God, but to win the
acclaim of the multitude. 'They believed in Him,' he says,
but they feared 'lest they should be put out of the synagogue,'[22] and they gave over their own salvation to others.

Truly, it is not possible for a man who is enslaved to the
glory of the present time to secure that which comes from
God. Wherefore He chided them, saying: 'How can you
believe who receive glory from one another, and do not seek
the glory which is from God?'[23] Vainglory is a kind of deep

---

17 John 5.23,21,17.
18 John 10.15.
19 John 10.30.
20 Mark 4.39; Matt. 8.3; Mark 9.25.
21 Matt. 5.21,22.
22 John 12.42.
23 John 5.44.

intoxication and therefore this passion makes its victim hard to convert.

Having cut away from heaven the souls of its slaves, it pins them to the earth and does not permit them to gaze on the true light, but persuades them to wallow continually in the mud, providing them with masters so powerful that they rule them without issuing orders to them. He who is stricken with this disease, even with no one bidding him, spontaneously does whatever he thinks may please his masters. Indeed, he puts on fine garments on their account and beautifies his face, doing this not for himself but for others, and he leads followers around to the marketplace in order to be admired by others. And all that he does he undertakes solely for the sake of the desire to please others. What keener suffering could there be than this—in order that others may admire him, he continually throws himself down headlong to ruin!

The words of Christ, in very truth, are sufficient to show the complete tyranny of this disease, but it also is possible to learn of it as follows. If you will ask any politicians who make lavish expenditures why they pour out so much gold and what so great an expenditure means to them, you will hear no other reply from them than that they desire to please the people. And if you should inquire again what in the world they mean by 'the people,' they will say: 'A nuisance completely confused and turbulent, and composed for the most part of senselessness, often completely tossed about in every direction like the waves of the sea, and quarreling because of a clash of opinions.' When, therefore, a man has such a master, who is there more pitiable than he?

For men of the world to be concerned about such matters is not so terrible, even though it may be a terrible thing; but for those who claim to have renounced the world to be sick with the same disease, or even with one more serious, this is the most terrible thing of all. The risk to men of the world is one of worldly goods, but the danger to the latter is to their souls. If they exchange the true faith for worldly glory and, in order that they themselves may be glorified, dishonor God, what excessive stupidity and madness would this procedure not show, I ask?

The other vices, in truth, though they inflict much harm, at least bring some pleasure, even if it is ephemeral and short. I say this, because the miser, and the drunkard, and the lustful have, together with the moral injury, some enjoyment, also, even though short; but those who are afflicted with vainglory always live a thoroughly bitter life, completely bereft of pleasure. They do not attain to what they very much desire— I mean fame in the eyes of the crowd. They only seem to enjoy it; actually, they do not enjoy it, because this is not fame at all. Therefore, this passion is said to be, not glory, but a thing empty of glory; hence, all the ancients have aptly called it vainglory.

Indeed, it is completely empty, possessing nothing bright and glorious within. Just as masks often seem to be bright and cheery but are empty within, and for this reason—though they are more beautiful than human countenances—they never capture anyone for their lover, so also, though much more wretchedly, popular acclaim has produced in us this passion so despotic and difficult to cure. It has merely a bright appearance, while that which is within is not only valueless but full of dishonor and cruel despotism.

'Whence, then, is this vice, so unspeakable and accompanied by no pleasure,' do you ask? Whence? Nowhere else than from a weak and mean soul. It is not possible for him who is captivated by love of fame easily to reflect on any great and noble thought; he must be base and mean and dishonorable and small. If a man does nothing for the sake of virtue, but only in order to be pleasing to men worthy of no consideration, and if on every occasion he bows to their erroneous and fallacious approval, how could he be worth anything? Take further notice. If someone should say to him: 'What do you think of the rabble?' it is very evident that he would say that he thinks they are capricious and not to be heeded. What then? If someone should say to him again: 'Do you choose to be like them?' it seems to me he would not wish to be so. Is he not excessively ridiculous, therefore, in seeking the acclaim of those whom he would never choose to resemble?

And if you should reply that [it would be impossible to resemble them, for] they are numerous and massed together collectively, it would be fitting for you, especially on that account, to frown upon them. If they are reprehensible taken individually, they will become more so when taken together. When they are taken collectively, the folly of each one becomes greater because it has been augmented by that of the crowd. Furthermore, if a man should take them one by one, he might sometimes even correct them; but when they are all together, he would not be able to do this easily, because their stupidity then is greater, and because they are driven like cattle and on all occasions follow one another's opinions. Tell me, then, will you show a preference for this acclaim of the mob?

Do not, I beg and beseech you. This has turned everything upside down; it has spawned greed, envy, false witness, treachery; it arms and infuriates those who have been wronged in nothing, against those who have done no wrong. And he who has fallen victim to this disease does not know friendship, or remember custom, or know how to show respect to anyone at all; but, having stripped his soul of all finer feelings, he is at war with all men, since he is inconstant and unfeeling.

The disease of anger, even if it is also despotic and hard to endure, does not always cause disturbance, but only when it has sources of irritation; that of vainglory, on the contrary, is ever-present. There is not a time, so to speak, when it is possible for it to cease, since reason does not prevent and dispel it; it is always present. Not only does it induce to sin, but, even if we happen to do right, it wrests this also from our hands; sometimes it is not possible to escape its domination and do right at all. Now, if Paul calls greed 'idolatry,'[24] what is it right to call its mother and root and source—I mean vainglory? Indeed, it is not even possible to find a term which matches its wickedness.

Well, then, beloved, let us rouse ourselves, and shed this evil garment, and tear it up and cut it off. Let us become free with true freedom, and let us recognize the nobility given to us by God. Let us frown upon the acclaim of the crowd. Nothing is so ridiculous and dishonorable as this vice, nothing so full of baseness and great infamy. So, for many reasons one may see that to desire glory is inglorious, and that true glory is to despise it, to give no thought to it, but both to speak and to do all things with an eye to what is pleasing to God.

Thus, in truth, we shall be able to receive our reward from Him who closely scrutinizes our affairs if we are satisfied with His gaze alone. Why, indeed, do we need the eyes of others, also, since He who will reward us always sees what is done by us? A servant performs all he does for the pleasure of his master and seeks for nothing more than his approving glance; he does not draw the eyes of others to his work, even if these others are great, but regards one thing only: how the master regards his work. Is it not strange, then, that we who have such a Master seek for another audience, who by their gazing can give us no aid, but instead, harm us and rob of merit all our toil?

Do not do this, I beg of you, but let us call as approver and spectator of our deeds Him from whom we have to receive our reward. Let us seek no reward from human approbation. If we should desire to have this glory we shall then attain it

24 Cf. Eph. 5.5.

when we seek only the approbation of God. For, 'Whosoever shall glorify me, him will I glorify,'[25] Scripture says.

Just as we most of all acquire riches when we despise them and seek wealth only from God, ('Seek ye first the kingdom of God,' He says, 'and all these will be added unto you,'[26]), so also with regard to glory. When the granting both of money and of honor is not dangerous to us, then God will grant the gift abundantly. It is not dangerous when it does not rule us, or possess us, or use us as slaves, but is with us as with masters and free men. It is on this account that He wishes us not to love them: that we may not be ruled by them. If we act rightly in this He will give them to us with great generosity, for what is clearer than the words of Paul: 'We do not seek glory from men neither from you, nor from others.'[27] And who is richer than he who has nothing and so possesses all things? When, as I have said, we are not ruled by them, then we shall rule them, then we shall receive them.

Well, then, if we desire to have glory, let us flee from glory; we thus shall be able, having kept the laws of God, to obtain possession of truly good things: both those here and those promised by the grace of Christ, with whom glory be to the Father, together with the Holy Spirit, forever and ever. Amen.

Homily 4 (John 1.1-3)

'In the beginning was the Word, and the Word was with God.'

Teachers do not impose many tasks at one time upon those children who are just entering upon their education, nor do they assign the work only once. They repeat the same short les-

25 1 Kings 2.30.
26 Matt. 6.33.
27 1 Thess. 2.6.

sons to them many times, so that what is said is easily re-
tained by their understanding; moreover, the children are
not overwhelmed at the start because of the multiplicity of
facts and the difficulty of remembering them. They are not
retarded in accumulating the information imparted to them,
as they would be if a certain lack of interest developed in
them because of the difficulty of learning.

Since I myself also wish to do what these teachers do, and
to make your work light, selecting little by little the things
on this divine table, I impart them to your souls in this way.
That is why I shall take the same words once more, not in
such a way as to repeat the same ideas, but only to add the
points that have been left out.

Come, then, let us once more bring our discussion to the
opening words: 'In the beginning was the Word, and the
Word was with God.' Why is it that, while all the other
Evangelists begin from the Incarnation (for Matthew begins:
'The book of the origin of Jesus Christ, the Son of David';[1]
and Luke tells us in the beginning the facts he learned from
Mary;[2] and Mark uses a similar approach by recounting from
this point of view the story of John the Baptist[3]), John
merely hints briefly at the Incarnation by saying further on:
'And the Word was made flesh.'[4] Why does he omit all the
other details—His conception, His birth, upbringing, growth
—and discourse to us about His eternal generation? What
the reason for this is I shall tell you now.

Since the other Evangelists had spent much time in out-
lining the details which pertain to His humanity, there would
be cause to fear lest some earthly minded individuals might,
in consequence, remain content with these teachings only,

1 Matt. 1.1.
2 Cf. Luke 1-2.
3 Cf. Mark 1.1-13.
4 John 1.14.

as indeed happened to Paul of Samosata.[5] It was, then, to draw up from this striving after things of earth those who were likely to relapse into it, and to direct them upward to heaven, that he deliberately made the introduction of his narrative open from on high and from the eternal existence. While Matthew entered upon his narrative from King Herod, Luke from Tiberius Caesar, and Mark from the baptism of John, he omitted all these details, mounted higher than all time and ages, and precipitated the understanding of his listeners on the words: 'In the beginning was.' And he did not allow it to halt in any place, or set any limitation on it, as they did in Herod, and Tiberius, and John.

Besides this, what may be mentioned as especially admirable is that he who began his discourse on a higher plane has not neglected the Incarnation, nor have [the other Evangelists] who hastened to begin their narrative with this subject been silent about the eternal existence; and very reasonably so. It was one Spirit who inspired the souls of all four, and therefore they showed great unanimity in their narratives.

And, beloved, when you hear 'Word,' do not consent to the opinion of those who declare that the Word Itself is a work of the Creator or of those who conclude that It is simply a word. Many, to be sure, are the words of God, which even angels carry out, but no one of them is God. They are all prophecies and commands (for it is customary in Scripture to call the laws of God, His commands, and prophecies, 'words'; and for this reason, in speaking of the angels, it adds: 'Strong powers, doing His word'[6]).

This Word, however, is a Being, a distinct Person, pro-

---

5 Paul of Samosata, Bishop of Antioch during the second half of the of the third century, was a heretic who denied the essential divinity of Christ and taught that He was merely a man, born of a virgin and inspired by God in an unusual manner. Cf. *Catholic Encyclopedia.*
6 Ps. 102.20.

ceeding from the Father Himself without alteration. He has indicated this, as I have said, by his appellation 'the Word.' Therefore, just as the expression 'In the beginning was the Word' reveals His eternity, so 'He was in the beginning with God' has revealed to us His co-eternity. Lest on hearing: 'In the beginning was the Word,' you might think that He was indeed eternal, but suppose that the life of the Father was older by some interval of time and might consequently concede that the Only-begotten had a beginning, he has added the sentence: 'He was in the beginning with God.' That is, He was as eternal as the Father Himself, for the Father was never without the Word but always God was with God, though each in His own Person.

'How is it, then,' you will say, 'that John said: "He was in the world," if He was indeed with God?' Because He was both with God and in the world. Neither the Father nor the Son is ever in any way limited. If, in truth, 'of His greatness there is no end'[7] and 'Of His wisdom there is no measure,'[8] it is plain also that there is no temporal beginning of His Being. Have you heard: 'In the beginning God created heaven and earth'?[9] What do you think of that 'beginning'? It is evident that it preceded all visible things. So, also, when you hear of the Only-begotten that 'He was in the beginning,' know that He existed before all intelligible things and before all ages.

Now, someone may say: 'But how is it possible for Him to be the Son of the Father and not be younger? It is inevitable for that which is begotten of someone to be subsequent to him from whom it proceeds.' We shall reply that this is, for the most part, a human way of speaking. And he who asks this question will ask others stranger still, and we ought not even listen to such things. Our discussion at present is

7 Ps. 144.3.
8 Ps. 146.5.
9 Gen. 1.1.

about God, not about human nature to which alone both the conclusions and the logic of such reasoning are applicable. Nevertheless, we shall discuss even these matters for the sake of strengthening the weaker among you.

Now, tell me, does the sunlight burst forth from the very substance of the sun, or from some other source? It must be acknowledged, unless one has been entirely bereft of his senses, that it comes from its substance. Nevertheless, although the light has its origin in the sun, we should not say that it could ever be subsequent to the substance of the sun, since the sun never has appeared without its light. But if, in the case of these bodies which are seen and felt, something appears to have its origin in something else and is not subsequent to it, why do you doubt this in the case of the invisible and ineffable Nature?

Surely, this same thing is true of It, but as is befitting that Being. It was on this account that Paul even referred to Him as 'Brightness':[10] to affirm both His proceeding from the Father and His co-eternity. Then, I ask, have not all the ages and all space come into being through Him? Anyone not insane must subscribe completely to this. Well, there is no gap, therefore, between the Son and the Father. And if there is none, He is not subsequent to Him but co-eternal with Him. Indeed, 'before' and 'after' are ideas signifying time. No one could conceive of such phrases apart from ages or time. And God is above times and ages.

But if you say that the Son had a beginning at all, be careful that you be not forced also to reduce the Father to a beginning by this argument and reasoning: an earlier beginning, but, nevertheless, a beginning. Now, tell me, if you suppose a limit and beginning for the Son, and thus if you go back from that to a previous time, do you not say that the Father preceded this? It is very evident that you do. Then, tell me, how long did the Father pre-exist?

10 Cf. Heb. 1.3.

Whether you say that the interval was little or great, you have reduced the Father to a beginning. It is quite clear that you will reply that the interval is small or large, only after you have estimated its extent; and it would not be possible to make a measurement if there were not a terminus at each end. Thus, you have allotted a beginning to the Father, also— at least as far as you can; consequently, not even the Father will be without beginning according to you. Do you perceive the truth of what the Saviour said, and that that statement of His is ever forceful? What is this? 'He who does not honor the Son does not honor the Father.'[11]

Now, I realize that what has been said is incomprehensible to many. On this account we often hesitate to start discussions based on logical reasoning because the rest of the people would not be able to follow them, and, if they should follow, they would not have anything definite or lasting [as a result]. 'For the thoughts of mortal man are fearful, and our counsels uncertain.'[12]

Still, I should like to ask of our opponents what the words mean which were once uttered by the Prophet: 'Before me there was no God, and after me there is none.'[13] If the Son is younger than the Father, how can the Father say: 'after me there shall be none'? You will not, therefore, also deprive the Only-begotten Himself of His substance, will you? Indeed, you must dare to do this, or else to accept the one Godhead with the distinct Persons of the Father and the Son.

Moreover, how is the phrase 'All things were made through him' true at all? If eternity is older than He, how would that which is before Him come into being through Him? Do you see to what sort of loose thinking the discussion has brought our opponents, once truth has been cast aside? Why, indeed, did not the Evangelist say that He derived His Being from

---

11 John 5.23.
12 Wisd. 9.14.
13 Cf. Isa. 43.10.

things that did not yet exist, as Paul declares about all other things when he says: 'He who calls things that are not, as though they were.'[14] Why, instead, did John say: 'He was in the beginning'? This, in truth, is the opposite to that [statement], and rightly so. God does not come into being nor is there anything prior to Himself, but the contrary ideas are the notions of the pagans.

Then, tell me this, also: Would you not say that the Creator immeasurably surpasses His works? Yet, since that which comes from things that are not is like them, where is the immeasurable superiority? And what meaning at all have the following: 'I am the first and the last'[15] and 'Before me there was no God formed'?[16] For, if the Son were not of the same Essence, there must be another God; and if He were not co-eternal, He would exist later than the Father; and if He did not proceed from the Father's Essence, it is evident that He must have been made.

Now, if they should say that these statements were intended to show the difference between Him and idols, why do they not agree that the words 'the only true God'[17] were said to differentiate Him from idols; how will you interpret the whole statement? 'After Me,' He declares, 'there is no other God.' He says this, not to cast aside the Son, but to affirm : 'There is no idolatrous God after Me,' not that there is no Son.

'Yes,' they say, 'but what then?' Will you so interpret: 'Before Me there was no God formed' as to maintain that there was no idolatrous god formed before, yet there was, nevertheless, a Son before Him? What kind of evil spirit would say this? I do not think that the Devil himself would say it.

On the other hand, if He is not co-eternal with the Father, how will you say that His life is without limit? For if He has a beginning dating from before creation, even if He

14 Rom. 4.17.
15 Isa. 41.4.
16 Isa. 43.10.
17 John 17.3.

be without end, He is not, nevertheless, infinite. Infinity must be limitless at both ends. Paul, to make this clear, said: 'Having neither beginning of days nor end of life,'[18] indicating in this way that He is both without beginning and without end. Just as the one has no limits so the other has none, for neither is there an end in one direction nor a beginning in the other.

Now, since He is Life, how was there ever a time when He did not exist? All would confess that Life exists always, both without beginning and without end, if it actually is Life, as, of course, it is. And if there is a time when it does not exist, how could it be the Life of the rest of living things if it ever did not exist?

'How is it, then,' you say, 'that John marked out a beginning by saying: "He was in the beginning"?' Tell me, did you pay attention to the words: 'In the beginning' and 'was,' and do you not understand: 'The Word was'? What! When the Prophet says of the Father: 'From eternity to eternity thou art, O God,'[19] it surely is not to set limits to Him that he says this? By no means, but he is affirming His eternity. Accordingly, consider John's text here in the same way. He was not setting limits when he said this. In fact, he did not say: 'He had a beginning,' but: 'He was in the beginning.' And by the word 'was' he leads you to reflect on the fact that the Son is without beginning.

'But see,' you say, 'the Father is spoken of with the article; the Son, without it.'[20] Then, what of the fact that the Apostle says: 'Of our great God and Saviour, Jesus Christ,'[21] and again: 'Who is over all things, God'?[22] For, behold, in this text he has also referred to the Son without the article. But

18 Heb. 7.3.
19 Ps. 89.2.
20 'Theòs ên ho Lógos.'
21 Titus 2.13.
22 Rom. 9.5.

he does this also with reference to the Father. Writing to the Philippians, he speaks as follows: 'Who, though he was by nature God, did not consider being equal to God a thing to be clung to.'[23] And again, to the Romans: 'Grace be to you and peace from God our Father and from the Lord Jesus Christ.'[24]

Besides, it was superfluous for the article to be added here, since in the line above it was consistently used with the word God. Just as, in speaking of the Father, he says: 'God is a Spirit,'[25] but because the article does not accompany the word 'Spirit' we do not on that account deny that God is without a body; so also here, even if the article is not placed with the Son, the Son is no less God on that account. How is that? Because, since he uses the word 'God' in both places,[26] he does not indicate that there is any difference in this Godhead, but quite the contrary. Once he had said: 'And the Word was God,' in order that no one might think that the Godhead of the Son was inferior, he at once predicated of Him characteristics recognized as marks of genuine divinity, both referring again to His eternity, by declaring: 'He was in the beginning with God,' and mentioning also His power of creating, for: 'All things were made through Him, and without Him was made nothing that has been made.' The latter power in particular, His Father frequently declares by the Prophets, is a characteristic mark of His own Essence.

Indeed, the Prophets repeatedly use this point in support of the Godhead, and not merely for Its own sake, but also in their struggle against the honor given idols. One says: 'The gods that have not made heaven and earth, let them perish';[27] And another: 'I stretch out the heavens by my hand.'[28] And

23 Phil. 2.6.
24 Rom. 1.7.
25 John 4.24.
26 Literally, 'he uses "God" and again "God." '
27 Jer. 10.11.
28 Isa. 44.24.

everywhere that this point is set down it is to show that it is indicative of the Godhead.

This Evangelist himself was not satisfied by these words, but also called Him both 'Light' and 'Life.' Well, then, if He was always with the Father, if He Himself created all things, if He Himself has directed and ordered all things (this is signified by 'Life'), if He illumines all things, who is so senseless as to say that the Evangelist was trying to show the inferiority of His Godhead by those very words by which in particular it is possible to prove His equality to and identity with the Father?

Then, let us not confuse the creature with the Creator, that we also may not hear: 'They worshipped the creature rather than the Creator.'[29] For, though they should say that this statement is made about the heavens, still, though speaking of the heavens, he has positively declared that we must not worship the creature, for that is the pagan error.

Therefore, let us not make ourselves subject to that curse. The Son of God came to earth for this reason: that He might convert us from this worship; for this reason He took on Himself the form of a slave, that He might free us from this slavery; for this reason He has been spat upon; for this reason He has been struck in the face; for this reason He has undergone the most shameful death. Let us not, then, make all these things useless, or return to our former impiety, or rather, to a much more serious one. Indeed, it is not equally wrong to worship the creature and to bring down, at least as far as we can, the Creator Himself to the worthlessness of the creature. For, of course, He Himself remains unchanged. 'Thou art the same,' says Scripture, 'and thy years have no end.'[30]

Therefore, let us glorify Him as we have learned from our fathers; let us glorify Him by our faith and our works. Pious teachings avail us nothing for salvation if our life has become

29 Rom. 1.25.
30 Ps. 101.28.

corrupted. Therefore, let us order it according to the will of God, establishing ourselves far from all shamefulness, injustice, and greed, as strangers and travelers and foreigners to things here. Even if one has much wealth and many possessions, let him use them in such a manner as a wayfarer who a little later will leave them, whether he wants to do so or not.

And even if a man may be wronged by another, let him not be angry forever; nay, rather, not even for a time. The Apostle has not given us more than one day to indulge in anger, since he says: 'Do not let the sun go down upon your anger.'[31] And rightly so, for it is not desirable for anything unpleasant to last even so short a time. If the night should overtake us, what has happened becomes magnified, since a huge fire of anger is piled up for us by our memory, and we scrutinize these things more keenly at our leisure. Therefore, before we obtain this pernicious leisure and kindle a more fiery blaze, he bids us extinguish the evil beforehand.

Swift, indeed, is the passion of anger and swifter than any fire. Wherefore, we need to be very quick in preventing its flame and in not permitting it to mount up on high. I say this because this disease, if allowed to grow, becomes the cause of many evils. Indeed, it has upset entire households, and completely destroyed long-standing friendships, and wrought irreparable tragedies in a brief space and in a moment of time. 'The wrath of his high spirits is his ruin,'[32] says Scripture.

Therefore, let us not allow the beast to be unbridled, but let us fasten on it a muzzle that is strong in every way; namely, the fear of the judgment to come. When a friend vexes you, or some member of your household stirs you to anger, consider your transgressions against God, and that, by the clemency you exercise toward those who have offended you, you may render that judgment of His milder for yourself.

31 Eph. 4.26.
32 Eccli. 1.28.

Scripture, in fact, says: 'Forgive, and you shall be forgiven,'[33] and so your passion will quickly depart.

Make the following consideration, also: [recall the time] when, having been carried out of yourself to the point of fury, you conquered yourself, and also the occasion when you were swept away by passion; compare both occasions, and in this way you will obtain much instruction.

Now, tell me: When did you consider yourself praiseworthy —when worsted or winning? When worsted, do we not accuse ourselves and feel ashamed—even if no one censures us—and repent heartily both of our words and of our deeds? But when we win out, do we not revel and exult as victors? Indeed, victory over anger is not to repay like for like (for this is total defeat), but for the man who has suffered wrong and heard evil of himself to bear it with equanimity. Victory consists in this: not to injure others but to bear injury.

Accordingly, when you have been angered, do not say: 'I certainly will get back at him—I certainly will seek revenge.' And to those who advise you to control yourself, do not reply: 'I will not allow that rogue to make a fool of me, and get away with it.' Indeed, no one will ever make a fool of you, except you yourself when you have been vindictive; and if someone does ridicule you, even when you have exercised self-control, he will be acting like a fool. But as for you, do not seek for the approbation of fools in your victory; consider it sufficient to have it from wise men.

Yet, why do I hold out to you a small and cheap theatre by mentioning to you the applause of men? Look straight to God, and He will praise you. It is not necessary for the man who is praiseworthy in His eyes to seek for honor from men. The latter often results from the flattery and the enmity of others, and brings no gain, but the approbation of God is free from this inconsistency and brings much advantage to him who wins it. Let us, then, seek after this praise.

---

33 Luke 6.37.

Do you wish to learn how great an evil anger is? Watch men quarreling in the marketplace. You will not be able easily to perceive the disgracefulness [of this passion] in yourself, since your reason is obscured and intoxicated with passion; but at a time when you are free from passion, look at your faults in others, since your judgment then is not clouded. See, I beg, the crowd surging around, with the angry men, like madmen, acting disgracefully in their midst. When passion boils up and pervades the heart and gets out of control, the mouth breathes out fire, the eyes send forth fiery glances, the face swells all over, the hands gesticulate in a disorderly manner, the feet leap about ridiculously and strike against those who are trying to impose restraint. And since angry men are bereft of their senses, as far as these reactions are concerned, they are no different from madmen; nay not even from wild asses that kick and bite. Truly, the angry man does not present a pleasing picture.

Next, after this very ridiculous behavior, on going home and coming to themselves these men feel increasing anxiety and a great deal of fear, as they wonder who in the world were the witnesses present when they were angry. Like madmen, they were unaware of the bystanders, but when they become sober, then they think about these details: whether friends, or enemies and opponents were the spectators. And this is so for they fear equally in both cases: if friends, because these will find fault with them and thus will cause them greater shame; if enemies, because these will gloat over them.

Moreover, if they happen to have exchanged blows with others, more terrible is the fear, lest, perchance, something very serious may befall the one struck: for instance, that fever consequent on the blows may bring on death, or a swelling, difficult to heal, may develop and place him in danger of the worst. 'And why, indeed,' they say, 'did I need to fight? What need of abuse and contention? Away with all these!'

And they end by cursing all the trifling pretexts which caused them to begin the quarrel.

Some who are more foolish blame the wicked spirits and the evil hour for what has happened. But the cause is not in the evil hour, for there is never an evil hour. Nor does the cause lie in a wicked demon, but in the wickedness of those who have been taken captive by the passion of anger. The latter draw even demons after them and bring on themselves every evil.

'But,' you will protest, 'the heart swells and is eaten away by insults.' Yes, I know; and that is why I admire those who conquer this terrible beast [of anger]. For, if we wish, it is possible to get rid of this passion.

Why, indeed, is it that when those in authority insult us we do not become angry? Is it not that fear, counterbalancing anger, has developed, frightening us and not permitting us even to begin to be angry? And why is it that our slaves, though they are insulted in countless ways, bear it all in silence? Is it not because they, also, have the same restraint placed upon them?

Now, do not think only of the fear of God, but that it is even God Himself who then treats you with contumely, God who bids you be silent, and you will bear all with equanimity. And say to him who is harassing you: 'Why should I be angry at you? Another restrains both my hand and my tongue.' The words will become, both for him and for you, an expression of true wisdom. Even now, for the sake of men we endure unendurable things and to those who have insulted us we often say: 'The other fellow insulted me, not you.'

Shall we not show this same care in the case of God? Otherwise, what sort of forgiveness shall we have? Let us say also to our soul: 'It is God who now insults us, and He restrains our hands; let us not leap up; let God not be less honored by us than men.' Did you shudder at these words? I wish you to shudder, not at the words only, but at the deed. God has bidden us not only to endure it when we are struck, but even to offer ourselves to suffer something worse.

However, we oppose Him with such violence that we not only do not expose ourselves to endure evil treatment, but even avenge ourselves, and often also take the initiative in laying unjust hands upon others. Moreover, we think we are worsted if we do not return like for like. And I say this because it is a terrible thing that we think we are victorious when, in fact, we are utterly vanquished. And when we are lying prostrate and receiving numberless blows from the Devil we think we are overcoming him.

Wherefore, I beseech you, let us understand what the true nature of the victory over anger is, and let us pursue this kind of victory. To endure ill treatment is to receive the crown. Well, then, if we wish also to be proclaimed victors by God, let us observe the rules, not of the pagan games, but those of God in these contests, and learn to endure all things with equanimity.

In this way we shall truly overcome our adversaries and win the rewards: both those granted here and those promised to us by the grace and mercy of our Lord Jesus Christ, through whom and with whom glory, power, and honor be to the Father, together with the Holy Spirit, now and always, and forever and ever. Amen.

Homily 5 (John 1.3-5)

'All things were made through Him and without Him was made nothing that has been made.'[1]

Moses, in beginning his narrative in the Old Testament, spoke to us of the things of sense and enumerated them with many details. 'In the beginning,' he said, 'God created the

---

1 John 1.3.

heavens and the earth';[2] then he added that light also was made, and then a second heaven,[3] and the nature of the stars, and every kind of living creature and—not to be tedious by naming them off one by one—everything else.

But this Evangelist, cutting all short, summed up in a line both these things and those Moses mentioned. This he did with good reason, since he was dealing with matters well known to his audience. He hastened at once to a greater theme and entered upon his main task, which was to speak, not about the works of the Creator, but about the Creator and Author of all things.

On this account, while Moses chose for his subject the inferior part of creation (for he did not discourse to us about the invisible powers) and dwelt on that, in detail, John, who was hastening to come to the Creator Himself, was justified in passing over both classes of things: not only those Moses spoke of, but also those about which he was silent—all of these he embraced in one short sentence: 'All things were made by Him.' And in order that you might not think that he meant only all those things explicitly mentioned by Moses he added: 'And without him was made nothing that has been made;' that is, no created thing, whether it be visible or merely intelligible, was brought into being without the power of the Son.

We shall not punctuate with a period after the word 'nothing,' as the heretics do. Thus, because they wish to say that the Spirit is a creature, they word it: 'That [which] has been made in Him was life.' But, read in this way, the sentence becomes unintelligible. In the first place, it was not the time here to make mention of the Spirit, and, even if he wished to do so, why did he make it so obscurely? How, indeed, is it certain that this statement was made with reference to the Spirit?

2 Gen. 1.1.
3 I.e., the sky.

Besides, we shall find that, according to their reading of this statement, it was not the Spirit, but the Son Himself, who came into being of Himself. But listen carefully, so that the meaning may not escape your understanding. And come, let us read it in their way for awhile, for in this way its strangeness will be more evident to us: 'That which has been made in Him was life.' They say that 'life' here means the Spirit. But this life also is discovered to be light, for he added: 'And the life was the light of men.' Well, then, according to them 'the light of men' here means the Spirit.

What then? When he goes on to say: 'There was a man, one sent from God, to bear witness concerning the light,' they must declare that this, too, is affirmed of the Spirit. The Person whom he first calls 'the Word,' going on to say that He is 'God' and 'life,' he also denominates 'light.' This 'Word,' he says, 'was life' and this 'life' was 'light.' Well, then, if the Word is Life, and this Word or Life became flesh, the Life, that is, the Word, was made flesh; 'and we saw his glory—glory as of the only-begotten of the Father—.' Now, if they say that here the Life means the Spirit, see what astonishing conclusions will follow. The Spirit will be incarnate, not the Son; the Spirit will be the only-begotten Son.

But, if they do not admit this, in escaping from this conclusion those who follow this reading stumble upon still another very strange conclusion. If they should concede that the statement is made of the Son, but should not punctuate nor read as we do, they will be actually declaring that the Son was begotten from Himself. If the Word was Life and 'that which was made in him was life,' He Himself was made in Himself and through Himself according to this reading.

Then, after saying something in between, he added: 'And we saw his glory—glory as of the only-begotten of the Father.' See, the only-begotten Son is also found to be the Holy Spirit according to the interpretation of those who make these statements, for it is about Him that John makes this entire exposition. And when the discussion veers away from the truth, do you see how false it becomes and to what strange conclusions it leads?

'What, then, is not the Spirit Light,' do you say? Yes, He is Light, but here the discussion is not about Him; as sometimes God is called a spirit, that is, said to be without a body, but God is not meant on all occasions when spirit is mentioned. Why do you think it strange if we say this about the Father? Similarly, we should not say, with regard to the Paraclete, that whenever spirit is mentioned the Paraclete is meant —yet this appellation of His is very well known—but, if some mention is made of the spirit, the Paraclete is not meant every time. Likewise, Christ is called 'the power of God and the wisdom of God,'[4] but if some mention is made of the power and wisdom of God, Christ is not always meant. So also here, even if the Spirit does give light, the Evangelist is not speaking of Him.

But, when we dispossess them of these astonishing ideas, they say, still with the same reading, once again striving in every way to take a stand against truth: 'That which has been made in him was life,' that is, 'that which has been made was life.' Then, what of the punishment of the Sodomites, and the flood, and hell,[5] and numerous other similar things? 'But our discussion is about the material creation,' they say. Certainly, for those things also are part of the material creation. But, that we may by adequate rebuttal refute their argument, let us address them directly. Tell me, is wood life? And is stone life? These inanimate and immobile things? Or is man altogether life? But who would say he is? For man is not self-existing, but a receiver of life.

Once again see the absurdity here, for here also we shall pursue the discussion along the same lines, so that from this

---

4 1 Cor. 1.25
5 'gehenna', i.e., the place of future punishment, the valley of Hinnon; in the New Testament, 'hell.'

part also we may learn their senselessness. By this interpretation they are saying nothing at all befitting the [Holy] Spirit. When they have been forced from their first stand, they adapt to men the same things which they considered before were worthily said of the Spirit.

However, let us examine also in this way their text itself. A creature is now said to be life; and then it is also light; and John came, bearing witness to it. Why, then, for is he not also light? But 'He was not the light,' [the Evangelist] says. Yet he himself also belonged to creation. How, then, was he not light? And how is it that 'He was in the world, and the world was made through him'? Was the creature in the creature, and the creature made by the creature? Further, how is it that 'The world knew him not'? Did the creature not know the creature? 'But to as many as received him he gave the power of becoming sons of God.'

However, enough of joking. I leave it to you to examine exhaustively into the utter monstrosity of these words later, that we ourselves may not seem to be discussing this simply to provoke laughter, and may not continue idly to waste time. If these words are spoken neither of the Spirit (and they certainly are not, as has been proved), nor of anything created, but they would still insist on the same reading of the text, the most absurd conclusion of all will follow, as we have said before: that the Son was begotten from Himself. Indeed, if the Son is the true Light, and this Light was Life, and Life was made in Him, it is quite unavoidable to draw this conclusion, according to their reading.

Therefore, putting this aside, let us proceed to the generally accepted reading and interpretation. And what is this? To finish the sentence at 'that has been made'; then to begin again from the following phrase, which reads: 'In him was life.' What he means is this: 'Without him was made nothing that has been made. No creatures that have been made,' he says, 'were made without Him.' Do you see how by this short addition all the absurd hurdles are surmounted? By premising that 'without Him was made nothing' and adding 'that has been made,' he includes things perceptible to the intellect, and at the same time excludes the [Holy] Spirit.

Indeed, because he said: 'All things were made through him and without him was made nothing,' he needed this addition in order that no one might say: 'Well, if all things were made through Him, the [Holy] Spirit also was.' 'I have in truth said,' he declares, 'that whatever is created was made through Him, even if it be invisible, even if bodiless, even if in heaven. For this reason I have not simply said, "all things," but "whatever has been made," that is, creatures. However, the [Holy] Spirit is not a creature.'

Do you perceive the precision of his teaching? He mentioned the creation of the world of sense, for Moses had taught this before him. Then, as he caused us to advance from there to higher things, I mean to incorporeal and invisible things, he excluded the Holy Spirit from all creation. So also Paul, deriving inspiration from this source, has said, 'For in Him were created all things.'[6] And see, here again, the same carefulness, since the same Spirit moved this soul, also. Lest anyone might exclude any created thing from the creation of God because of its being invisible, and that the Paraclete might not be confused with these, he, too, passing over things that are perceptible to sense and familiar to all, enumerates the things of heaven, saying: 'Whether Thrones, or Dominations, or Principalities, or Powers.' The word 'whether,' placed before each one, makes clear to us nothing else than that: 'All things were made through him and without him was made nothing that has been made.'

But, if you think the word 'through' implies inferiority, listen to [the Prophet] saying: 'In the beginning thou didst establish the earth and heaven is the work of thy hands.'[7]

6 Col. 1.16.
7 Ps. 101.26.

What is said of the Father as Creator is meant also of the Son; he would not have said it if he had not the same opinion of Him as of the Creator, and as not inferior to anyone. And if the words 'through Him' are used here, they are employed with no other view than that no one may subscribe to the idea that the Son is unbegotten.

Besides, in testimony that He is not inferior to the Father with respect to the dignity of the Creator, listen as He Himself declares: 'As the Father raises the dead and gives them life, even so the Son also gives life to whom he will.'[8] Accordingly, if it is also said of the Son in the Old Testament: 'In the beginning, O Lord, thou didst establish the earth,' the dignity of Creator is clearly referred to. And if you maintain that the Prophet really said this of the Father, but that Paul applied to the Son what was said of the Father, the same conclusion again follows. Paul would not have laid down that this expression was also proper to the Son if he were not very confident that His dignity was held in equal honor with the Father's. And I say this because it would have been an act of utter presumption to attribute things proper to the unique Nature [of God] to one inferior to and less than It.

However, the Son is in reality neither less than, nor inferior to, the Essence of the Father. Therefore, Paul had courage to say, not these things only, but also others similar to them. The expression 'from whom,' which you classify as possessing dignity worthy only of the Father, he also used of the Son, speaking as follows: 'from whom the whole body, supplied and built up by joints and ligaments attains a growth that is of God.'[9] And he was not satisfied with this only, but also refuted your argument elsewhere by using of the Father the expression 'through Him' which you say implies inferiority. He said: 'God is trustworthy, through him you have been

8 John 5.21.
9 Col. 2.19.

called into fellowship with his Son';[10] and again: 'through his will';[11] and elsewhere: 'For from him and through him and unto him are all things.'[12]

Further, the expression 'from whom' has been used, not of the Son only, but also of the Holy Spirit. And I say this because the angel said to Joseph: 'Do not be afraid to take to thee Mary thy wife, for that which is begotten in her is from the Holy Spirit.'[13] Likewise, the Prophet did not think it improper to apply to God the words 'in whom,' which properly belong to the Spirit, speaking as follows: 'In God we shall do mightily.'[14] And Paul said: 'Imploring in my prayers, that somehow I may at last in God's will have a prosperous journey to get to you.'[15] And again he used this expression of Christ, saying: 'In Christ Jesus.'[16] In short, frequently, even continually, we may find these expressions used for one another, and this would not happen if the same meaning did not underlie them in every instance.

But, that you might not now get the idea that the words, 'All things were made through him,' were said with reference to His miracles (for the rest of the Evangelists have discoursed about these), he added after these words: 'He was in the world and the world was made through him,' not, however, the Holy Spirit, for He is not a creature, but above every creature. Moreover, let us consider what follows. When John had said regarding creation: 'All things were made through him and without him was made nothing that has been made' he also added a word about His providence, saying: 'In him was life.'

Now, it was in order that no one might be incredulous as

10 1 Cor. 1.9.
11 Eph. 1.1.
12 Rom. 11.36.
13 Matt. 1.20.
14 Ps. 59.14.
15 Rom. 1.10.
16 A phrase which appears frequently in St. Paul.

to how so great and so many things were made through Him that he added: 'In him was life.' Accordingly, even as in the case of the spring which produces the fathomless depths [of the sea]—however much you drain off, you have in no way lessened the spring—so it is with the creative activity of the Only-begotten. However much you may believe has been accomplished and done through it, it is in no way lessened.

Rather, to use a more familiar illustration, I shall speak of the light, as he himself also has immediately gone on to do in these words: 'And the life was the light.' Accordingly, just as the light, however many men it has enlightened, is in no way lessened in its own brightness, so also God, both before creation and after it, remains intact, in no way lessened or wearied by the greatness of creation. Even if it were necessary for thousands of such worlds to be made—and even if their number were infinite—He Himself remains sufficient for all, not only to bring them forth, but also to conserve them after their creation. For the word 'life' here means not only creation, but also the providing for the conservation [of what has been created.]

Besides, this appellation introduces us to the doctrine of the resurrection, and commences to announce these wonderful good tidings. When Life has come to us, the power of death has been destroyed, and when the Light has shone for us, darkness is no more, but Life always remains in us and death cannot overcome it. Thus, what is said of the Father would also be properly said of this Light: 'In him we live and move and have our being.'[17] This is a point which Paul also made clear when he said: 'For in him were created all things, and in him all things hold together.'[18] Therefore, He also is called both 'Root'[19] and 'Foundation.'[20]

---

17 Acts 17.28.
18 Col. 1.16,18.
19 Cf. Rom. 15.12.
20 Cf. 1 Cor. 3.11.

However, when you hear: 'In him was life,' do not conceive of Him as made up of parts, for further on He says even of the Father: 'As the Father has life in Himself, even so He has given to the Son also to have life in Himself.'[21] Moreover, just as you would not say on this account that the Father is composed of various parts, so also you would not say it of the Son. Elsewhere [the Evangelist] says: 'God is light,'[22] and again: 'He dwells in light inaccessible.'[23]

He says all these things, not that we may get the idea that He is compounded of different substances, but that we may be led gradually upward to the most sublime doctrines. Since the average person would not easily understand how His life is self-existing, John first makes that easier statement, and then brings us, after that preparation, to the higher point. He who had said: 'He has given him to have life,'[24] also said: 'I am the life,'[25] and, again: 'I am the light.'[26]

But what kind of light is this, I ask? Not such as is perceived by the senses, but by the mind, enlightening the very soul. Since Christ was going to say: 'No one can come to me unless the Father draw him,'[27] the Evangelist therefore said here by anticipation that it is He Himself who gives light, in order that, even if you should hear some such thing about the Father, you would not say that it is true of Him alone, but also of the Son; for, 'All things that my Father has are mine,' He says.[28]

In the first place, then, the Evangelist taught us about creation. Next, he spoke also of the good things of the spirit which He by His coming has made available for us. And he subtly included these things in a single sentence when he af-

---

21 John 5.26.
22 John 1.5.
23 1 Tim. 6.16.
24 John 5.26.
25 John 14.6.
26 John 8.12.
27 John 6.44.
28 John 16.15.

firmed: 'And the life was the light of men.' Now, he did not say: 'was the light of the Jews,' but: 'of all mankind.' Not the Jews only, but also the pagans, came to this knowledge, and this light was set before them as common to all. And why did he not affirm this also of the angels, but said only: 'of men'? Because his discussion at this point concerned human nature, and he had come to announce the good tidings to men.

'And the light shines in the darkness.' He means the darkness both of death and of error. The light that can be seen by our eyes does not shine in the darkness, but apart from it. On the contrary, the Gospel has shone amid conquering error and has vanquished it. And when Christ Himself was in the midst of death, He so overcame it as to raise up those who had been already worsted by it. Therefore, since death did not overcome Him, nor did error, but He shines everywhere and gives light by His own power, for this reason he said: 'And the darkness grasped it not.' And this is so because, though it cannot be banished, it does not consent to dwell in souls that do not wish to be enlightened.

But, if He did not win all men over to Him, do not let this trouble you, for not by force and violence but by will and consent does God lead us on. Accordingly, do not shut the doors to this Light, and you will enjoy much happiness. This Light becomes present through faith, and when present, it subsequently shines with great abundance upon him who receives it; if you provide a pure life for it, it will remain continuously dwelling within you. 'If anyone love me, he will keep my word and the Father and I will come to him and will make our abode with him' He says.[29] Accordingly, just as it is not possible for one to derive enjoyment from a sunbeam if he does not open his eyes, so one may not share in this brightness in full measure if he does not open wide the eye of his soul and make it sharp-sighted in every respect.

How is this done? When we purge the soul of its evil in-

29 John 14.23.

clinations. Sin is darkness, and dense darkness, as is evident because it is committed rashly and thoughtlessly. In truth, 'Everyone who does evil hates the light and does not come to the light,'[30] and 'Of the things that are done in secret it is shameful even to speak.'[31] Therefore, even as in darkness one knows neither friend nor enemy, but is ignorant of all the properties of things, so also is it with sin. He who desires to possess more than his due does not distinguish friend from enemy, and the envious man looks upon his closest companion as an enemy, and the schemer has declared war on all without exception.

In a word, all who commit sin are no different from drunkards and madmen, with regard to not distinguishing the nature of things. And, even as at night, wood and lead and iron and silver and gold and a precious stone all look alike to us, since the light which makes them look different is not present, so also he who lives an impure life does not know the nobility of moderation or the beauty of wisdom. As I have just said, even if precious stones are present in darkness, they do not display their beauty, not because of their own nature, but because of the lack of perception on the part of those who are looking at them.

Now, this is not the only evil effect which follows upon us when we are in sin, but we then live continually in fear. Just as men walking through a moonless night tremble, even if no one who might inspire fear is present, so they who commit sin have no cause to take courage, even if no accuser be present, but they fear all things and are suspicious, goaded by conscience. All things are full of fear and terror for them; they suspect all things, they fear all things.

Well, then, let us flee from such a painful life. After this pain, death will follow, death that is deathless, for there is no end of punishment there. And while here, they are in

---

30 John 3.20.
31 Eph. 5.12.

no way different from the insane who occupy themselves with dreams of things that do not exist. And this is so because they who are not wealthy think they have riches, and they who do not enjoy pleasure think they do, and they do not perceive this foolishness as they ought until they are set free from this madness, until they are awakened from sleep. Wherefore, Paul enjoins upon all to be wary and be vigilant, and Christ likewise gives the same admonition. He who is careful and vigilant, even if he be caught by sin, quickly beats it off from himself. But he who is asleep and out of his wits does not perceive how he is possessed by it.

Well, then, let us not sleep. For it is not night time, but day. Therefore, 'Let us walk becomingly as in the day.'[32] Nothing is more unbecoming than sin. It is a lesser evil— considered in the light of what is unbecoming—to walk abroad naked than to go about committing sin or with offensive conduct. Going naked is not so great a fault, since, often, it may result from poverty; but nothing is baser and more dishonorable than the person who sins.

Then, let us reflect, also, on those who go before the law court because of their rapacity and greed, and think how base and ridiculous they appear, since they behave altogether shamelessly by lying and acting contumeliously. We ourselves are in so pitiable and wretched a state that we cannot endure to wear our cloak awkwardly or adjusted carelessly; even if it is another man we see with his garment askew, we straighten it. However, when all of us, and our neighbors, too, are walking upside down, we do not perceive it.

What, indeed, is more shameful, I ask, than a man having relations with a harlot? And what is more ridiculous than a wanton, a blasphemer, or a slanderer? Whence is it, then, that these things do not seem as shameful as to go naked? Merely from custom. No one ever willingly permits the one, but the others are brazenly done by all without shame. Surely,

---

32 Rom. 13.13.

if someone came into a group of angels, among whom no such thing ever has taken place, then he would realize clearly that such conduct is most ridiculous indeed.

Why do I say a group of angels? If in our royal palaces a man should bring in a harlot, and have relations with her, or if a man be overcome by drunkenness or be guilty of some other unbecoming conduct of the kind, he suffers the most serious punishment. If it is not permissible to do such brazen deeds in royal palaces, how much more completely shall we pay the penalty if we dare to do such things when the King is everywhere present and witnesses our actions?

Wherefore, I exhort you, let us show great gentleness and great purity in our lives. For we have a King who always sees all our actions. Therefore, in order that this Light may ever illumine us in abundance, let us attract its beams. Thus shall we enjoy the rewards both here and hereafter, through the grace and mercy of our Lord Jesus Christ, through whom and with whom glory be to the Father, together with the Holy Spirit, forever and ever. Amen.

Homily 6 (John 1.6-8)

'There was a man, one sent from God, whose name was John.'[1]

When in his preamble the Evangelist had told us the most important facts about the Word of God, he continued his narrative systematically and methodically, and came in due course also to the forerunner of the Word, named, like himself, John. And as you hear that the latter was 'sent from God,' remember in future that there is no merely human residue left in what he said. For he did not speak his own words, but every word he uttered was inspired by Him who sent him. That is why he is also called a messenger, since

---
1 John 1.6,

the excellence of a messenger consists in saying nothing of his own. Further, the word 'was' does not here mean his coming into existence, but refers to his office of messenger. That is why 'There was one sent from God' was said instead of 'He was sent from God.'

How is it, then, that some maintain that the words: 'He was by nature God,'[2] do not imply the Son's equality to the Father because the article is not added [to the word 'God']? Notice that here, also, the article is not used either. Well, do the words, therefore, not refer to the Father? If they do not, what shall we say to the Prophet who said: 'Behold I send my messenger before thy face who shall prepare thy way'?[3] These words, 'my' and 'thy' certainly indicate two Persons [in God].

'This man came as a witness, to bear witness concerning the light.'

'What is this,' someone may perhaps say; 'does the servant bear witness to the master?' Indeed, when you see Him not only attested by His servant, but also coming to him and being baptized by him with the Jews, will you not be still more astounded and puzzled? However, you must not be disturbed or confused, but marvel at His unspeakable goodness.

Yet, if one still remain perplexed and troubled, He will say also to him what He said to John: 'Let it be so now, for so it becomes us to fulfill all justice.'[4] And if he be still more perplexed, Christ will once more say to him, too, what He said to the Jews: 'I do not receive the witness of man.'[5] Well, then, if there was no need of this testimony, why was John sent from God? Not because there was need of his testimony (for this saying smacks of the worst blasphemy), but why? John the Evangelist himself gave the answer when he said: 'that all might believe through him.'

---

2 Phil. 2.6.
3 Mark 1,2.
4 Matt. 3.15.
5 John 5.34.

Now, Christ Himself, after saying: 'I do not receive the witness of men,' in order that He might not seem to the foolish to be contradicting Himself by saying at one time: 'There is another who bears witness concerning me and I know that the witness he bears concerning me is true,'[6] where He meant John [the Baptist]; and at another: 'I do not receive the witness of men,' at once added the explanation by saying: 'But I say these things that you may be saved.'

This was as if He said: 'I am God, and the true Son of God, and am of God's immortal and blessed substance, and so I need no one to bear witness to Me. Even if no one desired to do so, I should suffer no loss at all, as regards My substance, by this omission. But, since I am responsible for the salvation of mankind, for this reason I descended to such a degree of humiliation as to entrust to a man the testimony concerning Me.' Now, because of the worldliness and weakness of the Jews, faith in Him would in this way be made more readily acceptable to them and easier to digest. Therefore, just as He clad Himself in flesh lest, by advancing to the attack with His Godhead unrevealed, He might lose all men, so He sent a man as His forerunner in order that, since they would hear the words of a fellow human, the people might feel more at ease in coming to listen to him.

Indeed, because He had no need of that testimony, it was enough only to reveal Himself, to make known who He was, in His undisguised essence, to stupefy all men. But He did not do this, for the reason that I have just mentioned. He would, in truth, have destroyed all men, since no one could bear the onset of that unapproachable Light. Because of this, as I have just said, He even put on our flesh and entrusted the testimony about Himself to one of our fellow servants, since He directed all things for the salvation of mankind, not taking thought for His own dignity only, but also looking

6 John 5.32.

to what would be well received by and profitable to His hearers.

And, therefore, this is what He Himself intimated when He said: 'I say these things to you that you may be saved.' The Evangelist, also, after saying: 'To bear witness concerning the light,' has added, with the same meaning as his Master's: 'That all might believe through him.' In this he was all but saying: 'Do not think that John the Baptist came bearing witness for this reason: that he might add some weight to the trustworthiness of the word of the Lord. It was not for this, but that his fellow men might believe through him.' In fact, it is plain from what follows that he said this in the endeavor to remove even the possibility of that idea, for he added: 'He was not the light.'

Now, if it was not to remove this suspicion that he repeated this expression, he would be simply dragging in the phrase, and it would be tautology rather than a clarifying of his teaching. For, after saying that he was sent: 'To bear witness to the light' why did he say again: 'He was not that light'? Not purposelessly or without cause, but because for the most part, with us, the one bearing witness is greater than he in whose favor the guarantee is given, and the former seems oftentimes to be more worthy of trust. In order that no one might get this idea also about John, the Evangelist dispelled this evil notion right from the beginning. Tearing it up by the roots, he pointed out who it is that bears witness and who it is in whose favor the testimony is given, and how much difference there is between the One receiving and the one giving testimony. Having done this, and having pointed out His immeasurable superiority, he then continued confidently with the remainder of his treatise. Once he had taken pains to remove any ridiculous idea which might lurk in the minds of those who might be somewhat lacking in good sense, he then finally began to implant the word of teaching in all men in orderly sequence, easily and without impediment.

Let us pray, then, that for the future, keeping pace with the unfolding of this teaching and the correctness of our doctrine, our lives also may be pure and our conduct exemplary, since the former avail not at all if we do not have good deeds as well. Even if we should have faith in its entirety and a thorough knowledge of the Scriptures, if we should be empty and destitute of the protection derived from a good life, there would be nothing preventing us from being cast into the fire of hell and from being consumed forever by the inextinguishable flame. Indeed, just as those who have lived good lives will rise to life everlasting, so they who have dared to do the opposite will have everlasting punishment with no limits.

Wherefore, let us display all eagerness that we may not vitiate the reward in store for us from our steadfast faith, by the meanness of our deeds, but that, being in favor also because of them, we may behold Christ with confidence. No blessedness could be the equal of this. And may all, in order to reach the goal I have described, do all to the glory of God, to whom be glory together with the Only-begotten Son and the Holy Spirit forever and ever. Amen.

Homily 7 (John 1.9)

'It was the true light that enlightens every man who comes into the world.'

Dearly beloved children, the reason why we have fed you little by little with thoughts from the Scriptures, and have not poured them all out at once, is that we might make it easy for you to hold fast those already given to you.

And I say this for, in constructing a building when the first stones are not yet firmly fastened together, if a man sets others upon them, he renders the wall altogether unsound and easy to throw down. But, if he waits for the cement to set first, and then places the rest upon it gradually, he completes the whole house with safety, making it not a temporary structure, or easily destroyed, but durable. Let us also imitate these builders and let us build up your souls in the same way. For we are afraid lest, when the first foundation has just been laid, the adding of the next teachings may weaken the former, because your understanding is not sufficiently strong to hold all together firmly.

What is it, then, that is read out to us today? 'It was the true light that enlightens every man who comes into the world.' Now, in speaking above about John, the Evangelist had said that he came 'to bear witness to the light' and that 'he was sent.' Hence, lest anyone, upon hearing this, because the one bearing witness had come only recently, might suspect a like newness of the One to whom witness was borne, he appealed to our imagination and dispatched it to that Existence preceding every beginning, an existence which comes to no end and has no beginning.

'And, how is this possible,' you ask, 'since He is a Son? We are speaking about God, and do you ask 'how'? But are you not afraid, and do you not tremble? Yet, if someone should ask you: 'How will our souls and our bodies have life without end in the world to come?' you would laugh at the question on the ground that to seek such knowledge does not rightly belong to the human understanding. On the contrary, it is necessary only to believe and not to examine into what is said, since the power of the One speaking is sufficient guarantee of what has been said.

So, if we say that the Maker of souls and bodies, who immeasurably surpasses all creation, is without beginning, will you ask us how? And who would judge that this attitude is that of a balanced mind? Or of a sound reason? You have heard that 'It was the true light.' Why do you strive contentiously and in vain to compass by your reason this infinite life? It is not possible to do so. Why do you search for the unsearchable? Why do you scrutinize the inscrutable? Why do you seek into the incomprehensible? Inquire into the source of the sunbeams; you will not be able to find it; nevertheless, you do not wax indignant or feel vexed because of your weakness. How is it, then, that you have become rash and impetuous in greater matters than these?

John, the Son of Thunder, as he sounded forth on his spiritual trumpet, did not inquire further when he heard the word 'was' from the Spirit. And you, who do not share in his grace but merely give voice to your weak reasonings, strive contentiously to surpass the measure of his knowledge? For this very reason you will never be able even to approach the measure of his knowledge.

Such as this, indeed, is the strategy of the Devil; he leads those who are obedient to him beyond the bounds given to us by God, as if to much greater things. But when, having enticed us by these hopes, he has divorced us from the love of God, then not only does he add nothing more for the future (for how can he, since he is the Devil?), but he does not even permit us to return to the former circumstances where we lived safely and securely, but leads us wandering about everywhere, unable to come to rest anywhere.

In this way he also caused our first parent to be deprived of the abode of Paradise. After puffing him up by the promise of greater knowledge and honor, he forcibly separated him even from those things which he then had the right to enjoy with complete freedom. Indeed, not only was he not equal to God as [Satan] had promised him, but he even became subject to the despotic power of death. Not only did he gain no advantage from eating of the tree, but even destroyed in no small measure the knowledge which he then actually possessed, spurred on by the hope of obtaining greater knowledge. Then, indeed, a feeling of shame and a desire to be clad on account of his nakedness descended upon him who, before this trick, had not been subject to a feeling of shame. Indeed, the consciousness that he was naked and the need in future of the covering of clothes, and many other painful changes, were from that time forward natural to him.

In order that we, too, may not have something similar happen to us, let us be obedient to God, and let us remain faithful to those things which He has commanded us. Let us not beyond that be unduly inquisitive, that we may not be separated from the good things already granted to us, even as they were. In seeking to find the beginning of the Life that is without beginning they destroyed even the things which they could have had. Indeed, they did not find what they sought, since it was not possible to do so, and they lost the integrity of their faith in the Only-begotten.

Let us not change the ancient boundaries which our fathers set, but let us yield everywhere to the laws of the Spirit. And when we hear: 'It was the true light,' let us seek to find out nothing more. In fact, it is not possible to penetrate the meaning of these words further. If He begot in human fashion, it would be necessary that there be some interval between the one begetting and the begotten, but, since He begets ineffably and as befits God, leave out the words 'before' and 'after,' for these are terms belonging to time, and the Son is the Maker of all ages.

'Well, then,' you say, 'He is not the Father, but a brother.' Why is that necessary, I ask? If we had said that both the Father and the Son were from another source, then you would have a right to make this statement. But, inasmuch as we shun this impiety and say that the Father is without beginning and is not begotten, while the Son is without beginning but is begotten of the Father, why is it in any way necessary to pass from this idea to that impious statement? Not at all, for He is [the Father's] 'Brightness,' and brightness is understood to be simultaneous with the substance of which it is the brightness.[1]

And it is for this very reason that Paul has called Him so, namely, that you may not think that there is an interval between the Father and the Son. This point, then, has been cleared up by this expression,[2] but the words following it correct an absurdity which might arise in the minds of the foolish. 'For when you hear "brightness," ' he says, 'do not think that He is deprived of His own Person.' In truth, that impious belief is part of the insanity both of the Sabellians[3] and of the followers of Marcellus.[4] We do not talk as they do, however, but affirm that He exists also in His own Person. For this reason, when Paul had said that He is 'brightness,' he added that He is also 'the image of his substance,' in order that he might make it clear that the Son has His own Person and is of the same substance as that of which He is the image.[5]

Of course, it is not enough, as I have said before, to prove the teachings about God by one text; but it is desirable, when we have collected many, to choose what is fitting from each one. Thus we shall be able to arrive at praise worthy of Him; I say 'worthy,' to be sure, within my limitations. If someone should think that he is able to speak really worthily and should strive to do so, intimating thus that he knows God

---

1 Cf. Heb. 1.3.
2 I.e., 'brightness.'
3 The Sabellians, following the heretical teachings of Sabellius, a theologian of the early third century, recognized a distinction in the Trinity, not of Persons but of energies or modes, maintaining that the Deity is one Person. Cf. *Catholic Encyclopedia*.
4 Marcellus of Ancyra (d. 374), was at first a strong opponent of Arianism, and as such was present at the Councils of Ancyra and of Nicaea. In his zeal to combat Arianism he fell into the error of teaching that the trinity of Persons in the Godhead was not a permanent dispensation, but that God in the beginning was one personality from which at intervals the Son and the Holy Spirit proceeded and to which they will return at the consummation of all things, and the Godhead will again be an absolute unity. He was several times condemned for his teaching and died deprived of his see. Cf. *Catholic Encyclopedia*.
5 Cf. Heb. 1.1-3.

as He Himself knows Himself, then he would be most of all ignorant of God.

Therefore, since we know these things, let us continue to hold fast the things which 'they who from the beginning were eyewitnesses and ministers of the word have handed down to us'[6] and let us not meddle with them further. Two misfortunes will befall those who are sick with this disease: first, they will work hard fruitlessly, by seeking for things which it is not possible to find; second, they will incur the anger of God by striving to pass beyond the bounds He set. Now, what kind of anger this stirs up it is not necessary to learn from me, because you all know. Wherefore, avoiding the perversion of these men, let us tremble at His words in order that He may always protect us. 'To whom shall I have respect,' He says, 'but to him that is poor and little, and of a contrite spirit, and that trembleth at my words?'[7] Well, then, avoiding this destructive meddlesomeness, let us crush our hearts; let us grieve for our sins, even as Christ has enjoined upon us; let us have compunction for our offenses; let us carefully recall everything we dared to do in the past; let us earnestly strive to wipe these offenses out altogether.

Indeed, God has revealed to us many ways of doing this. 'Do thou first tell thy sins,' He says, ' "to justify thyself" ';[8] and again: 'I have said, I will confess my iniquity against myself, and Thou didst remit the guilt of my heart.'[9] For, the continual confession and remembrance of our sins avails not a little in lessening their gravity. There is still another more effectual way than this, namely, not harboring evil thoughts against anyone who has done wrong to us, forgiving the offenses of all who have offended against us.

Do you wish to learn a third way, also? Listen to Daniel

---

6 Luke 1.2.
7 Isa. 66.2.
8 Isa. 43.26.
9 Ps. 31.5.

saying: 'Wherefore, redeem thou thy sins with alms and thy iniquities with works of mercy to the poor.'[10] But there is still another way besides this, namely, perseverance in prayer and attending assiduously and earnestly to prayer to God. Fasting also brings to us no small palliation and remission of our sins, when it is joined with kindness toward others, and it quenches the fury of the anger of God. For, 'water quencheth a flaming fire and alms resisteth sins.'[11]

Let us, then, travel all these roads. If we are always on them, and if we spend our leisure in them, not only shall we efface past offenses, but we shall gain the greatest profit for the future. We shall not make it easy for the Devil to tempt us either to laziness or to destructive overactivity. In truth, through these and other imperfections he draws us on to foolish questionings and hurtful disputations, because he sees us idle or wasting time and taking no thought for virtue in our lives.

Let us block up this approach to him, let us be watchful, let us be wary, in order that, having worked a little in this short time, we may possess imperishable good things in the endless ages, through the grace and mercy of our Lord Jesus Christ, through whom and with whom glory be to the Father together with the Holy Spirit forever and ever. Amen.

Homily 8 (John 1.9-10)

'It was the true light that enlightens every man who comes into the world.'

Today there is nothing against resuming our study of the same words again, since last time we were prevented from reaching the whole text that was read, because we were explaining the doctrines involved.

---

10 Dan. 4.24.
11 Eccli. 3.33.

Well, where are they now who deny that He is true God? Here He is said to be 'the true light,' and elsewhere very 'truth' and very 'life.'[1] We shall explain the latter text more clearly when we come to it; for the present we must speak for awhile to your charity on the other part [of today's text].

If He enlightens every man who comes into the world, how is it that so many have remained unenlightened? For not all, to be sure, have recognized the high dignity of Christ. How, then, does He enlighten every man?

As much as He is permitted to do so. But if some, deliberately closing the eyes of their minds, do not wish to receive the beams of this Light, darkness is theirs. This is not because of the nature of the Light, but is a result of the wickedness of men who deliberately deprive themselves of the gift. Grace has been poured forth upon all: not refused to Jew, Greek, barbarian, Scythian, free, slave, male, female, old, young. It is sent to all alike, and calls all with equal honor. And they who do not wish to enjoy this gift ought rightly to attribute their blindness to themselves. When the way is open to all, and there is no one hindering, if some lovers of evil remain outside, they are destroyed by nothing else than by their own wickedness alone.

'He was in the world,' but not as conterminous with the world—perish the thought! Therefore, he added: 'and the world was made through him,' by this statement conducting you once more to the ageless existence of the Only-begotten. In truth, after hearing that all this is His work, even if a man is without feeling, even if inimical, even if hostile to the glory of God, he will be altogether compelled—willingly or unwillingly—to acknowledge that the Maker exists before His work. For this reason it always occurs to me to marvel at the madness of Paul of Samosata,[2] because he dared to oppose truth that was so evident, and he deliberately fell into

---

1 John 14.6.
2 Cf. Homily 4 n. 5.

error. He did not err in ignorance, but in spite of knowing [the truth] clearly, since he was afflicted in the same way as the Jews.

Now, they looked to the opinion of men and gave up the integrity of the faith, because, though conscious that He is the only-begotten Son of God, they did not acknowledge this, on account of the rulers—that they might not be cast from the synagogue. In like manner, it is said that he also gave up his own salvation to please a certain woman.[3] In truth, terrible, really terrible, is the tyranny of vainglory. It is capable of blinding the eyes, even of wise men, if they are not vigilant. If the taking of bribes can do this to them, this passion is much more powerful to do so. Wherefore, Christ also said to the Jews: 'How can you believe who receive glory from one another and do not seek the glory which is from the only God?'[4]

'And the world knew Him not.' Here he called the multitude 'the world': corrupt and engrossed by earthly things as it is—the vulgar, confused, and senseless crowd. But the friends of God and all the elect knew Him even before He was present in the flesh. Christ Himself said this of the patriarch, mentioning him by name: 'Abraham your father rejoiced that he was to see my day. He saw it and was glad.'[5] And to refute the Jews He said about David: 'How then does David in the spirit call him Lord, saying, "The Lord said to my Lord: Sit thou at my right-hand." '[6]

Often, too, in taking a stand against them, He reminded

---

3 Zenobia, Queen of Palmyra, supported and protected Paul of Samosata in his political ambitions; he seems to have shaped some of his heretical doctrines with a view to pleasing her Jewish susceptibilities. Cf. *Catholic Encyclopedia,* art. 'Paul of Samosata.'
4 John 5.44.
5 John 8.56.
6 Matt. 22.43,44.

them of Moses. And the chief Apostle does this also regarding the rest of the Prophets, for Peter declared that all the Prophets from Samuel on acknowledged Him and foretold His coming beforehand, as follows: 'And all the prophets who have spoken from Samuel onwards have also announced these days.'[7] Moreover, God appeared to Jacob and to his father and grandfather, and spoke to them, and promised to give them many great blessings which forthwith He did actually bestow.

'How is it, then,' you ask, 'that He said: "Many Prophets have desired to see what you see and have not seen it; and to hear what you hear, and they have not heard it"?'[8] Did they not, therefore, share in the knowledge of Him?' Without a doubt, they did. I shall try to make this fact clear from this very text, and according to which some maintain that the Prophets were denied this knowledge. Now, 'Many,' He says, 'have desired to see what you see.' It is implied that they knew that He was going to come to men and to perform the deeds which He did in fact perform. They would not have desired to see them if they had no knowledge at all of them. No one, to be sure, can conceive a desire for things which he has not in his mind. Therefore, they knew the Son of God and that He would come to men.

What, then, are the things which they did not know and what the things which they did not hear? Those which you now see and hear. And if some both heard His voice and saw Him, it was not in the flesh or as He mingled with men and addressed them with such freedom. He Himself, indeed, to make this plain, did not say simply: 'They desired to see Me.' But what? 'To see the things which you see.' He did not say: 'to hear Me.' But what? 'To hear the things which you hear.' So that, even if they did not see His coming in the

---

7 Acts 3.24.
8 Luke 10.24.

flesh, they knew that it was to come and were desirous of it; and they believed in Him, even without seeing Him in the flesh.

Therefore, when the heathen assail us, saying: 'What was Christ doing during the previous period when He was not visiting the race of men? And why in the world did He come so late to win our salvation, when He had neglected us for so long a time?' we shall reply that even before this He was in the world, and He foreknew His works, and was known to all who were worthy of this knowledge. And if, because not all then knew of Him, but He was known only to the upright and the virtuous, you should say that He was therefore not acknowledged, for the same reason even now you will not admit that He is worshiped by men, since not even now do all know Him. But, just as at present no one would utterly discredit those who know Him because of those who do not, so there ought to be no doubt, with regard to former times, that He was known to many men—nay, rather, to all those who were upright and exemplary.

But someone may say: 'And why did not all men give heed to Him? Why did not all then reverence Him, but only the just?'

I in turn shall ask: 'Why do not all men know Him now?' But why do I confine my remarks to Christ? Why, indeed, did not all men, either then or now, know His Father? Indeed, some say that all things are sustained by chance, while others attribute the guidance of the universe to evil spirits. There are still others who invent another god besides Him. Further, do some of these, even, declare blasphemously that God's power is exercised in opposition to the latter and think that His laws are those of some evil spirit? What then? Shall we in consequence say that He is not God because there are some who affirm this? And shall we agree that He is wicked because there are some who blasphemously declare that He is so?

Away with such nonsense and absolute madness! If we are going to define doctrine from the judgment of madmen, there is every reason to suppose that we also are mad to the uttermost degree of insanity. Again, no one will say that the sun is injurious to the eyes, judging by those who have diseased sight, but that it gives light, accepting the judgment of those who have healthy eyes. Further, no one will judge that honey is bitter because it seems so to the taste of the sick. Will some, however, guided by the decision of the feeble-minded, affirm that God either does not exist, or is wicked, or at one time exercises His providence and again does not do this at all? Who would say that such as these are sound, and not out of their senses and delirious and mad to the uttermost degree of insanity?

'The world did not know Him,' [the Evangelist] said. But they of whom the world was not worthy did know Him. Moreover, in saying that some did not know Him, he was also succinctly revealing the cause of their ignorance. For he did not simply say: 'No one knew Him,' but: 'The world did not know Him'; that is, those men who were devoted to the world and had a taste for the things of the world. Indeed, Christ also was accustomed to refer to them in this way, as when He said: 'Just Father, the world has not known thee.'[9] The world was ignorant not only of Him but also of His Father, as we have said.

In truth, nothing so clouds the mind as clinging to present things. Therefore, since you perceive this, separate yourselves from the world and be estranged from things of flesh as much as possible. Harm comes to you from these things, not in unimportant details, but with regard to the most important of your blessings. It is not possible for the man who eagerly clings to the things of the present life to be able truly to attain to heavenly things, but he who is striving for the latter must remain aloof from the former. 'You cannot serve

9 John 17.25.

God and mammon,' Scripture says,[10] since you must hold to the one and hate the other.

Now, actual experience in these matters shouts confirmation of this fact. Those, for example, who have laughed at the desire for money are in a particular way the ones who love God as He should be loved; likewise, those who stand in awe of the power of money are especially the ones who love Him less fervently. The soul once caught by the love of wealth will not easily or readily refrain both from doing and saying things which anger God, since it has become the slave of another master who enjoins commands opposite to those of God in all respects.

Well, then, come to your senses now and be vigilant and, reflecting whose servants we are, let us love only His sovereignty. Let us weep, let us bewail the former times when we were enslaved to Mammon. Let us cast off, once and for all, his yoke which is unendurable and heavy, and let us continue carrying that of Christ which is light and sweet.[11] Indeed, He enjoins on us no such commands as Mammon does. The latter bids us to be enemies to all men; Christ, contrariwise, to embrace and love all.[12] Mammon, having fastened us to mud and brick-making[13] (for that is what wealth is), does not permit us to relax a little, even during the night. But Christ frees us from this foolish and senseless preoccupation and bids us store up our treasure in heaven,[14] not gathering it by injustice to others, but by our own righteousness.

The former, after our many sweats and toils, cannot help us when we are being punished in the next world and enduring pain because of his commands, and he even will add fuel to the flame. But the latter, if he bids us give merely a

---

10 Luke 16.13.
11 Cf. Matt. 11.30.
12 Cf. Matt. 5.43,44.
13 Cf. above, p. 5.
14 Cf. Matt. 6.19.

cup of cold water, does not permit us to lose the reward and return, even for this deed, but repays it very generously.[15] How, then, is it not a mark of utter foolishness for us to forsake a rule, so mild and productive of such good things, and to become the slaves of a tyrant who is thankless, and unfeeling, and not at all able to assist, either here or there, those who obey him and give heed to him?

Moreover, this is not the only evil, not the only injury—that he does not assist those being punished—besides this he involves in countless misfortunes those who are subject to him, as I have just said. One may see that the majority of those who are punished in the next world are punished because they were enslaved to wealth and loved gold and did not share them with the needy. In order that we also may not suffer these punishments, let us disperse [our wealth], let us give to the poor, let us rid our souls both of troublesome cares here and of the dishonor awaiting us there as a result of these things. Let us store up righteousness in heaven instead of amassing wealth upon earth. Let us gather imperishable treasure, treasures which can accompany us to heaven, can be our stay when in danger, and render our judge merciful in that hour.

May it be that all of us, having a Judge well disposed both now and in that day, may enjoy with much freedom the good things made ready in heaven for those who love Him as they ought, by the grace and mercy of our Lord Jesus Christ, with whom glory be to the Father, together with the Holy Spirit, now and always, and forever and ever. Amen.

---

15 Cf. Matt. 10.42.

Homily 9 (John 1.11)

'He came unto His own, and His own received Him not.'

If you keep in mind the sermons we have delivered before this, we shall be more eager to continue the series, as though doing so in expectation of a great reward. If you remember what has already been said, you will in that way more readily understand the present talk. Thus, we shall not need to expend much effort, since you will be able to arrive at the meaning of the rest more swiftly because of your keen desire to add to your knowledge.

In truth, he who always forgets what has been taught will always need a teacher and never will know anything, but he who keeps what he receives and so adds the rest to it will soon be teacher instead of pupil. He will be useful, not only to himself, but also to all others. And I think this congregation will be especially so, judging by its great eagerness to hear [sermons]. Come, then, let us lay away in your souls, as in a safe treasury, the silver of the Lord, and let us expound the matters proposed for you for today, as the grace of the Spirit may provide.

Referring to former times, the Evangelist said: 'The world knew him not.' Then he came down in his discourse even to the time of the public life and said: 'He came unto His own and His own received Him not.' Here he was calling the Jews 'His own' as the chosen people, or perhaps even all men, as created by Him. Now, before this, appalled at the stupidity of the vast majority, and ashamed for the nature common to us all, he had said that the world which was made by Him did not know its Creator. So also here again, greatly distressed over the senselessness of the Jews and, in fact, of most men, he uttered the charge more forcibly, saying: 'His own received him not,' and that, too, though He had come to them.

Now, not he alone, but the Prophets also, said this same

thing in wonderment; and Paul also was later struck with astonishment for the same reasons. On the one hand, the Prophets cried out as follows, speaking in the person of Christ: 'A people that I had not known has served me; on first hearing it obeyed me. Children that are strangers have lied to me, strange children have faded away and have halted from their paths.'[1] And again: 'They to whom it was not told of him will see: and they that heard not will behold'[2] and: 'I was found by those who did not seek me; I appeared openly to those who made no inquiry of me.'[3]

Paul, writing to the Romans, likewise has said, 'What then? What Israel was seeking after, that it has not obtained; but the chosen have obtained it.'[4] And again: 'What, then, shall we say? That the Gentiles who were not seeking justice have secured justice; but Israel, by pursuing a law of justice, has not attained to the law of justice.'[5]

And this is so, for, in fact, [the unbelief of some Jews] gives great cause for astonishment. They were educated in the prophetic books, and so every day heard Moses speaking countless prophecies of the coming of Christ, and also the rest of the Prophets after him. They saw Christ Himself daily working miracles for them and mingling only with them, and neither allowing His disciples to depart in the direction of the Gentiles nor to approach the city of the Samaritans.[6] Further, they observed that He did not go there Himself, but said repeatedly that He was sent to the sheep of the house of Israel that were perishing.[7] Nevertheless, though they enjoyed the benefit of His miracles, and heard the Prophets daily, and had Him continually reminding them, so utterly did they

1 Cf. Ps. 17.45,46.
2 Isa. 52.15.
3 Rom. 10.20; quoting Isa. 65.1.
4 Rom. 11.7.
5 Rom. 9.30.
6 Cf. Matt. 10.5-7.
7 Cf. Matt. 15.24.

stultify and blind themselves that by no one of these things could they be persuaded to believe in Christ.

Some of the Gentiles, on the other hand, did believe, though they enjoyed none of these advantages. They never heard divine oracles—not even as much as might be spoken in a dream—but were always entangled in the myths of madmen (for that is what the philosophy of the pagans is). They unrolled and read[8] the nonsense of poets, and were enslaved to wood and stone. They knew nothing useful or sound, either for doctrine or living, since their life was more impure and corrupt than their doctrine. And how could it be otherwise? They would see their gods taking pleasure in every vice, and being worshiped by shameful words and more shameful deeds, and regarding this as festal honor. Moreover, when they read about the gods being honored by impure words and infanticides, they tried to emulate even such practices as these.

Nevertheless, though they had descended to the very depths of evil, suddenly, as if by some heavenly mechanism, they appeared to us shining forth from the very pinnacle of heaven. How, then, did this happen, and whence? Listen to Paul telling us. For that saint assiduously inquired into these matters and did not cease until he found the explanation of them and revealed it to all others. What, indeed, is it? And whence have the Jews such great hardness of heart? Listen to the one who has been entrusted with this mission,[9] as he speaks.

What, then, does he say to dispose of this difficulty felt by many? 'Ignorant,' he declares, 'of the justice of God and seeking to establish their own, they have not submitted to the justice of God.'[10] That is why they felt as they did. And once again, elucidating this same matter in another place,

---

8 I.e., opened the scrolls.
9 I.e., the conversion of the Gentiles.
10 Rom. 10.3.

he says: 'What then shall we say? That the Gentiles who were not pursuing justice have secured justice, but a justice that is from faith; but Israel, by pursuing a law of justice, has not attained to the law of justice. And why? Because they sought it not from faith. For they stumbled at the stumbling-stone.'[11]

Now, this means some such thing as follows: 'Their unbelief has become a cause of evil for the Jews. And pride has been its parent.' For before this time they possessed more than the Gentiles because they had received the Law, and had known God, and the other advantages which Paul mentions. After the coming of Christ they saw the Gentiles called to the faith with the same honor as they themselves, and that he of the circumcision had no more than he of the Gentiles after the latter had obtained faith. Therefore, falling into envy, they were stung to madness and refused to submit to the ineffable and superabundant mercy of the Lord. And this happened to them from no other cause than arrogance, wickedness, and hatred.

Now, why, you most foolish of all men, are you grieved at the care [shown by Providence] toward others? And how are your blessings made less by the fact that others have a share of the same ones in common with you? Surely, envy is blind and cannot readily perceive anything it should. Well, then, resentful because they are going to have companions sharing in the same privileges as they, they push the sword against themselves and cast themselves off from the mercy of God; and rightly so. 'Friend,' He said: 'I do thee no injustice. I choose to give to this last even as to thee.'[12]

Nay, they are not worthy of these words. For, even if that laborer did grumble, he could mention the whole day's work, and hardships, and heat, and sweat; but these—what have they to mention? Nothing, surely, but ease and dissolute-

---

11 Rom. 9.30-32.
12 Matt. 20.13,14.

ness and a thousand vices of which all the Prophets have continually charged and accused them, vices through which they, as well as the Gentiles, have come into conflict with God. And Paul, to make this plain, said: 'For there is no distinction of Jew and of Greek, as all have sinned and have need of the glory of God. They are justified freely by his grace.'[13]

He developed this whole point to advantage and very wisely, in that Epistle. Moreover, earlier in it he made them out to be worthy of still greater punishment. 'For whoever have sinned under the Law will be judged by the Law,'[14] he said; that is, more severely, since they have as accuser the Law as well as nature. And not for this reason alone [will they be punished], but because they have been the cause of God's being blasphemed among the Gentiles; 'For my name,' He said, 'is blasphemed through you among the Gentiles.'[15]

Accordingly, the Jews' chief grievance was this [calling of the Gentiles], for even to believers among the circumcised the thing seemed to be beyond belief. Wherefore, they even found fault with Peter, as he was returning from Caesarea, because he visited men who were uncircumcised, and ate with them.[16] Even after learning of the dispensation of God[17] they still wondered how 'on the Gentiles also the grace of the Holy Spirit had been poured forth,'[18] showing by their amazement that they never looked for this marvel. Therefore, since [Paul] knew that this especially was bothering them, he did everything to puncture their conceit and to free them from the vanity that was puffing them up.

---

13 Rom. 3.22-24.
14 Rom. 2.12.
15 Rom. 2.24; quoting Isa. 52.5.
16 Cf. Acts 11.3.
17 Among ecclesiastical writers the Greek word 'oikonomía' is used with several different shades of meaning. St. John employs it here in the sense of the universal plan of divine Providence—i.e., the will of God—in willing the salvation of all men, whether Jews or Gentiles.
18 Acts 10.45.

And see how he did this. After discoursing about the Gentiles, and showing that they had no excuse anywhere, or hope of salvation, and having accused them vehemently both of the perversity of their teachings and the impurity of their lives,[19] he shifted the discussion to the Jews. Moreover, after repeating all the texts from the Prophets in which he said that some of them were defiled and deceitful and hypocritical, and that 'they have all become worthless,' and no one among them sought God, but 'all have gone astray together,' and many similar things,[20] he added: 'Now we know that whatever the Law says, it is speaking to those that are under the Law; in order that every mouth may be shut, and the whole world may be made subject to God for all have sinned and have need of the glory of God.'[21]

Why, then, O Jew, do you exalt yourself? Why are you conceited? I say this, for your mouth has been stopped up, and your presumption has been taken away, and with the whole world you have become guilty, and you have been shown to be in need of being freely justified, just like other men. Therefore, even if you had conducted yourself virtuously and had much reason for confidence in God, you ought not to have envied those who were going to obtain pity and be saved by [God's] mercy.

Indeed, it is a mark of the worst envy to pine away over the good fortune of others, especially when this is going to happen without injury to you. If the salvation of the rest were actually destructive of your blessings, your grief might be reasonable; yet not even then would it be so to him who has learned to love true wisdom. But if, when another is punished your reward is not increased, or when another prospers your good fortune is not diminished, why do you rack your-

19 Cf. Rom. 2.1-16.
20 Cf. Rom. 3.10-18.
21 Rom. 3.19,23.

self with pain because someone else is winning salvation gratis?

Therefore, as I said, even if you were of good repute, you ought not to be envious because salvation redounds by grace to the Gentiles. But if you, who owe a debt to the Lord for the same offense and have yourself offended Him, begrudge the blessings of others and are resentful, as if you yourself alone deserved to have a share in grace, you are guilty, not only of envy and arrogance, but also of extreme folly, and will be liable to the most severe punishments of all. For, you have planted in yourself the root of all evils, namely, pride.

That is why the wise man also has said: 'Pride is the beginning of sin,'[22] that is, its root and source and mother. Thus it was that the first man fell from that state of blessedness; so also the Devil who deceived him had been cast down from that height of dignity. Therefore, the foul fiend, knowing that this sin of its own nature was sufficient to cast down even from heaven itself, traversed this road when he strove to drag Adam down from such a place of honor. Having puffed him up with the promise of equality with God, by this means he broke down his defenses and cast him down to the very depths of hell.

Indeed, nothing so estranges from the mercy of God and gives over to the fire of hell as the tyranny of pride. If we possess this within us, all our life becomes impure, even if we practice chastity, virginity, fasting, prayer, almsgiving, or any virtue whatsoever. 'Every proud man,' Scripture says, 'is an abomination to the Lord.'[23] Therefore, let us check this puffing up of the soul, and let us cut out this tumor, if we wish to be pure and be rid of the punishment prepared for the Devil. Indeed, listen to Paul declaring that the proud man must suffer those very penalties: 'Not a new convert,

---

22 Eccli. 10.15.
23 Prov. 16.5.

lest he be puffed up with pride and incur the condemnation passed on the devil.'[24] What is this condemnation?

'The same sentence,' he means; 'the same punishment.'

'How, then, may one escape from this terrible fate,' do you ask? If he ponder his own nature, and the multitude of his sins, and the greatness of the punishments in the next world, the transitoriness of things which seem beautiful here, but are just like grass and die more readily than the flowers of spring—if we continually revolve these reflections within ourselves and keep remembering those who lived the most virtuously, the Devil will not be able to overcome us easily, though he make a thousand attempts, nor will he be able even to begin to prevail over us.

May God, the God of the humble, He who is kind and merciful, Himself grant to you and to us a contrite and humble heart. For thus we shall also be able easily to excel in other respects, to the glory of our Lord Jesus Christ, through whom and with whom glory be to the Father, together with the Holy Spirit, forever and ever. Amen.

Homily 10 (John 1.11-13)

'He came unto His own, and His own received Him not.'[1]

Since God is merciful, beloved, and disposed to do good, He does and plans everything so that we may be bright with virtue. And since He wishes us to be virtuous, He tries to persuade us to this, but does not constrain or force anyone. Also, by bestowing benefits He draws all who are willing to be drawn and attracts them to Himself.

---

24 I Tim. 3.6, St. John Chrysostom, following one branch of Greek manuscript tradition for the New Testament, after 'condemnation' (*krima*) inserts 'and trap' (*kai pagida*). Cf. Merk. *loc. cit.*, 687.

1 John 1.11.

That is why some received Him when He came, while others did not. He does not wish to have as servant anyone who is unwilling or under constraint, but desires all to be His servants, willingly and of their own free choice, and with gratitude to Him for the privilege of serving Him.

Now, when men are so situated as to need the ministry of servants, they keep under the law of slavery even those who are not willing; but God, who is not in want, and is in need of nothing of ours, and who does all things only for the sake of our salvation, gives us complete freedom in this matter. Therefore, He brings to bear neither force nor necessity on anyone of those who are not willing [to serve Him]. Indeed, He has in view only our profit. To be won to this service, when unwilling, is equivalent to not serving at all.

'Then,' you say, 'why does He punish those who do not desire to listen to Him? And why did He threaten the punishment of hell for those who do not listen to His commands?' Because, even though we do not obey, He is very much concerned for us, since He is so good, and He does not stand aloof from us, even when we turn away and flee. However, when we have disdained the former way, that of His beneficence, because we are unwilling to traverse the path of persuasion and kindness, then He has introduced the other way—that of punishment and torture, which is very bitter, to be sure, but nevertheless salutary. When the former way is spurned, it is necessary to add the second.

Now, though law-givers establish many severe penalties for transgressors, we are not nevertheless hostile to them because of these. Rather, we even give them honor in return for the sanctions because, even though they were in need of nothing from us and often did not know who would profit by the assistance rendered by their written laws, they took thought for the good order in our lives by prescribing honor for those living in virtue, but restraining by punishments the undisciplined and those who might disturb the peace of the rest.

Now, if we admire and love them, ought we not marvel much more at God and love Him in return for the care He takes of us? Surely we ought to, for immeasurable is the difference between their and His solicitude for us. Truly ineffable and beyond all exaggeration is the wealth of His goodness. But notice: 'He came unto his own,' not because of His need (for the Deity, as I have said, is without wants), but for the sake of the benefit to His own. Yet His own did not receive Him when He came to His own in this way for their benefit, but even drove Him away; not only this, but they cast Him out of the vineyard and killed Him.[2]

Yet, not even for this did He rule them out from repentance. Even after such great transgression, if they were willing, He granted them to have their sins cleansed away by faith in Him, and to be made equal to those who had not committed any such wrong, but who especially loved Him. Moreover, I am not just saying these things, or saying them merely to persuade you. All the events in the life of blessed Paul loudly voice confirmation of this fact.

When he who hunted down Christ after the crucifixion and stoned His martyr Stephen with many hands[3] had repented and condemned his previous sins, and had become a follower of Him who had been hunted, straightway He listed him among His friends—even among those who held first place. He declared him a messenger and teacher of the whole world, though he had been 'a blasphemer, a persecutor, and a bitter adversary.'[4] Even so, Paul himself, exulting in the mercy of God, also spread these facts abroad and was not ashamed.

---

2 Cf. Matt. 21.39.
3 Cf. Acts 7.58. I.e., in guarding the clothing of those who were stoning Stephen, Paul was joining vicariously in the crime of these individuals.
4 1 Tim. 1.13.

He even set down in his writings, as if on a monument, the deeds he had dared to commit before. He pointed them out to all, thinking that it was better for his former life to be publicized to all men in order to make evident the greatness of the gift of God than to cover up His ineffable and indescribable mercy by shrinking from proclaiming his own sins to all.

He therefore recounted in detail his persecutions, his plots, his fights against the Church; on the one hand, saying: 'I am not worthy to be called an apostle, because I persecuted the Church of God';[5] and again: 'That Jesus came to save sinners of whom I am the chief;'[6] and once more: 'You have heard of my former way of life in Judaism; how beyond all measure I persecuted the Church of God and ravaged it.'[7]

Indeed, to give, as it were, some kind of return to Christ for His long-suffering toward him, by telling plainly what sort he was and what an enemy and foe He had saved, he very frankly revealed the battle which in the beginning he had waged with consuming zeal against Christ. And because of this he held out good hope even to those who had despaired of themselves. He actually said that Christ pardoned him for this reason: that in him, first of all, He 'might show forth all patience,' and the exceeding riches of His goodness, 'as an example to those who shall believe in Him for the attainment of life everlasting.'[8] I say this because the brazen deeds to which the Evangelist referred when he said: 'He came unto His own, and His own received Him not,' were [seemingly] too great for any pardon.

Whence came He who fills all things and is present everywhere? What sort of place did He leave empty of His presence, He who holds all things in His hand and rules them? He has,

5 1 Cor. 15.9.
6 1 Tim. 1.15.
7 Gal. 1.13.
8 1 Tim. 1.16.

indeed, left no place to go to another (for how should He?) but has brought it about [that 'He came'] by His coming down to us. Inasmuch as, though He was in the world, He did not seem to be present because of not yet being known, but later He revealed Himself, and chose to put on our flesh, [the Evangelist] called this revelation and descent 'a coming.' And it is surprising that the disciple was not ashamed of this humbling of his Master, but even wrote freely of the humiliation that was His. And this is no small proof of the honesty of his character.

Besides, if anyone feels ashamed he ought to be ashamed for those who offer insult, not for the person humiliated. Indeed, the latter has shone forth more brilliantly because of this, since even after the insult He displayed so much solicitude toward those who offered it. Moreover, they have appeared ungrateful and defiled among all men because they have driven out as an enemy and foe Him who came laden with such great benefits. And not only in this way were they harmed, but also by not obtaining what they obtain who receive Him. What do they obtain? 'To as many as received Him He gave the power of becoming sons of God,' he said.

Why is it, then, that you did not mention to us also, O blessed one, the punishment of those who did not receive Him, but merely said that they were His own and they did not receive Him when He came unto His own? Why did you not add what they will suffer for this and what sort of punishment they will undergo? Yet, by doing so you would have frightened them greatly and would have softened the hardness of their perversity by the threat. Why, then, were you silent? 'Now, what other penalty,' he replies, 'could be greater than that whereby the power of being sons of God is available to them, and they do not become so, but deliberately deprive themselves of such noble lineage and honor?'

Their punishment, however, will not be limited to that of failing to receive this benefit, but the unquenchable fire will also await them, and this he revealed more clearly as he continued. Meanwhile, he mentioned the ineffable rewards of those who did receive Him, and briefly set them forth in the following words: 'To as many as received Him he gave the power of becoming sons of God.' And whether they be slaves or freemen, whether Greeks or barbarians or Scythians, foolish or wise, female or male, children or old men, honorable or without honor, rich or poor, rulers or private citizens, all, he meant, would merit the same honor. Faith and the grace of the Holy Spirit, erasing the difference arising from worldly circumstances, have molded all to the same form and have impressed them with one royal stamp.

What could be comparable to this loving-kindness? A king who has been made of the same clay as we does not deem it fitting to enroll in the royal army his fellow men who share the same human nature with him, if they are slaves, though often they are superior to him in character; but the only-begotten Son of God has not considered it unworthy to enroll in the number of His family tax-collectors, and charlatans, and slaves, and persons less honorable than all these, and even many unsound in body and with countless infirmities.

Such is the power of faith in Him; such the greatness of His grace. And even as the element of fire, having come in contact with ore from mines, forthwith makes the ore true gold; so also, and even more, does baptism make those who have been washed in it golden instead of earthy, since the Spirit at that time falls like fire on our souls, both burning away 'the likeness of the earthy,'[9] and restoring 'the likeness of the heavenly,' freshly formed and shining, gleaming as if from the smelting furnace.

Why, then, did he not say: 'He made them sons of God,' but 'He gave them the power of becoming sons of God'? To show that we need to exert a great deal of effort so that the image of sonship, impressed on us in baptism, may remain

_____
9 1 Cor. 15.49.

entirely unsullied and intact; and at the same time to indicate that no one will be able to deprive us of this power unless we of our own accord deprive ourselves.

If those who have received from men authority in certain matters have nearly as much power as the donors of the authority, much more shall we who have obtained this honor from God be most powerful of all, if we do nothing unworthy of this power, because He who bestowed this honor upon us is both greatest and noblest of all. At the same time, he also wished to point out that grace does not come to men at random, but only to those who want and strive for it. In fact, it lies in their power to become sons. If they do not first wish it, the gift does not come, nor does it accomplish anything in them.

Well, then, since he has everywhere discounted the idea of force, and stressed voluntary choice and free will, he has spoken of this in this text, also. He did so because in the case of these mystical gifts themselves God's part is to give grace; man's, to provide faith. Yet, when that has been done, we still need to expend much earnest effort afterwards. It is not sufficient, in order to preserve the purity of our life, only to be baptized and to believe; if we are going to enjoy this brightness always, we must make our life worthy of it. God has made this depend on our will. Baptism results in our experiencing a mystical birth and purification from all our sins committed before it, but to remain pure subsequently, and to acquire no taint again after this, depends on our will and effort.

Therefore, he has reminded us of the manner of our birth, and by comparing it with human birth pangs has shown its superiority, saying: 'Who were born not of blood, nor of the will of the flesh, nor of the will of man, but of God.' Moreover, he did this in order that, reflecting on the cheapness and frailty of the former birth, that 'of blood and the will of the flesh,' and realizing the value and nobility of the second, which is of grace, we should therefore conceive great esteem for it—an esteem befitting the gift that has been bestowed—and so henceforth show much earnestness.

It is not a little to be feared that, having soiled this beautiful garment by our subsequent indifference and sins, we may be cast out of the inner room and the bridal chamber like those five virgins, the foolish ones,[10] or like him who did not have a wedding garment. The latter was one of the banqueters, because he himself also was invited; but when, after being invited and receiving so much honor, he was insulting to his host, listen to what kind of punishment he endured, how pitiable and deserving of many tears. Upon coming to share in that splendid banquet, not only was he shut out of the feast, but also, bound hand and foot alike, he was driven into the exterior darkness and subjected to perpetual and unlimited weeping and gnashing of teeth.[11]

Let us not, then, beloved, think that faith suffices for our salvation. If we do not give evidence of purity of life, but present ourselves clad in a garment unworthy of this blessed invitation, nothing will prevent us also from enduring the same sufferings as that wretched man. It is absurd that, while He who is both God and King is not ashamed to invite men who are worthless and beggars and good for nothing, but brings them even from the crossroads to His banquet, we show such indifference as not to become better because of such an honor. But even after the invitation we remain in the same wickedness, acting offensively toward the ineffable mercy of our host.

It was not for this that He summoned us to this spiritual and awful participation in the mysteries: that we should come clad in our former wickedness, but that, taking off the shameful garment, we might change to the clothing which they ought to wear who are guests in the royal palace. And

---

10 Cf. Matt. 25.1-13.
11 Cf. Matt. 22.11-14.

if we should not wish to act as befits that invitation, this conduct is not to the detriment of Him who has honored us but to our own loss. He does not cast us out of the august assembly of the invited guests; we cast ourselves out.

He, indeed, has done everything He ought to have done. I say this because He has made the marriage feast, and prepared the table, and sent messengers to invite us, and has received us when we came, and has given us every other honor. On the contrary, we have acted contumeliously toward Him, toward all those present, and toward the wedding by our soiled garments, that is, by our impure deeds. Hence, we deserve to be cast out. It is because He honors the wedding and the other guests that He drives away those who are brazen and impudent. If He suffered those clad in that garment [to remain], He Himself would seem also to be insulting the others. However, may it be that no one, neither we nor anyone else, may meet with such treatment from Him who has called us.

Therefore, all these things have been described in writing before they could occur, in order that, having been chastised by the threat of the written word, we might not permit this dishonor and punishment to materialize in deeds, but might make it rest in the words only, and might answer that invitation, each with a shining garment. May we all enjoy this boon through the grace and mercy of our Lord Jesus Christ, through whom glory, power, honor be to the Father, together with the Holy Spirit, now and always, and forever and ever. Amen.

Homily 11 (John 1.14)

'And the Word was made flesh, and dwelt among us.'

I wish to ask one favor of you all before I touch on the words of the Evangelist. Do not, I beg, refuse my request, for

I am asking nothing weighty or troublesome. And if you grant it, it will not only be useful to me who receive the favor, but also to you who grant it— and perhaps much more so to you.

What can it be, then, that I ask of you? Let each one of you, on some day of the week, even on the Sabbath itself, take in his hands the selection of the Gospels that is going to be read to you [at our next meeting]. Read it frequently as you sit at home in the time intervening, and often ponder with care the thoughts stored up in it and examine them well. Note what is clear and what obscure, and which thoughts seem to be contradictory, though they really are not. And when you have finally sampled all of it, thus prepared come to the sermon.

Indeed, both you and we shall derive no small profit from such effort. We shall not need to work much to make clear the significance of what is said, since your minds will have become familiar with the general tenor of the words. And because of this preparation you will become keener and more discerning, not only in hearing and learning yourselves, but also in teaching others.

As a matter of fact, many of those who have now come here are listening, indeed, but they have to become newly acquainted with everything: both with the words of the Gospel and with our comments on them. Hence, though we should continue preaching in this way for a whole year, they will not enjoy any great profit. How can they, indeed, when they have leisure for what is said only as a secondary interest: while in this place and for this short time.

Some, to be sure, allege business as excuse, and worries, and great preoccupation with public and private affairs. In the first place, this complaint is in itself no trivial indictment of them: that they are involved in such a volume of business and are continually so enslaved to worldly things that they do not have even a little leisure for the most necessary things of all. In the second place, social intercourse with friends, and also amusements in the theatre, would point an accusing finger at them, that these excuses are merely pretense and pretext; likewise, the parties which they make up for the sake of seeing horse races, in which they often spend entire days.[1]

You have associated with friends for a long time,[2] yet no one of them has ever alleged preoccupation with business as excuse for not following these pursuits. You are, then, always ready for these worthless occupations and can find abundant leisure for them; but, if you are required to turn your attention to the things of God, these seem to you to be so much more superfluous and worthless than everything else that you think you do not need to devote leisure time to them. Now, how do those who are so disposed deserve to breathe or to look at this sun?

Still another pretext, a most unreasonable one, is alleged by those who show this indifferent attitude in this matter, namely, that they cannot get books and have none. Now, as to the rich, it is ridiculous for us to bother with this excuse. But, since I believe that many of the poorer class have used it repeatedly, I should like to ask them this question: whether each one has not the tools of the trade at which he works—complete and in full—even if he be constrained by extreme poverty? Then, is it not strange that in the latter case they do not allege poverty as an excuse, but do everything in order not to be handicapped in any way? But when they might gain such [spiritual] profit, they lament their lack of leisure and their poverty.

Besides, even if some were that poor, it is still within their power not to be ignorant of what is contained in the sacred Scriptures, by reason of the reading continually made here.

1 The excessive preoccupation of St. John's contemporaries with the corrupt theatre of the day, and with other degrading and vicious forms of amusement, is commonplace knowledge and was a cause of deep concern to those responsible for the spiritual welfare of the faithful.

2 The text is corrupt here. The Benedictine editor brackets this clause.

And if this seems to you to be impossible, it is with reason that it seems so. Not many have come with a keen desire to hear what is said, but, having barely acquitted themselves of the obligation [of coming], out of consideration for the day,[3] they straightway return home. And if some should linger on, they are in no wise better than those who went off, since they are present here with us in body only.

However, not to burden you with charges any further or to spend the whole time in fault-finding, let us go to the words of the Evangelist; for it is time to employ the rest of the sermon on the text before us. Moreover, pay attention so that nothing of what is said may pass you by.

'And the Word was made flesh,' he said, 'and dwelt among us.' Having declared that they who received Him were 'born of God' and 'became sons of God,' he then set forth the cause and reason for this ineffable honor. It is that 'the Word became flesh' and the Master took on the form of the slave. He became the Son of Man, though He was the true Son of God, in order that He might make the sons of men children of God. In truth, to mingle the high with the low works no harm to the honor of the high, but raises the lowly up from its very humble estate. Accordingly, this is also true in the case of Christ. He in no wise lowered His own nature by this descent, but elevated us, who had always been in a state of ignominy and darkness, to ineffable glory.

Similarly, a king, in speaking with interest and kindness to a poor beggar, has not debased himself at all but has caused

---

3 From the first century on, the universal custom prevailed, and was soon considered obligatory, of assisting at liturgical gatherings (or assemblies) on Sunday, the principal event of which was the Mass. This is well attested for the first century, and numerous texts of the Fathers of the second, third, and fourth centuries bear witness to the Christian custom of assembling on Sunday and of celebrating the Eucharistic Sacrifice during the course of the assembly. In the early centuries the extent of the obligation to do so was not clear, but by the fourth century there are pronouncements of Church councils placing sanctions on those who failed in this obligation. Cf. E. Dublanchy, 'Dimanche,' *DTC* 4 (1924) 1334-1335.

the other to be esteemed and illustrious before all men. And if, in the case of the extrinsic dignity of man, the associating with a meaner person did no harm at all to him who bestowed the honor, much more is this so in the case of that pure and blessed Being, who has nothing extrinsic, or capable of increase or decrease, but possesses all good things immovable and fixed forever. So that when you hear: 'The Word became flesh,' do not be struck with consternation or downcast. His substance was not transformed into flesh (indeed, this is altogether impious even to think of), but remaining what He is, He thus took the form of a slave.

Why, then, did he use the expression 'was made'? In order to stop up the mouths of heretics. Since there are some[4] who say that all the details of the Incarnation were an appearance, an act, an allegory, to refute their blasphemy in advance, he added the expression 'was made,' desiring to affirm not that there was a transformation of His substance (away with that idea!), but His assuming of real flesh.

Just as when [Paul] said: 'Christ redeemed us from the curse of the law, being made[5] a curse for us,'[6] he did not mean this: that His substance, departing from His own glory, was existent as a curse (not even demons would think this—or even very foolish men, deprived by nature of reason—so much insanity has the idea, together with its impiety). He did not, then, mean this, but that, having accepted the curse that existed against us, He did not permit us to be accursed any more. Accordingly, here [John] also said: 'He was made flesh,' not that His substance changed into

---

4 The Docetae, a group of heretics who date back to apostolic times and whose teaching, that Christ only 'seemed' to be a man, to have been born, to have lived and suffered, aimed at destroying the meaning and purpose of the doctrine of the Incarnation. In the fourth and fifth centuries Docetism was concomitant to Gnosticism and Manichaeanism. Cf. *Catholic Encyclopedia.*

5 'genómenos': the translation 'being made,' found in the Challoner revision of Rheims-Douay, seems to fit the context better than the Confraternity's 'becoming.'

6 Gal. 3.13.

flesh, but that, after assuming flesh, His substance remained intact.

Now, if they should say: 'Being God, He can do all things so that He could even demean Himself into the substance of flesh,' we shall give them this answer: 'He can do all things as long as He remains God; but if He receives a transformation, and one for the worse, how would He be God? Change is out of keeping with that pure nature.' Wherefore, also, the Prophet said: 'All shall grow old as a garment and as raiment Thou wilt change them and they will be changed. But Thou art the same, and Thy years have no end.'[7]

In truth, this substance is above all change. There is nothing better than He so that by advancing He could come up to it. Why do I say 'better'? Not even equal, not even approaching Him somewhat. Well, then, there remains only His changing for the worse, if He should change. However, this would not be God. May the blasphemy come back upon the heads of those who say these things.

Indeed, he said 'was made' for this reason only: that you might not conceive the idea that it was merely an appearance. To prove this, consider in what follows how he clarified the word and dispelled that evil idea. He added: 'and dwelt among us,' all but saying: 'Do not conceive any strange idea from the expression "was made." For I did not mean a change of that unchangeable nature but its dwelling and habitation.' That which dwells cannot be the same thing as its dwelling, but must be something different. One thing dwells in another; otherwise the latter would not be a dwelling, for nothing dwells in itself. However, by 'different' I mean different in substance. By Their union and conjoining, God, the Word, and the flesh are one, not as a result of commingling or disappearance of substances, but by some ineffable and inexplicable union. But do not seek the how; it 'was made' in a way which He Himself knows.

---

7 Ps. 101.27.

What, then, is the dwelling where He dwelt? Listen to the Prophet saying: 'I will raise up the tabernacle of David that has fallen.'[8] Actually, it has fallen; our human nature has had an irreparable fall, and was in need of that powerful hand alone. For it was not possible to raise it up otherwise, unless He who fashioned it in the beginning stretched out a hand to it and formed it again from above by the regeneration of water and the Spirit.

Behold, pray, the awesome and ineffable character of the mystery. He dwells always in this tabernacle, for He put on our flesh, not to put it off again, but to have it always with Him. If this were not so, He would not have deemed it worthy of His royal throne and, bearing it [with Him], would not have had it adored by all the host above: the host of the Angels, Archangels, Thrones, Dominations, Principalities, Powers. What word, what intelligence, will be able to explain such a supernatural and awesome honor which has come to our race? What angel? What archangel? No one, anywhere, either in heaven or on earth. For such are the ordinances of God, and so great and extraordinary His benefits, that their accurate description defies not only the tongue of man but also the power of angels.

Wherefore, we also shall close our discussion for awhile with silence, having enjoined upon you in your turn to repay this great Benefactor of ours payment which will again redound to our entire advantage. And this repayment consists in caring for our souls with assiduity. This also is a work of His mercy that, though He is in need of nothing of ours, He says He receives repayment when we take care of our own souls. Therefore, it is a mark of utter madness and worthy of untold punishments not to make a return, to the extent we can, for such an honor, generously bestowed on us, and this, too, since profit redounds again to us by this means, and countless blessings await us on these conditions.

8 Amos 9.11.

Let us give glory to our merciful God for all these things, not only in word but much more in deed, in order that we may also obtain these blessings hereafter. May it be granted to all of us to attain to these through the grace and mercy of our Lord Jesus Christ, through whom and with whom glory be to the Father, together with the Holy Spirit, forever and ever. Amen.

Homily 12 (John 1.14)

'And we saw his glory—glory as of the only-begotten of the Father—full of grace and of truth.'

Perhaps it seemed to you last time that we were more bothersome and tiresome than was necessary, and that we were employing a somewhat sharp manner of speaking, and drawing out at too great length our indictment of the indifference of most of you. Now, if we had done this only through a desire to annoy you, each one of you would have reason to be indignant. But if, because we were thinking only of the help we could give you, we disregarded in our words what might gain your favor, even though you are unwilling to approve us for our forethought, at least you are bound to pardon such great affection as ours.

We have been very much afraid lest, while we were trying so hard [in addressing you], if you were unwilling to show the same effort in listening, the future judgment would be more severe for you. That is why we continually insist on your being attentive and keeping awake so that nothing at all of what is said may escape you. In this way you may both live with much confidence now, and in that day stand confidently at the tribunal of Christ. Accordingly, since but recently we have upbraided you enough, come, let us at the outset today proceed to the text itself.

'And we saw,' he said, 'His glory—glory as of the only-begotten of the Father.' After saying that we became sons of God and showing that this came about not otherwise than because the Word became flesh, he spoke of still another benefit resulting from this. Now, what is it? 'We saw His glory—glory as of the only-begotten of the Father.' We should not have seen it if we had not seen it in His Body that was like our own.

Indeed, though Moses shared the same nature with us, men of that time could not bear to look at his face which had merely become radiant. And even the just man needed the protection of a veil sufficient to shield the brilliance of that glory from him, and to show the face of their Prophet to them, with its radiance dimmed and, therefore, not dazzling to behold.[1] How, then, could we, creatures of clay and born of earth, endure the Godhead unveiled, when it is inaccessible to the very powers above? For this reason He dwelt among us, that we might be able to come to Him, and speak with Him, and be in His company without any fear.

And what is the 'glory as of the only-begotten of the Father'? Many of the Prophets also have been glorified; for example, Moses himself, Elias, Eliseus—the one encircled by a fiery chariot, the other taken up by one.[2] And after these Daniel,[3] and the three children,[4] and the many others who worked miracles, were glorified. Besides, certain angels appeared among men and revealed to those who saw them something of the brilliant light of their own nature. And not angels only, but also the Cherubim, were seen by the Prophet in great glory, and the Seraphim likewise. Therefore, the Evangelist, to draw us away from all these and make our minds depart from the brightness of creation and of our fellow slaves,

1 Cf. Exod. 34.29-35.
2 Cf. 4 Kings 2.11.
3 Cf. Dan. 14.42.
4 Cf. Dan. 3.92.

set us on the very pinnacle of blessedness. 'We saw the glory,' he said, 'not of a prophet, or of an angel, or of an archangel, or of the higher powers, or of any other created nature—if, that is, there is another—but of the Lord Himself, of the King Himself, of His own only-begotten Son, of Him who is the Ruler of us all.'

The word 'as' in this context does not express likeness or comparison, but affirms and unmistakably defines, as if he said: 'We saw glory such as it was fitting and probable for Him to have who is the only-begotten and true Son of God, the King of all things.' And this is a use of the word common to many (for I shall not refrain from strengthening the argument by appealing to common custom). It is not our purpose at present, to be sure, to speak with reference to the beauty of the words or the smoothness of the style, but only to help you, and therefore we have no inhibitions about strengthening our statement by quoting common practice.

Now, what is the custom of most men? Frequently, if they have seen a king most magnificently decked out and resplendent with precious stones, when they afterwards describe that beauty to others—its ornateness, its lavishness—they enumerate as many details as they can: the brilliance of the purple robe, the size of the gems, the whiteness of the mules, the gold ornamenting their yoke, the gleaming couch. But when, having listed these details and others besides, they find it impossible to do justice to all the splendor by their words, they straightway add this: 'Why is it necessary to say many words? In brief: he was as a king.' By this word 'as' they do not wish to indicate that he about whom they are making all these statements is like a king, but that he is a real king.

Well, then, it is in this way that the Evangelist also has used the word 'as,' desiring to declare that His glory is extraordinary and incomparably excellent. All others, indeed—angels, archangels, prophets—have performed all their actions as they were commanded, but He Himself has performed his with power befitting a king and lord. Moreover, the crowds also wondered at this, because He taught them 'as one having authority.'[5]

Angels, then, have also appeared upon earth with much glory, as I have said—for example, to Daniel, to David, to Moses—but they did everything as slaves subject to a master. But He Himself did all things as Lord and Ruler of all, even when appearing under a mean and lowly form. In truth, even when He was in this guise, creation nonetheless recognized its Master.

How? I say this for there was a star from heaven calling magi to adore Him,[6] and a great host of angels, thronging on all sides, ministering to their Master and praising Him in song. And suddenly other heralds appeared and all of them, meeting one another, announced this ineffable mystery: the angels to the shepherds; and the shepherds to the townspeople; Gabriel both to Mary and to Elizabeth; and Anna and Simeon to those who were in the Temple. Not only were men and women exalted with joy, but also the infant not yet come into the light of day— I mean that inhabitant of the desert, of the same name as this Evangelist—leaped in the womb of his mother, and all were uplifted with hopes for the future.[7]

Now, these things took place without delay at the time of His birth. But when He had revealed Himself more clearly, still other wonders, greater than the former, occurred. No longer star and sky, or angels and archangels, or Gabriel and Michael, but the Father Himself announced Him from heaven above, and, together with the Father, the Paraclete, who descended upon Him at His voice and remained upon Him.[8] Because of these events he truly said: 'We saw His glory— glory as of the only-begotten of the Father.'

5 Matt. 7.29.
6 Cf. Matt. 2.1-12.
7 Cf. Luke 1-2.
8 Cf. Mark 1.9-11.

Yet he said this not because of these things only, but also because of those which took place afterwards. It was no longer shepherds only, or widows, or aged men, who announced Him to us, but the very nature of [His words and deeds], sounding louder than any trumpet, and making themselves audible in such a way that their sound was at once heard even here.[9] 'His fame spread into all Syria,'[10] Scripture says, and He revealed Himself to all, and all things everywhere shouted out that the King of the heavens had come.

Indeed, the demons everywhere fled and withdrew, and the Devil hid himself and departed, and death itself was repulsed for a time and afterwards was completely routed. Further, every kind of disease was destroyed, and the tombs sent forth their dead; the demons departed from those possessed, and diseases from the sick. And it was possible to see wonders and miracles which the Prophets had with reason desired to see and did not see. Men could see eyes being fashioned and behold Him demonstrating to all, in a short space of time and on a more excellent part of the body, that enviable power which all have desired to see in operation, namely, that by which God fashioned Adam from the earth. It was possible to see limbs repaired and made whole when they had been paralyzed and crippled, withered hands moving, paralyzed feet suddenly leaping, blocked-up ears made open, and the tongue, which previously had been kept silent by muteness, now speaking aloud. Even as some skilled architect who restores a house fallen to decay with age, so He restored our common human nature. Like the architect, He supplied parts that had been broken off, fastened together the separated and disjointed portions, and raised up again that which had completely fallen down.

But what could one say of the refashioning of the soul, which is much more wonderful than that of the body? The

9 Antioch in Syria.
10 Matt. 4.24.

soundness of our bodies is a great thing, but much greater is that of our souls; in fact, as much greater as the soul is nobler than the body. And it is greater, not on this account only, but also because our bodily nature follows wherever the Creator wishes to lead it and does so without resistance, while the soul, being mistress of itself and having control of its deeds, does not obey God in all things unless it wishes. If it be unwilling and compelled by force [to obey], He does not will to make it beautiful and excellent, since such [conduct] is not virtue. However, He has to persuade it to become such because it wills and chooses to do so, and this is indeed more difficult than that other healing.

Nevertheless, He succeeds even in this, and every kind of wickedness has been driven away. Just as He changed bodies which were healed, not only to health, but even to the highest state of good health, so He not merely rid souls of the worst evil, but also brought them to the very pinnacle of virtue. The tax-collector became Apostle;[11] the persecutor and blasphemer and insulter was transformed into the world's herald;[12] the magi became teachers of the Jews; a thief was proclaimed a citizen of Paradise;[13] a harlot shone by reason of the greatness of her faith;[14] the Canaanite woman and the Samaritan—the latter also another harlot—one became the herald of her people, and having caught the entire city in her net, so brought them to Christ;[15] the other contrived by her faith and perseverance to drive out an evil spirit from the soul of her daughter.[16] And others much worse than these were straightway numbered in the ranks of the disciples.

All things were at once changed: both the diseases of the body and the afflictions of the soul. Moreover, they were

---

11 Matthew; cf. Matt. 9.9.
12 Paul cf. Acts 9.1-30
13 Cf. Luke 23.42,43.
14 Cf. Luke 7.40-50.
15 Cf. John 4.28-31.
16 Cf. Mark 7.24-30.

restored to health and the highest degree of virtue. And there were not two or three of these men, not five, or ten, or twenty, or a hundred only, but entire cities and nations were converted quite easily. What can anyone say [worthily] of the wisdom of the precepts, the virtue of the heavenly laws, the discipline of the angelic way of life? Such a life did He introduce to us, such laws did He establish for us, such conduct did He prescribe that those who made use of them would immediately become angels and like God, as much as is in our power, even if they happened to be the worst of men.

The Evangelist, therefore, summing up these wonders— those worked in bodies, those in souls, those in the elements, the precepts, those gifts (ineffable and more sublime than the heavens), the laws, the way of life, obedience, the future promises, His sufferings—gave voice to this utterance, wonderful and full of sublime teachings, saying: 'We saw his glory —glory as of the only-begotten of the Father—full of grace and of truth.'

Now, we marvel at Christ not only because of His miracles, but also because of His sufferings; for example, when He was nailed to the cross and was scourged, when He was struck, when He was spat upon and when He accepted blows on the cheek from those who had received benefits. And this is so, for even with reference to those things which seemed to be most ignominious, the same word was once more deemed worthy to be used, since even He Himself called His sufferings 'glory.'[17] And they were in truth evidences not only of providence and of love, but also of unspeakable power. When they took place, death was vanquished and the curse was destroyed; and demons were confounded and, after being led in triumph, were made a spectacle; and the handwriting of our sins was fastened to the cross.

Then, since these wonders were worked invisibly, others

17 Cf. John 12.23,24.

also took place visibly, to prove that He actually was the only-begotten Son of God and Lord of all creation. While the blessed Body still hung suspended, the sun withdrew its beams and the earth trembled and was completely in darkness.[18] Further, graves were opened, and the ground quaked and a multitude of the dead without number suddenly came forth and went into the city.[19] Though the stones of His tomb were fitted in place, and the seals still were intact, the dead man arose, He who had been crucified after being pierced with nails.[20] And after abundantly filling with a certain unconquerable and divine power the then eleven disciples, He sent them to men throughout the world, to be general physicians of all human nature. They were sent both to set right the life [of men], by spreading everywhere on earth the knowledge of the heavenly teachings, and also to destroy the despotism of the demons; likewise, to teach us of those great and ineffable blessings and to announce to us the immortality of the soul and everlasting life of the body, rewards both surpassing understanding and never to have an end.

[In writing today's text], then, this blessed Evangelist had in mind these thoughts, and more than these—things which he himself knew, but could not write, because the world did not have room for them. 'If every one of these should be written, not even the world itself, I think, could hold the books that would be written.'[21] Therefore, with all these thoughts in mind, he cried out: 'We saw His glory—glory as of the only-begotten of the Father—full of grace and of truth.'

Accordingly, it behooves those who have been deemed worthy of such sights and such sounds, and of profiting by so great a gift, to give evidence of a life also worthy of these

18 Cf. Luke 23.44,45.
19 Cf. Matt. 27.51-54.
20 Cf. Matt. 28.1-15.
21 John 21.25.

teachings, so as to enjoy the benefit also of the rewards
the world to come. Our Lord Jesus Christ came on this
account, too, that we might see not only His glory here, but
also the glory to come. Therefore, He said: 'I will that where
I am they also may be, in order that they may behold My
glory.'[22] Now, if this glory here has been so bright and splendid, what could one say of that other? It will not appear on
this corrupt earth, nor while we are in our perishable bodies,
but in that immortal and everlasting creation, and with so
much brightness that it is impossible to put it into words.
Oh, blessed, and thrice-blessed, and blessed many times over,
they who are deemed worthy to become beholders of that
glory! With reference to it the Prophet says: 'Away with the
impious that he may not behold the glory of the Lord.'[23]

May no one of us be cast out or forbidden ever to behold
it. If we are not going to enjoy it, it is time to say also on
our part: 'It were well for us if we had not been born.'[24]
Why, indeed, are we living? Why are we breathing? Why
do we exist, if we fail to obtain that sight? If we shall not
then be allowed to behold our Lord? If men who do not
behold the sunlight endure a life more bitter than any death,
what are they likely to suffer who have been deprived of that
Light? In the former case, suffering is limited to this privation
alone; but in the latter, it is not thus limited.

Yet, even if this were the only suffering [in the next world],
not even then would the extent of punishment be the same.
But the latter would be as much more severe as that Sun is
undoubtedly superior to the earthly one. However, actually
we must expect another punishment as well. He who does not
behold that Light must not only be borne away into darkness
but also be burned continually, and waste away, and gnash
his teeth and endure countless other terrible sufferings.

---

22 John 17.24.
23 Isa. 26.10.
24 Cf. Matt. 26.24,25.

Accordingly, let us not watch ourselves falling into everlasting punishment through omission and negligence in this short time, but let us be vigilant, let us live soberly, let us do and carry on everything so as to obtain that enjoyment, and be far from the river of fire which flows with great roaring before the dread tribunal. He who once has fallen in there must remain always, and there is no one who will rescue him from the punishment, not father, or mother, or brother.

Now, the Prophets themselves cry out these things, one saying: 'Brother does not redeem, will man redeem?'[25] And Ezechiel has revealed more than this, saying: 'If Noe and Job and Daniel stand they will not deliver their sons and daughters.'[26] There is only one bulwark there, which is that created by one's works, and it is not possible for him who is deprived of it to be saved otherwise.

Therefore, always preoccupied with these things and reflecting on them, let us purify our life and make it exemplary that we may behold the Lord with confidence and obtain the blessings promised, by the grace and mercy of our Lord Jesus Christ, through whom and with whom glory be to the Father, together with the Holy Spirit, now and always, and forever and ever. Amen.

Homily 13 (John 1.15)

'John bore witness concerning Him and cried: 'This was He of whom I said, He who is to come after me has been set above me because He was before me." '

Surely it is not in vain that we are hastening to our task? Surely we are not sowing on rocks? Surely the seeds which we cast do not lie hidden by the roadside and among thorns

---

25 Ps. 48.8.
26 Ezech. 14.14,16.

as they fall?[1] In truth, I am anxious for fear that our hus-
bandry may be unprofitable for us, and this although I myself
do not think I shall suffer loss as far as the reward for this
labor is concerned. For the plight of husbandmen is not
the exact counterpart of that of teachers like me.

Indeed, it often happens that the husbandman after his
year's toils, and that hard work of his, and sweat, if the
earth brings forth no fruit worthy of these pains will be able
to find no other source of consolation for his labors. But he
turns away with shame and sadness from the threshing floor
to his house and wife and children, because he can recover
no repayment for his long, patient industry.

However, in our case there is no such predicament in store
for us. Even if the earth, when cultivated, brings forth no
fruit—though we have left nothing undone—the Lord of
both of us and of the earth will not suffer us to go away with
empty hopes, but will give repayment. 'Yet, each,' Paul says,
'will receive his own reward according to his labor,'[2] not
according to the fruits of his labor. And listen to another corroboration of this: 'And you, son of man,' Scripture says,
'bear witness to this people, if so be they will listen, if so be
they will understand.'[3] Further, we may learn also through
Ezechiel that, provided the guardian gives warning as to
what it is necessary to avoid and what it is necessary to choose,
he delivers his own soul even if no one pay attention to him.[4]

Nevertheless, even with this strong encouragement—and
though we take heart because of the recompense awaiting
us—when we see our work in you not prospering, we feel
no better than those farmers who groan and weep and are
ashamed and embarrassed. For such is the tenderness of a
teacher; such, the solicitude of a father.

---

1 Cf. Matt. 13.3-23.
2 1 Cor. 3.8.
3 Cf. Ezech. 2.3,5.
4 Cf. Ezech. 3.19.

It was thus with Moses, though he might have rid himself of Jewish arrogance and might have received a more impressive sovereignty over another and much greater nation, [when God] said: 'Let me alone and I shall consume them and will make you a nation greater than this.'[5] Since he was a saint and servant of God, and a very true and loyal friend, he did not allow himself to listen to this word, but preferred to perish with those once assigned to his care, rather than to be saved apart from them and to be held in greater esteem. Such must he be who has the care of souls.

Now, a man who has small children does not wish to be called father of others, but only of those sprung from him. Hence, it is a disturbing thing that the disciples who have been entrusted to us are constantly exchanging places with those of others, and we are snatching at the guardianship now of these, again of those, and afterwards again of others, with a personal feeling for none.[6] However, may it never be necessary for us to suspect such behavior of you. Instead, we trust that you have an abundance of faith in our Lord Jesus Christ and of love for one another and for all.

We are speaking like this because we desire that you may grow more eager to listen to us and that your conduct may become more virtuous. If no mist of wrong-doing dims the eyes of your understanding and obscures its keenness and sharpness, your mind will then be able to plumb the full depths of the meaning of the words lying before us.

What, then, is the text proposed for us today? 'John bore witness concerning Him, and cried: "This was He of whom I said, He who is to come after me has been set above me because He was before me." ' This Evangelist is profuse in referring to John the Baptist throughout his Gospel and in

---

5 Cf. Exod. 32.10.
6 The Arian and other heresies contributed to making the times turbulent by creating warring factions among the unstable and excitable population of Antioch and other cities of the Empire.

applying his testimony everywhere. And he does this, not without reason, but very wisely, since all the Jews had great admiration for this man.

For instance, even Josephus imputes the war to the death of this man, because of whom, he points out, what was once a metropolis is now not even a city, and he goes on at great length with encomiums of him.[7] Therefore, in the hope of discomfiting the Jews by his agency, the Evangelist continually reminded them of the testimony of the Forerunner.

Now, the other Evangelists recalled the Prophets of olden times and referred their audience to each of the texts applicable to Christ. Of His birth they said: 'Now all this came to pass that there might be fufilled what was spoken to Isaias the prophet, saying, "Behold, the virgin shall be with child and shall bring forth a son." '[8] And when He was plotted against and sought out so diligently everywhere that the babes were slain before their time by Herod, they cited the words of Jeremias from a time long past: 'A voice was heard in Rama, weeping and loud lamentation; Rachel weeping for her children.'[9] Further, when He returned from Egypt again, they recalled the words of Osee, likewise: 'Out of Egypt I called my son',[10] and they did this throughout.

But this Evangelist, employing a more distinct and more recent testimony, as if crying out in an even louder voice than the others, repeatedly adduced, not those who had departed, not the dead only, but also this man living and acting, as he pointed Him out and baptized Him. In this the Evangelist was not trying to make the Lord worthy of faith by means of the servant, but was descending to the

---

7 Cf. Josephus, *A.I.* 18.113-120, where the destruction of the whole army of Herod at the hands of Aretas, King of Arabia Petraea, is accounted for as a punishment for the murder of John the Baptist. St. John Chrysostom, however, seems to be referring to the destruction of Jerusalem in his allusion.

8 Matt. 1.22,23; Isa. 7.14.

9 Matt. 2.18; Jer. 31.15.

10 Matt. 2.15; Osee 11.1.

weakness of his listeners. Just as, if He had not taken the form of a slave, He would not have been readily accepted, so if He had not trained beforehand by the voice of the servant the hearing of his fellow slaves, many of the Jews would not have accepted His teaching.

In addition to this, still another difficulty was being taken care of in a great and wonderful way. A person who says of himself something calculated to redound to his credit makes his testimony suspect and often gives offense to many of his hearers. Hence, another came to give testimony to Him. Besides, apart from these considerations, most men are somehow inclined to gravitate to the voice which is more ordinary and familiar to their ears, since they recognize it rather than the others. On this account the voice from heaven came but once or twice—that of John, frequently and continually.

Some, having mounted above the weakness of the crowd and so being rid of all the sensible appetites, were able to perceive the voice from above and therefore had no great need of a human voice. Because they obeyed the former in all things they were led by it. Others, on the contrary, still clinging to earth and befogged with many misty cares, had need of this more lowly voice. Thus, John, since he had stripped himself altogether of sensible appetites, did not therefore need human teachers, but was instructed from heaven. 'He who sent me to baptize with water,' he said, 'said to me, "He upon whom thou wilt see the Spirit descending he it is." '[11] But the Jews, still children, and not able to attain to that height, had a human teacher who did not speak his own words to them, but transmitted those which came to him from above.

What, then, did this Evangelist say? 'He bore witness concerning him, and cried.' What does the word 'cried' mean? 'With freedom,' he meant, 'with liberty, without any hesitation, did he herald the tidings.' And what did he

11 John 1.33.

herald? What is it that he testified and cried out? 'This was He', he said, 'of whom I said, "He who is to come after me has been set above me because He was before me." '

The testimony is indirect and still contains much that is lowly. He did not declare: 'This is the only-begotten Son of God.' But what did he say? 'This was He of whom I said, "He who is to come after me has been set above me because He was before me." ' It is here as with mother birds who do not at once or in one day teach their fledglings the whole art of flying. They lead them out only far enough to be outside the nest, and then, first persuade them to rest and next to fly. And on the day after this they add on another much more extensive flight, and thus gently and gradually lead them to the proper height. In the same way, also, the blessed John did not bring the Jews at once to the heights, but taught them for awhile to fly a little above the earth by saying that Christ was better than he.

Nevertheless, this was no small achievement for the moment, namely, that those who listened to such a wonderful man —I mean John—whom they clearly saw, one to whom they all ran and whom they thought to be an angel, were able to believe that He who had not yet appeared, or worked miracles, was better than John. For the moment, I repeat, he was striving to keep this matter straight in the minds of his hearers: that He to whom testimony was being given was greater than he who testified. He who was to come after was greater than he who came before. He who had not yet appeared was greater than he who was plainly to be seen and already famous.

And see how wisely he introduced the testimony. Not only did he point Him out as He appeared, but he foretold Him before He appeared. And the words, 'This is He of whom I said,' are those of a person speaking to that effect. Accordingly, Matthew likewise declared that, when all were coming to him, John said: 'I indeed baptize you with water.

But He who is coming after me is mightier than I, and the thong of His sandals I am not worthy to loose.'[12]

Why, then, did John speak thus even before He appeared? In order that the testimony to Him, when He should appear, might be readily accepted, since the minds of his hearers were already prepared by what had been said about Him, and so His mean disguise would not bother them. If they had seen Christ Himself, after having heard nothing at all, and if, after seeing Him, they heard such wonderful and great verbal testimony, at once the lowliness of His appearance would have been an obstacle to their accepting without question the greatness attributed to Him. Indeed, Christ affected such a humble and ordinary appearance that even Samaritan women and harlots and tax-gatherers had the courage to approach Him and converse with Him without any intimidation.

Therefore, as I said, if they had heard these words and seen Him at the same time, they would have ridiculed the testimony even of John the Baptist. But now, because of hearing them often before Christ appeared, and having their curiosity aroused by the statements made about Him, they had the opposite reaction. They did not cast aside the lesson taught by the words because of having seen Him of whom they gave testimony; on the contrary, because they believed what had already been said, they thought Him to be even more estimable.

Moreover, the expression, 'He who is to come after me,' means 'He who will preach after me,' not He who will be born after me. This, indeed, Matthew also gave us to understand, when he quoted John as saying: a man 'is coming after me,' not referring to His birth of Mary, but His coming to preach. If he were speaking of His birth, he would not have said 'is coming' but 'came,' for He had been born when John spoke those words. What, then, is the meaning of the expression, 'has been set above me'?

---

12 Matt. 3.11.

'Is in greater esteem, in greater honor. Now, do not think that because I came to preach ahead of Him, for that reason I am greater than He. In fact, I am much inferior—so much inferior, indeed, that I am not worthy to be enlisted in the office of His slave.' This is of a truth the meaning of 'has been set above me,' as Matthew made clear elsewhere when he said: 'The thong of His sandals I am not worthy to loose.' Besides, the fact that the statement 'has been set above me' does not refer to the way He came into being is plain from the next clause. If he wished to speak of that, the addition of the expression 'because he was before me' would be super-fluous. In truth, who is so foolish and senseless as not to know that He who was born ahead of him would be 'before him'?

On the other hand, if it refers to Christ's eternal existence, the expression means nothing else than: 'He who is to come after me existed ahead of me.' And besides the fact that such a statement would be ill advised, there was no point in adding on to it the clause beginning 'because.' And if this was actually what he wished to say, he should have said it differently; for instance: 'He who is to come after me existed ahead of me, because He was made before me.' One might rightly assign as a cause of a person's existing ahead [of someone else] the fact that he was made before the other. However, being made first is not the cause of prior existence.

Now, what we are saying is very reasonable. All of you, to be sure, know this: that not axioms, but facts that are not self-evident, are always in need of explanation. If the expression did indeed refer to existence, it would be quite evident that what has been made first must exist first. But since, on the contrary, the expression refers to dignity, this Evangelist with good reason offered this solution of an apparent diffi-culty. It was likely that many would be perplexed as to whence and for what reason 'He who is to come after has been set above,' that is, 'is manifestly of higher rank.' At once, then, he stated the answer to this question, and the reason is that

He existed before. 'For,' he said, 'it was not by some kind of promotion that He was set above me, after pushing me back when I was in first place,' but 'He was before me' even if He came later [in time].

'But how is it,' you say, 'that if the expression refers to His coming to men and to the glory which will accrue to Him thence, he spoke of the end not yet attained as if it had already taken place? He did not say "will be set," but "has been set." ' It was because those who are prophesying of the future are accustomed to speak frequently of future events as if of those that have taken place.

Isaias, indeed, in speaking of Christ's death, did not say: 'He will be led as a lamb to the slaughter,' which would refer to the future, but: 'He was led as a lamb to the slaughter.'[13] He was not yet incarnate; nevertheless, the Prophet spoke of what was to be as if it had taken place.

Further, David, in revealing the crucifixion, did not say: 'They will dig my hands and feet,' but: 'They have dug my hands and my feet' and 'They have parted my garments among them and on my vesture they cast lots.'[14] And with reference to the traitor who had not yet been born he spoke as follows: 'He that ate my bread has turned his heel against me.'[15] He also spoke in this way about the things that were to take place on the cross: 'They gave me gall for my food and in my thirst they gave me vinegar to drink.'[16]

Do you wish us to continue, or are these examples enough? I think so. Even if we have not spaded the whole width of the field, we have certainly thoroughly broken part of it up to a good depth, and this requires no less effort than that. Besides, we fear lest by keeping you here too long we may cause you to lose interest.

13 Isa. 53.7.
14 Ps. 21.17,19.
15 Ps. 40.10.
16 Ps. 68.22.

Wherefore, let us provide the proper sequel to our discussion. And what is the proper one? To give the proper glory to God, and it is the proper kind [if given] not in words only but much rather in deed. 'Let your light shine before men,' Scripture says, 'in order that they may see your good works and give glory to your Father in heaven.'[17] Indeed, nothing is more productive of light, beloved, than a virtuous life. One of the wise men also affirms this as follows: 'The ways of the just shine as the light.'[18] And they shine not only for those men themselves who kindle the light by their deeds and act as beacons on the straight path, but also for their neighbors.

Well, then, let us pour out oil for these lamps so that the flame may become higher, so that the light may appear richer. This oil not only has great strength now, but, even at the time when the offering of sacrifices was highly approved, its efficacy was commended more highly than theirs by far, for God said: 'I desire mercy and not sacrifice,'[19] and with good reason. That altar was lifeless, and this is living. Moreover, there, all that was lying thereon was consumed by the fire and ended in cinders and was dispersed in ashes and the smoke perished in the substance of the air; here, on the contrary, not so, but it bears other fruits.

And this Paul affirmed clearly, for in describing the treasures of the Corinthians he wrote as follows, referring to their love of almsgiving: 'The administration of this service not only supplies the wants of the saints, but overflows also in much gratitude to the Lord'; and again, 'glorifying God for

17 Matt. 5.16.
18 Prov. 4.18.
19 Osee 6.6. No doubt it was this text of Scripture that St. John here had in mind. But it also seems probable from the context that he was also using a clever play on words. The Greek *éleon,* ('mercy') and *élaion* ('oil') were pronounced in the same way in his day. So it is likely that he intended his audience to understand: 'I desire oil, and not sacrifice,' i.e., 'the oil of virtue.'

your obedient profession of the gospel and for the sincere generosity of your contributions to them and to all; while they themselves, in their prayers for you, yearn for you.'[20]

Do you see that [almsgiving] bears fruit in the giving of thanks, and praise of God, and continual prayers of those benefited, and warmer charity? Therefore, let us sacrifice, beloved, let us sacrifice every day on these altars. This sacrifice is greater than prayer and fasting and many other things, but only if it comes from just gain and just toil and is free from all greed and robbery and violence. And God accepts such offerings as these, whereas He turns away from and hates the others. He does not wish to be honored by the losses inflicted on others. Indeed, such sacrifice is impure and profane and would anger rather than conciliate God. Wherefore, it is necessary to take every precaution so as not to insult in the guise of worship Him who is being honored.

If Cain, who offered inferior things, though he had not wronged another man in these, paid the extreme penalty, when we offer something obtained by robbery and greed how shall we not receive more severe sufferings? That is why God even gave us an illustration of this command,[21] that we might show pity to, not torture, our fellow servants. A man who takes the goods of others and gives them to another has not shown mercy, but has inflicted wrong and acted unjustly to the last degree of injustice. Therefore, just as a stone could not produce oil, so harshness cannot produce mercy. Whenever almsgiving has such a root it is no longer almsgiving.

Wherefore, I urge not only that we look to this—how we may give to the needy—but also that we do not give what we have obtained by robbing others. 'When one prayeth, and another curseth, whose voice will the Lord hear?'[22] If we are

20 2 Cor. 9.12-14.
21 Cf. Matt. 18.23-35.
22 Eccli. 34.29.

careful so to conduct ourselves, we shall be able to obtain by the grace of God mercy and pity and pardon in abundance for the sins which we have committed during all this long time, and to escape the river of fire.

May it be that all of us, being delivered from that [penalty], may go up to the kingdom of heaven by the grace and mercy of our Lord Jesus Christ, through whom and with whom glory be to the Father, together with the Holy Spirit, now and always and forever and ever. Amen.

Homily 14 (John 1.16,17)

'And of His fullness we have all received, grace for grace.'

Last time we were saying that John explained away the doubt of those who would ask themselves how Christ, though coming later to preach, could have been set above [John the Baptist] and be more distinguished than he. This he did by adding the words: 'because He was before me.'

That was indeed one reason, but he added still another which he is now repeating. And what is it? 'Of his fullness,' he says, 'we have all received, grace for grace.' Moreover, along with these statements he made another one. And what is it? 'The law was given through Moses; grace and truth came through Jesus Christ.'

'Now, what is meant,' you say, 'by the expression: "Of His fullness we have all received" '? Indeed, we must discuss this point for awhile. 'Not by sharing with us,' says the Evangelist, 'does Christ possess the gift [of grace], but He Himself is both fountain and root of all virtues. He Himself is life, and light, and truth, not keeping within Himself the wealth of these blessings, but pouring it forth upon all others, and even after the outpouring still remaining full. He suffers loss in no way by giving His wealth to others, but, while always pouring out and sharing these virtues with all men,

He remains in the same state of perfection. On the other hand, whatever I possess is shared (for I received it from another).'

Besides, it is some small part of the whole, and like a small drop compared to a fathomless abyss and an infinite sea—though not even this example is adequate to illustrate what we are trying to say. If you remove a drop from the sea, the sea has been diminished by this amount, even if the diminution is imperceptible. In the case of that Fountain, on the contrary, it is not possible to say this; however much anyone draws from It, It remains in no way diminished.

Wherefore, we must go on to another example, for, though the latter is also inadequate, and cannot altogether clarify what we are seeking to explain, it leads, better than the former one, to the consideration now lying before us. Let us suppose, then, that there is a fountain of fire, and that from that source ten thousand lamps are enkindled, and twice as many, and three times as many, and many times more; does not the fire remain of the same fullness even after sharing its own strength with so many? Surely this is evident to all. Now if, among objects which are made up of parts and can be shared, and which are diminished by any subtraction, some such thing as this is discovered which, even after being shared with others, suffers no loss in its own substance, much more will this happen in the case of that incorporeal and simple Power. If, when that which is shared is a material substance, portions may be taken from it without dividing it, much more, when it is a question of a power—the power, too, of an incorporeal Being—that Power is not likely to suffer any division. And that is why John has said: 'Of His fullness we have all received,' and so linked his testimony with that of the Baptist. For, 'of his fullness we have all received' is a statement made, not by the Forerunner, but by the Disciple.

Now, what he meant is something like this: 'Do not think,' he said, 'that we who have been with Him for a long time, and have shared His salt and His table, testify in His behalf because of bias. John, also, who did not even know Him before this, who had not been with Him except when he was baptizing, when he saw Him in company with the others, cried out: "He was before me," since it was from Him he had received everything.' All of us, too: the twelve, the three hundred, the five hundred, the three thousand, the five thousand, the many thousands of Jews, the sum total of all the faithful—those who lived then, those at present, and those who will be—have received of His fullness.

But what have we received? 'Grace for grace,' he said. What for what? The new for the old. For, there was justice before and there is justice now: 'As regards the justice of the law, leading a blameless life.'[1] There was faith before and there is faith now: 'from faith unto faith.'[2] There was adoption of sons before and there is adoption of sons now: 'who have the adoption as sons,'[3] he says. There was glory before and there is glory now: 'If that which was transient was glorious, much more is that glorious which abides.'[4]

There was a law before and there is a law now: 'The law of the Spirit of life has delivered me.'[5] There was worship before and there is worship now: 'Whose worship,' [Paul] says, and again, 'Who serve God in spirit.'[6] There was a covenant before and there is a covenant now: 'I will make a new covenant with you, not according to the covenant which I made with your fathers.'[7] There was holiness before and there is holiness now. There was a baptism before and there is a baptism now. There was a sacrifice before and there is a sacrifice now. There was a temple before and there is a

1 Phil. 3.6.
2 Rom. 1.17.
3 Rom. 9.4.
4 2 Cor. 3.11.
5 Rom. 8.2.
6 Phil. 3.3.
7 Jer. 31.31.

temple now. There was a circumcision before and there is a circumcision now. So also there was grace before and there is grace now.

But the first-named as types, and the others as the reality, have kept the same name, but not the same meaning. Thus, even in pictures and images one that is done in black and white shades is said to be a man, and likewise one that has been done in realistic colors. Similarly, in the case of statues, both the gold one and the clay one are called statues, but the one as a model, the other as the real statue.

Do not, then, judge that things are the same because they have identical names, but do not decide that they are altogether different, either. In so far as a thing was a type, it was not completely divorced from truth. But, in so far as it continued to be shadow, it was less than the truth. Accordingly, what is the difference between all these pairs? Should you like us to choose one or two of the pairs I have mentioned, and to examine them? In this way the others also will be clear to you. And we shall all see that the types taught lessons suitable for children, while their realities belong to noble and great men; further, those precepts were given as to men, these as to angels.

Where, then, shall we begin? Do you wish to start from the adoption of sons itself? What, then, is the difference between that [of the Old Law] and this [of the New]? That was an honor in name, while here the actuality bears out the name. And about the former Scripture says: 'I have said: "You are gods and sons of the Most High, all of you",'[8] but about the latter: 'they were born of God.'[9] How and in what way? By the cleansing of regeneration and the renovation of the Holy Spirit. Moreover, after being called sons they still kept the spirit of bondage, but, though remaining slaves, they were honored, even so, by this appellation. However, we

8 Ps. 81.6.
9 John 1.13.

who are free receive the honor not in name only, but in deed. And this Paul has declared, saying: 'You have not received a spirit of bondage so as to be again in fear, but you have received a spirit of adoption as sons by virtue of which we cry: "Abba! Father!" '[10] Having been born from above and, so to speak, reformed, it is in this way that we have been called sons.

Again, if you examine the character of the holiness mentioned above[11]—what this is, and what that—you will again see a great difference. For they [of the Old Dispensation] were called 'holy' when they did not commit idolatry, or fornication, or adultery; but we become 'holy,' not only by refraining from these actions, but also by the possession of still greater things. To begin with, we obtain this gift[12] from the very visitation of the Spirit, and then [keep it by living] a way of life much more excellent than the Jewish one. And to prove that my words are not just empty talk, listen to what He says to them: 'Do not use divination nor purify your children, because you are a holy people.'[13]

Among them, therefore, this was holiness: to remain aloof from the customs governing the worship of idols. Among us, on the contrary, this is not so, but: 'That she may be holy in body and in spirit.'[14] . . . 'Strive for peace and for that holiness without which no man will see God;'[15] and 'Perfecting holiness in the fear of God.'[16] For the word 'holy' cannot have the same meaning in regard to all things of which it is predicated, since even God is called 'holy,' though not as we are.

Indeed, when the Prophet heard this word being uttered by the Seraphim, see what he said: 'Alas, woe is me, because

---

10 Rom. 8.15.
11 The character of the holiness of the Old Law and that of the New.
12 Sanctifying grace, at baptism.
13 Cf. Deut. 18.10.
14 1 Cor. 7.34.
15 Heb. 12.14.
16 2 Cor. 7.1.

I am a man of unclean lips and I dwell in the midst of a people that hath unclean lips.'[17] Yet, he was both holy and pure, but compared with the holiness of heaven we are all impure. Holy, in truth, are the angels, holy the archangels and the Seraphim and Cherubim, also, but there is still another difference between this holiness and that among us and among the higher Powers.

Now, I could go on to develop all the other points, but I see that my talk is extending to great length, and so, ceasing to go on further, we shall leave the rest for you to examine. It is possible for you when at home to compare these points and to study the difference between them, and similarly to go through the rest. 'Give an occasion to a wise man, and wisdom shall be added to him,' Scripture says.[18] Indeed, the beginning is ours, while the end will be yours. And now we must once again take up the thread of our discourse.

After saying: 'of His fullness we have all received,' he added: 'and grace for grace.' 'Not on account of your increase in numbers,' Scripture says, 'have I chosen you, but because of your fathers.'[19] If, then, it was not because of their own good deeds that they were chosen by God, it is evident that they obtained this honor by grace.

And we, too, have all been saved by grace, but not in the same way as they. It was not for the same reasons, but for much greater ones, and more sublime. Therefore, [the working of] grace in us is not the same as in them. Not only was pardon for our sins granted to us, since we shared in this with them —since all have sinned—but also justice, and holiness, and adoption of sons, and grace of the Spirit, much more splendid gifts and richer by far. Through this grace we have become dear to God, no longer merely as servants, but as sons and friends. That is why he said: 'grace for grace.'

17 Isa. 6.5.
18 Prov. 9.9.
19 Deut. 7.7.

In fact, even the very details of the Law came from grace, as well as the fact that we were created out of nothing. We did not receive this as a reward for good deeds previously done. How could we, indeed, when we did not yet exist? But God always takes the initiative in the giving of benefits. Now, not only was the being created out of nothing a work of grace, but also the power possessed by men, once they were created, to know at once what they ought to do and what they ought not. Then, too, the fact that they received this instinct as part of their very nature, and that the Creator entrusted to our keeping the inviolable tribunal of conscience, was the work of the greatest grace and ineffable mercy.

Further, the restoration of this [unwritten natural law] by a written Law, after it had been corrupted, was the work of grace. Moreover, the logical consequence was that they who transgressed the precept, once it had been given, be punished and dishonored; this, however, was not what took place, but, rather, reinstatement once more and pardon: not due, of course, but given out of mercy and grace. In proof that it was given out of mercy and grace, listen to what David says: 'The Lord works deeds of mercy and judgment for all that suffer wrong. He has made known his ways to Moses, his wills to the sons of Israel.'[20] And again: 'The Lord is good and righteous, he will give a law to sinners in the way.'[21]

Surely, then, the receiving of the Law is the work of mercy and compassion and grace. Therefore, after saying: 'grace for grace', he still more warmly insisted on the greatness of what had been given, and went on to say: 'The Law was given through Moses; grace and truth came through Jesus Christ.' Do you see how, slowly and gradually, word by word, both John the Baptist and the Disciple led on their hearers to the

---

20 Ps. 102.6,7.
21 Ps. 24.8.

most sublime knowledge after they had previously exercised them with more lowly things?

Now, the former, after comparing to himself Him who incomparably surpasses all, then proved His superiority by saying: 'who has been set above me,' adding: 'He was before me.' The latter, however, made a much greater [comparison], though still too little for the dignity of the Only-begotten. For he made the comparison, not to John, but to a man admired more than he by the Jews: I mean Moses. 'For,' he said, 'the Law was given through Moses; grace and truth came through Jesus Christ.'

See the wisdom of this. He made the comparison, not on the basis of appearance, but of deeds. For, if these were shown to be much greater, it was likely that even the senselesss would have to accept the verdict in approval of Christ. When the evidence consists of deeds which give grounds for no suspicion that they were done for some gain, or even of being done out of hatred, they make the verdict inescapable even for the senseless. Such things remain what the doers made them, when they come to light; wherefore, the testimony of these deeds is most of all above suspicion. And see how easy he made the comparison even for those who are somewhat weak. He did not play up the superiority with elaborate argument, but showed the difference by unadorned nouns, contrasting 'grace and truth' with 'Law,' and the verb 'came' with 'was given.'

Now, there is a great difference in each case. The latter— 'was given'—belongs to a servant who had received something from another and gave it to those to whom he was told to give; while the former—namely, 'grace and truth came'— belongs to a king who forgives all sins with authority and Himself provides His own gift. That is why He said: 'Thy sins are forgiven thee' and went on: ' "But that you may know that the Son of Man has power on earth to forgive sins"—he said to the paralytic, "Arise, take up thy pallet and go into thy house." '[22] Do you see how 'grace' comes through Him?

But consider 'truth,' also. Now, the above words, and those regarding the thief, and the gift of baptism, and the grace of the Spirit which was given through it, and many other words, too, are illustrative of 'grace,' but we shall see 'truth' more clearly if we examine the types of it. Anticipating the dispensation which was going to be fulfilled in the New Testament, the types sketched it in outline, like patterns, and Christ, when He came, executed the design.

Let us, then, consider the types briefly, for it is not opportune now to run through everything relating to the types, but, having become acquainted with some of them, from those types which I shall set before you you will also learn about the rest. Do you wish us to begin from the Passion itself? What does the type say? 'Take a lamb, by houses, and sacrifice, and do as he has enjoined and ordained.'[23] But Christ, not so; for He does not order this to take place. He Himself becomes the offering, presenting Himself to the Father as sacrifice and oblation.

See how the type was given through Moses, but the truth came through Jesus Christ. And again, on Mount Sinai, when the Amalecites were waging war on the Hebrews, the hands of Moses were propped up, held by Aaron and Hur standing on either side;[24] but Christ, when He came, Himself held His hands extended on the cross by His own power. Do you see how the type 'was given' and 'the truth came'? Again, the Law said: 'Cursed be he that abideth not in the words written in this book.'[25] But what does grace say? 'Come to me, all you who labor and are burdened and I will give you rest';[26]

---

22 Mark 2.9-11.
23 Cf. Exod. 12.3.
24 Cf. Exod. 17.9-12.
25 Deut. 27.26.
26 Matt. 11.28.

and Paul: 'Christ redeemed us from the curse of the Law, becoming a curse for us.'[27]

Therefore, since we enjoy such great grace and truth, I beseech you: Let us not become more lazy on account of the greatness of the gift. The greater the dignity of which we have been deemed worthy, so much the more are we obliged to practice virtue. He who has received slight benefits will not deserve so much blame, even if he does little of value. But he who ascends to the highest peak of honor, yet produces mean and paltry results, will merit so much greater punishment.

However, God forbid that we may ever entertain suspicions of such conduct in your regard. We trust in the Lord that you are winging your souls toward heaven, and raising them from the earth, and, though in the world, have no part in the things of the world. Nevertheless, even though we are confident of this, we do not cease continually exhorting you to the same. Even in pagan games it is not those who have fallen, not those who lie prone, that all the spectators urge on, but those who are up and doing, those who are still running. They stop paying attention to the former, feeling that they would be wasting their effort because they cannot spur them on by their shouts of encouragement, since they have completely lost all chance of winning a prize.

In our case, however, we can expect something worth while, not only of you who are spiritually vigorous, but also of those who have fallen away, provided they wish to regain their footing. For this reason, indeed, we are putting forth every effort, exhorting, finding fault, urging on, praising, so as to effect your salvation. Well, then, do not be annoyed at our persistent exhortation concerning your way of life. These are not the words of one charging you with laziness, but of one who has very high hopes in your regard.

27 Gal. 3.13.

Moreover, these words are, and will be, addressed not only to you, but also to us who speak them, for we ourselves also need the same teaching. In fact, even if it is spoken by us, yet nothing prevents it from being spoken also to us. If we discover a man who is in need of correction, the sermon sets him straight, whereas if a man is upright and free from wrong-doing, it leads him away as far as possible from wrong-doing. Yet, not even we ourselves are completely free from sins. Both the medicine and the remedies are intended for everybody and available to all. The healing effect, however, is not the same in every instance, but depends on the will of those who choose to make use of them [or not]. Wherefore, he who has applied the remedy as he ought has effected some cure, but he who has not applied it to his wound has caused the infection to increase and has made it liable to come to the worst of ends.

While we are being healed, then, let us not bear it ill, but much rather rejoice, even if the method of teaching cause bitter pain, since later it will produce for us the sweetest fruit of all. Therefore, let us do all to this end: that, being purified from the wounds and marks which the teeth of sin have imprinted on our soul, we may set out on the way to that eternal life, in order that, becoming worthy of the vision of Christ, we may not be given over in that day to the avenging and relentless powers, but to those who can lead us to the inheritance of heaven prepared for them that love Him.

May it be granted that all of us obtain this by the grace and mercy of our Lord Jesus Christ, to whom be glory and power forever and ever. Amen.

Homily 15 (John 1.18)

'No one has at any time seen God. The only-begotten Son, who is in the bosom of the Father, He has revealed Him.'

God does not wish us merely to listen to the words and phrases contained in the Scriptures, but to do so with a great deal of prudent reflection. Therefore, blessed David frequently prefixed to his Psalms the expression 'a meditation' and also said: 'Open thou my eyes and I will consider the wondrous things of thy law.'[1] And after him, his son also pointed out by way of instruction that one must seek for wisdom even as for silver, or, rather, to trade in it more than in gold.[2]

Moreover, the Lord, also, by urging the Jews to search the Scriptures,[3] made our study of them still more imperative. Indeed, He would not have spoken thus if it were possible to grasp them at once and from the first reading. No one would ever search out the meaning of what is evident, but only the meaning of what is obscure and found only after much seeking. It is for this reason, also, that He said that they are a hidden treasure: to spur us on to the search.

Now, He said these things to us in order that we might not approach the words of the Scriptures casually, but with great care. For, if someone should listen to what is written in them without examining into the meaning and should accept everything in its literal sense, he would get many strange notions about God. For example, he would learn that He is a man, and made of bronze, and angry, and hot-tempered and many ideas of Him still stranger than these.[4] But by examining the sense that lies hidden deep within he will rid himself of all these strange doctrines.

1 For example, Ps. 31, 43, and others; Ps. 118.18.
2 Cf. Prov. 16.16,
3 Cf. John 5.39.
4 Cf., for example, John 1.18; Apoc. 1.15.

To be sure, even the text lying before us now says that God has a bosom, a property which belongs to material bodies. But no one is so mad as to conceive the notion that He who is immaterial is a [material] body. Therefore, that we may grasp the whole matter with its spiritual connotation, come let us study this brief text from its beginning.

'No one has at any time seen God.' From what sort of thought sequence did the Evangelist arrive at this statement? Having shown the great superiority of the gifts of Christ and that there is an infinite difference between them and those dispensed through Moses, he wished to conclude by mentioning the probable cause of the difference. As Moses was a servant, he was the dispenser of more lowly things; but as Christ was Master and King and Son of a King, He provided much greater things for us, since He is always with the Father and continually beholds Him. For this reason, also, the Evangelist went on to say: 'No one has at any time seen God.'

What, then, shall we say to Isaias, the trumpet-toned, who affirmed: 'I saw the Lord sitting upon a throne high and elevated'?[5] Moreover, what shall we say to John himself, who testified: 'He said these things when he saw His glory.'[6] And what to Ezechiel? For he, al o, saw Him resting on the Cherubim.[7] And what to Daniel? For he likewise declared: 'The Ancient of days sat.'[8] And what to Moses himself, who said: 'Show me thy glory that I may know thee familiarly'?[9] Jacob also received his name because of this privilege when he was called Israel, for Israel means 'one who sees God.'[10] Indeed, others also have beheld Him.

---

5 Isa. 6.1.
6 John 12.41.
7 Cf. Ezech. 10.20.
8 Dan. 7.9.
9 Cf. Exod. 33.13.
10 Cf. Gen. 32.29, but the etymology seems at fault here: the name 'Israel' has, rather, the idea of 'striving with God.'

How is it, then, that John said: 'No one has at any time seen God'? He was affirming that all those instances were manifestations of His condescension, not the vision of pure Being Itself. If they had actually seen the very nature of God, they would not have beheld it under different appearances. For, that which is itself simple, and without shape, and not made up of parts, and not restricted by limits, does not sit nor stand nor walk about, since all these are functions of material bodies. However, He alone knows how He exists.

Now, to show this, God the Father declared by one of the Prophets: 'I have multiplied visions, and by the hands of prophets I have used similitudes,'[11] that is, I condescended to them; I did not appear as I was.' Since His Son was going to appear to us in the guise of real flesh, He gave them experience of this beforehand by allowing them to see the substance of God in the way in which it was possible for them to see Him.

However, what God actually is, not only have the Prophets not seen, but not even angels or archangels. If you ask them, you will not hear them reply anything about His substance, but only singing: 'Glory to God in the highest and peace on earth among men of good will.'[12] If you desire to learn something even from the Cherubim or Seraphim, you will hear the mystical melody of His holiness and that 'heaven and earth are full of His glory.'[13] If you inquire of the higher Powers, you will discover nothing else than that their one work is to praise God, for, 'Praise him, all his powers,' the Psalmist said.[14]

Therefore, the Son alone sees Him, and also the Holy Spirit. How, in truth, could created nature see the Uncreated? Indeed, if we cannot even succeed in seeing clearly any im-

11 Osee 12.10.
12 Luke 2.14.
13 Cf. Isa. 6.3.
14 Cf. Ps. 148.2.

material power whatsoever, even though it is created—and this often has been illustrated in the case of the angels—much less can we attain to the vision of the immaterial and uncreated Being. For this reason Paul, also, said: 'Whom no man has seen or can see.'[15]

Does this prerogative, then, belong to the Father only, and not also to the Son? Perish the thought! Certainly it also belongs to the Son. And to show that it does also belong to Him, listen to Paul making this point clear in the words: 'He is the image of the invisible God.'[16] Now, since He is the image of the invisible, He Himself also is invisible, since otherwise He could not be that image.'

But if he said elsewhere: 'God was manifested in the flesh,'[17] do not wonder, because the manifestation took place in the flesh, not in His substance. Furthermore, Paul also testified here that God Himself was invisible, not only to men, but also to the Powers above; having said: 'was manifested in the flesh,' he added: 'appeared to angels.'

So that He became visible to the angels as well, at the time when He put on the flesh. Before this, however, they did not see Him in this way, since His substance was invisible also to them. 'But how is it,' you will say, 'that Christ said: "Do not despise one of these little ones; for I tell you, their angels in heaven always behold the face of My Father in heaven" '?[18] Now, what is this? Has God a face and is it located in heaven? No one would be so mad as to affirm this. Well, what, then, is the meaning of what was said?

Just as, when He said: 'Blessed are the pure of heart, for they shall see God,'[19] He was speaking of mental vision—which is within our power—and also of thought about God, so, likewise, it may be said of the angels that, by reason of their

15 1 Tim. 6.16.
16 Col. 1.15.
17 1 Tim. 3.16.
18 Matt. 18.10.
19 Matt. 5.8.

pure and constant nature, they continually think of nothing else but God. That is also why He Himself again said: 'Nor does anyone know the Father except the Son.'[20] What then? Are we all in ignorance of Him? May that not be true, yet no one knows Him as the Son does.

Therefore, just as He has been seen by many, in whatever way vision of Him was possible for them, but no one has ever beheld His essence, so also we all now know God but no one knows His substance, whatever it is, except only He who has been begotten from Him. The knowledge the Evangelist means here is both clear vision and comprehension: such as the Father has of the Son. Indeed, 'Even as the Father knows Me, I also know the Father.'[21]

Wherefore, see, too, with what richness of meaning the Evangelist spoke. When he declared: 'No one has at any time seen God,' he did not then simply say that the Son who has seen Him revealed Him, but added something else— more than the mere seeing—in the words: 'who is in the bosom of the Father.' To be in God's bosom is a much greater thing than to see Him. Indeed, he who merely sees may not have altogether accurate knowledge of what appears, but he who is in His bosom would be ignorant of nothing at all.

Therefore, in order that when you hear: 'No one knows the Father except the Son,' you may not say that, although He has greater knowledge of the Father than anyone else has, He does not know how great He is, for this reason the Evangelist declared that He is in the bosom of the Father, and Christ Himself said that He knows Him as the Father knows the Son.

Therefore, inquire of anyone who may object to this: 'Tell me, surely the Father knows the Son?' And he will reply unequivocally that He does—if he is not utterly mad. After this let us ask him this question, also: 'What? Does He see Him as a clear vision and know Him with accurate knowledge

20 Matt. 11.27.
21 Cf. John 10.15.

and understand clearly what He is?' And to this also he will altogether assent. 'From this, then, draw the conclusion that the Son is clearly comprehended by the Father.' He Himself said: 'Even as the Father knows Me so also I know Him.' And elsewhere: 'Not that anyone has seen the Father, except him who is from God.'[22]

That is also the reason, as I have said, why the Evangelist mentioned the Father's bosom: to clear up the whole matter for us by this one word. [It implies] that They have full conformity and agreement of substance, that Their knowledge is identical, that Their power is equal. For, the Father would not have anyone distinct from His own essence in His bosom, nor would any other have dared—since he was a slave and an ordinary person, to be himself in the bosom of the Lord, for this is a prerogative only of His own Son who is on terms of complete equality with Him who begot Him and is in no way inferior to Him.

Moreover, do you wish to learn as well about His eternity? Listen to what Moses said about the Father. When he had inquired what he should answer if he should be asked by the Egyptians who it was that had sent him, he was bidden to say: 'He who is sent me.'[23] Now, the words 'He who is' mean that He exists always, and is without beginning, and that He really exists, and exists as Lord and Master. The words 'was in the beginning' also signify this, since they imply the attribute of existing always. Therefore, John has used this expression here to show that the Son is in the bosom of the Father, without beginning and forever.

Further, in order that you may not think, because of the identity of the name, that He is one of the sons who have become so by grace, in the first place, the article is added to distinguish Him from the sons in the order of grace. And if this is not sufficient, but you still look down to earth, listen to

22 John 6.46.
23 Exod. 3.14.

a stronger word than this: 'only-begotten.' And if after this you still look below, 'I shall not refrain from even uttering a human expression about God' [says St. John], 'I mean "the bosom," but only do not, therefore, suspect anything unworthy of Him.'

Do you see the mercy and providence of the Lord? God has Himself described by unworthy expressions in order that thus you may understand clearly, and think great and sublime thoughts of Him; and do you still remain earth-bound? But tell me: Why was reference made here to 'the bosom'—that gross and carnal word? That we might conceive the suspicion that God is a material body? Perish the thought! By no means did he intend that. Why, therefore, was it mentioned? If neither the real Sonship of the Son is established by it, nor that God is not a material body, the expression has been thrown in superfluously, fulfilling no purpose. Why, then, is it mentioned? I shall not try to avoid listening if you ask this question.

Is it not very clear that it was for no other reason than that by it we might grasp the idea of the reality of the Only-begotten and His co-eternity with the Father? 'He has revealed,' he said. What has He revealed? 'No one has at any time seen God'? 'There is but one God?' But this both Moses and the other Prophets cry out without ceasing: 'The Lord your God is one Lord,'[24] and Isaias: 'Before me there was no God formed, and after me there shall be none.'[25]

Besides this, then, what else do we learn from the Son as He is 'in the bosom of the Father'? What from 'the Only-begotten'? First, that even these very words manifest His power; second, we have received a much clearer teaching and know that 'God is spirit' and that 'they who worship Him must worship in spirit and in truth.'[26] We learn, too, the fact itself that it is impossible to see God and that no one knows Him

24 Deut. 6.4.
25 Isa. 43.10.
26 John 4.24.

except the Son; and that He is the Father of the true and Only-begotten; and whatever other truths have been mentioned of Him.

Now, the expression 'he has revealed' indicates the clearer and more evident teaching which he gave, and which He directed not only to the Jews but to the whole world. Whereas not even all the Jews paid attention to the Prophets, the whole world would both give way to and obey the Only-begotten of God. Well, then, here the use of this word 'reveal' makes evident the greater certainty of His teaching, and for this reason He is called both Word and Angel of Good Counsel.

Therefore, since we have been deemed worthy of a greater and more perfect teaching, no longer through Prophets, but through the Son of God preaching to us in these latter days, let us give evidence of a much better life and one more worthy of the honor. It would be strange if, while He condescends to such an extent that He no longer wills to speak to us through servants, but through Himself, we show no greater effects of this than our predecessors. To be sure, they had Moses as instructor, but we have the Lord of Moses. Well, then, let us give evidence of a philosophy [of life] worthy of this honor and let us not have anything in common with the earth. It is for this reason that He has furnished us with teaching from above, from heaven, in order that He may remove our thoughts thither, that we may become imitators of our Teacher according as we are able.

'But how,' you will say, 'is it possible to become imitators of Christ?' If we do all things for the common good and do not seek our own interests. 'Christ,' Paul said, 'did not please himself, but as it is written, "The reproaches of those who reproach thee have fallen upon me." '[27] 'Let no one seek his own interests.'[28]

---

27 Rom. 15.3; Ps. 68.10.
28 1 Cor. 10.24.

Now, one is seeking his own interests [in the right way], if he looks to those of his neighbor, for our neighbor's good is ours. 'We are one body, but severally members of one another.'[29] Let us not, then, act as if we were widely separated, and let no one say: 'Such a one is not a friend of mine, or a relative, or a neighbor, nor have I anything in common with him. How shall I approach him? How shall I address him?' Even if he is not a relative, or a friend, he is still a man, sharing the same nature with you, having the same Master, a fellow slave and living in the same tent—for he has been born in the same world. And if he also shares the same faith, lo, he has also become your member. Indeed, what sort of friendship would ever be able to create as much unity as the kinship of faith?

Now, we must have for one another an intimacy, not merely like that which friends must have for one another, but as much as member must have for member. One could never find any relationship closer than this kind of friendship and fellowship. Even as you would not be able to say: 'Whence is my relationship and kinship with this [limb]?' for that would be a ridiculous question, so neither would you be able to say this about your brother. 'We were all baptized into one body,'[30] Paul says, Why 'into one body'? So that we may not be separated, but keep the condition of one body by association and friendship with one another.

Accordingly, let us not despise one another that we may not neglect ourselves. 'For no one ever hated his own flesh,' he said; 'on the contrary he nourishes and cherishes it.'[31] It is for this reason that God gave one house for all of us— this world; distributed all created things equally; kindled one sun for all; stretched above us one roof—the sky; set up one table—the earth. And He also gave another much

29 Rom. 12.5.
30 1 Cor. 12.13.
31 Eph. 5.29.

greater table than this,[32] but this, too, is one—those who partake of the mysteries understand what I say. He has bestowed one manner of generation, the spiritual, for all; one fatherland for all—that in heaven; we all drink from the same chalice. He has not bestowed more abundant and more honorable largesse upon the rich and meaner and less upon the poor, but has called all equally; He has furnished temporal things as generously as spiritual.

Then, whence comes the great inequality of conditions in life? From the greed and arrogance of the rich. But, brethren, let this no longer be. While the general and more necessary things are drawing us together to the same end, let us not be driven asunder by earthly and mean things— I mean wealth, and poverty, and bodily kinship, and enmity, and friendship. All these things are shadow and less than shadow for those who have the bond of love from on high. Let us, then, preserve this unbroken, and nothing will be able to approach us from the evil spirits who shatter such great unity.

May it be that we all may attain to this by the grace and mercy of our Lord Jesus Christ, through whom and with whom glory be to the Father, together with the Holy Spirit, now and always, and forever and ever. Amen.

Homily 16 (John 1.19-27)

'And this is the witness of John, when the Jews sent to him from Jerusalem priests and Levites to ask him, "Who art thou?" '[1]

A terrible thing is envy, beloved, terrible and ruinous to those who envy, but not to those who are envied. It harms

---

32 Holy Eucharist.

1 John 1.19.

and destroys them first, like some deep-seated and fatal poison within their souls. And if it should in some way do harm to those who are envied, the hurt is trifling and worth nothing, and brings greater gain than loss. Moreover, not only as regards envy, but also in all other vices, not the one who endures evil, but he who does evil, is the one who receives harm.

Now, if this were not so, Paul would not have exhorted his disciples to endure injustice rather than to act unjustly in the words: 'Why not rather suffer wrong? Why not rather be defrauded?'[2] He knew well that ruin pursues, without exception, not the one who endures evil, but the one who does it. And it is, of course, prompted by the thought of the envy of the Jews that I am saying all this. Those very men who had streamed out of the cities to John and who had then both accused themselves of their own sins and accepted baptism from him, afterwards—as if moved by some sort of qualms —sent to ask him: 'Who art thou?'

Truly a 'brood of vipers, and serpents'[3] and worse—if there is anything worse! 'Evil and adulterous generation,'[4] and perverse, after being baptized did you then become vainly curious and act officiously toward the Baptist? What folly can be more unreasonable than that of yours? How was it that you came out to him? How was it that you confessed your sins? How was it that you flocked to him as he was baptizing? How was it that you questioned him about what you must do? You did all these things illogically if you did not know the reason and purpose for them. However, the blessed John said none of these things, nor did he blame or censure, but answered them with all kindness.

And the reason why he did this is worth learning, so that their wickedness may be plain and evident to all. Frequently,

---

2 1 Cor. 6.7.
3 Cf. Matt. 23.32.
4 Cf. Matt. 12.39.

John testified to the Jews concerning Christ, and when he baptized them he continually recalled Him to those present and said: 'I indeed baptize you with water. But He who is coming after me is mightier than I. He will baptize you with the Holy Spirit and with fire.'[5]

It was, therefore, human passion which they felt in John's regard. Agitated in mind by the glory of the world, and looking to the things pertaining to outward show, they thought that it was not fitting for him to be inferior to Christ. Now, it was obvious that John had much to recommend him; first, his noble and estimable family, for he was the son of a high-priest; then, his way of life and austerity, his disdain of all human things, for, despising clothing and table and dwelling and food itself, he had spent the time before this in the desert.

But in regard to Christ, everything was quite the opposite; His family was ordinary, as they often taunted Him, saying: 'Is not this the carpenter's son? Is not his mother called Mary? And his brethren James and Joseph?'[6] Further, the native land which seemed to be His was so disgraceful that even Nathanael said: 'Can anything good come out of Nazareth?'[7] Besides, His way of life was ordinary and His garments were no better than those of most men. He did not bind a leather girdle about Himself, nor have His garment made of hair, nor eat honey and locusts, but He lived like most other men, and was present at the banquets of wicked men and publicans so as to draw them to Him. And the Jews, becoming aware of this, censured Him on this account, also, as He Himself declared: 'The Son of Man came eating and drinking, and they say, "Behold a glutton and a wine-drinker, a friend of publicans and sinners." '[8]

When, therefore, John repeatedly sent them from himself to

5 Matt. 3.11.
6 Matt. 13.55.
7 John 1.46.
8 Matt. 11.19.

Him who seemed to them to be inferior, they became ashamed and bore it ill. They preferred to have him as teacher, though they did not dare to say this openly, but sent to him, hoping through flattery to induce him to confess that he was Christ. Now, it was not men of low estate that they sent as they did to Christ, for, in the desire to catch Him they sent servants to Him, and again, Herodians, and such as these.

In this instance they sent priests and Levites, and not merely priests, but those from Jerusalem, that is, those held in greater honor (for the Evangelist did not reveal these details without design). And they sent them to ask: 'Who art thou?' Now, indeed, his family was well known to all, so that all even said: 'What then will this child be?'[9] And this saying went abroad through the whole of the hill county. And when he came forth again to the Jordan, all the cities were on the move and—both from Jerusalem and from all Judea—went to him to be baptized. Yet, these now questioned him, not out of ignorance (how could they be ignorant, when he was revealed in so many ways?), but wishing to lead him on to what I have mentioned.

Hear, then, how this blessed one replied to the intention with which they asked, not to the question itself. When they asked: 'Who art thou?' he did not at once say what it was possible to say straightforwardly: 'I am the voice of one crying in the desert.' What did he say? He removed the suspicion which they held. When asked, ' " Who art thou?" he acknowledged and did not deny; and he acknowledged, "I am not the Christ." ' And see the wisdom of the Evangelist. Three times he said the same thing, revealing both the virtue of the Baptist and the wickedness and folly of his adversaries.

Now, Luke also says that when the people suspected that he was the Christ, he again removed the suspicion. This is the duty of the prudent servant: not only not to steal his Lord's glory, but even to refuse it when offered by the crowd.

9 Luke 1.66.

However, the people arrived at this suspicion through simplicity and ignorance, but these men derived their suspicion from an evil mind, and questioned him as I have described, hoping, as I said, by flattery to allure him to the object for which they were striving. For, if they did not have this hope, they would not have at once gone on to another question. They would rather have been indignant at his making reply as if to a dissenter, and not replying to the question, and would have said: 'We did not suspect that you are [the Christ], did we? We did not come to ask this question, did we?'

But, as if caught and detected, they went on to another question and said: ' "What then? Art thou Elias?" And he said: "I am not." ' They hoped as well that Elias also would come, as Christ likewise stated. For, when the disciples were asking: 'Why then do the scribes say that Elias must come first?'[10] He Himself said: 'Elias indeed is to come and will restore all things.'

Next, they asked: ' "Art thou the Prophet?" And he answered, "No." ' Now, he was indeed a prophet. Why, then, did he deny it? Once more he was mindful of the intention of his questioners. For they hoped that a certain pre-eminent prophet would come, because Moses had said: 'A prophet like me will the Lord, your God, raise up for you from among your own kinsmen; to him you shall listen.'[11] But this Prophet was the Christ. For this reason they did not say: 'Art thou a prophet?'—inferring 'one of many.' But they used the article, 'Art thou the Prophet?'—that one, they meant, who was foretold by Moses. Thus it was that he denied, not that he was a prophet, but that he was that Prophet.

'They, therefore, said to him, "Who art thou? that we may give an answer to those who sent us. What hast thou to say of thyself?" ' Do you see that they were becoming more vehement, and pressing him hard, and repeating their questions,

---

10 Matt. 17.10.
11 Deut. 18.15.

and not desisting from them? And that he, who had before mildly removed their false suspicions, then laid down the truth? For he said: 'I am the voice of one crying in the desert, "Make straight the way of the Lord," as said Isaias the prophet.' Since he had uttered something great and exalted about Christ, because of their suspicious attitude he took refuge at once in the Prophet, authenticating his words by citing this source.

'And they who had been sent were from among the Pharisees,' he said. And they asked him, and said to him, "Why, then, dost thou baptize, if thou art not the Christ, nor Elias, nor the prophet?" ' Do you see that I was not mistaken when I said that they wished to lead him on to this point? But they did not, indeed, say it outright from the beginning, that they might not be detected by everybody. Next, when he said: 'I am not the Christ,' once more wishing to conceal what they were scheming within, they went on to Elias and the Prophet. And as he said that he was not any one of these, finally, at a loss, tearing off the mask, they revealed their deceitful, wily purpose with its face uncovered, and said: 'Why, then, dost thou baptize, if thou art not the Christ?' Then, once more wishing to disguise their purpose, they added the others, also; I mean Elias and the Prophet. For, since they did not succeed in tripping him up by flattery, they hoped to be able to force him by accusation to say what was not true, but they were not strong enough.

Oh, the madness! Oh, the arrogance and unbridled meddlesomeness! You were sent to learn from him who he was and whence, and surely you will not make rules for him? For this, once more, was the purpose of those who were forcing him to acknowledge that he was the Christ. Nevertheless, he did not even now grow indignant, nor did he say some such thing as might have been expected, as: 'Are you dictating to me and legislating for me?' But once again he displayed great moderation. 'I baptize with water,' he said; 'but in the midst of you there has stood one whom you do not know. He it is who is to come after me, who has been set above me, the strap of whose sandal I am not worthy to loose.'

What, finally, would the Jews have to say in reply to these words? The indictment of them is thence inescapable; the condemnation is without hope of pardon; they themselves have cast the vote against themselves. How, and by what means? They considered that John was honest and, for that reason, trustworthy, so that not only when he was giving testimony about others did they believe him, but also when he was speaking about himself. If they were not so disposed they would not have sent to learn from him the details about himself. Indeed, you know that generally, when people speak about themselves, we believe only those persons whom we think to be most truthful.

Further, not only were their words a stumbling-block, but also the frame of mind with which they accosted him, for they had come to him with great eagerness, even if later they changed. And both these things Christ affirmed when He said: 'He was the light burning; and you desired to rejoice for awhile in his light.'[12] Moreover, his answer made him yet more worthy of belief. For, 'He who does not seek his own glory is truthful, and there is no injustice in him.'[13] Indeed, he did not seek his own glory, but referred them to another.

Now, they who were sent were of the number of those whom they trusted and held the first places, so that there was nowhere an excuse for them, or pardon for the unbelief which they manifested to Christ. Why did you not accept what was said about Him by John? You sent those who held the first places, you questioned him through them, you heard what the Baptist answered. They displayed every solicitude, examined into everything, and named off all whom you sus-

---

12 John 5.35.
13 Cf. John 7.18.

pected [him to be]; nevertheless, he very freely acknowledged that he was not the Christ, or Elias, or the Prophet.

Besides, he did not even stop here, but showed also who he was, and discoursed about the nature of his own baptism, [saying] that it was unimportant and insignificant and possessed of nothing more than water. Then he affirmed the superiority of the baptism given by Christ. And he also adduced Isaias the Prophet, who had testified previously— a long time before—and had called Him Lord and named John the Baptist as his servant and minister.[14]

What, then, remained further? Was it not to believe in Him about whom testimony was given, and to prostrate before Him and acknowledge that He is God? The character and philosophy of the one giving testimony made it evident that his testimony was not that of flattery, but of truth. Moreover, this is plain also from the fact that no one prefers his neighbor to himself, and, if it should be possible to obtain rightful honor for himself, he would not be willing to surrender it to another, especially in the case of such great honor. So that, if Christ were not God, even John would not have given up in His favor the right to his testimony. If he spurned this honor from himself, as being too great for his nature, he surely would not have attributed it anew to another nature which was also undeserving of it.

Now, 'in the midst of you there has stood one whom you do not know.' He said this because it is likely that Christ was mingling with the people, as one of the multitude, inasmuch as He taught meekness and humility at all times. And the 'knowledge' he here meant was exact information, for example, who He was and whence He had come. But he immediately added: 'He it is who is to come after me,' all but saying: 'Do not think that all is finished after my baptism. If it were complete in itself, another would not come after

14 Cf. Isa. 40.3.

me to provide another baptism, but this one of mine is a preparation for, and forerunner of, that other. Mine is the shadow and image; another must come who will add to it the reality.' So that the very expression 'come after me' showed His dignity in a special way. For, if the first baptism were perfect of its kind, it would not require a successor.

'He has been set above me,' that is, 'in greater honor, more esteemed.' Then, that they might not think that it was by comparison that He had superior dignity, wishing to demonstrate that there could be no real comparison, he added: 'whose sandal I am not worthy to loose.' That is, not merely has He been set above me, but in such a way that I am not worthy to be numbered among the least of His servants, for, to loose the sandal belongs to the lowest rank of servitude in [the scale of] labor.

Now, if John was not worthy to loose His sandals—John, than whom there was no one greater 'among those born of women'[15]—where shall we rank ourselves? If he who was equal to the world, nay rather, greater than it (Paul says: 'of whom the world was not worthy'),[16] declared that he was not worthy to be named among the lowest of His servants, what shall we say who are laden with countless sins and who are as far from the virtue of John as earth is from heaven?

On the one hand, then, he said that he was worthy not even to loose the strap of His sandal. On the other hand, the enemies of truth mouth such insane ravings as to maintain that they are worthy to know Him as He knows Himself.[17] What worse insanity than this? What more mad than this presumption? Well did the wise man say: 'The beginning of pride is not to know the Lord.'[18] Not even the Devil would have been cast down and become the Devil—he who was

---

15 Matt. 11.11.
16 Heb. 11.38.
17 Eunomius, Bishop of Cyzicus (d. 395), taught that there was nothing in divine things that might not be grasped by human reason. His followers, the Anomoeans, are meant here. For a fuller treatment cf. art. 'Eunomianism' in *Catholic Encyclopedia*.
18 Cf. Eccli. 10.14.

not a demon before—if he had not been sick with this sickness. It deprived him of that well-known position of trust, it sent him into hell, it became for him the cause of all evils. For, through it, it is possible for all the virtue of the soul to be corrupted, even if it discovers there almsgiving, prayer, fasting, any virtue whatsoever. 'Pride among men is impure before God,'[19] Scripture says.

Therefore, not only impurity or fornication commonly defile those guilty of them, but also pride, and much more so than they. Why? Because, even if fornication is an indisputable evil, still, at the same time the sinner has lust to plead as excuse, but pride can discover no possible justification, or any pretext whatsoever, by which it may attain to even a shadow of pardon. Indeed, it is nothing else than perversion of mind and a most serious disease, begotten nowhere else than from insanity.

Nothing is more senseless than a proud man, though he be admired as wealthy, though he be possessed of prolific knowledge of profane things, though he be established in power, though possessed of all the things which seem desirable among men. And if the unhappy and wretched man who is proud of things that are really good loses the reward of all those things, how would the man not be most ridiculous of all who vaunts himself for things that are nothing and puffs himself up on account of a shadow and the flower of the field (for such is the glory of the present life)? He is acting like a man who is poor and blind, one always pining away with hunger, but who would take pride if he should perchance happen to see a beautiful dream one night.

O unhappy and wretched man, while your soul is corrupted by a most grievous disease and you are poor to the lowest degree of poverty, do you plume yourself because you have such or such a number of talents of gold? Or because you have a large number of slaves? But these are not yours. If

19 Cf. Luke 16.15.

you do not believe my words, learn from the experiences of your predecessors.

Moreover, if you are so intoxicated as not to learn from what has happened to others, wait a little while and you will know, from what happens to you, that none of these things is of help to you when, lying at the last gasp, and being master of not even one hour, or of a brief moment, you will unwillingly leave these possessions to those around you, and often to those to whom you do not wish [to leave them]. Many have not had the chance to make provision about these things, but have gone off suddenly. Though they indeed wished to have the enjoyment of them, they were not permitted to do so, but were dragged off, both giving up the possession of these things to others and giving place, perforce, to those to whom they were unwilling to yield.

In order that we may not endure such suffering, let us here, while we are still vigorous and in good health, give over these possessions to our own city.[20] In this way only shall we be able to enjoy them; but otherwise, not at all. In this way we shall lay them up in a secure and safe place. In that place there is not, there is not a single thing with the power to deprive us of them: death is not there, or wills, or succession of heirs, or sycophants, or schemes. But he who departs thither, carrying with him many possessions, can there enjoy the fruits thereof forever. Who, then, is so wretched as not to wish to revel in riches which will be irrevocably his?

Well, then, let us give over our wealth, and let us store it up there. We shall not need asses, or camels, or wagons, or ships for such storage; and I say this because God has freed us of this difficulty. But we need only the poor, the maimed, the crippled, the sick. These have been commissioned with this transfer. These dispatch our wealth to heaven. These bring the possessors of such wealth to the inheritance of everlasting good things.

---

20 Heaven.

May we all obtain this inheritance by the grace and mercy of our Lord Jesus Christ, through whom and with whom glory be to the Father, together with the Holy Spirit, now and always, and forever and ever. Amen.

Homily 17 (John 1.28-34)

'These things took place at Bethany, beyond the Jordan, where John was baptizing. The next day John saw Jesus coming to him, and he said, "Behold the Lamb of God who takes away the sin of the world!" '[1]

It is a very good thing to be sincere and open in speaking, and to make everything else secondary to the confession of Christ. So great and wonderful is it that the only-begotten Son of God confesses before His Father the man who does this, although the exchange of service is not equal. You confess upon earth, while He confesses in heaven; and you, before men, while He, before His Father and all the angels.[2]

Such a man was John, not with an eye to the multitude, or to glory or to any other human consideration, but treading upon all these things, with befitting freedom he announced to all men the tidings about Christ. And this is the reason why the Evangelist made note of the place: to show the courageous outspokenness of the loud-voiced herald. It was not in a house, or in a corner, or in a desert, but when he had taken over the Jordan, in the midst of the multitude, while the whole audience was made up of those who had been baptized by him (these Jews came to him as he was in the act of baptizing), that he voiced that wonderful confession regarding Christ. His words were replete with sublime and great and ineffable teachings, and asserted that he was not worthy to loose the strap of His sandal.

1 John 1.28,29.
2 Cf. Luke 12.8.

How, then, did the Evangelist note the place? He went on to say: 'These things took place at Bethany.' Some more accurate copies say: 'In Bethabara,' for Bethany was not 'beyond the Jordan,' or in the desert, but somewhere near Jerusalem.[3]

He specified the places for still another reason. Inasmuch as he was going to narrate events which were not ancient, but had happened a short time previously, he was making witnesses of those who had been present and had seen them, and also was drawing proof from the very names of the places. Feeling confident that he was adding nothing to the words uttered by the Baptist, but was narrating all the facts simply and truthfully, he appealed to the testimony of the places, which was, as I have said, no unimportant corroboration.

'The next day he saw Jesus coming to him and he said, "Behold the Lamb of God who takes away the sin of the world." ' The Evangelists have divided between them the period [when these events took place]. Matthew, on the one hand, passing quickly over the time preceding the imprisonment of John the Baptist, hurried on to what followed, but John the Evangelist not only did not hurry, but particularly dwelt on these events.

Thus, the former remained silent about the period after Jesus had come back from the desert, omitting, for example, what John said and what the Jews who were sent to him said, and everything else, and passed on at once to the imprisonment. For, he said: 'When Jesus heard that John had been delivered up he withdrew from there.'[4] But not so with John; on the contrary, he was silent with regard to the desert journey as described by Matthew. He related the

---

3 I.e., Bethany, the home of Martha and Mary, was a village near Jerusalem, but there was another place of the same name on the other side of the Jordan where the baptism of Christ took place. Cf. note on John 1.28 in Confraternity edition.
4 Matt. 4.12.

events following the return from the mountain,[5] and after narrating many details, then added: 'For John had not yet been put into prison.'[6]

'But why,' you say, 'did Jesus come to him now, and why did He do this, not once only, but also this second time?' Matthew asserted that he had to come there at first for the sake of being baptized. To show this, therefore, Jesus also went on to say: 'So it becomes us to fulfill all justice.'[7] But John [the Baptist] showed that this was the second time that He had come, and that it took place after His baptism, when he said: 'I beheld the Spirit descending as a dove and it abode upon him.'[8]

Why, then, did he come to John? In truth, He did not go by chance, but approached him [purposely], for the Evangelist said: 'He saw him coming to him.' For what reason, then, did He come? So that, since he had baptized Him with many others, no one might conceive the suspicion that He hastened to go to John for the same reason as that for which the others went, namely, for the confession of sins and to wash in the river for repentance. And so, He came for this reason, and at the same time to give John an opportunity to dispel this suspicion again. By saying: 'Behold the Lamb of God, who takes away the sin of the world,' he removed this suspicion entirely.

Now, it is clear that He who is so pure that He can take away the sins of others was not present to make a confession of sins, but to give an opportunity to that admirable herald, both to reiterate to his hearers more clearly by a second utterance the words he had formerly spoken and to add still others. The word 'Behold' is used because many had been frequently seeking Him on account of what had been said, and for a

---

5 Where Christ had delivered the Sermon on the Mount.
6 John 3.24.
7 Matt. 3.15.
8 John 1.32.

long time before this. Therefore, he pointed out that He was present in person by saying: 'Behold'—meaning: 'This is He who has been looked for of old. This is the Lamb.'

Moreover, he called Him a lamb, to recall to the Jews the prophecy of Isaias and His prefiguration at the time of Moses, in order that from the type he might the more readily conduct them to the reality. That other lamb, however, did not completely remove the sin of anyone, but this removed the sin of the whole world. For when the latter was running the risk of being destroyed, He snatched it quickly away from the anger of God.

'This is He of whom I said: "After me there comes one who has been set above me." ' Do you see how he here explained what he had said previously? Having said 'Lamb,' and that 'He takes away the sin of the world,' he then said: 'He has been set above me.' By the word 'above' he meant the taking away the sin of the world, the baptizing in the Holy Spirit. 'For my coming has no more significance than to announce the universal Benefactor of the world and to provide the baptism of water. But His coming is in order to purify all men and to dispense the power of the Paraclete.'

'He has been set above me,' that is, 'He has appeared brighter than I, because He was before me.' Let those who have accepted the insane teachings of Paul of Samosata[9] be ashamed, since they are opposing such manifest truth.

'And I did not know Him.' See how he here rendered his testimony above suspicion, showing that it was not derived from human affection, but proceeded from divine revelation. Yet, 'I did not know Him,' he declared. How, then, would you be a trustworthy witness? And how could you instruct others if you yourself did not know Him? He did not say: 'I do not know Him,' but 'I did not know Him.' Thus, for this reason he would be most deserving of trust, for how could

---

9 Cf. above, Homily 4 n. 5.

he have been currying the favor of one whom he did not know?

'But that he may be known to Israel, for this reason have I come baptizing with water.' Now, John himself did not need baptism, and that ablution of his had no other purpose than to prepare the way for faith in Christ for all other men. He did not say: 'I have come baptizing that I may purify those who have been baptized'; not: 'that I may set free from sins'; but: 'that He may be known to Israel.'

However, tell me, was it not possible without baptism to preach and attract the crowds? Yes, but by no means as easily. All men would not come together in crowds if the preaching took place without baptism. They would not discern [Christ's] superiority without comparison. The multitude indeed went out, but not to hear what he said. Why, then? To confess their sins and be baptized. And when they were present, they were given instruction about the teachings regarding Christ and the difference in His baptism. Moreover, though this [baptism of John] was holier than the Jewish one, and therefore all men ran after it, it nevertheless was imperfect.

How, then, did you know Him? 'By the descent of the Spirit,' he said. And again, lest anyone might think that He stood in need of the Spirit, even as we do, hear how he removed this suspicion, also, by pointing out that the descent of the Spirit took place only for the sake of announcing Christ. Having said: 'And I did not know Him,' he added: 'But He who sent me to baptize with water said to me, "He upon whom thou wilt see the Spirit descending and abiding upon him, He it is who baptizes with the Holy Spirit."' Do you perceive that this was the function of the Spirit here: to point out Christ?

Now, to be sure, the testimony of John was above suspicion. But, wishing to make it more trustworthy, he gave it the support of God and the Holy Spirit. Since he had given testimony so great, and awesome, and sufficient to terrify all hearers—namely, that Christ Himself alone takes away the sin of the whole world, and that the greatness of the gift is adequate for such a great expiation—he ended by setting forth the proof of this. And the proof is that He is the Son of God, and that He did not need baptism, and that the purpose of the descent of the Spirit was only to make Him manifest.

Indeed, it was not within the power of John to give the Spirit, and those who were baptized by him plainly said this: 'But we have not even heard that there is a Holy Spirit.'[10] Christ, then, did not need baptism—not John's nor any other's; rather, baptism was needful of the power of Christ. In fact, that which was lacking was the chief of all blessings, namely, for the baptized to be deemed worthy of the Spirit. Therefore, He added this valuable gift of the Spirit when He came.

'And John bore witness, saying, "I beheld the Spirit descending as a dove and it abode upon Him. And I did not know Him. But He who sent me to baptize with water said to me, He upon whom thou wilt see the Spirit descending and abiding upon Him, He it is who baptizes with the Holy Spirit. And I have seen and have borne witness that this is the Son of God." ' He repeated the phrase: 'I did not know Him,' not undesignedly, or without reason, but because he was His kinsman according to the flesh.

'Behold,' [the angel] said, 'Elizabeth thy kinswoman also has conceived a son.'[11] Accordingly, in order that he might not seem to be favoring Him through kinship, he repeated the phrase: 'I did not know Him.' And this statement was true with good reason, for he had spent the whole time previously in the desert, and was away from his father's house.

---

10 Acts 19.2.
11 Luke 1.36.

How, then, if he did not know Him before the descent of the Spirit, and if he then recognized Him for the first time, did he seek to prevent Him before His baptism, by saying: 'It is I who ought to be baptized by thee'?[12] This statement indicated that he knew Him very well. Still, in all likelihood he did not know Him before, or, at any rate, not long before. The miracles which took place when He was a child, such as those regarding the magi, and others like them, happened long before, when John himself also was still a child. Moreover, since a long period had elapsed in the meantime, He probably was unknown to all. If He had been known, John would not have said: 'That He may be known to Israel, for this reason have I come baptizing with water.'

Thence, in short, it is plain to us that those miracles which some ascribe to Christ's childhood are false, and merely products of the imagination of those who bring them to our attention. If He had worked miracles beginning from His early youth, neither would John have failed to recognize Him, nor would the rest of the crowd have needed a teacher to reveal Him.

Actually, John himself said that he had come for this reason: 'That He may be known to Israel.' Further, it was for this reason once more that he declared: 'It is I who ought to be baptized by Thee.' And later, when he recognized Him more clearly, he announced Him to the multitudes, saying: 'This is He of whom I said, "After me there comes one who has been set above me because He was before me." ' Also, since 'He who sent me to baptize with water' sent me for this reason: 'that He might be made known to Israel,' He Himself revealed Christ to John even before the descent of the Spirit.

Therefore, even before He appeared, John said: 'He is to come after me who has been set above me.' He did not know

---

12 Matt. 3.14.

Him, then, before coming to the Jordan and baptizing all men. But, when He was about to be baptized, then he recognized Him, inasmuch as the Father revealed Him to His Prophet. And when He was being baptized the Spirit showed Him to the Jews, on account of whom the descent of the Spirit took place.

In order that the testimony of John might not be rejected when he said: 'He was before me,' and 'He baptizes with the Spirit,' and 'He judges the world,' the Father sent His voice announcing Christ to be His Son, and the Spirit came upon Him, in order to focus the voice on the head of Christ. In fact, it was because the one was baptizing and the other was being baptized—lest any of the bystanders might think that the words were said of John—that the Spirit came, to forestall such a suspicion. So that, when he said: 'I did not know Him,' he meant the time before, not that proximate to, the baptism. Otherwise, how was it that he tried to prevent Him and said: 'It is I who ought to be baptized by Thee'? Further, how was it that he made other similar statements about Him?

'How was it, then, that the Jews did not believe,' do you say? 'John was not the only one who saw the Spirit in the form of a dove.' Because, even if they did see it, such things need not only the eyes of the body, but, more than these, the vision of the understanding, to prevent the incidents being considered as vain illusions. If, indeed, they who had seen Him working miracles and touching with His own hands the sick and the dead and thus restoring them to life and health were so drunk with malice that they asserted the opposite of what they had seen, how would they dispel the unbelief by the mere visit of the Spirit?

Yet, some say that not all of them saw, but only John and those who were better disposed. Even if it was possible for mortal eyes to see the Spirit descending, as it were, in the form of a dove, it was not altogether necessary for the event to be clearly evident to all. Indeed, Zachary saw many things with his bodily eyes,[13] and David,[14] and Ezechiel,[15] and yet they had none to share the vision. Moreover, Moses had knowledge of many things, such things as no one else knew. And not all the disciples were worthy of the Transfiguration on the Mount.[16] Not even all of them shared in the vision of the Resurrection; this Luke clearly indicated by saying that He showed Himself to 'Witnesses designated beforehand by God.'[17]

'And I have seen and have borne witness that this is the Son of God.' Now, where was it that he bore witness that 'this is the Son of God?' He did indeed call Him 'Lamb' and say that He was going to 'baptize with the Spirit,' but nowhere did he say that He is the Son of God. And the other Evangelists likewise did not record that after the baptism he said anything, but went on at once to tell of the miracles that took place after the imprisonment of John, and kept silence regarding the intervening time.

From this it is reasonable to conclude that both these details, and many more besides, have been omitted, and this our Evangelist himself has plainly said at the end of his Gospel.[18] So far were they from conjuring up anything creditable about Him that they all, with unanimous agreement, and with careful accuracy, set forth the details which might seem dishonorable, and you would not find any one of them omitting anything of the kind. As for His miracles, they conceded some of them to certain Evangelists to relate, others to others, and they were all silent about still others.

Now, it is not undesignedly that I am saying these things, but to confute the shameless deceit of the pagans. This is

---

13 Cf. Luke 1.
14 Cf. 2 Kings 5.
15 Cf. Ezech. 1.
16 Cf. Matt. 17.1-2.
17 Acts 10.41.
18 John 21.25.

surely a sufficient proof of the truthfulness [of the Evangelists],
and of their saying nothing merely for the sake of currying
favor. By this argument, together with others, you will be
able to arm yourselves against these others.[19] But be on your
guard, for if the physician can give accurate information with
regard to his profession, and the shoemaker, and the weaver,
and, in a word, all craftsmen, with regard to theirs, it is
ridiculous if he who professes to be a Christian is unable to
utter a word in defense of his own faith. Yet, the absence of
the former ability merely does harm to men's wealth, while
the neglect of the latter destroys our very soul. Nevertheless,
we are so perversely disposed as to devote all our zeal to the
former, and to despise, as if worth nothing, those essentials
which are the foundation of our salvation.

It is this that prevents the pagans from quickly realizing
the absurdity of their error. Inasmuch as, relying on false-
hood, they make every effort to obscure the baseness of their
teachings, while we who are the guardians of truth cannot
even open our mouth, what will prevent them from despising
the great weakness of our doctrine? Will they not get the idea
that our teaching is deceitful and foolish? Will they not
blaspheme Christ as a dissembler and deceiver who makes
use of the stupidity of the majority to advance His deceit?
And we are responsible for this blasphemy if we are not
willing to be on the alert to speak in defense of righteousness,
but rate such matters as superfluous, and concern ourselves
about the things of earth.

To be sure, an admirer of a dancer, or of a charioteer, or
of a contender against wild beasts runs every risk and makes
every effort so as not to come off worsted in disputes concerning his favorite. Moreover, these men string together long
commendations, building up a defense against those who
find fault with them, and casting countless jibes at their opponents. But, when arguments are proposed about Chris-

---

19 The Gentiles.

tianity, they all bow their heads, and rub them, and yawn, and, when laughed at, withdraw.

Now, are you not deserving of unmitigated anger if Christ appears less honored among you than a dancer? For, while you have thought up countless defenses of their deeds—even though all of these are somewhat base—you do not even exert yourself to give any thought and care to the wondrous deeds of Christ, although they have drawn the world to Him.

We believe in the Father and the Son and the Holy Spirit; in the resurrection of the body; in everlasting life. Well, then, some pagan may say: 'Who is this Father?' And: 'Who is the Son?' And 'Who the Holy Spirit?' Or: 'How is it that when we speak of three gods you accuse us of polytheism?' What will you say? What will you answer? How will you meet the onslaught of these questions? And what if, when you are silent, he should proffer that other question and ask: 'Lastly, what is the resurrection? Shall we arise in this body once more? Or will it be in another besides this? And if in this one, what use is there in its being destroyed?' What will you say in reply to these?

Further, what if he should say: 'Why did Christ appear when He did instead of before that? And did it seem best to Him to provide at that time for the human race, but during all the rest of time did He neglect us?' Or if he should line up still other questions besides, more weighty than these? But it is not expedient to ask many questions in succession and to be silent about the answers, lest in this way we harm the more simple [among you]. What has been said already is sufficient to shake off your sluggishness. What then? If they inquire into these things and you absolutely cannot bear even to listen to these words, tell me, since we are responsible for such error on the part of those who sit in darkness, shall we undergo only a slight punishment?

We should like, if you enjoyed a great deal of leisure, to bring before all of you the book of a certain foul pagan philosopher written against us, and also that of that other older one,[20] in order, in this way at least, to arouse you and draw you out of your excessive apathy. If they were so ready to speak against us, what pardon ought we to deserve if we do not even know how to ward off their attacks made upon us? Moreover, why have we been brought forward?

Do you not hear the Apostle saying: 'Be ready always with an answer to everyone who asks a reason for the hope that is in you.'[21] And Paul also gave the same admonition, when he said: 'Let the word of Christ dwell in you abundantly.'[22] But what do those who are more irrational than drones say in reply? 'Blessed be every simple soul,' and 'He that walketh in simplicity walketh confidently.'[23] Now, it is a cause of all kinds of evils that many do not know how to use the testimony of Scripture rightly. 'Simple' does not mean here 'irrational,' or refer to the man who knows nothing, but the blameless, the man who does no evil, the prudent. If it were otherwise, it was vain to hear: 'Be therefore wise as serpents and simple as doves.'[24]

But why should I say these things, since this discussion is beside the point? In addition to what we have mentioned, other things also are not right with us, I mean those pertaining to our life and conduct. In every way we are wretched and ridiculous and always ready to blame one another, but hesitant to correct our own faults, which we blame or censure when we see them in others.

Wherefore, I beseech you that now at least we pay heed to ourselves, and not stop at finding fault only, for this is not sufficient to appease God. Let us strive to show a change for the better in all respects, in order that, having lived here for the glory of God, we ourselves may also enjoy future

---

20 Not to be identified with absolute certainty.
21 1 Peter 3.15.
22 Col. 3.16.
23 Prov. 10.9.
24 Matt. 10.16.

glory. And may we all attain this by the grace and mercy of our Lord Jesus Christ, to whom be glory and power for ever and ever. Amen.

Homily 18 (John 1.35-41)

'Again the next day John was standing there, and two of his disciples. And looking upon Jesus as He walked by, he said, "Behold the Lamb of God!" And the two disciples heard him speak, and they followed Jesus.'[1]

How sluggish is human nature and how liable to meet with a bad end, not by reason of nature's constitution, but by reason of the sluggishness of its will. And on this account Paul, in writing to the Philippians, said: 'To write you the same things indeed is not irksome to me, but it is necessary for you.'[2]

Now, once the earth has received the seeds, it is immediately fruitful and does not need a second sowing. But in the case of our soul this is not so; one must be content, when he has often sown and given it much care, to be able once only to derive fruit. In the first place, the words sink with difficulty into the mind because it is very hard under the surface, and is thick with numberless thorns, and there are many scheming foes to steal away the seed. In the second place, when it has been planted and rooted, the same care is still needed so that the seeds may come to maturity and, having done so, remain undamaged and receive no harm from any source.

Further, in the case of seeds, when the plant has reached maturity and has attained its full strength, it readily resists blight and drought and all other pests. In the case of doctrine, however, this is not so, but even after the whole has been perfectly worked out, frequently a single storm and flood comes on, and it is destroyed, either by the force of discontent,

1 John 1.35-37.
2 Phil. 3.1.

or by the plotting of men who know how to deceive, or by various other trials borne in upon it.

Indeed, I have spoken thus, not without purpose, but so that when you hear John again uttering the same words as before you will not rate them as nonsense or consider them vain and boring. Of course, when he spoke the first time he wished to be heard, but since many, because of their deep apathy, did not pay attention to his words from the beginning, he roused them from sleep by repeating his message again. Now, consider; he had said: 'After me there comes one who has been set above me'; and 'I am not worthy to loose the strap of his sandal'; and 'He will baptize [you] with the Holy Spirit and with fire,'[3] and that the Spirit was seen descending as a dove and abiding upon Him, and he bore witness that 'this is the Son of God.'

No one paid attention or asked a question or said: 'Why do you say these things, and about whom, and for what reason?' Again, he had said: 'Behold the Lamb of God who takes away the sin of the world.' Not even thus did he penetrate their insensibility. For this reason, finally, he was forced to say the same words again, as if softening some hard and unyielding soil by cultivating it. By his word, as it were by a plow, he stirred up the hard-packed mind so that the seeds might settle down deeply. Accordingly, it is for this reason that he did not make his speech long, either, because he was striving for one thing only: namely, to lead them on and to unite them with Christ. He knew that when they had accepted this, and had been convinced, they would not have any further need of his testimony to Him. And this is what actually took place.

If the Samaritans said to the woman, after hearing Him: 'We no longer believe because of what thou hast said, for we have heard for ourselves and we know that this is in

3 Matt. 3.11.

truth the Saviour of the world, the Christ,'[4] much more quickly would the disciples have been won over, as did, in fact, actually happen. Indeed, after they had come and heard Him for one evening, no longer did they return to John, but they chose Christ so completely that they took upon themselves the task of John, and themselves heralded Him. 'He found his brother Simon,' the Evangelist says, 'and said to him, "We have found the Messias," (which interpreted is Christ).'

Now, kindly consider this fact, too—that when he said: 'He it is who is to come after me, who has been set above me,' and: 'I am not worthy to loose the strap of His sandal,' he won no one over. But, when he spoke about the Redemption and brought his speech to a more humble level, the disciples followed Christ.

Further, this is not the only conclusion that emerges from this incident, but we may also observe that most men are attracted, not so much when something great and sublime is said about God, as when mention is made of His kindness and mercy or of something conducive to the salvation of those who are listening. So, these men merely heard that He takes away the sin of the world and at once they ran to Him. 'If it is possible to be set free from the charges against us, why do we delay?' they said. 'He is present who will free us without effort of ours. Is it not, then, utter senselessness to defer accepting the gift?' Let the catechumens listen to this—those who are putting off to their last breath their own salvation.[5]

'Once more,' he declared, 'John stood and said, Behold the Lamb of God!' Christ said nothing, but John said all. And this is what takes place in the case of the bridegroom.

---

4 John 4.42.
5 Adult baptism was the more common practice in the Christian society contemporaneous to St. John, and prospective Christians frequently deferred the reception of the sacrament to the hour of death, because of the fear of sinning under its obligations.

He himself does not say anything to the bride for awhile, but waits there in silence. Others point him out to her, and still others hand over the bride to him. Now she is merely presented to him and he goes away, not after having won her by his own efforts, but after another has given her over to him. But, when he has taken the bride thus given, he so captivates her that she does not think any more of those who arranged the betrothal.[6]

This has happened also in the case of Christ. He came to betroth the Church; He Himself said nothing, but only came. But His friend John placed in His right hand that of the bride, entrusting to Him by his words the souls of men. When He had accepted them, He afterwards so captivated them that they did not return further to the one who had entrusted them to Him.

Now, this is not the only observation to be made here; there is something else. Even as in nuptials the maiden does not go to the bridegroom, but he hastens to her, even if he be the son of a king, while she is of low estate and an outcast —nay, even if he is going to betroth a serving-maid. So also it happened here. Human nature did not go up to heaven, but He Himself came to it, rightly despised and worthless as it was, and when the espousals had taken place He did not permit it to remain longer here, but took it away and brought it to His Father's house.

Now, why did John not take his own disciples to one side and speak to them about these things, and then hand them over to Christ, instead of saying to them publicly in the presence of all: 'Behold the Lamb of God'? In order that the work might not seem one of intrigue. For if, after having been exhorted privately by him, they went away [to

---

6 Some ancient pagan marriage customs still persisted in Christian marriage. A well-known part of these rites, and one considered most essential, was the joyful, and at the same time solemn, procession escorting the bride from her father's house to that of the bridegroom. St. John seems to be referring to some such custom here.

Christ], as if doing a favor for John, they would perhaps turn quickly back from Him, also. But now, having received their discipleship by means of instruction given in general, they remained thereafter steadfast disciples, since they had not followed, because of a desire to please their teacher, but purely with a view to their own profit.

Indeed, the Prophets and all the Apostles proclaimed Him when He was not present: the former, before His coming in the flesh; the latter, after the Ascension. But this man alone proclaimed Him in person. For this reason, also, he called himself 'the friend of the Bridegroom,'[7] since he alone was present at the nuptials. And this is so, for he arranged and completed all the details, and he himself provided a starting-point for the ceremony.

'And looking upon Jesus as He walked by, he said, "Behold the Lamb of God!" ' He made this statement to show that he bore witness not only by his voice but also by his eyes, for he looked with admiration upon Christ, rejoicing and exulting. And for awhile he did not speak in exhortation, but simply gazed admiringly and in astonishment at His presence. Then he revealed to them all the gift for the sake of which He had come, and the method of purification. For 'the Lamb' signifies both these things.

Now, he did not say 'who will take away' or 'who has taken away,' but 'who takes away the sins of the world,' since He is always doing this. When He suffered He did not then only take away sins, but from that time up to the present He takes them away, not that He is continually being crucified (for He offered one sacrifice for sin), but He is always purifying through that one sacrifice.

Therefore, just as 'the Word' means to us His election, and 'the Son' signifies His exalted dignity in comparison to the rest, so also 'the Lamb' and 'the Christ' and 'the Prophet' and 'the true Light' and 'the Good Shepherd,' and any other

7 John 3.29.

epithets applied to Him with the addition of the article, imply an important distinction. This is so because there were many lambs and prophets and Christs and sons, but the article removes Him far from the company of all of those. And not only has He been safeguarded by this article, but also by the addition of the 'the Only-begotten,' for He has nothing at all in common with the creature.

Now, the tenth hour may seem to someone too late a time of day to be adapted to a discussion of this kind (and I say this, for that was then the time, since 'It was about the tenth hour,'[8] the Evangelist says). Such a man seems to me to be very much in error. In the case of most men, to be sure, and especially those enslaved to the flesh, probably the time after dining[9] is not very suitable for any serious matters because of the heart's being weighted down by food. But here was a man who partook not even of common food, but spent the evening with as much sobriety as we do the morning, or, rather, with much more (for in our case, whatever of the evening's food is still left within us often distracts our soul with imaginations, but he weighed down his vessel with none of these). And so, it was likely that he might speak about such matters in the late afternoon. Besides, he lived in the desert beyond the Jordan. Thither all repaired for baptism with much trepidation, caring little then for the necessities of life, as also happened when they remained with Christ for three days and were without food.[10]

Now, it is the part of a zealous herald and earnest husbandman not to leave off until he sees that the word which has been planted has taken root. Why in the world, then, did he not travel everywhere in Judea proclaiming Him, instead of taking up his stand beside the river, waiting for Him

8 About 4:00 P.M.
9 The chief meal of the day was customarily taken at about the ninth or tenth hour, that is, between 3:00 and 4:00 P.M. It was a lengthy meal, ordinarily lasting several hours, sometimes longer.
10 Cf. Matt. 15.32.

to come and waiting to point Him out when He did come? Because he wished Him to be proclaimed through His works. His own endeavor, meanwhile, was merely to make Him known and to persuade at least some men to hear about eternal life.

Moreover, he relinquished to Him the greater testimony: that, namely, made by His works, even as He Himself said: 'I do not receive the witness of man, for the works which the Father has given me to accomplish, these very works that I do bear witness to me.'[11] See, now, how much more effective this was. When he had struck a small spark, the fire straightway began to flame high. Those, indeed, who previously did not heed his works, later said: 'All things that John said are true.'[12] And besides, if he said these things as he went round about, the developments which transpired might have seemed to be the result merely of some human effort, and his preaching would be beset by suspicion.

'And the two disciples heard him speak and they followed Jesus.' Now, John indeed also had still other disciples, but they not only did not follow [Jesus] but even were jealous of Him. 'Rabbi,' they said, 'he who was with thee beyond the Jordan, to whom thou hast borne witness, behold he baptizes and all are coming to him.'[13] And once again they came and accused Him: 'Why do we fast, whereas thy disciples do not fast?'[14] However, those who were more noble than the rest tolerated no such reaction as this, but as soon as they had heard they followed Him.

Moreover, they followed Him, not as though scornful of their former teacher, but as though fully convinced by him. And they provided striking proof that they were doing so because of a correct interpretation of his arguments. They did

11 John 5.34,36.
12 John 10.42.
13 John 3.26.
14 Matt. 9.14.

not act as they did as a result of being urged—a course of action which could be viewed with suspicion—but when he merely had foretold the future, and said that Christ would baptize by the Holy Spirit, they followed Him. Accordingly, they did not desert their master, but, rather, desired to learn what Christ had to offer more than he.

Further, notice that their eagerness was accompanied by reverence. When they had approached Jesus, they did not at once question Him about essential and important matters, and they did not converse with Him publicly, in front of everybody, openly and casually, but they made haste to have a talk with Him in private. They knew that the words of their teacher proceeded not from false modesty, but from truth.

'Now Andrew, the brother of Simon Peter, was one of the two who had heard John and had followed him.' For what reason, then, did the Evangelist not also make known the name of the other person? Some say it was because the writer was the other follower, but others deny this and say that the latter was not one of the chosen [disciples]. Therefore, it was not necessary to mention more than the bare facts about him. What use in learning his name, when the Evangelist did not even mention the names of the seventy-two? Now, it is possible to observe this practice also in Paul: 'And we have sent along with him,' he said, 'the brother who is in the gospel.'[15]

Besides, he made mention of Andrew for another reason. What, then, is it? In order that, when you hear that when Simon heard, in company with him, the words: 'Come, follow me, and I will make you fishers of men,'[16] he was not perplexed by this paradoxical promise, you will know that his brother had already laid the foundation of his faith.

15 Cf. 2 Cor. 8.18,22.
16 Matt. 4.19.

Now, 'Jesus turned round and seeing them following him, said to them, "What is it you seek?"' From this we are taught that God does not forestall our will by His gifts, but when we take the initiative, when we furnish the will, then He gives to us many means of salvation. 'What is it you seek?' What is this? Did He who knows the hearts of men, He who is intimately present to our thoughts, did He ask this? Yes, but not in order to learn (for how could that be?), but in order that by the question He might make them more at ease with Him, and might impart to them greater confidence and show them that they were worthy of listening to Him.

It is likely that they were embarrassed and afraid, since they were unknown to Him and had heard the things which their master testified about Him. Therefore, to free them from all these things: their shame, their fear, He asked the question and did not permit them to go in silence to His house. Yet, the same thing would have taken place even if He had not asked the question. They would have continued to follow Him and, walking in His steps, would have reached the house. For what reason, then, did He ask the question? To accomplish what I have said; namely, to reassure their minds, which were timid and still anxious, and to cause them to take courage.

Not only by following Him did they show their good will, but also by asking a question. Though they had not yet learned anything at all from Him or heard Him, they called Him 'Master,' numbering themselves among His disciples, and showing the reason for which they had followed Him, namely, in order to hear something of profit. And notice, I pray, their prudence. They did not say: 'Teach us about doctrines or some other important matter'; but what?—'Where dwellest thou?' As I have said before, they wished to say something quietly to Him and to hear something from Him, and thus to learn.

Therefore, they did not delay, nor did they say: 'By all means we shall come tomorrow, and we shall listen to you speaking in public, but they proved how eager they were to hear Him by not being deterred even by the time of day. And I say this for, as it happened, it was near sunset, since 'It was about the tenth hour,' the Evangelist said.

This was also the reason why Christ did not tell them the appearance of His dwelling, or its location, but drew them on to follow Him by showing that He had accepted them. And for this reason, likewise, He did not say any such thing as: 'It is not a good time now for you to come to my dwelling. Be among my listeners tomorrow if you wish something, but now go home.' On the contrary, He spoke as if to friends and those who had been acquainted with Him for a long time.

How is it, then, that He said elsewhere: 'The Son of Man has nowhere to lay his head,' while here He says: 'Come and see where I dwell'?[17] Because the expression 'has nowhere to lay his head' signifies that He did not possess His own lodging, but not that He did not stay in a dwelling. And this is so for the parable [that precedes][18] also means this.

To resume: The Evangelist said that they stayed with Him that day, but he did not go on to explain why, because the reason was evident. It was only to obtain instruction that they followed Him and that Christ drew them to Himself. And so profusely and eagerly did they profit by it even in one night that they both came immediately in search of others as well.

Well, then, let us also be taught from this to consider all things less important than hearing the divine Word, and to think no time inopportune. And let us learn never to neglect this pursuit, even if we must go into another's house, or even

17 Luke 9.58.
18 'The foxes have dens, and the birds of the air have nests.'

if it is necessary for an obscure man to become familiar with the great, or even if it is at an untimely hour of the day, or at any time whatsoever. Therefore, let food, and bathing, and banqueting, and the other necessities of life have a definite time; but let instruction about the philosophy from above have no set hour—let all the time belong to it. 'In season, out of season, reprove, entreat, rebuke,'[19] Scripture says. And the Prophet: 'On His law he will meditate day and night.'[20] And Moses, too, bade the Jews to do this continually.

To be sure, the necessities of life—I mean baths and banqueting—even if essential, nevertheless, if continually indulged in, make the body weak, but the soul's instruction, however much it is prolonged, makes the soul which receives it so much the stronger. As it is, we consume all our time in trifles and foolish nonsense. At dawn, and in the afternoon, and at noonday, and in the evening itself, we idly sit together and have set apart places in which to do this. But if we hear the divine teachings once or twice in the week, we are nauseated, we become satiated.

What, then, is the reason? We are ill disposed in soul. We have vitiated all its desire in striving for these things. Because of this it has no strong appetite for spiritual food. And this also, among other things, is a great proof of its sickliness, that it does not hunger or thirst, but has an aversion to spiritual food and drink. And if in the body this symptom[21] is an indication of serious indisposition and causes ill health, much more is it so in the soul.

'How, then, shall we be able to restore it to strength, when it has thus lost ground and slackened its pace? By doing what and saying what?' you ask. By seizing upon the divine words of the Prophets, the Apostles, the Evangelists, and all the others. Then we shall know that it is much better to feed on

19 2 Tim. 4.2.
20 Ps. 1.2.
21 Aversion to food and drink.

these things than on worthless nourishment—for this is what we must call social gatherings and idle conversation at the wrong time.

Now, which is better, I ask you, to discuss the affairs of the marketplace, those of the law courts, those of the army— or those about heaven and [the time] after our departure from here? Which is more noble: to talk about one's neighbor and the business of one's neighbor, and to be busy about the affairs of others, or to search into the affairs of the angels and those which are important to us personally? The affairs of your neighbor are not yours at all, but those of heaven are.

'But,' you object, 'one can exhaust these topics by discussing them once.' Then, why do you not think this about the subjects of your vain and foolish conversations? Indeed, though you spend your whole life in these, you think that you have by no means exhausted the discussion of these matters.

But I have not yet mentioned considerations much more serious than these. Even people of the more respectable type converse with one another about the last-mentioned subjects, but there are others, still more careless and negligent, who bandy about in their conversation mimes and dancers and charioteers, sullying their hearing, corrupting their soul, exciting their nature to frenzy by these stories, bringing every kind of evil image into their mind by such conversation.

At the same time as the tongue utters the name of the dancer, the soul instantly conjures up an image of his face, his hair, his soft clothing, the famous personage himself, more effeminate than these details. Once again, someone else fans the flame from another direction, bringing into the conversation a harlot and her words, her dress, her flashing eyes, her languorous expression, her curly tresses, her smooth cheeks, and darkened eyelids.

Did you not feel any emotion as I was enumerating these

details? But do not be ashamed, do not be worried about this, because the compelling influence of your human nature causes this [reaction] and affects the soul in proportion to the suggestiveness of the details narrated. Now if, as I was speaking, you felt the stirrings of emotion at what you heard, despite the fact that you were in church and far removed from the reality [pictured by my words], consider what it is likely that they experience who are seated in the very theatre, utterly shameless, absenting themselves from this august and honorable assembly, and quite unashamedly looking at and listening to those things.

At this point some scatterbrained person may perhaps say: 'If the compelling influence of nature affects the soul in this way, why in the world do you make no allowance for it and find fault with us?' I do so because, on the one hand, it is the effect of the movements of nature for a man to be tempted upon hearing of these things; on the other, it is a fault no longer of nature, but of the will, if he actually goes to listen to such. Even so, if a man is caught in the midst of fire he must be destroyed, and the weakness of nature, to be sure, is responsible for this; but nature does not also lead us to the fire and to the destruction therefrom, for this would be the work only of a perversion of the will.

Therefore, I am determined to abolish and correct this abuse so that we may not deliberately throw ourselves down headlong, or thrust ourselves into the pit of evil, or hasten of our own accord onto the pyre; and also that we may not be responsible for setting ourselves down in the fire prepared for the Devil.

May all of us, indeed, rescued both from this fire and from that other, proceed to the very bosom of Abraham by the grace and mercy of our Lord Jesus Christ, with whom glory be to the Father, together with the Holy Spirit, forever and ever. Amen.

Homily 19 (John 1.41,42)

'He found first his brother Simon and said to him, "We have found the Messias" (which interpreted is Christ). And he led him to Jesus.'

In the beginning, when God had made man, He not only did not abandon him, but gave to him woman as a helpmate and caused her to dwell with him, knowing that they would gain much profit from this companionship. What matter that the woman did not make use of this advantage as she should have?

In spite of this, if one examines closely into the nature of the matter, he will perceive that, for those who are wise, a great deal of benefit results from such companionship. Not only is this so in the case of wife and husband, but also if brothers share the same dwelling, they likewise will derive profit from this. And therefore the Prophet has said: 'Behold how good and how pleasant it is for brethren to dwell together in unity.'[1]

Moreover, Paul urged the early Christians 'not to forsake their assembly.'[2] And he did so for this is a way in which we are different from the animal kingdom. We have built cities and marketplaces and houses for this reason: in order that we may be united together with one another, not only in our dwelling places, but also in the bond of love. Since the Creator has made our nature dependent and not self-sufficing, God has fittingly directed that the assistance we derive from living with one another should supply for what is thus wanting to us.

Marriage was instituted for this reason: that what was lacking to the one [partner] might be supplied by the other, and that their nature, incomplete in itself, might thus become so self-sufficient that it would be able, even though mortal, to

1 Ps. 132.1.
2 Cf. Heb. 10.25.

immortalize itself for a long time through a succession of descendants. And I might continue further in this discussion to show that, when the association we have with one another is lawful and pure, those who take part in this relationship derive profit as a result. However, there is here another important consideration, in the light of which, indeed, we have made these assertions.

After Andrew had remained with Jesus and had learned what he did learn, he did not keep his treasure concealed for himself, but hastened to run quickly to his brother to share with him the good things which he had received. However, why did John not tell what the matters were which Jesus discussed with them? And also, whence is it clear that it was in order to hear these things that they stayed with Him?

We explained this not long ago,[3] but it is possible to learn it as well from the text read out today. See—what did he say to his brother? 'We have found the Messias (which interpreted is Christ).' Do you perceive that he proved by these words how much he had learned in a short time? And I say this because he showed the power of the Teacher who persuaded them, and their own enthusiasm from the start, and also their pondering carefully about these things from the very beginning.

Indeed, this is the statement of a soul who has felt a keen longing for His presence. Having long awaited His coming from on high, and so becoming overjoyed at His long-awaited appearance, it hastens to share the good news with others. This is a mark of brotherly kindness, of loving kinship, of genuine good will: to hasten to stretch out a helping hand to one another in spiritual matters. Furthermore, notice also that he added the article to the word as he used it. He did not say 'Messias,' but 'the Messias'; hence, they were awaiting one certain Christ, who had nothing in common with

3 Cf. Homily 18, pp. 179-182.

others. See likewise, pray, the docile and obedient disposition
of Peter from the beginning. He hastened to Him at once
with no delay. 'He led him to Jesus,' the Evangelist said.

But let no one despise his docility because he did not first
weigh his brother's words and then accept them. In fact, it
is likely that his brother had spoken of these things to him
in greater detail and at length, but the Evangelist everywhere cut short many details, seeking brevity. Besides, he did
not make the downright statement: 'He believed,' but: 'He
led him to Jesus'—to hand him over to Him for the future,
so that he might learn all from Him. Then, too, the other
disciple also was there and vouched for what he said.

Now, John the Baptist, after saying that He is 'the Lamb'
and that 'He baptizes with the Holy Spirit,' entrusted his
disciples to Christ so that they might have this doctrine
clarified. And Andrew would much more have done this,
doubting his ability to make the entire explanation and
drawing Peter to the very Source of light with so much zeal
and joy that nothing at all could delay or put him off.

He continued: 'But Jesus, looking upon him, said, "Thou
art Simon, the son of John; thou shalt be called Cephas"
(which interpreted is Peter).' From this time on, He began
to reveal His Godhead and gradually to make it known by
His predictions. He acted thus both in the case of Nathanael
and in that of the Samaritan woman. Prophecies convince
no less than miracles, and do not seem to be boastful. Even
if His miracles were calumniated by the stupid ('By Beelzebub,'
they said, 'He casts out devils)'[4] no such charge was ever made
about His prophecy. Accordingly, in the case of Simon and
also of Nathanael, He used this method of teaching, but in
that of Andrew and Philip He did not do this. Why in the
world was this? Because they had the testimony of John,
which was no small preparation, and Philip, on seeing the

---

4 Matt. 12.24.

others present with Jesus, received reliable evidence of their faith.

'Thou art Simon the son of John; thou shalt be called Cephas (which interpreted is Peter).' His foreknowledge of the future was thus guaranteed by His present [knowledge]. Since He named Peter's father, it was plain that He foreknew the future, also; moreover, this prediction of the future carried with it an implication of praise. This was not the act of a flatterer but of a seer who was foretelling the future, one whose testimony was confirmed by that means. But, in the case of the Samaritan woman, notice how He supplemented His revelation with a serious accusation. He said: 'Thou hast had five husbands, and he whom thou now hast is not thy husband.'[5] Thus, His Father devoted a large portion of His discourse to prophecy when He took a stand against the cult of images. 'Let them[6] tell the things that shall come to thee'; and again: 'I have declared and have saved; and there was no strange one among you,'[7] and throughout the entire prophecy He stressed this point.[8]

Prophecy is indeed especially the work of God which the demons would not be able to imitate, even if they should strive very hard. In the case of miracles, there also might be delusion, but foretelling the future with accuracy is a prerogative of His pure nature alone. Moreover, if demons have ever done this, they were merely deceiving the more stupid, whence, also, their oracles are always easily unmasked.

Now, Peter made no reply to these words, for he did not yet know anything clearly, but still was learning. And notice that the prediction was not yet complete. He did not say: 'I shall change your name to Peter and on this rock I will build My Church,' but: 'Thou shalt be called Cephas.' The

---

5 John 4.18.
6 Astrologers.
7 Cf. Isa. 47.13; 43.12.
8 I.e., that only God has power to foretell the future.

former speech would be indicative of too great power and authority. And Christ did not all at once and from the beginning show His power in all respects, but spoke for awhile in somewhat humble fashion. When, indeed, He had given proof of His Godhead, then He spoke more authoritatively and said: 'Blessed art thou, Simon, for My Father has revealed this to thee'; and again: 'And I say to thee, thou art Peter and upon this rock I will build My Church.'[9]

As we have said, therefore, He called him by this name, and James and his brother He called 'Sons of Thunder.' Why, then, did He do this? To show that He it is who gave the Old Testament and changed names, calling Abram Abraham, and Sarai Sara, and Jacob Israel.[10] He appointed the names of many from their birth, like Isaac, Samson, and others mentioned in Isaias and Osee.[11] He appointed the names of still others even after their name had been received from their parents, both in the examples mentioned above and in that of Josue, son of Nun.[12]

Now, it was the custom among the ancients to give names also from the attendant circumstances, as, in truth, Elias[13] did. This did not happen without reason, but that they might have in the name a memorial of the loving-kindness of God, in order that by the names a continual reminder of the prophecy might be implanted in those who heard them. Thus, indeed, He gave John his name in his infancy.[14] Those in whom virtue was going to shine from their earliest youth received their names from that time, while the name was

---

9 Matt. 16.17,18.
10 Cf. Gen.17.5,15; 35.10.
11 Cf. Isa. 8.3; Osee 1.4,6,9.
12 Cf. Num. 13.17.
13 The reference to Elias in this connection is obscure. Possibly, as Savile conjectures, the reading should be rather *Hē Leía* ('Lia'). Cf. Gen. 29-30 for the account of how Lia, the wife of Jacob, named her sons according to the circumstances of their birth.
14 Cf. Luke 1.14.

given afterwards to those who were destined to be famous later.

At that time, however, each one received a different name, while now we all have the same one: that which is greater than all, namely, to be called Christians and sons of God, His friends and His body. This name can stir us more than all those famous ones and make us more desirous of the practice of virtue. Well, then, let us not do things unworthy of the honor of our name, considering it the greatest honor that we are called Christ's. For, so Paul called us.[15]

Let us ponder and reverence the greatness of our name. A person who is said to be of the family of a distinguished general or else of some eminent man is proud when he hears of the one or the other [distinction]. He considers the name a great honor, and makes every effort not to bring defamation by his carelessness upon the one whose name he bears. Shall not we who are called by the name not of a general, or of some earthly ruler, or of an angel, or of an archangel, or of the Seraphim, but of the King of all these Himself, give up even our life itself, so as not to affront Him who has honored us?

Do you not know how much honor the imperial divisions of shield-bearers and spear-men—those close to the emperor's person—enjoy? So, let us also who have been deemed worthy to be near Him—actually much nearer, as much closer to Him than the above-mentioned as the body is to the head —let us use every means to imitate Christ.

What, therefore, did Christ say? 'The foxes have dens, and the birds of the air have nests, but the Son of Man has nowhere to lay his head.'[16] If, then, we should require this of you, it would perhaps seem to most of you burdensome and inconsiderate. Therefore, because of your weakness,

---

15 Cf. 1 Cor. 3.23.
16 Luke 9.58.

I dispense with this exact imitation, but I do expect you not to be attached to wealth.

Further, just as I refrain from demanding the extreme practice of virtue, because of the weakness of most of you, so also I expect you to refrain from the extreme practice of vice, and much more so. I do not censure those who have houses, and fields, and wealth, and slaves, but I wish you to possess these things in a safe way and as you ought. Now, what does 'as you ought' mean? In the manner of masters and not of slaves, so as to rule them and not be ruled by them, so as to use them and not abuse them.

They are called 'things to be used' for this reason: that we may use them for necessary services, not that we may store them up; the latter is what a slave does, the former, what a master does. To keep is the part of a slave, while to spend is the part of a master and of one who has much authority. You did not receive wealth for this reason, that you might bury it, but that you might distribute it. If God wished it to be stored up He would not have given it to men, but would have permitted it to remain lying in the ground.

However, since He wishes it to be expended, He therefore permitted us to have it, that we might share it with one another. Now, if we keep it to ourselves, we are no longer masters of it. But if you wish to increase it and hoard it on that account, even in this case this is the best way: to disperse and distribute it everywhere. No increase is possible without expenditure, or wealth without outlay.

Now, one may see this also in temporal affairs. It is thus with the merchant, thus with the farmer: the latter expending seeds; the former, wealth. And this is so, for the one sails the sea to disperse his possessions, while the other toils the whole year, casting his seeds and cultivating them. But here there is no need of any one of these things: of preparing a vessel, or of yoking oxen, or of plowing land, or of being anxious about the variability of the weather, or of fearing a shower of hail; here there are no waves, no cliff. This sailing and this sowing need one thing only: the casting out of material things; then that well-known Husbandman will do all the rest, about whom Christ says: 'My Father is the husbandman.'[17]

Is it not strange, then, that when, on the one hand, it is possible to receive all things without any toil at all, men are apathetic and indifferent; while, on the other hand, where there is need of many labors, many toils and anxieties, there they display every indication of zeal, although, afterwards, the outcome of these hopes is uncertain.

Let us not, I beseech you, let us not be insensible to such a degree as this with regard to our own salvation. But, spurning the more burdensome things, let us hasten to the easier and more profitable ones, that we may also attain to the good things to come, by the grace and mercy of our Lord Jesus Christ, with whom glory be to the Father, together with the Holy Spirit, now and always, and forever and ever. Amen.

Homily 20 (John 1.43-49)

'The next day He was about to leave for Galilee, and He found Philip. And Jesus said to him, "Follow me." Now Philip was from Bethsaida, the town of Andrew and Peter.'[1]

For the man who seeks diligently there is a reward in store, the proverb says.[2] Moreover, Christ gave us to understand something more than this when He said: 'He who seeks, finds.'[3] And in this connection it occurs to me to wonder how it was that Philip followed after Christ.

Andrew, to be sure, was persuaded after he had heard

---

17 Cf. John 15.1-2.

1 John 1.43,44.
2 Cf. Prov. 14.23.
3 Matt. 7.8.

of Him from John, and Peter from Andrew. But Philip, having acquired information from no one—except only that Christ said to him: 'Follow me'—at once obeyed, and did not turn back, but even became a herald announcing Him to others. Hastening to Nathanael, he said: 'We have found Him of whom Moses in the Law and the Prophets wrote.' Do you see that he had a mind given to earnest thought, and had been assiduously studying the words of Moses and awaiting the coming of Christ? And this is so because the expression 'We have found' is always used of persons who have been engaged in some kind of search.

On the next day Jesus departed for Galilee. He did not call anyone who had not first joined His company. And He acted in this way not without purpose, but in keeping with His wisdom and prudence. When men were not disposed to seek His company, if He Himself put pressure on them to follow Him, they would perhaps even have turned away from Him. But as it was, when they had chosen of their own volition to follow Him, they would remain faithful in future. Yet He did explicitly call Philip, because he was rather well known to Him before, for, since he had been born and brought up in Galilee, He was better acquainted with him.

It was, then, after He had acquired some disciples that He went to hunt out the rest; and He drew Philip and Nathaniel to follow after Him. In the case of Nathanael, however, there was nothing remarkable [in his answering the invitation], because the fame of Jesus had traveled up and down the whole of Syria.[4] The truly remarkable thing was with regard to Peter and James and Philip—not only that they believed in Him before witnessing His miracles, but also that they believed even though they were from Galilee, whence no prophet came, nor was it possible for any good to come, for the people of Galilee were somewhat

4 Matt. 4.24.

boorish and rustic and dull. Indeed, Christ also showed His power from the very circumstance that He took the select group of His disciples from this unpromising place.

It is probable, then, that Philip followed Jesus, after he had both seen those who were with Peter and heard of Him from John, and it is also likely that the voice of Christ worked some effect in him, for He knew those who would be suitable [for His purpose.] The Evangelist, however, cut all these details short. To sum up: that the Christ was going to come, Philip knew, but that this was the Christ he did not know; and I maintain that he heard about Him from Peter or from John. And John also mentioned his village in order that you might learn that 'the weak things of the world God has chosen.'[5]

'Philip found Nathanael, and said to him: "We have found him of whom Moses in the Law and the Prophets wrote, Jesus the son of Joseph of Nazareth." ' He said these things to make his announcement credible—as it would be if based on Moses and the Prophets—and by this means to confound his hearer. Since Nathanael was sincere and would examine everything honestly, both as Christ testified and the event proved, with reason did he send him to Moses and the Prophets to identify in that way Him who was being announced. And though he said that He was the son of Joseph, do not be disturbed, for He was still thought to be his child.

And whence is it clear, Philip, that this is He? What evidence can you give us? It is not enough merely to say so. What sign do you see? What miracle? It is not without risk to believe unquestioningly in such matters. What proof have you?

'The same as Andrew,' he says. When Andrew was not able to show forth the riches which he had discovered, because he could not do justice to his treasure in words,

---

5 1 Cor. 1.27.

he led his brother to what he had found. This, accordingly, Philip did also. Now, He did not say that He is the Christ and that the Prophets had foretold Him, but he drew him to Jesus knowing that he could not leave off afterwards if he should taste His words and His teaching.

'And Nathanael said to him, "Can anything good come out of Nazareth?" Philip said to him, "Come and see." Jesus saw Nathanael coming to him, and said of him, "Behold a true Israelite in whom there is no guile!" ' Because he said: 'Can anything good come out of Nazareth?' Christ praised and commended the man! Yet, ought he to have been censured? By no means. The statement is not that of one who does not believe, nor is it deserving of blame, but of praise. How, and in what way? Because he had examined into the prophecies more carefully than Philip. And this is so because he had heard from Scripture that Christ must come from Bethlehem and from the city in which David was. This belief, indeed, prevailed among the Jews and, also, the Prophet had proclaimed it of old, saying: 'And thou, Bethlehem, art by no means least among the princes of Juda, for from thee shall come forth a leader who shall rule my people Israel.'[6] Therefore, when he heard that He was from Nazareth, he was troubled and in doubt, since he found that the announcement of Philip was not in agreement with the words of the prophecy.

But see his prudence and fairness even in his doubt. He did not at once say: 'You are deceiving me, Philip, and lying. I do not believe you, I will not go. I have learned from the Prophets that Christ must come from Bethlehem, but you say He comes from Nazareth. Well then, this is not He.' No, he said none of these things. But what did he do? He also went to Him, but showed his carefulness about the Scriptures and the straightforwardness of his character by still not accepting the One who was from Nazareth. Yet

6 Mich. 5.2; Matt. 2.6; John 7.42.

he manifested the great desire which he had for the coming of Christ by not rejecting the messenger who brought the tidings. He considered that it was possible that Philip was making a mistake about the place.

Notice, further, please, how mildly the denial was made, and that it was put in the form of a question, for he did not say: 'Galilee produces nothing good'—but what? 'Can anything good come out of Nazareth?' And Philip also was very prudent. Though he had been doubted, he was not vexed nor did he bear it ill, but persisted, wishing to bring the man [to Christ] and showing us from the beginning the self-control becoming an Apostle. It was for this reason, also, that Christ said: 'Behold a true Israelite in whom there is no guile!' And so, though there is such a thing as a lying Israelite, this was not such a one, for He meant his judgment was unbiased. He spoke it neither to gain favor nor to show hostility.

Now, the Jews, when asked where Christ should be born, said: 'In Bethlehem,' and produced the proof, saying: 'And thou, Bethlehem, art by no means least among the princes of Juda.' Yet it was before they had seen Him that they gave this testimony, but when they had seen Him they concealed the evidence through envy, saying: 'As for this man, we do not know where he is from.'[7] Not so, Nathanael; he continued to hold the opinion which he had about Him from the beginning, namely, that [the Messias] was not from Nazareth.

Why, then, did the Prophets call Him the Nazarene? From His being brought up in that place and living there. Moreover, Christ refrained from saying: 'I am not from Nazareth, as Philip reported to you, but from Bethlehem,' so as not to make Philip's account questionable at the outset; besides this, because, even if He did convince him, this would not have furnished sufficient evidence that He was the

---

7 John 9.29.

Christ. Even if He was from Bethlehem, what prevented Him from failing to be the Christ, like the others who were from there? Therefore, He did not advert to this point at all, but did something which was most capable of winning Nathanael over: He showed that He was invisibly near them as they were conversing.

Therefore, when Nathanael said: 'Whence knowest thou me?' He said: 'Before Philip called thee, when thou wast under the fig tree, I saw thee.' See what a well-balanced and steadfast man he was. When Christ said: 'Behold a true Israelite,' he was not puffed up at the praise, he did not grasp at commendation, but continued seeking and searching more carefully and desired to learn something definite. Therefore, he still continued to inquire in human fashion, but Jesus replied as God. And this is so because He said: 'I know you from the beginning,' and [implied] that He knew the uprightness of his character, not as a man might, by being in company with him, but He already had known him before, as God does.

'And just now I saw thee under the fig tree,' when no one else was present there, but only Philip and Nathanael, and they were carrying on their entire conversation in private. Accordingly, the Evangelist specifically mentioned that it was when He had seen him from afar that He said: 'Behold a true Israelite,' in order to show that Christ had uttered these words before Philip drew near, so that the evidence was above suspicion.

For this reason, also, He spoke of the time and the place and the tree. If He said only: 'Before Philip came to you I saw you,' it might perhaps have been suspected that He Himself had sent Philip to him, and so was saying nothing noteworthy; but now, by speaking of the place where he was when accosted by Philip, and the name of the tree, and the time of the conversation, He showed that He unquestionably was speaking from foreknowledge.

And not only did He make evident His foreknowledge, but also He gave him instruction in another way. He recalled to him the things that had just been said, for example: 'Can anything good come out of Nazareth?' And it was most certainly because of this that Nathanael completely accepted Him, and also because He did not find fault with him for saying these words, but praised and approved him. Therefore, he also knew from this that He was really the Christ: both by reason of His foreknowledge and by reason of His accurately analyzing his state of mind, something that belonged to One who wished to show that He knew what was in his mind. Besides this, there was His refraining from blaming, and even praising, a statement he seemed to have made against Him. Therefore, though He asserted that Philip had called him, He omitted to mention what was said to him, and what he replied, leaving it to his conscience, because He did not wish to censure him further.

'What, then? Was it only before Philip called him that He saw him, or did He not also see him before this with His sleepless eye?' Surely He saw him, and no one would deny this, but it was extremely necessary to speak as He did for the moment. What, then, did Nathanael do? Since he had received the unmistakable proof of His foreknowledge, he proceeded to make his confession of faith, and, as he had showed his exactitude by his previous delay, so he revealed his candor by his subsequent submission. The Evangelist said: 'He answered him and said, "Rabbi, thou art the Son of God, thou art the King of Israel." ' Do you perceive how his soul at once became overjoyed and embraced Jesus with words? 'Thou art,' he said, 'the Expected One, He who has been sought.' Do you perceive that he was thunderstruck, amazed, leaping and bounding with joy?

So we, also, ought to rejoice, since we have been deemed worthy to know the Son of God and to rejoice not only mentally, but in our very actions as well. And what is the part of those who rejoice? To obey Him who is known. Moreover, it is the part of those who obey to do what He wishes, since, if we are going to do the things which move Him to anger, how are we showing that we rejoice?

Do you not see, even in private homes, when a man is entertaining one of his loved ones, how he joyfully puts forth every effort, bustling about in all directions and, even if it should mean expending all his possessions, sparing nothing so as to please the visitor? But if a man, though he had invited a guest, should pay no attention to him and should neglect to do what would make him comfortable, even if he should say, times without number, that he welcomes his coming, he would never be believed by his guest; and rightly so, for this must be shown by deeds.

Well, then, since Christ also has come to us, let us show that we rejoice, and let us not do any of the things which make Him angry. Let us adorn the dwelling into which He comes, for this is the conduct of those who rejoice. Let us set before Him the meal which He wishes to eat, for this is the conduct of those who rejoice exceedingly. But of what kind is this meal? He Himself says: 'My food is to do the will of him who sent me.'[8] Let us feed Him, hungry; let us give drink to Him, thirsty.[9] Even if you give but a cup of cold water, He accepts it, for He loves you;[10] and things that come from loved ones, even if they happen to be small, seem great to the lover.

Only, do not be hesitant; even if you contribute two oboli, He does not turn away, but accepts them, as if they were great wealth. Since He is not in want of anything and does not accept these things because of need, He is likely to measure all, not by the size of what is given, but by the intention of the giver. Only show that you love Him who

---

8 John 4.34.
9 Cf. Matt. 25.34,35.
10 Cf. Mark 9.40.

has come, that you are earnestly striving in all things because you rejoice at His presence. See how He Himself feels toward you. He came because of you, He laid down His life for your sake, and after all this He does not refuse to act as a suppliant toward you. 'On behalf of Christ, therefore,' Paul says, 'we are acting as ambassadors, God, as it were, appealing through us.'[11]

'And who is so mad,' you say, 'as not to love his Lord?' I also say this, and I know that no one of us would deny his love of Him in word or thought. However, not by words only, but also by deeds, does the loved one wish love to be shown. If we should say that we love, but should not do what lovers do, it is ridiculous, not only before God, but even in the sight of men. Therefore, since the profession [of our love for God] by words alone, and the denial of it by deeds, is not merely senseless but even harmful to us, I beseech you, let us make our confession by deeds, in order that we likewise may obtain acknowledgment from Him in that day when He will confess before His Father those who deserve it,[12] in Christ Jesus our Lord, through whom and with whom glory be to the Father, together with the Holy Spirit, now and always and forever and ever. Amen.

Homily 21 (John 1.49-2.4)

'Nathanael answered him and said, "Rabbi, thou art the Son of God, thou art King of Israel." Answering, Jesus said to him, "Because I said to thee that I saw thee under the fig tree, thou dost believe. Greater things than these shalt thou see." '[1]

---

11 2 Cor. 5.20.
12 Cf. Matt. 10.32,33.

---

1 John 1.49,50.

We need much care, dearly beloved, much vigilance, so as to be able to plumb the depths of sacred Scripture. It is not possible to discover its meaning merely incidentally, or while we are asleep, but we have need of careful scrutiny, and of earnest prayer as well, that we may be able to penetrate a little the sanctuary of the sacred mysteries.

Today, also, you see, it is no trifling question which lies before us, but one, further, which requires much earnest study. When Nathanael said: 'Thou art the Son of God,' Christ replied: 'Because I said to thee that I saw thee under the fig tree, thou dost believe. Greater things than these shalt thou see.'

What, then, is the point in these words that needs an explanation? The fact that when Peter, after witnessing such great miracles and hearing such sublime teaching, had confessed: 'Thou art the Son of God,' he was called blessed because he had received the revelation of this from the Father.[2] But when Nathanael said this same thing, even before the miracles and before Christ's teaching he heard no such commendation. On the contrary, as if he had not said as much as he ought to say, he was led on to something greater. What, then, was the reason for this?

It was because both Peter and Nathanael said the same words, but both did not have the same meaning, for Peter confessed the Son of God as true God, while Nathanael confessed Him as a mere man. And whence is this clear to us? From what he said immediately afterwards, for, when he had said: 'Thou art the Son of God,' he added: 'Thou art King of Israel.' But the Son of God is not King of Israel only, but of the whole world.

Now, Nathanael's meaning is evident, not merely from this, but also from what follows. Christ made no further statement to Peter, but, as if his faith was complete, He said that He would build· His Church upon his confession. In

---

2 Cf. Matt. 16.13-20.

the other case, however, He did no such thing; just the opposite. As if the greater and better part were lacking to this confession, He added the remaining words. And what did He say? 'Amen, amen, I say to you, you shall see heaven opened, and the angels of God ascending and descending upon the Son of Man.' Do you perceive how He gradually led him up from the earth and made him think of Him no longer merely as man? For, how can He be a mere man to whom the angels minister and upon whom angels ascend and descend? For this reason He said: 'Greater things than these shalt thou see,' and to illustrate this He brought in the ministry of angels.

Moreover, what He meant is some such thing as this: 'Does it seem to you, Nathanael, to be a great thing, and is that why you affirmed that I am King of Israel? What, then, will you say when you see the angels ascending and descending upon Me?' By this means He was persuading him to confess Him Lord of the angels as well. It was as upon the King's own Son that the royal ministers ascended and descended: at the time of the Crucifixion, again at the Resurrection and the Ascension, and even before that, when they came and ministered unto Him, as when they announced the good tidings of His birth and cried out: 'Glory to God in the highest and peace on earth';[3] and also when they came to Mary, when they came to Joseph.

And in this instance He did something which He repeated many times. He uttered two prophecies, and at once proved one of them true, to confirm by that which was at hand the other which was yet to take place. This is true, for some of the things that were said had immediate corroboration: for example, 'Before Philip called thee, when thou wast under the fig tree, I saw thee'; while others were still going to happen or had taken place in part: for instance, the descent and ascent of the angels, that at the Crucifixion, that at

---

3 Luke 2.14.

the Resurrection and the Ascension. And by His words He made the event itself credible even before it took place. If a man had had proof of His power in events already accomplished, when he heard also from Him about future events he would more readily accept this prophecy.

What, then, did Nathanael do? He made no reply to this. Therefore, Christ also finished His discourse to him at this point, permitting him to think over privately the things that had been said, and not wishing to pour out everything at once. Having cast the seeds into fertile soil, He permitted them to develop for a while at leisure. And in another place, likewise, to illustrate this, He said: 'The kingdom of heaven is like a man who sowed good seed in his field; but while men were asleep, his enemy came and sowed weeds among the wheat.'[4]

'And on the third day a wedding took place in Cana of Galilee. Now Jesus too was invited to the marriage. And the mother of Jesus also was there and his disciples.' I have just said that He was rather well known in Galilee;[5] therefore, they invited Him to the marriage and He went. He did not consider His own dignity, but our benefit. Indeed, He who did not disdain to take on Himself the form of a slave would much more not have thought it unworthy to attend the wedding of slaves, and He who reclined together with publicans and sinners would, much rather, not refuse to recline with those who were present at the marriage. To be sure, they who invited Him did not have the opinion of Him which He merited; nor did they invite Him as some prominent personage, but merely as one of many guests and as an acquaintance. This the Evangelist implied by the words: 'And the mother of Jesus was there, and also his disciples.' Therefore, just as they invited her and His disciples, they also invited Jesus.

4 Matt. 13.24,25.
5 Cf. Homily 20, p. 194.

'And the wine having run short, the mother of Jesus said to him: "They have no wine." ' Here it is worth while to examine how it came about that His Mother became aware of the greatness of her Son. He had not yet actually performed any miracle, for 'This first of his signs Jesus worked at Cana of Galilee.'

Now, if it should be objected that the mere addition of the words 'at Cana of Galilee' is not sufficient proof that this was the first of His miracles—since it may have been the first miracle worked there, but not altogether the first (it is likely that He had performed others elsewhere)—we shall say in reply what we have said before. What, then, is this? What John had said: 'And I did not know him. But that he may be known to Israel, for this reason have I come baptizing with water.'

Now, if He had been working miracles from His early youth, the Israelites would not have needed another to make Him known. When He did come among men, by means of His miracles He became well known, not only to the inhabitants of Judea, but also to those in Syria and beyond, and accomplished this in three years only.[6] Actually, He would not have needed these three to reveal Himself, for even from the first, His fame at once traveled everywhere.

If, I repeat, He who within a short time, because of the number of His miracles, became so famous that His name was familiar to all, had worked wonders in boyhood from His earliest youth, with much more reason He would not have been forgotten in this longer period. The things which happened would have seemed to be more amazing, since they were done by a boy, and the time would also have been double, or triple, or much more. However, He worked no wonder as a boy except that single one which Luke narrated: that at the age of twelve He sat listening to the teachers,

6 Cf. Matt. 4.24.

and by reason of His questions appeared to be out of the ordinary.[7]

But for another reason, also, it was right and reasonable that He did not begin His miracles at once from His earliest youth, since people would have thought the phenomenon an illusion. If, when He had reached manhood, many actually did have this suspicion, they would have had it much the more if He had worked wonders when still only a lad. Then, those consumed by envy would have hurried Him to the cross more quickly and before the appointed time, and the actual details of the Redemption would not have been believed.

'Then how did His Mother become aware of the greatness of her Son?' you say. He had, of course, recently begun to reveal Himself, and was manifested by John and also by His own words to His disciples. But even before all these things, the conception itself, and all the events connected with the nativity, made her aware of the greatness of her Son. She heard all these things about her Son, [the Evangelist] says, 'and kept them in her heart.'[8]

'Why, then,' you say, 'did she not allude to these things before this?' Because, as I have said, it was at this time that He finally entered upon the beginning of His public life. Indeed, before this He lived as if He were an ordinary man; consequently, His mother did not venture to mention anything of the kind to Him. But when she had heard that John had come for His sake and that he had borne witness to Him as he had done, and that He had disciples, then, finally, taking heart, she called on Him and, the wine failing, she said: 'They have no wine.'

Now, she desired both to obtain a favor for them and to enhance the favor itself because it would be bestowed by her Son. Or perhaps she even was prompted by some human

7 Cf. Luke 2.46.
8 Cf. Luke 2.51.

motive, as His brethren were when they said: 'Manifest thyself to the world.'[9] This, then, was why He replied somewhat emphatically: 'What wouldst thou have me do, woman? My hour has not yet come.' Yet, as evidence that He reverenced His mother very much, listen to Luke telling how He was subject to His parents,[10] and John the Evangelist himself showing how solicitous He was of her even at the time of the Crucifixion.[11]

Now, when parents in no way hinder—or forbid—the things of God, it is necessary and fitting to be submissive, and not to do so is very dangerous, but if ever they make some ill-advised request, and stand in the way of a spiritual good, it is not safe to obey. And that is why He here answered as He did. Elsewhere, too, He said: 'Who are my mother and my brethren?'[12] For they did not yet have a proper opinion of Him. But because she was His Mother, after the manner of other mothers she expected as His Mother to have His obedience in all respects, while her place was to reverence and adore Him as her Lord. That is why, therefore, He then replied as He did.

9 John 7.4.
10 Cf. Luke 2.51.
11 Cf. John 19.25-27.
12 Mark 3.33. The very human interpretation here placed by St. John Chrysostom on the relations between Christ and His Mother during the public life in no way implies a belittling of the Blessed Virgin, devotion for whom was already solidly established by the fourth century on firm foundations laid in the lifetime of the Apostles. St. John himself is careful to guard against any such false notion by repeated reference to her exalted dignity and to the love and honor Christ invariably showed toward her. His words to His Mother on the occasions which St. John mentions in this and the following homily, have, as a matter of fact, provided matter for much careful exegesis down to the present. During the fourth and fifth centuries there is evidence of a tendency for a certain type of popular veneration for the Virgin Mother to run to extravagant lengths. Such prudent moderation as St. John showed here in the discussion of her prerogatives was calculated to place a curb on such excess and to safeguard that genuine love for and devotion to the Mother of God, which had become an integral part of Christian life. For an excellent and comprehensive treatment of the subject, cf. E. Dublanchy, 'Marie,' DTC 9 (1927) esp. 2433-2447.

Indeed, picture to yourself what it was like when all the people and the crowd were standing around Him, and the multitude was hanging on His words, and His teaching was being set before them, for her to come there and seek to draw Him away from His preaching and to speak with Him in private; not to come within, but to bring Him outside, alone, to her. That is why He said: 'Who are my mother and my brethren?' It was not in scorn of His Mother—perish the thought!—but in order to be of the greatest help to her and not permit her to have thoughts of Him below His dignity. If He took care of the others and exerted every effort so that the proper estimation of Him might be instilled in them, much more would He do this in the case of His Mother.

Since it was possible that though she had heard this from her Son she might not have allowed herself to be convinced in that way, but might still have thought herself worthy of first consideration on all occasions because of being His Mother, He therefore replied as He did to those who gave the message. Otherwise, He could not have led her up from this earthly attitude to that perfection which is hers, if she expected always to be honored as by her Son, but did not look for Him to come as her Lord.

Now, in today's text it was for this reason that He said: 'What wouldst thou have me do, woman?' And no less for still another important reason. And what was that? So that the miracle about to take place might not be doubted. It was desirable that the request for it be made by those in need of it. And why was this? Because favors that are granted by the intervention of friends frequently give offense to those who perceive this, even in important matters. But, if they who are in need make the request themselves, then the wonderful result is not colored by suspicion, approval is sincere, and great benefit is derived.

To illustrate what I mean: If some reputable physician,

upon entering the dwelling where many are ill, should hear nothing from the sick or from their attendants, but should be summoned only by his own mother, he would be looked upon askance by the sick and would also be a source of annoyance to them. Moreover, neither they nor any of those in attendance would know that he could effect some really great benefit.

That is why He then objected: 'What wouldst thou have me do, woman?'—to instruct her not to make requests in just this way in future. He intended, to be sure, that honor be shown both to Himself and to His Mother, but much more was He taking thought for her soul's welfare and for the advantage of mankind for whose sake He had even clothed Himself in the flesh. These words were not, then, those of one speaking censoriously to His Mother, but of divine Providence, both directing her destiny and arranging that His miracles take place with befitting dignity.

Now, even apart from other considerations, this seeming rebuke itself can provide evidence in a special way that He held her very much in honor. By His vehemence itself He proved that He greatly respected her. How this was and in what way He showed it we shall discuss in our next sermon.[13] Therefore, keep these things in mind also when you hear a certain woman saying: 'Blessed is the womb that bore thee, and the breasts that nursed thee.' Then, when He answers: 'Rather, blessed are they who do the will of my Father,'[14] reflect that those words, too, are said with the same sentiment. The reply is not that of one rejecting his mother, but of one who shows that her motherhood would not have been of profit to her if she herself were not virtuous and obedient.

Now, if the fact that Christ was born of her was of no advantage to Mary without her own spiritual excellence, much less will it be of profit to us if we have a father, a

13 Cf. Homily 22, pp. 214-215.
14 Luke 11.27.

brother, a child who is virtuous and noble, while we ourselves are far removed from his virtue. David indeed said: 'No brother can redeem, shall a man pay the price of his ransom?'[15] Our hope of salvation must depend on no one else, but only on our own good deeds, together with the grace of God.

Obviously, if her motherhood of itself benefited the Virgin, it would also have been of advantage to the Jews, for Christ, according to the flesh, was their kinsman. It would have benefited the city in which He was born, and it would also have helped His brethren. In actual fact, as long as His brethren neglected themselves, the dignity of their kinship did not benefit them, and they were arraigned with the rest of the world, but when they shone by their own virtue, then they became objects of praise. His city, however, both fell and was burned, profiting not at all by its distinction; and his kin according to the flesh were slain and perished very pitifully, gaining no profit for salvation from their kinship with Him.

The Apostles, on the other hand, appeared greater than all men, because they sought the true and excellent way of relationship with Him—that of obedience. From this, therefore, we learn that we have a universal need of faith and of an upright and virtuous life, for only these will be able to effect our salvation. And though for the most part His relatives were held in esteem on all sides and were called 'kinsmen of the Lord,'[16] we do not even know their names, but both the lives and the names of the Apostles are reverenced everywhere.

Well, then, let us not be puffed up at nobility of birth according to the flesh, but, even if we have countless admirable ancestors, let us ourselves strive to excel their

---

15 Ps. 48.8.
16 Cf. Eusebius, *Ecclesiastical History* 1.7, in *Fathers of the Church* 19, trans. R. J. Deferrari (New York 1953), 64 n. 22.

virtues, knowing that we gain nothing for the judgment to come from the efforts expended by others, but on this account our judgment will be even more severe. Though we are of good ancestry and have the good example of our house, we do not imitate our teachers in this respect.

Moreover, I am now saying these things because I see many non-Christians, when we bring them to the faith and urge them to become Christians, taking refuge in their relatives and ancestors and family, and saying: 'All my kinsmen and friends and household are faithful Christians.' What, then, is this to you, wretched and unhappy soul? It is particularly to your dishonor that out of respect for your numerous household you do not run to the Truth.

Again, certain others, though of the faithful but living careless lives, when urged to virtue allege this same pretext, saying: 'My father, and grandfather, and great-grandfather, were, as it happens, respected and virtuous.' But this especially condemns you, because, though descended from such, you have performed deeds unworthy of your race. Listen to what the Prophet said to the Jews: 'Israel[17] served for a wife and was a keeper for a wife';[18] and, again, Christ said: 'Abraham your father rejoiced that he was to see my day. He saw it and was glad.'[19] Indeed, people everywhere point out the deeds of our ancestors, not only not to praise us, but even for our greater blame.

Therefore, since we know these things, let us also do everything so that we may be able to be saved by our own works, in order that, having foolishly deceived ourselves by our hopes in others, we may not then learn that we have been deceived when this knowledge will be of no help to us. For Scripture says: 'In the underworld who shall confess to thee?'[20]

17 I.e., Jacob.
18 Osee 12.12.
19 John 8.56.
20 Ps. 6.6.

Well, then, let us here repent so as to obtain everlasting good things. And may all of us obtain them by the grace and mercy of our Lord Jesus Christ, through whom and with whom glory and power be to the Father, together with the Holy Spirit, forever and ever. Amen.

Homily 22 (John 2.4-10)

'What wouldst thou have me do, woman? My hour has not yet come.'[1]

Preaching really entails hard work, and this fact Paul made plain when he said: 'Let the presbyters who rule well be held worthy of double honor, especially those who labor in the word and in teaching,'[2] But you are responsible for making this toil light or heavy. If you despise my words or, though you do not despise them, do not embody them in your deeds, my toil will be heavy, because I am laboring fruitlessly and in vain.

But if you pay attention and make my words manifest in your deeds, I shall not even be aware of the perspiration, for the fruit produced by my work will not permit me to feel the laboriousness of the toil. And so, if you wish to spur on my zeal and not to extinguish it or make it weaker, show me the fruit of it, I beseech you, in order that, viewing the leafy crops, sustained by hopes of a rich harvest and calculating my wealth, I may not be sluggish in engaging in this promising task.

It is, to be sure, no trifling question that lies before us today, also. When the Mother of Jesus said: 'They have no wine,' Christ replied: 'What wouldst thou have me do, woman? My hour has not yet come.' Yet, though He uttered these words, He did what His mother said. Now, this

1 John 2.4.
2 1 Tim. 5.17.

action, no less than the preceding words, provides matter for discussion. Therefore, calling to our aid Him who worked this miracle, let us with His assistance come to the solution of the problem.

Now, not only has this statement been made in this context, but the same Evangelist further in his Gospel clearly said they were not able to lay hold of Him, 'because his hour had not yet come.'[3] And again: 'No one laid hands on him because his hour had not yet come.'[4] And once more: 'The hour has come! Glorify thy Son.'[5] I have brought together all these texts, taken from this Gospel as a whole, that I may give one explanation for all of them.

What, therefore, is the meaning of the words? It was not because Christ was by necessity subject to time that He said: 'My hour has not yet come,' nor would He carefully watch the hours (for how could the Maker of time, the Creator of ages and generations, be so restricted?). But by these words He wished to make it plain that He does all His works at the fitting time, since there would be confusion and disorder resulting from them, if He did not perform each at the appointed time, but mixed all things together: birth, and resurrection, and judgment.

And besides, take note: It was necessary for the universe to come into existence, but not all at the same time; and for man and also woman, but not even these at the same time. It was necessary for the human race to be condemned to death and for the resurrection to take place, but there is a considerable interval between. It was expedient for the Law to be given, but not grace at the same time, but for each to be dispensed at its own time.

Christ, then, was not subject to the necessity of time— He who pre-eminently established the order of time—since

3 Cf. John 8.20.
4 John 7.30.
5 John 17.1.

He was also its Maker. But John here quoted Christ as saying: 'My hour has not yet come,' to show that He was as yet by no means known to the majority of men, and that He had not even gathered the entire group of His disciples. Andrew was following Him, and with him Philip, but no one else;[6] not even all these knew Him as they ought, nor did His Mother or His brethren, for after many miracles had taken place the Evangelist said this about His brethren: 'Not even his brethren believed in him.'[7]

Furthermore, those at the wedding did not know Him, for surely they would have come to Him and would have entreated Him when they were in need. For this reason He said: 'My hour has not yet come. I am not yet known to those who are present and they do not even know that the wine has failed. Let them perceive this first. Indeed, I ought not to hear this even from you. You are My mother and so you may cause the miracle to be called in question. Now, those who are in need must come to Me, and this is necessary, not because I need this [request], but that they themselves may accept what happens with wholehearted assent. If a man knows that he has been in want, when he gets what he asks he feels much gratitude; but, if a man does not perceive his need, he will not perceive clearly and distinctly the favor done him.'

'But,' you will ask, 'when He had begged off by saying: "My hour has not yet come," why did He do what His Mother asked?' It was especially in order that His action might be sufficient proof, to his opponents and to those who thought He was subject to time, that the contrary was true. If He was subject to time, how was it that, when the appointed

---

6 An inaccuracy. John has mentioned Peter and Nathanael as also among His disciples above. Cf. John 1.40-51. Matthew indicates (4.18-22) that John and James were called at the same time as Peter and Andrew, though he does not include the miracle at Cana in his narrative at all. Cf., also, Mark 1.16-22 and Luke 5.8-12.

7 John 7.5.

hour had not yet come, He did what He did? Besides, He acted thus to honor His Mother that He might not seem to gainsay her entirely; also, to avoid acquiring the reputation of powerlessness, and in order not to put His Mother to shame, when so many were present, for she had brought the servants to Him.

Then, too, even though He said to the Canaanite woman: 'It is not fair to take the children's bread and to cast it to the dogs,'[8] He granted her request after saying this, being moved at her perseverance. Yet, He had also said the following words: 'I was not sent except to the lost sheep of the house of Israel'; nevertheless, after saying this, He healed her daughter.

From this we learn that even if we are unworthy of receiving our request, often we make ourselves worthy by our perseverance to do so. That is why His Mother both persevered and wisely brought the servants to Him, so that the request might come from more people. It was for this reason that she added the words: 'Do whatever he tells you,' for she knew that His begging off from her request proceeded, not from impotence, but from His modesty and from His reluctance to perform the miracle rashly and without cause; and therefore she brought the servants.

'Now six stone water jars were placed there, after the Jewish manner of purification, each holding two or three measures. Jesus said to them, "Fill the jars with water. And they filled them to the brim." ' Not without design did the Evangelist say: 'after the Jewish manner of purification,' but in order that unbelievers might not conceive the suspicion that, if there were dregs remaining in the jars, when water was then poured in and mixed, it became very thin wine.

Since Palestine is arid, and frequently it was not possible to find springs and fountains of water, they always filled the water jars with water, so as not to be obliged to run

8 Matt. 15.26.

to the river if they were in need of purification, but that they might have the means of purification near at hand.

Now, why did He not perform the miracle before they were filled, which would have been a much more wonderful miracle? Of two possibilities—to change existing material to another kind of substance or to create the very existence of that which has no being—the latter is more wonderful. But it would not, if done thus, be credible to many. For this reason, indeed, He deliberately curtailed the greatness of His miracles so that they might be more readily accepted.

'But why was it,' you will say, 'that He Himself did not produce the water and then show the wine, but bade the servants to do so?' Once more for the same reason, and that He might have those who had drawn the water as actual witnesses that the miracle had really taken place and that what was done was no delusion. If some were impudently to deny it, the attendants would be able to say to them: 'We drew the water.'

Besides, He was also refuting the teachings that would spring up against the Church. Since there are some who say that there is another creator of the world, and that the visible works are not God's, but those of another god in opposition to Him,[9] to silence their mad ravings He performed most of His miracles by means of already existing substances. If there were a creator opposed to Him, He would not have used the other's materials for the proof of His own power. Actually, however, to show that it is He who changes the water in the vines and converts the rain through the root into wine, He did in an instant at the wedding what takes place in nature over a long period of time.

Now, when they had filled the water jars, 'He said, "Draw out now and take to the chief steward." And they took it

---

9 A pithy summary of the fundamental error of the Manichaeans; cf. art. 'Manichaeism' in *Catholic Encyclopedia*.

to him. Now, when the chief steward had tasted the water after it had become wine, not knowing whence it was (though the attendants who had drawn the water knew), the chief steward called the bridegroom, and said to him, "Every man at first sets forth the good wine, and when they have drunk freely, then that which is poorer. But thou hast kept the good wine until now." '

Here, again, some belittle this testimony by saying: 'The group was made up of drunken men, and the perception of the judges was dull and able neither to comprehend what had happened nor to pass judgment on what was being done, so that they did not know whether the product was water or wine, for the chief steward himself showed by what he said that they were intoxicated.' This, indeed, is most ridiculous of all; besides, the Evangelist has already dispelled this suspicion of theirs, for, he said, it was not the guests who were the judges about the water made wine, but the chief steward, who was sober and had not yet tasted anything.

All of you, of course, know this, that it is those who have been entrusted with the management of such banquets who, above all, remain sober, since it is their sole responsibility to manage all the details of the feast in a seemly and orderly fashion. Accordingly, it was this sober judgment which He called to witness what had happened, for He did not say: 'Pour out the wine for the guests,' but: 'Take to the chief steward.'

'Now when the chief steward had tasted the water after it had become wine, not knowing whence it was (though the attendants who had drawn the water knew), the chief steward called the bridegroom.' Why did he not call upon the attendants? If he had done so, the miracle would thus have been revealed. It was because not even Jesus Himself revealed what had taken place; He wished the power of His miracles to be made known slowly and gradually.

If, therefore, it had been attested then, the attendants

would not have been believed when they should relate
these happenings. On the contrary, they would have been
thought mad when testifying later to such power in One
who seemed to most men to be an ordinary man. They themselves knew the thing clearly by experience, for they would
not deny the evidence of their own hands, but they were
not enough to convince others. For this reason He Himself
did not even reveal it to all, but only to one who was best
able to understand what had taken place, reserving for the
future the clearer understanding of it.

After the manifestation of His other miracles, this one
would also be believed. At least, when He later healed the
official's son, the Evangelist made it plain by what he said
there that this miracle was already more clearly known. It
was especially for this reason that the official called upon
Him, namely, because he knew about the miracle, as I have
mentioned. And John showed this when he said: 'Jesus came
to Cana of Galilee where he had made the water wine';[10]
yes, and not merely wine, but the finest wine.

Indeed, [the products of] such wonders worked by Christ
are much more beautiful and better than those produced in
the course of nature. So also in other cases, when He straight-
ened the lame limb of a body, He rendered it stronger than
a healthy one. Accordingly, not merely the attendants would
testify that the product of the miracle was not only wine but
the finest wine, but the bridegroom and the chief steward as
well. And those who drew the water would bear witness that
the wine was made by Christ.

Hence, even if the miracle had not then been revealed,
it would not have been possible to conceal it forever, since
He had stored up so many important pieces of evidence for
it ahead of time in anticipation of future needs. He had
the attendants as witnesses of His making the water wine, and

10 John 4.46.

the chief steward and the bridegroom of its becoming good wine.

Now, it is likely that the bridegroom said something in reply to these words of the chief steward, but the Evangelist, hastening on to the more important details of his narrative, after merely sketching this miracle in outline, hurried past the rest. In truth, the important thing was to know that He made the 'water wine, and good wine; what the bridegroom said to the chief steward he thought it was not important to add. Indeed, many details of the miracles, once somewhat obscure, have become better understood with the passage of time, through being narrated by those who have had more accurate knowledge of them from the beginning.

At that time, therefore, Jesus made wine from water, and both then and now He does not cease changing wills that are weak and inconstant. There are men no different from water: cold and weak and inconstant. Accordingly, let us bring to the Lord those who are thus disposed, so as to cause their will to change and become like wine, so that it no longer is inconstant, but steadfast, and they become a cause of rejoicing both for themselves and for others. And who are they who are cold, unless it is those who are attached to the passing things of this life, who do not scorn the luxury of this world, who are infatuated with glory and power? All these things are passing, never constant, always bearing us down hill precipitately. And this is so, because today a man is rich; tomorrow, poor. Today he appears with a herald, and purse, and chariot, and many attendants; frequently, on the following day he has taken his abode in prison, forsaking to another, unwillingly, that show of grandeur.

Again, he who fares sumptuously and is glutted cannot retain for one day—however much he strains his stomach— the [feeling of] satiety caused by this food, but, when it has been dispersed, he is forced to partake of still other food.

Indeed, he is hardly different from a flowing stream. Even as when the flowing water has now passed on, still other takes its place, so here also, when the present food has passed on, we must once more supply other. Moreover, the nature of living things is such as never to succeed in remaining static, but always to be in a condition of flux and swift change.

Now, in the case of delicate living, this flux, this swift change is not the only effect; it also gives rise to many others. By its violent course it strips off the strength of the body and sweeps away the virility of the soul. The force of river floods, to be sure, commonly undermines the banks and causes them to collapse, but not so easily as delicate living and wantonness sweep away all the bulwarks of our health.

Even if you have recourse to a physician's office, and go there for a consultation, you will discover that all the causes of disease really stem from that source. Frugality and a simple table are the mother of health. Consequently, even physicians have defined it so, since they define health as not being satiated, for 'moderation in food is health,' meaning that to eat sparingly is the mother of health.

Now, if abstinence is the mother of health, it is plain that eating to repletion is the mother of sickness and ill health, and brings forth diseases defying the skill of physicians themselves. And this is so, because pain in the feet, and headaches, and blindness, and pains in the hands, and trembling, and paralysis, and jaundice, and lingering burning fevers, and many others in addition to these (there is not time to run through them all), are not from abstinence and a life of self-denial, but have been caused by gluttony and satiety.

Further, if you similarly wish to seek out the diseases of the soul which spring thence, you will see that greed, sloth, melancholy, laziness, licentiousness—in short, every kind of folly has its beginning from there. The souls addicted to delicate living become no better after banquets of this kind than asses that are torn asunder by wild beasts like these vices.

Shall I also tell how many sufferings and pains they have who are addicted to voluptuousness? It is not possible to go over them all, so I shall describe all under one head. They never taste of the table, I mean this sumptuous one, with pleasure. Abstinence, in truth, as it is the mother of health, is also the mother of pleasure; and repletion, as it is the source and root of diseases, is also provocative of disgust. Where there is satiety, it is not possible for desire to exist, and if desire is lacking how could there ever be pleasure? Therefore, not only should we find the poor more prudent and healthier than the rich, but even enjoying more happiness.

With all these things in mind, let us flee drunkenness and soft living, not only that at our tables but also every other kind in the affairs of life. Let us substitute for that pleasure the enjoyment to be derived from spiritual things. Let us delight in the Lord, according to the Prophet who said: 'Make the Lord thy delight and He will grant thee what thy heart seeks,'[11] in order that even here we may enjoy the good things to come, by the grace and mercy of our Lord Jesus Christ, through whom and with whom glory be to the Father, together with the Holy Spirit, forever and ever. Amen.

Homily 23 (John 2.11-22)

'This first of his signs Jesus worked at Cana of Galilee.'[1]

Mighty and vigorous, the Devil presses to the attack, laying siege on all sides to our salvation. It is, therefore, necessary to be watchful and awake and to wall off his approach in all

---

11 Ps. 36.4.

---

1 John 2.11.

directions. If he discovers even a small opening, he thereupon prepares a broad entrance for himself and gradually introduces his whole power. Well, then, if we have regard for our salvation, let us refuse him entrance in small ways in order that thereby we may check great ones beforehand. I say this because it would be extreme folly if, while he displays so much zeal to destroy our souls, we do not even show an equal amount for our own salvation.

It is not just by chance that I am saying these things, but because I fear that this wolf, unperceived by us, may even now be taking up his stand in the midst of our chapel,[2] and from it may seize as his prey a lamb which by its slothfulness, or his wicked plotting, has been beguiled from the flock and from listening. If his wounds were perceptible, or if the body received his blows, it would not be a difficult task to cope with such treachery. But, since the soul is invisible, and it is the soul that receives the wounds, we have need of much vigilance so that each one may prove himself. 'For who among men knows the things of a man save the spirit of the man which is in him?'[3]

Now, my preaching is addressed to all and provides a remedy in common for those who need one, but it is the duty of each one of my listeners to take what is suited for his affliction. I do not know who are the sick, who the healthy. Therefore, I discuss subjects of every sort and suited to every ill: now censuring greed, and again delicate living; at another time, attacking licentiousness; now praising and encouraging almsgiving, then again each of the other good

---

2 By the fourth century Christian assemblies were regularly held in a special place appointed for the purpose, though at times the assemblies, if large, collected in the open air. Since the Peace of Constantine, many large, often elaborate, churches had been built for liturgical worship. In addition, assemblies were held in the numerous martyrs' shrines which had been built in localities sacred to the memory of these martyrs. *The Homilies on the Gospel of St. John* were probably delivered in the principal church of Antioch, a beautiful edifice built by Constantine.

3 1 Cor. 2.11.

works. I fear that, if my words are concerned about one thing only, I may, all unaware, be treating one illness, while you are struggling with others.

If but one person were present here, I should not think it very necessary to make my sermon so many-sided. But, since in such a large crowd it is likely that there are many ills, it is not unreasonable for me to vary my teaching, for the sermon which includes all will surely find its own usefulness. In fact, this is the reason why Scripture itself also is many-sided, and speaks to us of numberless matters, since it is addressed to the common nature of mankind.

Indeed, in such a great crowd as this all the diseases of the soul must be represented, even if not all are in every man. Well, then, having purified ourselves of these, let us thus listen to the divine words, and let us hear with attentive minds the text read to us today. And what is it? 'This first of his signs Jesus worked at Cana of Galilee,' the Evangelist said.

I recently mentioned that some maintain that this was not the first. 'Why was it the first,' they say, 'if the phrase "at Cana of Galilee" occurs? Surely he meant that this was the first sign He worked at Cana.' However, I would not split hairs about the point, though we have shown before this that He did, at any rate, begin the miracles after His baptism. But it seems to me that we must not affirm too positively whether this or another was the first of the signs worked after His baptism.

'And he manifested his glory.' How can this be said and in what way did He do so? Not many paid attention to what had taken place, except the attendants and the chief steward and the bridegroom. How, then, did He manifest His glory? A part of it, at least. Moreover, if not all then heard of the miracle, they were all going to hear of it later, for even to the present it is reverenced and has not been forgotten.

However, from the text that follows it is clear that on

that day not all knew it. After saying: 'He manifested his glory,' the Evangelist added: 'And his disciples believed in him,' while before this they, too, merely admired Him. Do you perceive that it was very necessary to work His miracles at a time when well-disposed and observant persons were there to see what was taking place? For these would more readily believe and accurately observe what happened.

Now, what means of making Him known was there besides His miracles? Adequate instruction, and prophecy, and admiration inspired in the souls of His hearers so that they would pay attention with a right disposition to what happened, if their soul was already favorably disposed. For this reason, indeed, the Evangelists have often mentioned in other contexts that it was on account of the perversity of the men who dwelt in a place that He failed to perform some miracle.

'And after this he went down to Capharnaum, he and his mother, and his brethren, and his disciples. And they stayed there but a few days.' Why, then, did He go with His Mother to Capharnaum? He neither worked any miracle there, nor were the inhabitants of that city among those who were well disposed toward Him; they were even of the exceedingly corrupt. In truth, Christ made this clear when He said: 'And thou, Capharnaum, shalt thou be exalted to heaven? Thou shalt be thrust down to hell.'[4] Why, then, did He go there?

It seems to me that since He intended to go up to Jerusalem shortly, it was for this reason He went to Capharnaum at that time, so as to avoid bringing His brethren about with Him everywhere, and also His Mother. Accordingly, after going to spend a little time with His Mother out of devotion to her, He again resumed His miracles when He had settled her once more at home. That is why the Evangelist said that after a few days: 'He went up to Jerusalem.' It was some days before the Pasch, then, that He had been baptized.

---

4 Luke 10.15.

And when He went up to Jerusalem what did He do? A deed
of great authority. He cast out those notorious merchants,
the money-changers, those who sold doves and oxen and
sheep, and who frequented the Temple for that purpose.

Now, another Evangelist said that as He cast them out He
said: 'Do not make the house of my Father a den of thieves,'[5]
but John said: 'A house of business.' They were not, however,
contradicting one another, but showing that He cleansed
the Temple twice. Further, it is clear that both expressions did
not refer to the same occasion, and that He did this once at
the beginning [of His public life] and again as He was going
to His very Passion. And that is why, employing very vehement words on the latter occasion, He used the term 'den,'
whereas at the beginning of His miracles He did not do
so, but preferred to use a mild rebuke. Hence, it seems likely
that He cleansed the Temple twice.

'And why,' you will say, 'did Christ do this very thing
and show indignation against these men such as He did not
seem to show anywhere else—not even when men insulted
and taunted Him and called Him a Samaritan and a
demoniac? He was not satisfied with mere words, but also
took up a little whip and drove them out with it.'

Moreover, the Jews, on occasions when others received
some benefit, complained and were angry, but now, when
it was reasonable for those who had been rebuked to be
furiously indignant, they did not react thus toward Him. In
fact, they did not find fault with Him or insult Him, but what
did they say: 'What sign dost thou show us, seeing that thou
dost these things?' Do you see their excessive envy and how
the benefits done to others were a greater source of irritation
[than insults]?

When, to resume, He said that they were making the
Temple a 'den of thieves,' it was to show that the wares
sold were the products of theft and of rapacity and of greed

---

5 Matt. 21.13.

and they were growing rich from the misfortunes of others; but when He called it a 'house of business,' it was to show that their business was impious. Why did He do this? Because He was going to heal on the Sabbath, and to do many similar things, which would seem to them to be transgressing the Law; and also in order that He might not seem to be doing these things like some enemy of God, who has come out of opposition to the Father. By this action He corrected any such suspicion of theirs. For, He who had shown such zeal for the house would not withstand the Lord of the house who was worshiped in it.

The preceding years, in which He lived according to the Law, were in truth sufficient to show His respect for the Law-giver and that He did not come in opposition to the Law. But, since it was likely that those years were forgotten because of the passage of time—years which were not known to all because of His being brought up in a poor and ordinary home—and since, besides, all types of men were present (a large multitude had come there because the festival day was at hand), He cleansed the Temple, even though at great personal risk. Indeed, He not merely cast them out, but also overturned the tables, and poured out the money, giving them to understand by this that He who endangered Himself for the sake of the honor of the house would not despise the Master of the house.

Moreover, if He were playing the hypocrite in doing these things, He would have needed only to admonish them. But it was a very daring thing to place Himself in danger as well. It was no trifle both to expose Himself to such great resentment on the part of the merchants, and to stir up against Himself a mob of traders who were full of brutality, by insulting them and causing them loss. This was not the action of a hypocrite, but of one choosing suffering for the sake of the honor of His House.

Not only by what He did, in this instance, but also by

what He said, He showed His harmony with the Father, for He did not say 'the holy house,' but 'the house of my Father.' Notice that He even called Him Father without their becoming angry, for they thought He was talking merely in a general way. But when He went on to speak more clearly so as to establish the idea of His equality [with the Father], then they were provoked to anger.

What, then, did they say? They said: 'What sign dost thou show us, seeing that thou dost these things?' Oh, what utter madness! Indeed, was a miracle needed to stop the evil practices and to rid the house of such shame? And was not the exhibition of such zeal for the house of God the greatest sign of His virtue? On the other hand, they who rightly understood derived instruction from this. 'His disciples remembered,' the Evangelist said, 'that it is written, "The zeal for thy house has eaten me up." ' But the others did not remember the prophecy, and so kept saying: 'What sign dost thou show us?'

At the same time, they lamented that their base gain had been wrested from them, and hoped in this way to check Him, wishing to elicit a miracle and to prosecute Him for what had taken place. Therefore, He did not give them a sign and when, before this also, they had come and asked for one, He gave the same answer: 'An evil and adulterous generation demands a sign, and no sign shall be given it but the sign of Jonas.'[6] Then, however, He answered more clearly, but now more ambiguously; and this He did because of their extreme hardness of heart. He who anticipates and gives signs to those who do not ask for them would not have turned away from those who asked, unless He saw that their mind was wicked and treacherous and their will, corrupt.

Indeed, consider the question itself from the outset: how full it was of evil. Although they ought to have commended

---

6 Matt. 16.4.

Him for His earnestness and zeal and should have marveled because He exhibited such solicitude for His house, they censured Him instead, saying that to engage in trade there was allowed and that He might not do away with the traffic unless He performed a miracle for them.

What, then, did Christ reply? 'Destroy this temple, and in three days I will raise it up.' Many such things He said which were not clear to those who heard them at the time, but would be to others afterwards. And why did He do this? That when the fulfillment of the prophecy came He might be proved to have foreseen beforehand events to happen later. And this, accordingly, happened in the case of this prophecy, for the Evangelist said: 'When he had risen from the dead, his disciples remembered that he had said this, and they believed the scripture and the word that Jesus had spoken.'

At the time when He said it, some were at a loss as to what its meaning was, while others were contentious, saying: 'Forty-six years has this temple been in building, and wilt thou raise it up in three days?' When they said forty-six years, it is plain that they meant the later building, for the earlier was completed in twenty years.[7]

Why, then, did He not explain the riddle and say: 'I am not speaking of this temple but of my body.' Why did the Evangelist, writing his Gospel later, interpret what Christ said, while He Himself was silent at that time? Why, I repeat, did He remain silent? Because they would not have accepted His explanation. If not even His disciples could understand what had been said, much less could the multitude. 'When Jesus had risen from the dead,' the Evangelist said, 'his disciples remembered that he had said this, and they believed the scripture and the word.'

Indeed, there were two considerations proposed to them at that time: one was that of the Resurrection; the other,

---

7 Cf. 1 Esdras 6.15.

greater than this, whether He who dwelt within the temple was God. He was speaking of both enigmatically when He said: 'Destroy this temple, and in three days I will raise it up.' Moreover, Paul said that this is no small proof of His Godhead, in the following words: 'who was foreordained Son of God by an act of power in keeping with the holiness of his spirit, by resurrection from the dead, Jesus Christ.'[8]

But why, both in the latter and in the former texts did He give this sign, and also in others—at one time saying: 'If I be lifted up'; and 'When you have lifted up the Son of Man, then you will know that I am he'; and again: 'No sign shall be given it, but the sign of Jonas';[9] and here, once more: 'In three days I will raise it up'? Because this especially is the proof that He was not an ordinary man; namely, that He was able to set up a trophy over death and so quickly terminate its long tyranny and relentless warfare. That is why He said: 'Then you will know.'

'Then'—when is that? 'When, after rising from the dead, I draw the world to myself, then you will know that I did these things also as God and as the true Son of God, to make amends for the wrong done to my Father.'

But why in the world did He not reply with the kind of signs needed to stop the evil instead of merely declaring that He would give a sign? Because by doing the former He would have angered them more, but by the latter He struck them with wonderment. Nevertheless, they made no reply to this, for He seemed to them to be saying something incredible and they did not even continue questioning Him, but disregarded the statement, as something impossible.

Now, if they possessed understanding, even if at that time it seemed to them to be incredible, afterwards when He had performed many miracles, then they would have approached and questioned Him. Then they would have thought it

---

8 Rom. 1.4.
9 John 12.32; 8.28; Matt. 12.39.

worth while for their doubt to be removed. Actually, they were without understanding, for they did not even pay attention to some of the things He said, while they listened to others with ill-disposed minds. And it was for this reason, also, that Christ spoke obscurely to them.

The next question to be investigated, however, is: how was it that the disciples did not know that it was necessary for Him to rise from the dead? Because they had not yet been deemed worthy of the grace of the Spirit. Therefore, though they were continually hearing His words about the Resurrection, they did not understand, but were debating among themselves what in the world this meant. And this is so because it was a very strange and contradictory statement that someone could resurrect himself and would rise from the dead in this way. For this reason Peter, also, was rebuked, when, since he knew nothing about the Resurrection, he said: 'Far be it from thee.'[10]

Further, Christ did not reveal it to them clearly before it took place that they might not be estranged at the beginning and doubt His words, both because these were very paradoxical, and because they did not yet know who He was. No one would disbelieve things that were made known with the supporting evidence of deeds, but it is likely that some would disbelieve those averred by word alone. That is why at first He allowed what He said to remain obscure.

But when His words were proved true by experience, then finally He gave both understanding of His words and sufficient grace of the Spirit to help them to accept everything straightway, for He said, 'He will bring all things to your mind.'[11] Indeed, they who cast aside in only one evening their reverence for Him, and not only fled but also asserted they did not know Him, hardly would have remembered the things said and done during the whole time if they had not enjoyed an abundance of grace of the Spirit.

---

10 Matt. 16.22.
11 John 14.26.

'But,' you will say, 'if they really were going to hear these things from the Spirit, what need was there for them to be with Christ, since they were not going to understand His words? Because the Spirit did not teach them, but recalled the things which Christ had first spoken to them. In fact, His being sent to recall the words of Christ to men's minds contributed not a little to the glory of Christ.

In the beginning, indeed, the onrush of the grace of the Spirit, so rich and abundant, came from the goodness of God, but later the retaining of the gift came from their own virtue. They manifested an exemplary life, and abundant wisdom, and great toils, and scorned the present life, and thought nothing of human things, but were above all. Flying high like a kind of light-winged eagle, they reached to heaven itself by their deeds, and by these obtained possession of the ineffable grace of the Spirit.

Well, then, let us also imitate them, and let us not extinguish our lamps, but keep them bright by almsgiving. It is by this means that the brightness of this fire is preserved. Let us, then, put oil in our vessels as long as we are here. It is not possible to buy it when we have taken our departure hence, or to receive it from any source other than the hands of the poor. Let us, therefore, collect it from there in great abundance, that is, if we wish to enter in with the bridegroom; if we do not do this, we must remain outside the bridal chamber. It is impossible, I repeat, even if we perform countless good works, to enter the portals of the kingdom without almsgiving.

Therefore, let us give an example of it very generously so that we may enjoy those ineffable blessings. May it be that all of us shall obtain these, by the grace and mercy of our Lord Jesus Christ, to whom be glory and power everywhere, now and always, and forever and ever. Amen.

Homily 24 (John 2.23-3.4)

'Now, when he was at Jerusalem for the feast of the Passover, many believed in his name.'[1]

Some of the men of that day clung to error, while others
adhered to the truth; even of these latter, some accepted it
for a little while, but cast it aside again. And Christ spoke in
parables and compared these to seeds, not lying deeply, but
with their roots above the surface of the earth, and they, He
declared, quickly perish.

The Evangelist also was referring to these in this passage
when he said: 'When he was at Jerusalem for the feast of
the Passover, many believed in his name, seeing the signs
that he was working. But Jesus himself did not trust himself
to them.' For those disciples were more dependable who came
to Him, not only by reason of miracles, but also because of
His teaching. Miracles, indeed, attracted the more slow-
witted, but prophecies and teaching, the more intelligent.
And those who were won over by teaching were, in truth,
more steadfast than those won by miracles. Christ has even
called them blessed, saying: 'Blessed are they who have not
seen, and yet have believed.'[2]

That the others were not of His true disciples the next
words show, for the Evangelist added: 'Jesus did not trust
himself to them.' Why? 'In that he knew all men and because
he had no need that anyone should bear witness concerning
man, for he himself knew what was in man.' What this
means is as follows: He who dwells in the very hearts of
men and enters into their minds did not give heed to outward
words. Knowing clearly that the fervor of these men was
transient, He did not feel confidence in them as full-fledged
disciples, nor did He entrust all His teachings to them as if
they were already firm believers.

1 John 2.23.
2 John 20.29.

Now, to know what is in the hearts of men belongs to Him who 'has fashioned the heart of each of them,'[3] that is, to God, for 'Thou only,' Scripture says, 'knowest hearts.'[4] He did not, then, need witnesses in order to know the minds of His own creatures; therefore, He did not have confidence in them by reason of their inconstant faith. Men who know neither the present nor the future often both say and confide everything without hesitation to those who treacherously approach them, and who will presently forsake them, but not so Christ, for He clearly knows all secrets.

Such men they were, indeed, as many are now, who have the name of being of the faith, but actually are very inconstant and easily led. Therefore, Christ even now does not entrust Himself to them but hides many things from them. Even as we have confidence not merely in friends, but in true ones, so it is with God. Listen to what Christ actually said to His disciples: 'No longer do I call you servants, for you are my friends.'[5] Whence is this and why? 'Because all things that I have heard from my Father I have made known to you.'

It was for this reason that He did not give signs to the Jews when they asked: because they were asking to tempt Him. Now as well as then, therefore, is it not characteristic of those tempting Him to ask for miracles? Even now there are some who seek for them and say: 'Why do miracles not also occur now?' But if you are faithful as you ought to be, and if you love Christ as you ought to love Him, you have no need of miracles; they are given for those who disbelieve.

'How was it, then,' you will say, 'that they were not given to the Jews?' They were, indeed, given to them especially. But if there was an occasion when, even though asking for signs, they did not receive them, miracles were not granted them because they did not ask for them in order to be rid of their unbelief, but to strengthen their wickedness.

---

3 Ps. 32.15.
4 Cf. 3 Kings 8.39.
5 John 15.15.

'Now there was a certain man of the Pharisees, Nicodemus by name, a ruler of the Jews. This man came to Jesus at night.' Nicodemus again put in an appearance in the middle of the Gospel, and spoke in defense of Christ; for he said: 'Does our Law judge a man unless it first give him a hearing?' And the Jews were angry with him and said: 'Search the scriptures and see that out of Galilee arises no prophet.'[6] Further, after the Crucifixion, he exercised great care about the burial of the Lord's body, as the Evangelist said: 'And there also came Nicodemus (who at first had come to Jesus by night), bringing a mixture of myrrh and aloes, in weight about a hundred pounds.'[7]

And even in today's text he was well disposed toward Christ, not, indeed, as much as he ought to have been, nor in the proper frame of mind, but still held back by Jewish weakness. Moreover, that is why he came at night, since he was afraid to do so by day. But the mercy of God, even so, did not reject him, or censure him, or deprive him of His teaching, but even discoursed with him very kindly and revealed to him the most sublime teachings, obscurely, to be sure, but nevertheless revealed.

Actually, he was much more worthy of pardon than those whose actions were dictated by malice. They were beyond all excuse, while he himself, though deserving of censure, did not merit it as richly as they. How is it, then, that the Evangelist said nothing like this about him? He did, indeed, say elsewhere that many of the rulers believed in Him, but because of the Jews they did not acknowledge Him, that they might not be put out of the synagogue.[8] But here all this was only hinted at by referring to his presence 'by night.'

What, then, did Nicodemus say? 'Rabbi, we know that thou hast come a teacher from God, for no one can work

---

6 John 7.51,52.
7 John 19.39.
8 Cf. John 12.42.

these signs that thou workest unless God be with him.' Nicodemus still was clinging to earth, still had a human opinion of Him, and spoke as of a prophet, thinking nothing exceptional about Him, though aware of His miracles.

'We know that thou hast come a teacher from God.' Why, then, do you come at night and in secret to Him who speaks the things of God? To Him who has come from God? Why do you not speak out with boldness? But Jesus did not say this nor rebuke him, for 'A bruised reed he will not break and a smoking wick he will not quench.'[9] And the same writer said again: 'He will not wrangle nor cry aloud.'[10] And once more Christ said: 'I have not come to judge the world, but to save the world.'[11]

'No one can work these signs that thou workest unless God be with him.' But he still was talking like the heretics, saying that Christ received His power from outside Himself and needed the help of others in doing the things He did. What, then, did Christ reply? See His excessive condescension. He did not say: 'I need no aid from others, but I do all things with my own power for I am the true Son of God and have the same power as He who begot me,' but He avoided this for a time since it was difficult for His hearer. As I always say, and now repeat: The object which Christ strove to attain was not so much to make known His own dignity as to convince men that He was doing nothing in opposition to His Father.

Therefore, He often appeared to be measuring His words to their limited understanding, but not so in His deeds. When He worked a miracle, He acted with complete independence and said: 'I will; be thou made clean'; 'Talitha, arise';[12] 'Stretch forth thy hand;' 'Thy sins are forgiven thee';[13]

9 Isa. 42.3; Matt. 12.20.
10 Matt. 12.19.
11 John 12.47.
12 Mark 1.41; 5.41.
13 Matt. 12.13; 9.5.

'Peace, be still'; 'Take up thy pallet, and go to thy house'; 'I say to thee, go out of the man, thou unclean spirit';[14] 'Let it be done to you according to your faith';[15] 'If anyone say anything to you, you shall say that the Lord has need of it';[16] 'This day thou shalt be with me in paradise'[17]; 'you have heard that it was said to the ancients, Thou shalt not kill; and that whoever shall murder shall be liable to judgment. But I say to you that everyone who is angry with his brother shall be liable to judgment'; 'Come, follow me, and I will make you fishers of men.'[18]

Now, in each instance we see that He spoke very authoritatively. Moreover, in face of the deeds [that accompanied His words] no one would have called in question the things that transpired. Indeed, how could they? If what He said did not turn out and did not receive fulfillment in accordance with His commands, someone of their number might have been able to say that His commands were foolish. But, since they did eventuate, the unquestionable fact of the accomplishment of the events silenced them even against their will.

On the other hand, on the basis of His words alone, they frequently took occasion in their impudence to judge Him guilty of foolishness. Indeed, this was true here in the case of Nicodemus, when Christ did not speak of sublime things plainly, but by speaking in riddles raised him up from his earthly thoughts and taught him that He is sufficient to Himself for manifesting His miracles. The Father has begotten Him, complete and sufficient to Himself, and with no imperfection.

But let us see how He brought him to this very conclusion. Nicodemus said: 'Rabbi, we know that thou hast come a teacher from God, for no one can work these signs that thou

---

14 Mark 4.39; 2.12; 5.8.
15 Matt. 9.29.
16 Mark 11.3.
17 Luke 23.43.
18 Matt. 5.21; 4.19.

workest unless God be with him.' He thought that he was uttering something complimentary when he said this of Christ. What, then, did Christ say? He showed that Nicodemus had neither approached the entrance of proper knowledge nor did he stand even in the portico, but was still wandering somewhere outside the palace—not only he, but any other who might make such statements. He taught him that a man who held to this opinion of the Only-begotten had not yet come near true knowledge of Him.

What did He say? 'Amen, amen, I say to thee, unless a man be born again, he cannot see the kingdom of God'; that is, 'Unless you are born again and accept My teachings exactly, you are wandering outside and are far from the Kingdom of God.' However, He did not say this in so many words.

In order to make His words less troublesome, He did not address them explicitly to him, but said indefinitely: 'Unless a man be born,' as if to say: 'Whether it be you or anyone else at all who has such ideas about Me, he is somewhere outside the Kingdom.' Unless He had said these words with the idea of conveying this thought, the reply was irrelevant to the statement [of Nicodemus.] Indeed, if the Jews had heard these words, they would have gone away, after laughing Him to scorn. But Nicodemus showed his thirst for knowledge in this instance, also.

Now, it was for this reason that Christ often spoke obscurely, because He wished to make His hearers more inclined to ask questions and to cause them to be more attentive. What has been said with its meaning obvious often escapes the listener, but what has been said obscurely makes him more curious and eager. He meant, that is: 'Unless you are born again, unless you receive the Spirit by the laver of regeneration, you cannot conceive the proper idea of Me. For this idea you have is not spiritual but carnal.' He did not speak in this way, however, to avoid frightening one who had merely voiced as best he could ideas he had picked up. Instead, He raised him unsuspectingly to greater knowledge, when He said, 'Unless a man be born again.'

Some say that the word *ánōthen* ('again') here means 'from heaven,' while others say, 'from the beginning.' It is not possible for him who has not been born thus, He said, 'to see the kingdom of God.' By the latter words He meant Himself and showed that not merely that which is seen exists, but that we need other eyes to see Christ.

When Nicodemus had heard these words, he said: 'How can a man be born when he is old?' Do you call Him rabbi, and say that He has come from God, yet not accept His words, but address your Teacher with language which gives rise to much confusion? This word 'how' is the expression of doubt and does not belong to those whose faith is firm, but to those who are still of the earth. Sara, for example, was offering derision by her question, when she said, 'How';[19] and many others who used this question have fallen away from the faith.

In this way, also, heretics persevere in heresy, hunting down this expression everywhere. Some say: 'How was He made flesh?' while others: 'How was He born?'—subjecting that infinite Being to the weakness of their reasoning. Therefore, they who are aware of this must flee such untimely curiosity. Those who so question will not know the 'how' and they will fall away from the true faith. Therefore, Nicodemus, also, in his perplexity sought to learn the way this would be done (for he was conscious that what was said was addressed even to him).

He was confused and disturbed and in distress, since he had approached as if to a man, but was hearing things greater than would be heard from a man and which no one had ever heard. He was rapt for awhile by the sublimity of

19 Cf. Gen. 18.10-14.

His words, but was in the dark and badly shaken, whirling about in every direction and steadily falling away from faith. He therefore persisted in reiterating the impossibility [of being born again], so as to urge Him on to clearer teaching, and asked: 'Can a man enter a second time into his mother's womb and be born again?'

Do you see how, when a man wrests spiritual things to his own reasoning, he both utters absurdities and seems to be raving and intoxicated, since he is unduly examining the words, beyond what is pleasing to God, and does not accept the deposit of faith? He has heard of spiritual generation, but did not understand that it was of the Spirit. Instead, he dragged what was said down to the lowliness of the flesh and thus made a great and sublime teaching depend upon the natural sequence [of birth]. So, in the end, he trumped up foolish trifles and ridiculous questions. Therefore, Paul also has said: 'The sensual man does not perceive the things that are of the Spirit of God.'[20]

Nevertheless, even at this point Nicodemus maintained his respect for Christ. He did not scoff at what had been said, but, though he thought it was impossible, he was silent; for there were two sources of doubt: such a birth and the Kingdom. Indeed, the name of the Kingdom had not been heard by the Jews at any time, nor had such a birth as this. Meanwhile, he halted at the first part of Christ's statement which most of all had shaken his thoughts.

Therefore, since we know these things, let us not examine into the things of God by reasoning and let us not submit divine things to the order prevailing among us, nor subject them to the necessity of nature, but let us think of them all reverently, believing as the Scriptures have said. He who is curious and meddlesome gains no profit; in addition to not finding what he seeks he will pay the extreme penalty. You

---

20 1 Cor. 2.14.

have heard that He begot Him; believe what you have heard, but do not seek out 'how'; and do not on this account deny the begetting. This would be the part of utter senselessness.

In truth, when Nicodemus had heard of begetting—not that ineffable one, but the one according to grace—he did not think anything great of it, but something human and earthly. He was, therefore, blinded and plunged in doubt. Then, how much punishment will they not merit who scrutinize and meddlesomely inquire into that most awesome begetting which sets at naught both reason and understanding in all respects?

Now, nothing makes one so dizzy as human reasoning, which says everything from an earthly point of view, and does not allow illumination to come from above. Earthly reasoning is covered with mud. Therefore, we have need of streams from above, so that, when the mud has fallen away, whatever part of the reason is pure may be carried on high and may be thoroughly imbued with the lessons taught there. This takes place when we manifest both a well-disposed soul and an upright life. For it is possible, it is possible, I repeat, for the mind to be darkened also by corrupt habits, and not only by untimely curiosity.

That is also why Paul said to the Corinthians: 'I fed you with milk, not with solid food, for you were not yet ready for it. Nor are you now ready for it, for you are still carnal. For since there are jealousy and strife among you, are you not carnal?'[21] And in the Epistle to the Hebrews, also, and elsewhere, too, one may see Paul saying that this is the cause of evil teachings, for the diseased soul cannot see anything great accurately, but, as if clouded by some rheum, is subject to the most acute dim-sightedness.

Let us, then, purify ourselves; let us kindle the light of knowledge; let us not sow among thorns. Indeed, what the

21 1 Cor. 3.2.

number of the thorns is you know, even if we should not tell you. You have often heard Christ giving the name of 'thorns' to anxiety about the present life and the deceit of riches,[22] and rightly so. Even as thorns are without fruit, so also are these; even as thorns pierce those who touch them, so also these evils; and even as thorns are easily destroyed by fire and hateful to the husbandman, so also the things of the world. Further, just as among thorns wild beasts are hidden, and vipers, and scorpions, so also in the deceit of riches.

But let us apply the fire of the Spirit that we may consume the thorns and put to flight the wild beasts, that we may provide cleared seed land for the husbandman; and after purifying it, let us water it with spiritual streams. Let us plant the fruitful olive, the most easily cultivated tree, ever green, illuminating, nourishing, giver of health.

All these qualities almsgiving has and is as a seal on those who possess it. Not even death, as it approaches, dries up this plant, but it ever remains, enlightening the mind, nourishing the sinews of the soul, rendering its strength more powerful. If we always possess this, we shall be able with confidence to behold the Bridegroom and to enter the bridal chamber.

May we all obtain this by the grace and mercy of our Lord Jesus Christ, with whom glory be to the Father, together with the Holy Spirit, now and always, and forever and ever. Amen.

Homily 25 (John 3.5)

'Jesus answered: "Amen, I say to thee, unless a man be born again of water and the Spirit, he cannot enter into the kingdom of God." '

22 Cf. Matt. 13.22.

Small children who go to school every day both receive instruction and recite lessons, and do this without ceasing. Nay, at times they even add nights of study to days, a thing which you force them to do for the sake of passing and temporal ends.

However, we do not require of you who have reached manhood as great effort as you impose upon your children. Not every day, but only on two a week, do we urge you to attend to our words for a short part of the day, so that the task is a light one for you. Furthermore, it is with the following end in view that we are only gradually analyzing the content of the Scriptures. We hope that it may be possible for you to receive them with ease, and store them in the treasury of your mind, and thus strive to remember them all, so that you may be able also to repeat them accurately; unless, that is, you should be very sluggish and slothful and lazier than a small boy.

But come, let us take up the passage following our last text. Let us see how, when Nicodemus had fallen into error, both by distorting Christ's words to mean earthly birth, and by saying that it is impossible for an old man to be born again, Christ explained more clearly the manner of this birth. Even so, it was a manner which offered difficulty for one who was inquiring with a carnal point of view, but which, nevertheless, had the power to raise up the hearer from his earthly-mindedness.

What, indeed, did He say? 'Amen, I say to thee, unless a man be born again of water and the Spirit, he cannot enter into the kingdom of God.' By these words He meant something like the following: 'You say that this is impossible, but I affirm that it is quite possible, so much so that it is even necessary and one cannot be saved without it.'

Now, God has made things that are necessary very easy for us. Earthly birth—that according to the flesh—is of the earth; therefore, heavenly things have been walled off from it. What has that which belongs to earth in common with heaven? But the birth which is of the Spirit easily opens for us the vaults above. Hear ye, as many of you as are outside the Light; shudder, groan. Fearful is the threat, fearful the sentence. 'It is not possible,' He asserted, 'for him who has not been born of water and the Spirit to enter into the kingdom of heaven, because he bears the garment of death, of the curse, of destruction.' He has not yet received the Master's stamp; he is a stranger and a foreigner; he does not possess the King's watch-word. 'Unless a man,' He said, 'be born again of water and the Spirit, he cannot enter into the kingdom of heaven.'

But Nicodemus did not even thus understand. For nothing is worse than to relegate spiritual things to human reasoning. This also was what kept him from placing a lofty and sublime interpretation [on the words]. We ourselves are called 'faithful' precisely for this reason: in order that, having put aside the weakness of human reasoning, we may come to the sublimity of faith, and that we may entrust the greater part of our welfare to the teaching of faith. If Nicodemus had done this, he would not have thought the thing impossible.

What, then, did Christ say? To lead him away from this idea which was dragging him earthward, and to show that He was not speaking of this kind of birth, He said: 'Unless a man be born again of water and the Spirit, he cannot enter into the kingdom of heaven.' Now, He spoke these words because He wished to attract him to the faith through fear of the threat, and to persuade him not to think that the thing was impossible. He was also striving to separate him from his notion about rebirth according to the flesh.

'I mean another kind of birth, Nicodemus,' He said in effect. 'Why do you drag the meaning down to earth? Why do you subject the thing to the force of nature? This bringing forth is superior to such pangs and has nothing in common with you. This is truly called birth, but shares in the name only; it is different in reality. Do not think of the usual kind of intercourse; I am introducing another kind of childbirth into the world; I desire that men be born in another way; I have come to bring a new method of procreation. I did fashion [man] of earth and water; that which was fashioned did not become useful but the vessel was perverted. I no longer wish to fashion him of earth and water, but of water and the Spirit.'

Now, if someone ask: 'How of water?' I in turn ask: 'How of earth?' For, how was the clay transformed into the different parts of the body? And how were they of the same substance? Earth was a single substance, but the things that were made of it were various and manifold. Whence bones, and nerves, and arteries, and veins? Whence membranes and organic vessels, and cartilage, and tissues, liver and spleen, and heart? Whence skin, and blood, and phlegm, and bile? Whence such great activity? Whence the various colors? These things do not belong to earth or clay.

How is it that earth sprouts, upon receiving seeds, while flesh, upon receiving seeds putrefies them? How is it that earth nourishes things cast upon it, while flesh is nourished by them, but does not nourish them? For example, earth, upon receiving water, makes it wine; while flesh, upon receiving wine, often changes it to water. Whence, therefore, is it evident that these things come from the earth, since the earth acts contrariwise to the body, according to what has just been said?

I cannot discover this by reason, but accept it only by faith. Well, then, if things that are of everyday experience, and tangible, need faith, much more the things that are so mystical and spiritual. Even as the earth which is soulless and powerless has acquired strength by the will of God, and such wonderful things have come from it, so also when the Spirit is present to the water, all these marvellous wonders, beyond the power of reason, easily take place.

Well, then, because you do not see these things do not disbelieve them, inasmuch as you do not see your soul, yet believe you have a soul, and that the soul is something apart from the body. Christ, however, did not use this illustration to persuade Nicodemus, but another. Even though this is bodiless, the soul I mean, He did not on that account bring it into the discussion, because Nicodemus was still somewhat slow of understanding.

He adduced another example which neither partakes of the denseness of bodily things nor rises to the nature of incorporeal things, namely, the onrushing of the wind. First, He began with water, which is lighter than earth, but denser than wind. For, just as in the beginning the earth underlay [creation] as the elemental substance, but all was of the Creator, so also water now underlies as element and all is of the grace of the Spirit; and then 'Man became a living soul,' while now 'a life-giving spirit.'[1] But there is a great difference between the two. The soul does not give life to another, while the Spirit not only lives by His own power, but also gives life to others. It was thus, indeed, that the Apostles even raised the dead.

Moreover, at the time when creation was taking place, man was fashioned later [than inanimate things], but now quite the contrary; the new man is created before the new creation. This is so because he is born first and then the world is transformed. And just as in the beginning He fashioned him perfect, so also now He creates him without blemish. Yet, at that time, He said: 'Let us make for him a helper,'[2] but here no such thing. Will he who has received the grace of the Spirit need any other help? How much need of assistance in future has he who fills out the body of Christ?

At that time He made man to the image of God, but

---

1 1 Cor. 15.45; cf. Gen. 2.7.
2 Gen. 2.18.

now He has made him one with God Himself. Then He bade him to rule over the fishes and wild beasts; now He has lifted up our first-fruits above the heavens. Then He gave him life in paradise; now He has opened up heaven to us. Then man was formed on the sixth day, when the age of creation was even about to be completed, but now, on the first day and in the beginning, as light was also created. From all these considerations it is plain that the effects accomplished belong to another, better, life and a condition which has no end.

The first creation, indeed, was from clay: that of Adam; and the one after his was from his rib, namely, that of woman; and the one after hers was from his seed, namely, that of Abel; nevertheless, we cannot attain to the understanding of any one of these, or depict in words what took place, even though they are very earthly. How, then, shall we be able to give explanations of the spiritual birth, that of baptism, which is much more sublime than these? And how can we require proofs of this wonderful and strange bringing-forth, since even angels were present at this birth when it occurred? Yet, no one would be able to tell the manner of that wonderful birth by baptism. They, in truth, have merely been present, doing nothing, but only seeing what took place. Father and Son and Holy Spirit do all.

Let us, then, believe the Word of God, for it is more worthy of belief than is sight. Sight often is mistaken, but it is impossible for the other to fall into error. Let us, then, believe it. Since it has brought into being things that did not exist, it would be trustworthy also when it speaks of their nature. What, then, does it say?—That what is accomplished is a birth. And if someone should say to you: 'How?'—silence him by the word of Christ which is the greatest proof and a clear one.

Moreover, if someone should ask: 'Why has water been mentioned as necessary for baptism?'—let us also in our turn ask why earth at the beginning was employed for the forming of man. For, it is altogether clear to all men that even without earth it was possible for Him to make man. Well, then, do not be overinquisitive.

However, that the part which water plays is essential and indispensable you may learn from the following: When, on one occasion, the Spirit had come down before the water [was poured], the Apostle did not remain satisfied with that, but as if the water was necessary and not superfluous, see what he said: 'Can anyone refuse the water to baptize these, seeing that they have received the Holy Spirit just as we did?'[3]

What, then, is the function of the water? This, also, I shall presently tell you, as I unfold to you the mystery concealed here. The rite, to be sure, conveys some other ineffable lessons, but of the many I shall now speak to you only of one. What, then, is this? In it the divine covenant is fulfilled: burial and death, and resurrection and life, and all these take place at once. When we immerse our heads in the water, just as if in a grave, the old man is buried, and, having sunk down, is entirely hidden once for all; then, when we emerge, the new man rises again. Just as it is easy for us to be immersed and to emerge [from the water], so it is easy for God to bury the old man and raise up the new. This is done thrice that you may learn that the power of the Father and of the Son and of the Holy Spirit performs all this.

Further, in proof that what has been said is not conjectural, listen to Paul saying the following: 'We were buried with him by means of baptism into death'; and again: 'Our self has been crucified with him'; and once more: 'We have been united with him in the likeness of his death.'[4] Moreover, not only is baptism called the cross, but the cross, baptism. 'With the baptism with which I am to be baptized, you shall be baptized,' He said; and again: 'I have a baptism to

3 Acts 10.47.
4 Rom. 6.4,6,5.

be baptized with' which you know not.[5] Even as we are easily baptized and emerge again, so also, after dying, He easily rose again when He wished; nay rather, much more easily, even if, by a mystery, for three days He awaited the dispensation of Providence.

Therefore, since we have been deemed worthy of such mysteries,[6] let us manifest a life worthy of the gift: the noblest way of life. And, you who have not yet been deemed worthy of them, do everything so as to become worthy, that we may be one body, that we may be brethren. As long as we are separated in this, even if a man be one's father, or brother, or anyone else, he is not yet a real kinsman, if separated from the heavenly relationship.

Indeed, what help is there in being united in our earthly family if we are not bound together by the spiritual one? And what profit is there from close kinship upon earth, if we are strangers in heaven? The catechumen is a stranger to the believer, for he does not have the same Head; he does not have the same Father; he does not have the same city, or food, or clothing, or table, or dwelling, but all are different.

Now, I say this for all the possessions of the former are on earth; those of the latter are in heaven. Christ is the King of the latter; sin and the Devil, of the former. Christ is the food of the one; that of the other is rotten and corrupt. And, once more, the garment of the one is the work of worms; that of the other is the Lord of angels. The city of the one is heaven; of the other, earth. Since, then, we have nothing in common, tell me, in what shall we share? But, have we provoked the same travail and come forth from one womb? Still, this is not productive of the most perfect relationship. Let us, then, hasten to become citizens of the heavenly City. How long shall we remain in exile when we ought to recover our ancient fatherland?

---

5 Mark 10.39; Luke 12.50.
6 I.e., have been baptized.

Indeed, the risk is not for a trifling stake, for, if it should happen—and may it not!—that, death coming upon us unexpectedly, we depart from here uninitiated,[7] even if we have earthly blessings without number, nothing else will welcome us than hell, and the poisonous serpent, and unquenchable fire, and indissoluble bonds. But, may it not be the fate of anyone listening to these words to be tried by that punishment.

And we shall not be thus tried if, having been deemed worthy of the mysteries, we build on that foundation gold and silver and precious stones. In this way we shall be able, on departing thither, to appear rich, since we do not leave behind possessions here, but transfer them to safe treasuries there by the hands of the poor, inasmuch as we lend them to Christ. We owe many debts there, not of money, but of sins. Let us, then, lend Him our wealth so that we may receive pardon for our sins. For it is He Himself who acts as judge.

Let us not overlook Him here, hungry, in order that He Himself may feed us there. Here let us clothe Him, that He may not send us forth naked from the safe refuge with Him. If we give Him to drink here, we shall not say with the rich man: 'Send Lazarus to dip the tip of his finger in water and cool our tongues.'[8] If here we receive Him into our homes, there He will prepare many mansions for us. If we go to Him when He is in prison, He Himself will free us also from our bonds. If, when He is a stranger, we take Him in, He will not look down upon us as strangers when we are in the Kingdom of heaven, but will give to us a share

---

7 I.e., 'unbaptized.' Here St. John Chrysostom was speaking against those who were deliberately putting off their reception of baptism until the hour of death in order to avoid being responsible for the obligations incumbent on a Christian during life. This practice, all too common in his day, caused those guilty of it also to be guilty of presuming on God's mercy. Hence, they were liable to the punishments mentioned here. He did not include in their number, of course, those who remained unbaptized through invincible ignorance.

8 Luke 16.24.

in the heavenly City. If we visit Him when He is sick, He Himself will quickly free us also from our infirmities.[9]

Accordingly, as persons who receive great things and give little, let us give even that little, that we may secure the great. While it is yet time, let us sow, that we may reap. When the winter descends, when the sea is no longer navigable, we are no longer able to trade. And when will it be winter? When that great and notorious day may come. Then we shall no longer sail this great and vast sea, for that is what the present life is like.

Now is the time of sowing; then, that of reaping and gaining profit. If a man does not cast seeds at the time for sowing, but sows in the reaping season, besides accomplishing nothing he will also be ridiculous. But, if the present is the time for sowing, it should be a time, not of collecting but of dispersing for the future. Well, then, let us scatter abroad in order that we may gather in; let us not wish to collect now, that we may not destroy the harvest. This time, as I have said, summons us to sow and to dispense and to spend, not to collect and to store away.

Let us not, then, forego the opportunity, but let us cast down a rich sowing, and let us be sparing of none of our possessions, that we may receive them back with abundant recompense by the grace and mercy of our Lord Jesus Christ, with whom glory be to the Father together with the Holy Spirit forever and ever. Amen.

Homily 26 (John 3.6-11)

'That which is born of the flesh is flesh; and that which is born of the Spirit is spirit.'[1]

---

9 Cf. Matt. 25.31-46.

---

1 John 3.6.

The only-begotten Son of God has deemed us worthy of great mysteries—great ones, and such as we do not deserve, but such as were fitting for Him to give. In the light of our merit, not only are we unworthy of the gift, but even deserving of punishment and torture.

Since He did not look to this, not only did He set us free from punishment, but also endowed us with a life much more splendid, brought us to another world, made us another creature. 'If then any man is in Christ, he is a new creature.'[2] What sort of new creature? Listen to Him as He says: 'Unless a man be born again of water and the Spirit, he cannot enter into the kingdom of God.'

We were entrusted with paradise and did not prove worthy of our sojourn there, and yet He brought us to heaven. In the first [trial] we were not found faithful, yet He entrusted to us a greater. We were not strong enough to refrain from one food, yet He provided nourishment from above. In paradise we did not remain steadfast, yet He opened heaven to us. With reason has Paul said: 'Oh, the depth of the riches of the wisdom and of the knowledge of God.'[3]

No longer is there a mother, no longer travail, nor the couch, and carnal intercourse, but the forming of our nature is from above, of the Holy Spirit and water. Moreover, the water succeeds to the task, becoming a means of birth for that which has been begotten. As the womb is to the embryo, so the water is to the believer, since he is formed and shaped in the water. In the beginning, to be sure, God said: 'Let the waters bring forth crawling creatures having life.'[4] From the time when the Lord came forth from the waters of the Jordan, the water brings forth no longer 'crawling creatures having life,' but rational souls bearing the Holy Spirit. And that statement made of the sun: 'Like a bridegroom advanc-

2 Cor. 5.17.
3 Rom. 11.33.
4 Cf. Gen. 1.20.

ing from his bridal chamber'[5] might be more fittingly said of the faithful, for they send forth beams much more brilliant than its rays.

However, that which is formed within the womb needs time, while this is not so in the case of the water, since all takes place in a single moment. Where the life is perishable and takes its beginning from carnal corruption, that which has been begotten is slow in forming (such is the nature of bodies; in time, they acquire their finished form). But it is not so with spiritual things. Why? Because they are perfectly formed from the start.

However, when Nicodemus upon hearing these words [of Christ] was altogether disquieted, see how He revealed to him the ineffable meaning of this mystery, and made clear what previously had been obscure to him. 'That which is born of the flesh is flesh; and that which is born of the Spirit is spirit,' He said. He led him away from all the things of sense and did not permit the explanation of the mystery to be scrutinized by his bodily eyes. For, 'we are not talking about flesh but Spirit, Nicodemus,' He said. By these words He directed his gaze upward for awhile. 'Do not, then, look for things of sense; for the Spirit would not appear to these eyes. And do not think that the Spirit brings forth flesh.'

'How, then,' someone may say, 'was the flesh of the Lord begotten?' Not from the Spirit only, but also from flesh. Therefore Paul, also making this clear, said: 'born of a woman, born under the law.'[6] The Spirit formed Him in this way, and not from nothing, since in the latter case what need would there be of the womb? As a matter of fact, He did form Him of the flesh of a Virgin, but how, I cannot explain. Now, this took place that no one might think that the Child was of another nature than ours. If there are

---

5 Ps. 18.6.
6 Gal. 4.4.

some who do not believe in such a birth—though it has actually taken place—how would they have avoided falling into such impiety, if He had not taken on the flesh of the Virgin?

'That which is born of the Spirit is spirit,' He said. Do you perceive the dignity of the Spirit? He is represented as doing the work of God. He had said above, of a truth: 'They were born of God,' but here, that they are born of the Spirit. 'That which is born of the Spirit,' He said, 'is spirit.' He meant, that is, 'He who is born of the Spirit is spiritual.' In this context He did not mean birth in the material order, but that in the order of honor and grace.

'Well, then, if even the Son is born in this way, what superiority has He to men who are born thus, also? And how is He only-begotten? Truly, I also have been born of God, though not of His essence. Well, then, if not even He is of His essence, how, therefore, is He different from us? Nay, in that case, surely, He will be found to be less than the Spirit? For generation of this kind takes place by the grace of the Spirit. In that event, surely, in order to remain the Son, He needs the aid of the Spirit? Yet, how is this different from the teachings of the Jews?'

When Christ, then, had said: 'That which is born of the Spirit is spirit,' since He saw that Nicodemus was once more disturbed, He steered the conversation to an illustration perceptible to the senses. 'Do not wonder,' He said, 'that I said to thee, "You must be born again." The wind blows where it will.' Now, by saying 'Do not wonder' He took note of the other's trouble of soul, and recalled to his mind a material object that is somewhat unsubstantial. For, by saying 'That which is born of the Spirit is spirit' He had begun to lead him away from things of the flesh.

But when he did not understand what in the world it was that He meant by 'That which is born of the Spirit is spirit,' He finally conducted him to another illustration. In this He neither brought him to the crassness of corporeal things nor discoursed purely of incorporeal things (for the other was not able to understand if he heard them). But by choosing something between the corporeal and the incorporeal— namely, the onrush of the wind—He led him on from there. In regard to the wind He said: 'Thou hearest its sound but dost not know where it comes from or where it goes.'

Now, when He said: 'The wind blows where it will,' He did not say this as if the wind had a kind of free will, but with the meaning that its onrush takes place unhindered and with power. Holy Scripture also is apt to speak in this way of incorporeal things, as when it says: 'For creation was made subject to vanity—not by its own will.'[7] Accordingly, the expression 'blows where it will' is that of one showing the impossibility of restraining the wind, and that it streams forth everywhere, and that there is no one who can prevent it from being carried here and there; but it is dispersed very freely, and no one is strong enough to turn aside its onset.

'And thou hearest its sound,' that is, its roaring and howling. 'But dost not know where it comes from or where it goes. So is everyone who is born of the Spirit.' 'For if,' He said, 'you cannot explain the violence nor know the way of this wind, which you perceive both by hearing and by touch, how is it that you inquire into the working of the divine Spirit, when you do not even understand that of the wind, though you hear its sound?'

Furthermore, the expression 'blows where it will' was also used to establish the power of the Paraclete. And what He meant is some such thing as this: 'Indeed, if no one restrains the wind, but it is carried where it wills, much more will laws of nature be unable to restrain the working of the Spirit; neither the limits of carnal birth nor any other such thing.'

But it is also clear that the expression, 'Thou hearest the

7 Rom. 8.20.

sound,' was said of the wind, for, in addressing the unbeliever and one who did not know the working of the Spirit, He would not have said: 'Thou hearest its sound.' Therefore, just as the wind is not seen, though it gives forth a sound, so spiritual birth is not seen by bodily eyes. Yet the wind is truly a material body, even if very unsubstantial, for that which is subject to perception is a body. Well, then, if you are not troubled about a bodily object, when you do not see it, and do not doubt it for that reason, why, then, when you hear about the Spirit, do you become confused and require so many proofs, though you do not do so in the case of a bodily object? What, then, did Nicodemus do? He still persisted in his Jewish obtuseness, even when the matter was so clearly illustrated to him.

When he once again said doubtfully: 'How can these things be?' finally Christ replied to him more rebukingly: 'Thou art a teacher in Israel and dost not know these things?' See how He nowhere accused the man of malice, but merely of slowness and stupidity. Now, someone may inquire: 'What did this spiritual birth have in common with Jewish teachings?'

What, indeed, did it not have in common? Tell me. The first man, and the woman born from his side, and the barren women, and the things effected by the waters—for example, that with regard to the fountain on which Eliseus buoyed up the iron,[8] that with regard to the Red Sea which the Jews crossed,[9] that with regard to the pool which the angel stirred,[10] that with regard to the Syrian Naaman who was cleansed in the Jordan[11]—all these foretold, as types, the birth and purification that would take place in the future.

Also, the words of the Prophets hinted at the manner of this birth: 'A generation to come shall be declared to the

8 Cf. 4 Kings 6.6.
9 Cf. Exod. 14.10-22.
10 Cf. John 5.4.
11 Cf. 4 Kings 5.1-14.

Lord, and shall proclaim his justice to people yet to be born which the Lord hath made.'[12] Likewise: 'Thy youth is renewed like the eagle's.'[13] And: 'Be enlightened, Jerusalem; behold thy King cometh.'[14] Again: 'Blessed are they whose transgressions are forgiven.'[15]

Further, Isaac also was a type of this birth. For, tell me, Nicodemus, how was he begotten? Was it in accordance with the law of nature? By no means. The manner of his birth was midway between the latter and the other:[16] in accordance with the law of nature, on the one hand, because resulting from cohabitation, but not in accordance with natural law on the other hand, because he was born 'not of blood.'[17]

Moreover, I shall show that such births foreshadow not only this spiritual birth but also the Virgin Birth, for, since it would not be easy for anyone to believe that a virgin could bring forth, barren women conceived; and then, not barren women only, but also aged women. Yet, for woman to be born of a rib was much more wonderful than these instances. But, since Eve's birth was of olden time and long past another new and prophetic kind of birth took place later: that of barren women, preparing the way for belief in the Virgin Birth.

He was, therefore, recalling these truths to him when He said: 'Thou art a teacher in Israel and dost not know these things? We speak of what we know, and we bear witness to what we have seen; and our witness you do not receive.' The latter words He added to make His teaching additionally credible by means of them and to condescend to the other's weakness by His way of speaking.

But what is the meaning of what He said? 'We speak of

12 Cf. Ps. 21.32.
13 Ps. 102.5.
14 Cf. Isa. 60.1.
15 Ps. 31.1.
16 Cf. Gen. 18.9-15.
17 John 1.13.

what we know, and we bear witness to what we have seen.'
Now, since among us the sight is more trustworthy than the
other senses, and if we wish to convince someone we say: 'I
have seen with my own eyes,' not 'I know by hearsay'; therefore even Christ was speaking to him in a somewhat human
fashion, and thereby made His words more credible. And it
is plain from the context that it was this, and nothing else,
that He wished to establish, and that He did not mean that
the thing seen is a sensible object. Having said: 'That which
is born of the flesh is flesh; and that which is born of the
Spirit is spirit,' He added: 'We speak of what we know, and
we bear witness to what we have seen.' But this had not
yet taken place. How, then, could He say: 'What we have
seen'? Is it not quite clear that He was referring to knowledge
that is exact and cannot be mistaken?

'And our witness you do not receive.' Surely, therefore,
He says 'What we have seen' of Himself and His Father, or
of Himself alone. Yet, the expression 'You do not receive'
is not that of one who is displeased, but of one stating a fact.
He did not say: 'What could be more senseless than you
who do not accept the teachings that have been so clearly
expounded by Me?' On the contrary, showing every consideration both by deed and word, He said nothing of this, but
mildly and gently foretold the future.

By this mode of action He was giving us also the example
of unceasing gentleness, and teaching us not to show dis-
pleasure, not to be indignant, when we preach to men and
do not persuade them. For it is not possible for the angry
man to achieve anything; rather, he renders it more difficult
to persuade others. Therefore, we ought to refrain from
anger and thus make our teaching more acceptable to all,
not only by not showing anger, but also by not ranting.
Noisy speech is the fuel of anger.

Well, then, let us hobble the horse that we may subdue
the horseman; let us clip the wings of anger, and no longer

will the evil rise to its peak. Fierce is the passion of anger, fierce, and capable of stealing away our souls. For this reason it is necessary to shut off its approach on all sides. And this is so because it is ridiculous to be able to tame wild beasts yet to allow our own minds to be savagely angry.

Anger is a strong fire, consuming all things, for it both wastes the body, and corrupts the soul, and renders a man odious and base to look upon. And if it were possible for the angry man to see himself at the time of his anger, he would not need any other admonition, for there is nothing less pleasing than an angry countenance. Anger is an intoxicant, or, rather, more dangerous than an intoxicant and more wretched than a demon.

But if we take care not to rant, we shall discover the noblest way to a good life. Therefore, Paul writes to do away with ranting as well as anger, saying: 'Let all wrath and clamor be removed from you.'[18] Well, then, let us obey this teacher of all philosophy, and when we are angry with our servants, let us recall our own sins, and let us be shamed at their forbearance. Moreover, when you angrily insult one of them and he bears the outrage in silence, and when you act indecorously and he acts wisely, accept this in place of any reproof. Even if he is a servant, he is a man with an immortal soul, and honored with the same gifts as you by our common Lord.

Further, if he who is equal in honor with us in the greater and more spiritual things so mildly bears offenses from us, through a certain human, lowly and humble excellence, what pardon and how much excuse would we deserve, if we should not be able—or rather, not be willing—to act wisely through the fear of God, as he does through fear of us?

Therefore, considering all these things, and recalling our sins, and the common sharing of human nature, let us take

18 Cf. Eph. 4.31.

care to speak gently everywhere, in order that, being humble
of heart, we may find rest for our souls, both now and hereafter.[19] May all of us attain to this by the grace and mercy of
our Lord Jesus Christ, with whom glory be to the Father,
together with the Holy Spirit, now and always, and forever
and ever. Amen.

Homily 27 (John 3.12-16)

'If I have spoken of earthly things to you, and you do not
believe, how will you believe if I speak to you of heavenly
things? And no one has ascended into heaven except him
who has descended from heaven: the Son of Man who is
in heaven.'[1]

I now declare and will keep repeating something that I
have often said. And what is this? That when Jesus is at the
point of arriving at teachings that are sublime He frequently
restrains Himself in consideration of the weakness of His
hearers, and does not dwell for long on subjects befitting His
greatness, but rather on those which condescend to their
lowliness.

If the sublime and the great is even said once, it is sufficient to establish that dignity as far as is possible for us to
hear it, but unless things that are more lowly and approaching
the understanding of the hearers were spoken repeatedly,
lofty ideas would not easily be grasped by the ordinary listener.
It is on this account, accordingly, that more of His words were
lowly than sublime.

However, in order that this might not be the cause of
harm in still another way by keeping the disciple fastened
to earth, He did not merely expound the more lowly ideas

19 Cf. Matt. 11.29,30.

1 John 3.12,13.

without stating the reason for which He spoke thus; as He has done here also. When He had said what He did about baptism and the birth by grace taking place upon earth, though He desired also to speak of that mysterious and ineffable generation of His, He put it off and did not continue. And then He asserted the reason why He did not continue. What is this? The dullness and weakness of His listeners. He implied this when He said: 'If I have spoken of earthly things to you, and you do not believe, how will you believe if I speak to you of heavenly things?' So that, where He spoke in limited and earthly terms, it must be attributed to the limitations of His hearers.

Now, the phrase 'earthly things' here refers to the wind, according to the opinion of some. That is: 'If I have given examples taken from earthly things and you do not even thus believe, how will you be able to grasp those more sublime?' Moreover, if He here referred to baptism as earthly, do not wonder. He called it so, either because it is accomplished on earth, or else He gave it this appellation by comparison with His most awesome generation. In truth, even if birth by baptism is heavenly, still, when compared with that unique filiation which proceeds from the substance of the Father, it is earthly.

Furthermore, it was with reason that He said not: 'You do not understand,' but: 'You do not believe.' When a person balks and does not readily accept things which it is possible for the mind to receive, he may with reason be accused of stupidity; when he does not accept things which it is not possible to grasp by reason but only by faith, the charge is no longer that of stupidity, but of incredulity. Therefore, to divert Nicodemus from scrutinizing His words by reason, He pricked him more severely by accusing him of incredulity.

But if we must accept by faith our [spiritual] birth, what would they deserve who inquire by reason into the generation of the Only-begotten? Nevertheless, someone may ask: 'Why did He say these things if His hearers were not going to believe them?' It was because, even if they did not believe, those who were to come after them would accept and profit by them.

Having pricked him very severely, then, He went on to show that He knew not only these things but others as well, much more numerous and greater than these. Wherefore, by His next words He made this also clear by saying: 'And no one has ascended into heaven except him who has descended from heaven: the Son of Man who is in heaven.' 'But what connection,' you say, 'has this with the preceding?' A very close connection and one entirely in harmony with His foregoing words. Since Nicodemus had said: 'We know that thou hast come a teacher from God,' He set him right on this very point, as if to say: 'Do not think that I am a teacher like the many Prophets who are of the earth. I am now come from heaven. None of the Prophets, indeed, has ascended there, but I dwell there.'

Do you see how even what seems to be most sublime is yet most unworthy of His greatness? He is not only in heaven, but also everywhere else, and fills all things. Yet He scaled His remarks to the weakness of His listener, out of a desire to lead him gradually upward. In this place, however, He did not mean only His humanity by 'the Son of Man,' but here called His entire Person, so to speak, by the name of its lesser part. And I say this, for it was His custom frequently to name the whole from His Godhead, and as often to name it from His humanity.

'And as Moses lifted up the serpent in the desert,' He said, 'even so must the Son of Man be lifted up.' Now, once again this seems to be foreign to what precedes, but actually it is very pertinent. For, having said that the greatest benefit comes to men by baptism, He now mentioned in addition the gift responsible for this and not inferior to it, namely, that received through the Cross. Just as Paul, also, in addressing the Corinthians, placed these benefits side by side when he said: 'Was Paul crucified for you? Or were you baptized in the name of Paul?'[2] Most of all, these two things show His unspeakable love: that He suffered for His enemies, and that, having died for His enemies, He gave them by baptism full pardon for their sins.

Further, why did He not say plainly: 'I am going to be crucified,' instead of sending His hearers to the ancient figure?[3] In the first place, that they might learn that the old order was akin to the new, and not foreign to the latter; next, that you might know that not unwillingly did He go to His Passion; and, besides, that you might learn that no lasting harm was His as a result of it, and salvation for many was brought forth from it.

In fact, He conducted us to the ancient story to forestall anyone's saying: 'How is it possible for those who believe in the Crucified One to be saved, inasmuch as He Himself was possessed by death?' It is possible, for, if the Jews escaped death by looking upon the brazen image of a serpent, with much greater reason would those who believe in the Crucified One enjoy an even greater benefit. For the crucifixion took place, not by reason of the impotence of the Crucified, and not by reason of the superior strength of the Jews; it was because 'God loved the world' that His living Temple was crucified.

'That those who believe in him may not perish, but may have life everlasting.' Do you perceive the reason for the crucifixion and for the salvation proceeding from it? Do you perceive the relationship of the figure with the reality? In the former, the Jews escaped death, but it was temporal death; in the latter, the faithful escape eternal death. In the former, the uplifted serpent healed the bites of serpents; in the latter, the crucified Jesus healed the wounds inflicted

2 1 Cor. 1.13.
3 I.e., the brazen serpent; cf. Num. 21.6-9.

by the spiritual dragon. In the former, he who looked with these eyes of earth was healed; in the latter, he who gazes with the eyes of his mind lays aside all his sins.

In the former, there was the uplifted brass fashioned in the likeness of a serpent; in the latter, the Lord's body formed by the Spirit. A serpent inflicted the bite in the former, and a serpent healed it; so also in the latter, death destroyed and death saved. But the destroying serpent possessed poison, while the Saviour was free from poison. And here similarly once more: the death which destroyed us had sin as the serpent has poison, but the death of the Lord was free from all sin just as indeed the brazen serpent was, of poison. Scripture says: 'Who did no sin, neither was deceit found in his mouth.'[4] And this it is also which Paul said: 'Disarming the Principalities and Powers, he displayed them openly, leading them away in triumph by force of it.'[5]

Moreover, as a great athlete, when he makes his victory more splendid because of having lifted up his opponent on high and hurled him down again, so Christ, with the whole world looking on, cast down the powers opposing Him, and having healed those smitten in the desert, He freed them from all wild beasts by hanging suspended on the cross. However, He did not say 'must be suspended,' but 'must be lifted up,' since, for the sake of His hearer, He used an expression which seemed to be somewhat more acceptable, yet close to the type.

'For God so loved the world that he gave his only-begotten Son, that those who believe in him may not perish, but may have life everlasting.' He meant, that is: 'Do not wonder that I am going to be lifted up that you may be saved. This seems best to the Father and He Himself has so loved you as to give His Son in behalf of slaves, even ungrateful slaves.' And He does this though a man would not even do it for

---

4 1 Peter 2.22.
5 Col. 2.15.

his friend, nor would one readily do it for the sake of a just man; as Paul made clear when he said: 'For scarcely in behalf of a just man does one die.'[6] But he spoke at greater length since he was addressing the faithful, while in our context Christ spoke more briefly—since His words were addressed to Nicodemus—yet more emphatically.

Indeed, each section of His statement has great force. By the words 'so loved' and 'God [loved] the world' He indicated the extent of His love. The distance between was great—infinite, rather—since He who is immortal, infinite, immense, limitless has loved those made of earth and ashes, weighted down with countless sins, always offending, ungrateful. Again, His next words are likewise full of meaning as He continued: 'so that he gave his only-begotten Son.' That is, it was not a slave, not a messenger, not an archangel that He gave, He declared. Indeed, who would show such solicitude for his child as God showed for ungrateful slaves?

Nevertheless, He did not refer to the Passion in very explicit terms, but only by indirection. The benefit to be derived from it, however, He pointed out clearly and without equivocation, as follows: 'that those who believe in him may not perish, but may have life everlasting.' Since He had said 'must be lifted up' and thus hinted at His death, in order that His hearer might not become dejected by His words if he should think about Him in a human way and conclude that death for Him was final, notice how He set this straight by saying that He who was given was the Son of God and that He was the means of life, even of eternal life.

Now, He who provided life for others by His death would not Himself be in the power of death forever. For, if they who believe in the Crucified do not perish, far more will it be that He Himself who was crucified will not perish. Indeed, He who freed others from destruction will much more

6 Rom. 5.7.

certainly be free from it Himself. He who makes life available for others will gain it much more abundantly for Himself. Do you perceive that there is in all this discussion a need of faith? He declared that the Cross is a source of life, a fact which reason would not readily accept. Indeed, even now there are heathen who, by laughing at it, corroborate what I say. But faith, going beyond the weakness of reason, would readily both accept and keep it.

Now, whence has 'God so loved the world'? For no other reason at all but of His own goodness. Well, then, let us give heed to His love; let us be ashamed at the excess of His mercy. He did not spare even His only-begotten Son for our sake, while we spare even our wealth to our own ruin. He Himself gave His own Son for us, while we do not even despise money for Him—indeed, not even for ourselves. And how could this merit forgiveness?

If we see a man risking danger and death for us, we show him preference before all men, and count him among the first in the number of our friends, and entrust all our possessions to him, and declare that they are his rather than ours. In truth, we think that we are not even thus making a worthy return to him. However, we do not keep even this measure of gratitude toward Christ. He has given His life for us, and poured forth His precious Blood for the sake of us who are neither grateful nor good, while we do not pour out even our money for our own advantage, but disregard Him who died, naked and forsaken, for us.

Now, who will save us from the punishment to come? In truth, if God were not to be our judge, but we were to sit in judgment on ourselves, should we not cast the vote against ourselves? Should we not condemn ourselves to the fire of hell for allowing Him who has given His life for us to waste away with hunger?[7] But why do I speak merely of money?

---

7 I.e., in the person of the poor; cf. Matt. 25.35.

If we had ten thousand lives, ought we not lay them all down for Him? Yet, not even in that way would we be doing anything worthy of His generosity.

He who takes the lead in generous giving demonstrates his goodness clearly, while the recipient of his generosity, whatever return he makes, is paying a debt, but not bestowing a favor. And this is especially true when he on whose side the generosity begins is the benefactor of his enemies. Indeed, he who repays him makes a return to his benefactor, and at the same time he himself enjoys the fruit of it once more.

However, not even these considerations influence us, but we are so wanting in sense that we encircle slaves and mules and horses with golden collars, and disregard the Lord as He goes about naked, passing from door to door, ever standing by the wayside with hands extended; frequently, we even look at Him with a harsh gaze. Yet He endures this very treatment for our sake, for He gladly goes hungry that you may dine and remains naked that He may furnish for you the covering of the garment of immortality. Nevertheless, not even in the light of this do you give away any of your garments—though some of them are moth-eaten, others, stored in a chest, are an excessive source of worry to their possessors; while He who has given you these and everything else goes about naked.

Suppose, on the contrary, you do not store them in a chest, but make a fine showing while you wear them? Tell me: what is the advantage in that? For they will not admire you when you are clad in these garments, but only when you give them away to the needy. If you wish to be admired, you will enjoy acclaim without measure when you clothe others. Then God, also, will praise you, along with men. But now, no one will praise, but all will bear you ill-will, as they see your body decked out, but your soul neglected. Harlots, also, have this kind of raiment; frequently their garments are more expensive and more lavish than is usual.

But the soul's adornment belongs only to those who live in
virtue.

I say these things continually, and I will not cease from
them, not so much from solicitude for the poor as for your
souls. For the poor will have assistance—if not from us, then
from another source. And if they do not have assistance,
but perish with hunger, their loss is not great. Indeed, what
harm did Lazarus suffer from poverty and wasting away
with hunger? No one, in truth, will rescue you from hell
except the assistance which you obtain from the poor. But
we shall say the same words as those addressed to the rich
man, who is forever consumed by fire and will obtain no
assuagement.[8]

However, God grant that no one may ever hear these
words, but that you may go to the bosom of Abraham, by
the grace and mercy of our Lord Jesus Christ, through whom
and with whom glory be to the Father, together with the
Holy Spirit, forever and ever. Amen.

Homily 28 (John 3.17-21)

'For God did not send his Son into the world in order to
judge the world, but that the world might be saved through
him.'[1]

Many of those men who are somewhat inclined to heap up
sin upon sin, and, abusing the mercy of God, to indulge in
excessive negligence, utter such words as these: 'There is
no hell; there is no judgment; God forgives all our sins.'
To silence them a certain wise man has said: 'Say not: "The

---

8 'Son, remember that thou in thy lifetime hast received good things,
and Lazarus in like manner evil things; but now here he is comforted
whereas thou art tormented' (Luke 16.25).

---

1 John 3.17.

mercy of the Lord is great, he will have mercy on the multitude of my sins." For mercy and wrath quickly come from him: and his wrath looketh upon sinners.'[2] And again: 'According as his mercy is, so his correction'[3] is abundant.

'And where,' you say, 'are the proofs of His mercy, if we receive the punishment of our sins according as they deserve?' In testimony that we shall receive punishment 'as they deserve,' listen to the words both of the Prophet and of Paul. The former declared: 'You render to everyone according to his deeds,'[4] and the latter: 'Who will render to every man according to his works.'[5]

But it is also clear from this fact that the mercy of God is, nonetheless, great. God has shown great mercy to these men in apportioning our affairs into two divisions of life— the present life and the future life—making the former occur amid a succession of trials; the latter, in a place of crowns. How, and in what way? Because, though we have committed many and grievous sins, and have not ceased, from youth to the last extremity of old age, to sully our souls with their incalculable evil, He has demanded of us the accounting for no one of these sins, but has granted pardon for them by the laver of regeneration, and has endowed us with justice and holiness.

'Then,' you say, 'what if a man, deemed worthy of the mysteries from his earliest youth, should commit countless sins after this?' Such a man is certainly deserving of greater punishment. For we do not pay the same penalty for the same sins, but the penalty is much more severe when we offend after partaking of the mysteries. Paul made this clear, when he said: 'A man making void the Law of Moses dies without any mercy on the word of two or three witnesses; how much

---

2 Eccli. 5.6,7.
3 Eccli. 16.13.
4 Ps. 61.13.
5 Rom. 2.6.

worse punishments do you think he deserves who has trodden under foot the Son of God, and has regarded as unclean the blood of the covenant through which he was sanctified, and has insulted the grace of the Spirit?'[6] Such a one, therefore, will be deserving of greater punishment.

He has, nonetheless, opened the portals of repentance even to this man and has granted him to wash away his offenses in many ways, if he desires. Therefore, consider how great proofs these are of His mercy: both to remit sin by grace, and after grace has been received, not to punish the sinner, even though he is worthy of punishment, but to give him opportunity and time for making amends. That is why Christ uttered these words to Nicodemus: 'God did not send His Son into the world in order to judge the world, but that the world might be saved through Him.'

In truth, there are two comings of Christ: that which has already taken place and the future one. And the two are not for the same ends; the former has taken place, not that He might judge our deeds, but that He might remit them, while the second will take place, not that He may remit, but that He may judge. Of the former, therefore, He said: 'I have not come to judge the world but to save the world.'[7] And of the second coming: 'But when the Son of Man shall come in the glory of his Father, he will set the sheep on his right hand, but the goats on the left, and the former will go into everlasting life, while the others, into everlasting punishment.'[8]

Yet the first coming also was for judgment according to the rule of justice. Why? Because, before His coming there were the natural law, and prophets, and then written law, and formal teaching, and numberless promises, and manifestation of signs, and punishments and retributions, and many other

6 Heb. 10.28,29.
7 John 12.47.
8 Cf. Matt. 25.31,33,46.

things capable of setting men straight—and to demand an accounting was a logical consequence of these. However, since He is merciful, He did not then demand an accounting, but merely granted pardon. Whereas, if He had made an accounting, all men would straightway have been violently carried off. Scripture says: 'All have sinned and have need of the glory of God.'[9] Do you perceive the ineffable excess of mercy? 'He who believes in the Son is not judged; but he who does not believe is already judged.'

Now, if He did not come to judge the world, how is he who does not believe already judged, if the time of judgment is not yet here? Either He said this because unrepented unbelief is itself a punishment—for to be outside the Light is, even in itself, a very great punishment—or He was foretelling the future punishment. In fact, just as the murderer, even if he has not yet been condemned by the decision of the judge, has been condemned by the nature of his deed, so also the unbeliever. Indeed, on the day when Adam ate of the tree he died. Thus, to be sure, the sentence was: 'The day you eat of the tree you will die.'[10] Yet he remained alive. How, then, did he die? By the sentence, and by the nature of his deed. For he who has made himself subject to punishment is under the penalty: if not in actual fact, yet by the sentence.

Moreover, lest someone, having heard the words: 'I have not come to judge the world,' might think he could sin with impunity, and become more careless, He forestalled this negligent attitude by saying 'is already judged.' Since the judgment was to come, and not yet present, He brought the fear of the penalty near at hand and referred to the punishment as already come. Now, this very fact is an evidence of His abundant mercy: that He not only gives His Son, but

9 Rom. 3.23.
10 Gen. 2.17.

even postpones the time of the judgment, in order that sinners and unbelievers may have an opportunity to wash away their sins. 'He who believes in the Son is not judged': 'he who believes,' not he who questions; 'he who believes,' not he who curiously inquires.

What, then, if the believer should be guilty of an impure life and deeds that are not good? Paul declared that these, most of all, are not sincere believers, for 'They profess to know God, but by their works they disown him.'[11] Besides, in this place He meant this: 'He is not judged in this one respect; but, though he is not punished for unbelief, he will pay a more severe penalty for his deeds because of having at one time believed.'

Do you see how, having begun with fearful truths, He returned again to the same? He began by saying: 'Unless a man be born of water and the Spirit, he cannot enter into the kingdom of God.' And here, once more, He said: 'He who does not believe in the Son is already judged,' that is: 'Do not think that the delay is of any help to him who has become subject to the penalty, if he does not repent. For he who does not believe is no better off than those who have been already judged and punished.'

'Now this is the judgment: the light has come into the world, yet men have loved the darkness rather than the light.' He meant, that is: 'They are punished because of this: that they have not been willing to shun darkness and run to the Light.' Here at last He took away their last line of defense. 'For, if I had come,' He said, 'inflicting punishment and demanding an accounting of men's deeds, they would have had this to say: "We ran away because of that." But now, I have come to drive away darkness and bring them to the Light.' Who, then, would pity the man who does not wish to go from darkness to the Light? 'For, though they can lodge

---

11 Titus 1.16.

no charge against Me, but rather have received countless blessings,' He said, 'they run away from Me.'

And elsewhere, too, He accused them of this and said: 'They have hated me without cause.' And again: 'If I had not come and spoken to them, they would have no sin.'[12] He who, in the absence of light, sits in darkness may perhaps receive pardon; but he who, after the light has come, remains in the darkness gives evidence against himself of a perverted and contentious will. Next, since what He said would seem to be incredible to most men (surely, no one would prefer darkness to light), He also assigned the reason why they had this affliction. What, then, is this? 'For their works were evil,' He said. 'For everyone who does evil hates the light, and does not come to the light, that his deeds may not be exposed.'

Now, He did not indeed come to judge and search out, but to pardon and to remit sins, and to give salvation by faith. How was it, then, that they fled from Him? For if He had gone to the tribunal and had taken His seat as judge, their words would have been somewhat reasonable. Indeed, he who is conscious to himself of evil usually flees from his judge, but transgressors run to him who grants pardon. Well, then, if He came to pardon, it was likely that they especially would run to Him who were conscious to themselves of many sins; and this actually did happen in the case of many. And I say this for publicans and sinners came and dined with Jesus.

What, then, do these words mean? He was speaking with reference to those who choose to remain altogether in evil. For He Himself came for this reason: to forgive past sins and to afford protection against future sins. Yet, since there are some so weak and slothful in the practice of virtue that they wish to remain in wickedness to their last breath, and

12 John 15.25,22.

never to cease from it, He was plainly ridiculing these men here. 'Because, in truth, Christianity requires both correctness of doctrine and an upright life, they are afraid,' He said, 'to come over to us, because they do not wish to live a blameless life.'

No one, to be sure, would condemn a man living [sincerely] in paganism. If he has gods such as these and religious practices as shameful and ridiculous as his gods, he is but performing actions in keeping with these teachings. But men of God, if they live indifferently, have all kinds of censurers and accusers; so great is the admiration of the truth even on the part of its enemies.

Well, then, notice how precisely He worded what He said. He did not say: 'Everyone who has done evil does not come to the light,' but: 'Everyone who always does it, that is, who always wishes to be befouled with the mire of sin, does not wish to subject himself to My laws, but, remaining outside them, shamelessly commits fornication and does all the other things that are forbidden. If he comes here, he is very plainly identified, as a thief is, on coming into the light. For this reason he flees My rule.' Yet, it is possible to hear many pagans even now saying that they cannot come to our faith for this reason: because of not being able to refrain from drinking, and fornication, and such sins as these.

'What, then,' you will say; 'are there not also Christians who do evil, and pagans who live in accordance with the true philosophy?' Yes, there are, on the one hand, Christians who do evil, and I know them; on the other hand, if there are pagans living uprightly, this I do not know so clearly. Moreover, do not speak to me of those who are well behaved and seemly by nature, for this is not virtue; but tell me of the man who endures the fierce onslaught of his passions, yet lives in an exemplary manner.

However, you would not be able to tell me of such. For,

if the promise of the Kingdom, and threats of hell, and other teachings of the kind, with difficulty keep men in virtue, those who believe in none of them would hardly seek for virtue. And if some do pretend to virtue, they do it for the sake of reputation. But, if a man does it for outward show, when he can hide from view, he will not shrink from giving in to his evil tendencies. However, lest we seem to some to be contentious, let us grant that there are some living righteously among pagans, because this in no wise gives the lie to my words. For they refer to what generally happens, not to what takes place rarely.

But see how Christ deprived them[13] of all defense from the other direction also when He said: 'The Light has come into the world,' for 'they did not search for it themselves, did they?' He meant: 'They did not grow weary, did they? They did not toil in order to find it, did they? The Light itself came to them, and they did not, even so, run to it.' And if they object that there are even certain Christians who are living wickedly, I should reply that He said this, not with regard to those who have been Christians from the start and have received from their ancestors the practice of piety, although these often have been separated from the true teachings by a wicked life. However, I think that He was now speaking not with reference to them, but about those of the pagans and of the Jews who ought to be converted to the true faith. For He pointed out that no one living in error would choose to come to the faith without having first outlined an upright way of life for himself; while no one would remain in unbelief without having first chosen to live altogether in evil.

Further, do not tell me that some individual is chaste and does not steal, since these things of themselves are not virtue. For what use is it if he has these good points but is enslaved

---

13 I.e., pagans apparently living a good life.

by vainglory, and through human respect remains in error. This, in truth, is not living an upright life. For, he who is enslaved to reputation is no less guilty than a fornicator; indeed, he does much more evil and more serious, than the latter.

But, to resume, tell me someone who, even while remaining with the pagans, is rid of all passions and free from all evil. Indeed, you cannot. And you are not able to do so, for those among them who have had great things to boast of— because they have risen above wealth and palate, as they say—have most of all been enslaved by love of praise; and this is the root of all evils. It was in this way that the Jews also remained in error. And [Christ] therefore accused them as follows: 'How can you believe who receive glory from one another?'[14]

Now, why do you think He did not speak about these matters to Nathanael, to whom also He revealed truth; why did He not converse with him at length? Because not even he came to Him with such eagerness [as that of Nicodemus]. The latter set this task for himself and chose as the time of his audience the period which others have for repose. The former, on the contrary, came to Him at the persuasion of another. Yet He did not spurn him even so, but said to him: 'You shall see heaven opened, and the angels of God ascending and descending.'

To Nicodemus, however, He said none of these things, but discoursed about the Incarnation and everlasting life, speaking differently to each one, according to the disposition of each. Since the first was versed in the sayings of the Prophets and was not so fearful, it was sufficient for him to hear only as much as he did. But since the latter was still held back by fear, He prudently did not reveal everything to him, but stirred his mind so as to cast out fear by fear, by

14 John 5.44.

saying that he who does not believe is judged and that persistence in unbelief proceeds from the consciousness of a wicked life.

Nicodemus, indeed, made much account of the praise of men and respected it more than [eternal] punishment ('Even among the rulers many believed in him, but because of the Pharisees they did not acknowledge it'[15]). And so He upbraided him on this account, and showed by what He said that 'It is not possible for him who does not believe in Me to persist in unbelief for any other reason except that he lives an impure life.' Further on, He said: 'I am the Light,'[16] but here: 'The Light has come into the world.' In the beginning, He spoke somewhat obscurely, but later, more clearly. Nevertheless, the man was held back by the thought of the praise of men. Therefore, Christ also did not allow Himself to speak freely, as was fitting.

Well, then, let us flee vainglory, for this passion is more despotic than all the others. From it come greed and desire for wealth; thence, hatred and enmity and quarrels. For he who desires more than he has will be able to rest nowhere. In fact, he desires more for no other reason than for the love of empty praise. Indeed, tell me, why do many men surround themselves with a multitude of eunuchs, and crowds of slaves, and a great display? Not for the sake of utility, but in order that bystanders may witness this untimely display.

Well, then, if we cut off this passion, we shall destroy the other limbs of the evil as well, together with the head, and nothing will prevent us from dwelling on earth as if in heaven. Not only, in truth, does it impel its victims to evil, but even insinuates itself into the virtues; and when it is not able to dislodge us from there it wreaks much damage on our very virtue, forcing us to perform virtuous acts and depriving us of their fruits. For he who looks to vainglory,

15 John 12.42.
16 John 8.12.

whether fasting or praying, or giving alms, loses the reward of the good action.

What could be more pitiable than this punishment, especially since it happens that a man is mortifying himself in vain and fruitlessly, and so becomes a laughing-stock, and is deprived of the glory of heaven? For it is not possible for him who has his heart set on both to attain both [kinds of glory]. Yet it is possible to attain both if, indeed, we really desire, not both but the one from heaven. However, it is not possible for him who desires both to attain both.

Therefore, if we wish to attain to glory, let us flee from the praise of men and desire only that coming from God. Truly, in this way we shall attain to the former as well as to the latter. May we all enjoy this by the grace and mercy of our Lord Jesus Christ, through whom and with whom glory be to the Father, together with the Holy Spirit, forever and ever. Amen.

Homily 29 (John 3.22-30)

'Jesus and his disciples came into the land of Judea, and he stayed there with them and baptized.'[1]

Nothing could be clearer or stronger than truth; just as nothing could be weaker than lying, even if it is shrouded in wrappings without number. Even thus covered, it is easily detected and readily dissipated. Truth, on the contrary, stands forth without concealment to all who wish to look upon her beauty.

Indeed, she does not desire to be hidden, nor does she fear danger, nor tremble at intrigues, nor desire the praise of men, nor is she subject to any human considerations. She stands above them all, receiving the assault of countless deceits and remaining unsubdued; protecting as in a safe

---

1 John 3.22.

refuge those who flee to her and doing this by the superiority of her own power; avoiding concealed pitfalls, while revealing openly to all her own resources.

This, to be sure, Christ made clear when He addressed these words to Pilate: 'I have always taught openly, and in secret I have said nothing.'[2] He said this at that time,[3] but now He was putting the words into practice. 'After these things, Jesus and his disciples came into the land of Judea, and he stayed there with them, and baptized.' Now, in festive seasons He went to the city, in order that in the course of them He might set forth His teachings and supplement them by His miracles. But when the festive seasons were ended, He frequently went to the Jordan, since many gathered there also.

Moreover, He always sought out much-frequented places, not in order to make a show, nor because of a desire for honor, but in the endeavor to make His assistance available to more people. Yet, further on, the Evangelist said that Jesus did not baptize, but His disciples,[4] from which it is plain that here also he meant by this statement that they alone were baptizing. 'But why,' you will ask, 'did He not baptize?' John the Baptist said, in anticipation of this: 'He will baptize you with the Holy Spirit and with fire;'[5] however, the Spirit had not yet been given. With reason, therefore, He did not baptize, but His disciples did so, in the desire to draw many to the doctrine of salvation.

And why, once the disciples of Jesus were baptizing, did John not cease doing so, but continue on his own to baptize,

---

2 John 18.20.
3 I.e., during His Passion.
4 John 4.2. According to another reading noted by Savile, this sentence of St. John Chrysostom has an interpolation at the beginning which reads: 'Now, if the Evangelist said here that Christ was baptizing, he did not make this statement with the meaning that He Himself was baptizing, but that the work performed by the disciples included the Teacher; and I say this because further on He said,' etc.
5 Luke 3.16.

and why did he persist in this until he was cast into prison? For, the words: 'John was also baptizing in Aennon,' followed by: 'For he had not yet been put into prison,' plainly indicate that he did not stop doing this until then. 'Why,' you will ask, 'did he continue baptizing until then? Indeed, he would have shown that the disciples of Jesus were of greater prestige if, when they began to baptize, he himself refrained. Why, then, did he continue baptizing?'

He continued to do so that he might not rouse his own disciples to greater resentment and make them more contentious. For if, when he kept proclaiming Christ over and over again, and ever retired from first place in favor of Him and made himself so much less than He, he still could not persuade them to go over to Him, he would have made them much more contentious, if he had, besides, ceased to baptize.

And that is why Christ began to preach in full vigor only when John was out of the way. Indeed, I think that for this reason the death of John was allowed and took place very speedily, so that the mind of the multitude might come over altogether to Christ, and no longer be split into contrary opinions about both leaders.

But besides this, even while baptizing, he did not cease to admonish them continually and to point out the great and holy prerogatives of Jesus. He was baptizing for no other reason than that they might believe in Him who was to come after him. Well, then, how would a man who was so preaching have made the disciples of Jesus appear to be worthy of esteem if he ceased?

Indeed, if he ceased baptizing he might, contrariwise, have seemed to do so because of envy or anger, but by continuing to preach he made his testimony stronger. For he did not seize upon the glory for himself, but sent his listeners off to Christ. And so he assisted Him no less than His disciples did—even much more—because his testimony was proportionately above reproach, as his reputation was greater than theirs in the eyes of all. Actually, the Evangelist said this in effect, in the words: 'There went out to him all Judea and all the region about the Jordan and they were baptized by him.'[6] And even though the disciples [of Christ] were baptizing, many still did not desist from flocking to him.

Now, if someone should inquire what greater efficacy the baptism of the disciples had than that of John, we reply that it had no greater power. For, each one alike was without the grace of the Spirit, and all had a single purpose in baptizing: to bring the baptized to Christ. Moreover, in order that they might not be obliged to gather together those who ought to believe, by hastening in search of them—as Simon's brother did to him, and Philip to Nathanael—they were appointed to baptize, so that by this means all would be brought to them effortlessly and they would prepare the way for the future faith.

Now, the text that follows makes clear that each of these baptisms had no more value than the other. What, then, is this text? 'There arose a discussion about purification between some of John's disciples and a Jew.'[7] For the disciples of John, ever disposed to be envious of the disciples of Christ and of Christ Himself, when they saw them baptizing, began to argue with those who were baptized on the ground that the baptism they administered had more value than that of the disciples of Christ. And, laying hold of one of those who had been baptized, they sought to convince him, but they did not succeed. Notice how the Evangelist said by implication that they were the ones who hastened to the attack, and it was not their victim who started the quarrel. He did not say: 'A certain Jew had a discussion with them,' but: 'A

---

6 Matt. 3.5.
7 The singular, as found in St. John Chrysostom, is that of the Greek New Testament, though the plural, ('the Jews,' which is the reading in the Confraternity translation) is supported by a strong manuscript tradition. Cf. Merk, annotation on John 3.25.

discussion about purification arose between some of John's disciples and a Jew.'

Reflect, also, on the Evangelist's mildness. He did not use furious language, but softened the charge as much as he could, saying merely that a discussion arose, since the text that follows makes it clear that the remarks had been made from envy, though he composed this text also in mild terms. For he said: 'They came to John and said to him, "Rabbi, he who was with thee beyond the Jordan, to whom thou hast borne witness, behold he baptizes and all are coming to him," ' that is, 'He whom you baptized.' This is what they implied when they said: 'to whom thou hast borne witness,' as if to say: 'He whom you pointed out and made famous is daring to do the same things as you.'

They did not, however, say 'whom you baptized,' for surely they would have been forced also to recall the Voice sent down from above and the descent of the Spirit. But what did they say? 'He who was with thee beyond the Jordan, to whom thou hast borne witness,' that is, 'He who filled the position of disciple, who had no greater prestige than we, this man has cut Himself off from you and is baptizing.' Not only by this fact did they think to nettle him, but also by putting his standing in question. So they said: 'All are coming to Him.' From this it is evident that they had not convinced the Jew with whom they had held the discussion. Moreover, they spoke in this way because they were still imperfectly disposed and were not yet purified of a love of empty fame.

What, then, did John reply? He did not find fault with them severely, lest they might break away once more from him and work some other evil. What did he say? 'No one can receive anything unless it is given to him from heaven.' Now, do not wonder that he spoke somewhat belittlingly of Christ, for it was not possible to give the entire doctrine right from the start to those afflicted with such a malady [as envy].

But he desired for the moment to terrify and frighten them by showing that they were contending against none other than God when they contended against Him. Gamaliel, indeed, also said this: 'You will not be able to overthrow it. Else perhaps you may find yourselves fighting even against God';[8] and John himself here was, in a subtle way, leading up to this. For, one who spoke the words: 'No one can receive anything unless it is given to him from heaven' meant by them nothing else than that they were attacking unassailable truths and that in consequence they were to be rated as enemies of God.

What, then? Did not Theodas and his followers 'receive' from themselves?[9] Yes, they did. But at once they were dispersed and perished. The works of Christ, however, were not such as these. Hence, he gently gave them counsel, teaching them that He who was showing Himself superior to them was not a mere man, but God. Therefore, they must not be surprised if His works became far-famed and all came to Him, for such developments were divine and it was God who was bringing them about. Indeed, if He were not, such things would never have been so potent. 'Everything human, to be sure, is ephemeral and changing, and quickly passes, and perishes; but these things are not so; therefore, they are not of men.'

Further, notice how, inasmuch as they had said: 'To whom thou hast borne witness,' John then turned this, too, against them, though they thought they were bringing it forward to the disparagement of Christ. For, having first shown that glory did not come to Him from his testimony, he then silenced them from their own words. 'No one can receive anything unless it is given to him from heaven,' he said.

---

8 Acts 5.39.
9 Cf. Acts 5.34-36: 'Some time ago there rose up Theodas, claiming to be somebody, and a number of men, about four hundred, joined him; but he was slain and all his followers dispersed and he was brought to nothing.'

What does this mean? 'If you subscribe altogether to my testimony,' he said, 'and think that it is true, you know that especially by reason of it you must not prefer me to Him, but Him to me. For, what testimony did I give? I call on you as witnesses of it.'

Therefore, he went on: 'You yourselves bear me witness that I said: "I am not the Christ but have been sent before him." Well, then, if it was out of esteem for my testimony that you brought forward those arguments to me, when you said: "To whom thou hast borne witness," not only is He not made inferior by receiving my testimony, but He is to be held in greater esteem by reason of it. Besides, the testimony was not mine, but that of God. And so, if I seem to you to be trustworthy, consider that, among other things, I said: "I have been sent before him." '

Do you perceive how he showed gradually that the Voice [which spoke at the baptism] was divine? What he meant is something like this: 'I am a servant and I speak the words of Him who sent me, not giving way to Christ to win human favor, but giving my service to His Father who sent me. Surely, I did not do Him a favor by my testimony, but I said what I was sent to say. Do not, then, on this account think that I am something great. Indeed, this proves that He is something great. For He is the Lord of all things.' And to show this he went on once more to say: 'He who has the bride is the bridegroom; but the friend of the bridegroom, who stands and hears him, rejoices exceedingly at the voice of the bridegroom.'

Now, how is it that he who said: 'I am not worthy to loose the strap of His sandal,' now declared that he was His friend? It was not to exalt or praise himself that he said this, but out of a desire to show that he himself also was especially promoting this,[10] and that these things were taking

---

10 I.e., Christ's increasing popularity.

place, neither against his will nor to his distress, but with his whole-hearted co-operation. Besides, he desired to show that it was especially with a view to this that he was exerting every effort. And these things he very modestly implied by the appellation of 'friend.'

The servants of the bridegroom do not rejoice and take pleasure in such things as his friends do. He did not, then, mean that he was to be esteemed equally (perish the thought!), but said that he was His friend, out of a desire to show the abundance of his joy, and at the same time to condescend to their weakness. He had implied, to be sure, that he was His servant by saying: 'I have been sent before him.' On this account, accordingly, and because they thought that he was vexed at the turn of events, he called himself 'the friend of the bridegroom': to prove that not only was he not vexed, but even rejoiced very much.

Well, then,' he meant, 'inasmuch as I have come to bring about this very thing, I am proportionately far from being distressed at what has been done, since, if it were not done, I would be exceedingly distressed. If the bride had not come to the Bridegroom, then I would have been aggrieved; but not now,' he said, 'since my task has been accomplished. And this is so for, when His affairs prosper, it is I who prosper, for what I wished has taken place, and the bride recognizes the Bridegroom. Indeed, you yourselves also bear witness to this when you say: "All are coming to him." In truth, this is the object for which I have been striving, and for this end I have been performing all my works. Wherefore, at seeing this outcome I rejoice, and am glad, and leap for joy.'

Now, what is the meaning of the text: 'Who stands and hears him rejoices exceedingly at the voice of the bridegroom'? He has shifted his discourse from the parable to its underlying theme. Since he had called to mind bride and bridegroom, he pointed out how the espousals take place, namely, by word and instruction. For thus it is that the Church is espoused to

God. Wherefore, Paul also has said: 'Faith depends on hearing, and hearing on the word of God.'[11] 'At this Voice, then, I rejoice.'

He used the words 'who stands' with a purpose: to show that his office had ceased and that, when he had given over the bride to Him, henceforth he must stand and listen to Him. He also desired to show that he was a minister and servant, and that the aspirations of his fair hope and joy had reached fulfillment in what had been done. Therefore, to make this clear he also added the words: 'This my joy, therefore, is made full,' that is, 'The work has been accomplished by me as it ought to have been done, and in future I can accomplish nothing more.'

Next, to curb not only their present jealousy but also that which might be suffered in future, he proceeded to speak also of the future, making his words credible by the things already said and done. For this reason he went on to say: 'He must increase, but I must decrease,' that is, 'My fame is at a standstill and has ceased for the future, while His is on the increase. Therefore, what you have feared is not only an actuality, but is going to become much more so. Indeed, it is this which most of all makes my reputation famous: on this account, in truth, have I come, and I rejoice that His interests have made much progress and that those developments have taken place for the sake of which I have performed all my actions.' Do you perceive how, calmly and with great wisdom, he soothed their anxiety, and extinguished the fire of envy, and showed that they were attempting the impossible? This is a method by which evil can generally be checked.

It was for this reason that in the plan of Providence these things took place while he was still living and baptizing: that they might have him as a witness to Christ's pre-eminence, and have no excuse if they did not believe. John did

---

11 Rom. 10.17.

not come of his own accord to say these things, nor at the request of outsiders; they themselves made the inquiry and listened to the answer. Moreover, if he had spoken of his own accord, they would not even then have believed him when in answer to their inquiry they heard Him reply that they already had his testimony in disparagement of himself. Similarly, the Jews also deprived themselves of all excuse, especially for this reason; namely, that they sent messengers to him, from their homes, and, when they heard what they did hear, they did not believe.

What, then, are we taught from this? That vainglory is the cause of all evils, for it led them to envy. When they had quieted down a little, the latter once more roused them to action, and therefore, going to Jesus they said: 'Why do thy disciples not fast?'[12] Let us then, beloved, flee from this passion. For, if we flee from it we shall escape hell. Indeed, its fire seizes on the vainglorious in particular, so much has vainglory extended its rule everywhere and despotically taken possession of every age and every dignity.

It has thrown churches into confusion, it spoils political affairs, it upsets entire homes, and cities, and peoples, and nations. And why do you wonder if it has come even into the desert and displayed its great power even there? Those who have bade farewell many times to wealth and to all the empty display of the world, and who associate with no one, and who have subdued the more imperious lusts of the body, frequently have lost the merit of all these as a result of being caught by vainglory. On account of this vice the Pharisee who had expended effort on many things went off with less to his credit than the publican who had worked hard at nothing but committing sins by the thousand—and all because of this disease of vainglory.[13]

However, it is no task to castigate the vice (for all men

12 Matt. 9.14.
13 Cf. Luke 18.9-14.

agree in that); the object to be sought is how to overcome it. How, then, do we overcome it? If we exchange true glory for vainglory. For, just as we scorn earthly wealth when we look to other riches, and despise this life when we fix our mind on that much better one, so also we shall be able to reject the glory here when we fix our mind on that glory which is holier by far than this; namely, real glory. In truth, the former is vain and foolish, with a name empty of substance, while the latter is true, and from heaven, and has as eulogists not men, but angels, and archangels, nay, rather, it has even men also, together with Him.

If you look to that theatre, if you have learned the lesson of those crowns, if you lean on the applause from that quarter, it will never be possible for the things of this world to hinder you, nor will you esteem present things as great, nor will you seek for those that pass. And this is so, for in the royal palace no guard who stands near the king, ignoring the one who wears a diadem and sits on the throne, wastes his time on the cries of crows, or the noise of flies and gnats as they flit about and buzz. The praises of men, indeed, are no better than these.

Well, then, since we know the worthlessness of human values, let us gather all things into a safe treasury, and let us seek the glory which lasts and is inviolable. May all of you obtain this glory by the grace and mercy of our Lord Jesus Christ, through whom and with whom glory be to the Father, together with the Holy Spirit, now and always, and throughout the endless ages of eternity. Amen.

Homily 30 (John 3.31-34)

'He who comes from above is over all. He who is from the earth belongs to earth, and of the earth he speaks.'[1]

---

1 John 3.31.

The love of glory is a terrible things, terrible and prolific of many evils. It is a kind of thorn, hard to remove; or a wild beast, impossible to tame; a many-headed monster, taking up arms against the very ones who feed it. Just as the worm gnaws through the wood by which it is generated, and the rust feeds on the iron whence it proceeds, and moths feed on wool, so also does vainglory destroy the soul that feeds it. Wherefore, we must be very much in earnest if we are to get rid of this disease.

Indeed, notice here again what long incantations John chanted over his disciples who were afflicted with this disease, and with difficulty he mollified them. Besides the words upon which we have already commented, he showered them with still others. With what kind? He said: 'He who comes from above is over all. He who is from the earth belongs to earth, and of the earth he speaks.' He meant: 'Since you are spreading my testimony everywhere, and saying that I am more worthy of belief, it is necessary for you to know this: that it is not possible for Him who comes from heaven to be rendered worthy of belief through the agency of one who dwells on earth.'

But what is the meaning of the expression: 'is over all'? And what did he wish to indicate by it? The meaning is as follows. By this expression he made it clear that Christ needs no one, but is Himself sufficient to Himself and that He is incomparably greater than all men. Further, he said that he himself 'is from the earth and speaks of the earth,' not in the sense that he was drawing on his own ideas, as he preached, but in the way that Christ said: 'If I have spoken of earthly things to you, and you do not believe.'

Christ referred to baptism in this way, not because it was of earth, but because He was using it in contrast with His ineffable generation. So also in this context, when John said that he was speaking of the earth, He was comparing his teaching with that of Christ. For, 'speaking of the earth' means nothing else than 'My teachings are small and of little account, and of little value, compared with His, and are such as are suitable for earthy nature to receive.' For, in Him 'are hidden all the treasures of wisdom.'[2] That he was not speaking of human reasoning is plain from the context.

'He who is from the earth belongs to earth,' he declared. Yet, not everything he had was from the earth, but his chief possessions were from heaven. And I say this because he had a soul and he had his participation in the Spirit and these possessions were not from the earth. How is it, then, that he asserted that he himself was from the earth? In this he was saying by implication nothing else than: 'I am little, and worthy of no consideration, inasmuch as I come from clay and have been born on the earth; but Christ comes to us from above.'

Accordingly, having first snuffed out this passion[3] by all these words, he finally spoke about Christ with more confidence. Before this it would have been vain to give vent to such ideas, since they would never be able to secure a place in the minds of his listeners. But when he had drawn out the thorns, he finally began to cast the seed with confidence, and said: 'He who comes from heaven is over all. And he bears witness to that which he has seen and heard, and his witness no one receives.'

Since he had said something great and sublime about Him, once again he brought his words to a lowlier level, for the words, 'that which he has seen and heard,' are expressed in a somewhat human fashion. Christ did not, of course, come to the knowledge of what He knows by perceiving it by sight or hearing. He possessed everything in His nature, as He came forth perfect from the Father's bosom, and did not

---

2 Col. 2.3.
3 I.e., vainglory.

need a teacher. For He said: 'As the Father knows me, I know the Father.'[4]

What, then, is the meaning of the expressions, 'what he has heard,' 'he speaks,' and 'he bears witness to what he has seen'? Inasmuch as it is by these senses that we accurately learn everything, and we seem to be reliable instructors in regard to those things which we either perceive by sight or learn by hearing—recounting them without elaboration or lying—John wished to give this impression here when he said: 'That which He has seen and heard.' That is, none of His teachings is false, but all are true. So, in truth, we also often ask inquisitively: 'Have you heard? Have you seen?' And if this is affirmed, the information given is considered to be without question.

Now, He Himself said: 'As I hear, I judge'; and: 'The things that I heard from my Father, these I speak'; and: 'We bear witness to what we have seen,'[5] and many other similar things. These He asserted, not that we might imagine that He uttered His words only after instruction (for to think this is the furthest extreme of madness), but He spoke in this way that nothing of what He said might be called in question by the hard-headed Jews. Since they by no means held the opinion of Him that was fitting, He continually referred them to His Father and thus established what He said as true.

Now, why do you wonder that He referred them to His Father, since He often also had recourse to the Prophets and the Scriptures? For example, when He said: 'It is they that bear witness to me.'[6] Surely, then, we should say that He is inferior to the Prophets, since He drew on them for testimony to Himself? Perish the thought! It is because of the imperfection of His hearers that He conducted His words along these paths and declared that He said what He did

4 John 10.15.
5 John 5.30; 8.26; 3.11.
6 John 5.40.

after hearing it from His Father. It was not that He needed someone to teach Him what to say, but that they might believe that nothing of what was said was false.

Now, what John meant was some such thing as the following: 'I need to hear His teachings, for He comes from above, heralding heavenly truths which He Himself alone knows clearly.' The words 'He has seen and heard' truly mean this. 'And His witness no one receives.' Yet He also had disciples and many were attentive to His words. How was it, then, that John said that 'no one' received them? Here he said this in the sense of 'few,' because, if he meant 'no one,' how could he have added: 'He who receives his witness has set his seal on this, that God is true'?

Here he was also upbraiding his own disciples on the ground that they were not going to give him much credence in the future, for it is plain from later texts that they did not believe his words even after this. Indeed, it was on this account that even while in prison he sent them from there to Him, in order that he might bind them more closely to Him. Moreover, at that time they had difficulty in believing as Christ also implied when He said: 'And blessed is he who is not scandalized in me.'[7] Well, then, John said: 'And His witness no one receives,' for no other reason than to safeguard his own disciples, saying in effect: 'Do not think that, since only a few will believe in Him, His words are false for this reason.' For, he said, 'He bears witness to that which he has seen.'

At the same time, he said this also as a reproach to the Jewish insensibility. Moreover, the Evangelist at the outset leveled this reproach also at them, when he said: 'He came unto his own, and his own received him not.'[8] Now, this is not His fault, but those who did not receive Him are answerable for it.

---

7 Matt. 11.6.
8 John 1.11.

'He who receives his witness has set his seal on this, that God is true.' Here he also inspired them with fear, for he made it clear that he who does not believe Him is unbelieving, not only toward Him, but toward the Father also. Therefore, he also added the words: 'He whom God has sent speaks the words of God.' Therefore, 'Since he utters His words, both he who believes has faith in Him and he who does not believe is unbelieving toward Him.'

Now, the words 'has set his seal on' mean 'has shown.' Having said this, he added, to increase their fear still more, 'that God is true,' to indicate that a man could not disbelieve Christ without accusing of falsity God who had sent Him. Since, then, none of His teachings is separate from those of the Father, and all His are the Father's, he who does not listen to Him does not listen to Him who sent Him. Do you perceive how John confounded them by these words, also? For, thus far they thought it no great thing not to listen to Christ. And it was for this reason that he pointed out that such great danger threatened unbelievers, in order that they might be convinced that they who do not listen to Christ are refusing to listen to God Himself.

Next, he continued with the following words, condescending to the lowliness of their understanding and saying: 'For not by measure does God give the Spirit.' Once more, as I have said, he brought his speech down to a lower plane, varying it and making it more readily comprehensible for those who were then listening. For it was not possible otherwise to arouse them and increase their fear. If, indeed, he said anything great and sublime about Him, they would not have believed it but would have regarded it with scorn. Therefore, he referred everything to the Father, speaking of Christ the while, as if of a man.

But what is the meaning of the words: 'Not by measure does God give the Spirit'? He wished to point out that we all have received the operation of the Spirit in measure, for here 'Spirit' means His operation, since it is this which is imparted. But He possesses the entire operation of the Spirit, without measure and in its fullness. Now, if the operation of the Spirit which He possesses is without measure, much more so is His substance. You perceive that the Spirit is without limit? Well, then, how would it be right to hold in question Him who has received the operation of the Spirit in its entirety, who knows the things of God, who said: 'We speak of what we have heard, and we bear witness to what we have seen'?[9] For He says nothing which is not of God and nothing which is not of the Spirit.

And for the moment John did not speak explicitly of the Word of God, but made his teaching authoritative by referring to the Father and the Spirit. His listeners knew that God exists, and they understood that the Spirit exists—even though they did not have the right idea of Him; however, they did not know that the Son exists. That is why he continually referred them to the Father and to the Spirit, so as to establish the truth of his words from Them.

If, putting aside this explanation, one should examine the passage on its face value, it truly falls quite short of the true dignity of Christ. It was not by reason of the fact that He possesses the operation of the Spirit that He was worthy of their faith, since He does not need support from that source, but is Himself sufficient to Himself. But, for the moment, John was refuting the suspicion [that Christ was inferior] entertained by imperfect men, because he wished to lead them up gradually from their state of imperfection.

I mention these details in order that we may not run quickly over the things lying hidden in the Scriptures, but may observe also the point of view of the speaker, the imperfections of the audience, and many other details in them. Indeed, teachers do not say all things as they desire, but say many things as the dispositions of imperfect listeners

9 John 3.12.

demand. Wherefore, Paul also said: 'I could not speak to you as to spiritual men but only as carnal. I fed you with milk, not with solid food.'[10] He meant: 'I wished, indeed, to speak as to spiritual men, but I was not able.' How was that? It was not because he himself was unable, but because they were not able to listen as spiritual men. So John also wished to teach his disciples certain great truths, but they could not yet bear to accept them; for this reason he dwelt chiefly upon less sublime ideas.

It is necessary, then, to interpret everything with care. We must do this, for our spiritual weapons are the words of the Scriptures. If we do not know how to fit on the armor and to arm our disciples well, the armor has its own strength, but it cannot help those who receive it. For example, let us suppose we have a strong breastplate, and a helmet, and a shield, and a spear. Then, suppose someone takes these weapons and places the breastplate around his feet, and the helmet over his eyes instead of his head, and does not hold the shield in front of his chest, but obstinately tries to fit it around his feet. Surely, he will not be able to enjoy any benefit from these weapons? On the contrary, will he not actually suffer harm from them? Certainly; it is obvious. However, it is not by reason of the weakness of the weapons, but because of the person who does not know how to use them well. Thus it is in the case of the Scriptures, also. If we throw their orderly array into confusion, they will have their own power even so, but we shall gain no assistance.

Though I say these things to you continually, both in private and in public, I accomplish nothing further. I am saying this because I see you spending all your time in temporal affairs, while you do not even partake of spiritual things in sleep. For this reason our life is ineffectual, and even while striving in behalf of truth, our efforts are not

10 1 Cor. 3.1,2.

of much avail; we are a laughing-stock to the heathen, and to the Jews, and to the heretics.

If, while you were negligent with regard to other affairs, you showed the same slackness also in spiritual things, not even in that case would your conduct be deserving of excuse. But, as it is, each one is keener than a sword in temporal affairs—both those who pursue the arts and those who engage in political affairs. In essential and spiritual things, on the contrary, we are most sluggish of all, treating less important works as if essential, while considering as not even slightly important those works which we ought to rate as most important of all.

Or do you not know that what has been written [in the Scriptures] has been composed, not for the sake of men of olden times, but on our account? Do you not hear Paul saying: 'These things were written for our correction, upon whom the final age of the world has come, that through the patience and the consolation afforded by the Scriptures we may have hope'?[11]

Now, I am aware that I am speaking without effect, but I shall not cease speaking. For by acting in this way I shall be justified before God, even if there be no one listening to me. To be sure, he who addresses an attentive audience has the consolation of speaking to receptive listeners. However, he who continues to preach, and, though not listened to, does not cease speaking, would be deserving of more credit, because, in accordance with what seems best to God, he is performing his duty completely, even though no one is paying attention.

Nevertheless, even if we obtain a greater reward from your failure to listen, we desire our reward rather to be lessened, and your hope of salvation to be increased, since we consider your well-being a great reward. Moreover, we

---

11 1 Cor. 10.11; Rom. 15.4.

are now saying these things, not to make our discourse unpleasant and burdensome, but to show you the grief we experience over your sluggishness.

May it be that all of us, being rid of this, may possess an eager desire for spiritual things and attain to the blessings of heaven, by the grace and mercy of our Lord Jesus Christ, with whom glory be to the Father, together with the Holy Spirit, forever and ever. Amen.

Homily 31 (John 3.35-4.12)

'The Father loves the Son, and has given all things into his hand. He who believes in the Son has everlasting life; he who is unbelieving towards the Son shall not see life, but the wrath of God rests upon him.'[1]

The great advantage of moderation can be demonstrated in all affairs of life. Thus, in mastering the arts we have not learned everything at once from our teachers. Similarly, we have constructed our cities by degrees, setting them up slowly and gradually. By this means we keep order in our life.

Moreover, do not be surprised if this quality is so important in the things of this life, since you will also find that in the things of the spirit the power of this prudent moderation is great. Thus the Jews were able to be rid of idolatry, by being persuaded slowly and gradually, and hearing no lofty teaching in the beginning with regard either to doctrine or to practice. Thus, after the coming of Christ, when it was the time for somewhat more sublime teaching, the Apostles won over all men by refraining at first from teaching anything too deep. And Christ adopted this practice toward most men from the start. So John also has done now [in the text we are considering], speaking of Christ as if merely

---

1 John 3.35,36.

of an unusual man, and only indirectly including lofty ideas.

Commencing in this way, indeed, he said: 'No one can receive anything of himself.' Next, having brought in something lofty by saying: 'He who comes from heaven is over all,' once more he brought his discourse down to a lower level, saying, among other things: 'Not by measure does God give the Spirit'; then he added: 'The Father loves the Son and has given all things into his hand.'

Next, knowing the benefit derived from the mention of punishment, and that most men are convinced not so much by being made aware of rewards as by the threat of punishment, he finally concluded his discourse at this level by saying: 'He who believes in the Son has everlasting life; he who is unbelieving towards the Son shall not see life, but the wrath of God rests upon him.' Here once more he referred the mention of punishment to the Father, for he did not say: 'The wrath of the Son,' though He is the Judge, but threatened them with the Father, desiring to frighten them more.

'Is it not, therefore, enough to believe in the Son.' you will say, 'to have eternal life?' By no means. Listen to Christ making this point clear by saying: 'Not everyone who says to me, "Lord, Lord," shall enter into the kingdom of heaven.'[2] Furthermore, blasphemy against the Spirit is sufficient, even of itself, to cast into hell. But why do I mention only part of the doctrine? Even if one believes in an orthodox manner in the Father and the Son and the Holy Spirit, but does not live a moral life, he does not gain profit from his faith for his salvation.

Therefore, even when He says: 'Now this is everlasting life, that they may know thee, the only true God,'[3] let us not think that the knowledge mentioned is of itself sufficient for salvation for us. We also need uprightness of life and

2 Matt. 7.21.
3 John 17.3.

character, for, if he did say here: 'He who believes in the Son has everlasting life,' he put still more forcibly what follows. Indeed, it was not only from rewards but also from their opposite that he selected matter for his discourse. And notice how. For he added: 'He who is unbelieving towards the Son shall not see life, but the wrath of God rests upon him.'

Nevertheless, not even from this statement do we conclude that faith alone is sufficient for salvation. The words of the Evangelists, which frequently treat the subject of conduct, make this clear. For this reason he did not say: 'This alone is everlasting life,' or: 'He who just believes in the Son has everlasting life,' but in each case he showed that, if a man fulfills a certain condition, he has everlasting life. However, if an upright life does not accompany faith, severe punishment will follow.

He did not say 'awaits him,' but 'rests upon him,' to indicate that the wrath of God will never be separated from him. He has added this clause which shows that it settles on him perpetually, in order that you may not think that the words 'shall not see life' mean temporal death, but may believe that the punishment is everlasting. And he did this to induce them by these words to go over to Christ. Therefore, he did not give them this admonition in private, but in common and as convincingly as he could. He did not say: 'If you should believe,' and: 'If you should not believe,' but stated what he said in the third person so as to place it beyond misunderstanding.

This he did even more emphatically than Christ. Christ said: 'He who does not believe is already judged,' while John said: ['He who is unbelieving toward the Son] shall not see life, but the wrath of God rests upon him.' And it was very fitting for him to do this. For it was not the same for a person to speak about himself, as for another to do so about him. They would have thought that Christ, on the one hand, was saying these things out of ambition and was boasting, but John was free of this suspicion. And if Christ later also made use of more forcible language, it was only when they finally had a high opinion of Him.

'When, therefore, Jesus knew that the Pharisees had heard that Jesus made and baptized more disciples than John—although Jesus did not baptize, but his disciples—he left Judea and went again into Galilee.' He Himself, then, did not baptize, but the informers, wishing to arouse the envy of their hearers, reported that He did. 'Why, then, did He go away?' you will say. It was not because of cowardice, but to cut short their malice and to soften their envy.

It was indeed possible for Him to hold His aggressors in check, but He did not wish to do this continually, in order not to weaken faith in the Incarnation. For if, after being overcome, He repeatedly escaped [miraculously], many would have held this doctrine in question. Therefore, He did many things in a somewhat human way. For, just as He wished it to be believed that He was God, so also he wished it to be believed that, being God, He assumed human flesh.

For this reason even after the Resurrection He said to the disciple: 'Feel me and see; for a spirit does not have flesh and bones, as you see I have.'[4] That is why also He found fault with Peter when he said: 'Far be it from thee, O Lord; this will never happen to thee.'[5] Thus, this consideration was an object of very great concern to Him.

Indeed, this doctrine forms no small part of the teachings of the Church, and is its chief doctrine with regard to our salvation and the one through which all things have come to exist and are directed. Through it death has been destroyed, and sin has been removed, and the curse has vanished, and countless blessings have come into our lives. Therefore, He was most desirous that the divine dispensation be believed

---

4 Luke 24.39.
5 Matt. 16.22.

in, since it is the root and source of innumerable blessings for us. But, while making provision for His humanity, He did not wish His divinity to be overshadowed. So, after withdrawing [into Galilee], He continued to follow the same course of action as before.

Now, He did not withdraw to Galilee without purpose, but went to perform a significant mission among the Samaritans. Moreover, He went not merely to do this, but with the prudence befitting Himself and so as to leave to the Jews no ground for shameless justifying of themselves. The Evangelist, to imply this, has added: 'Now he had to pass through Samaria,' showing that He was going there incidentally to His journey. Further, the Apostles [subsequently] did the same thing. For, just as it was when they were persecuted by the Jews that they went to the Gentiles, so also Christ, when they had driven Him away, took the Gentiles in hand, as He did, too, in the case of the Syrophoenician woman.

In fact, this happened in order to deprive the Jews of all ground of complaint and not to allow them to say: 'He has abandoned us and has gone over to the uncircumcised.' For this reason, also, His disciples later used to say to justify themselves: 'It was necessary that the word of God should be spoken to you first, but since you judge yourselves unworthy of eternal life, behold, we now turn to the Gentiles.'[6] And He Himself, again: 'I was not sent except to the lost sheep of the house of Israel.' And, once more: 'It is not fair to take the children's bread and to cast it to the dogs.'[7] But, since they had driven Him away, they had opened the door for the Gentiles.

Even so, He did not go to them by preference, but incidentally. Incidentally, then, 'He came to a town of Samaria called Sichar, near the field that Jacob gave to his son

---

6 Acts 13.46.
7 Matt. 15.24,26.
8 Cf. Gen. 48.22; Jos. 24.32.

Joseph.[8] Now Jacob's well was there.' Why is the Evangelist precise about the place? In order that, when you hear the woman saying: 'Our father Jacob gave us this well,' you may not be unfamiliar with the information. For that is the place where Levi and Simeon and their followers, roused to anger because of the wrong done to Dina, perpetrated that terrible slaughter.[9]

At this point it is also appropriate to tell whence the Samaritans originated. I say this, because the entire region is called Samaria. From what source, then, did they derive this name? The mountain is called Semer from the man who had taken possession of it,[10] as Isaias also said: 'And the head of Samaria, Ephraim.'[11] The inhabitants, however, were called, not Samaritans, but Israelites. But as time went on, they transgressed against God, and during the reign of Phacee, Theglathphalasar went up and seized many cities.[12] After attacking and killing Ela, he gave the kingdom over to Osee.[13]

Later, Salmanasar came and captured other cities and made them subject and tributary.[14] However, though Osee at first yielded, he revolted afterwards from subjection and took refuge in the aid of the Ethiopians.[15] The Assyrian learned this, and, having made an expedition and taken them captive, forbade the nation to remain there any longer, because he suspected the possibility of another such revolt.

9 Cf. Gen. 34.
10 Cf. 3 Kings 16.24.
11 Isa. 7.9. The Challoner revision of Douay-Rheims reads: 'The head of Ephraim is Samaria.' The Benedictine editor notes that the latter reading agrees with the Septuagint, Hebrew, and Vulgate versions, and accounts for the slight discrepancy here by suggesting that the writer was probably quoting from memory. The minor inaccuracies to be found in the passage that follows would seem to support this theory.
12 Cf. 4 Kings 15.29.
13 This is a slight departure from the facts as related in 4 Kings 15.30.
14 Cf. 4 Kings 17.3-6.
15 Actually, the Egyptians; cf. 4 Kings 17.4. In the following details of the history of the Samaritans St. John Chrysostom draws on 4 Kings 17 *passim*.

These inhabitants, moreover, he transported to Babylon and Medea and, having brought from various regions the people dwelling in that vicinity, he caused them to dwell in Samaria so that his power might be safeguarded for the future, with loyal inhabitants in possession of the place.

When these things had taken place, God, wishing to show His power and that He had given over the Jews not because of any lack of power on His part, but because of the sins of those whom He had surrendered to their enemies, sent lions upon the barbarians, and these preyed on the entire nation. This was reported to the king, and he sent a certain priest to give to them the laws of God. Nevertheless, not even then were they freed entirely from their impiety, but only partly. However, as time went on they turned away from idols and worshiped God. When things had reached this point, the Jews, finally returning, showed a contentious spirit towards them as foreigners and enemies,[16] and named them 'Samaritans' after the mountain.

Moreover, the Jews had a great aversion toward them ever afterwards. They did not recognize all the Scriptures, but accepted Moses only and did not make much account of the other Prophets. However, they strove aggressively to force themselves into the Jewish noble line, and showed honor to Abraham and wrote him down as their ancestor, since he was from Chaldea. They also called Jacob their father, since he was a descendant of the former. The Jews as well as all other [peoples] detested them.

That is why they taunted Christ by saying: 'Thou art a Samaritan, and hast a devil.'[17] And because of this attitude, it was a Samaritan that Christ brought to the man who went down from Jerusalem to Jericho as the one 'who took pity on him,'[18] that is, the man of no account, despised, con-

---

16 Cf. Eccli. 50.27,28.
17 John 8.48.
18 Luke 10.37.

temptible in their eyes. And of the ten lepers, he calls the one [who returned] a 'foreigner' for this reason, that 'he was a Samaritan.'[19] Further, He Himself gave the following instruction to His disciples: 'Do not go in the direction of the Gentiles, nor enter a town of Samaritans.'[20]

It was not merely for the sake of the history of the place that the Evangelist recalled Jacob to our minds, but also to call attention to the casting out of the Jews that had taken place before this time. In the time of their ancestors, in truth, they occupied the region instead of the Samaritans. For the latter had laid waste the possessions won by the ancestors of the Jews, because of the sluggishness and disobedience of those Jews who then held them. Thus, there is no profit in being descended from noble ancestors, if the descendants do not happen to be of like character. The barbarians, indeed, after being punished once, straightway returned to the Jewish worship; while the Jews, though subjected to such great chastisements, did not acquire wisdom even as a result of this.

Christ, then, came to this place, scorning as always to indulge in a soft and easy life, and following by preference one that was laborious and painful. He did not use beasts of burden, but traveled on foot so strenuously that He was tired out from the journey. Invariably He taught us to work with our hands, to be simple, and not to want many possessions. Therefore, He wishes us to be strangers to superfluities so that we even do without many actual necessities. For this reason He said: 'The foxes have dens, and the birds of the air have nests; but the Son of Man has nowhere to lay his head.'[21] And that is why He spent frequent periods in the mountains and in the deserts, not only by day, but also by night. David, indeed, foretold this when he said:

---

19 Luke 17.16,18.
20 Matt. 10.5.
21 Matt. 8.20.

'From the brook by the wayside he will drink,'[22] to show the simplicity of His way of life.

Moreover, John also pointed this out here: 'Jesus therefore, wearied as he was from the journey, was sitting at the well. It was about the sixth hour. There came a Samaritan woman to draw water. Jesus said to her, "Give me to drink"; for his disciples had gone away into the town to buy food.' From this text we learn both His endurance with regard to journeys and His disregard of food, and also how casually He treated the matter of food.

The disciples, indeed, were taught to manage their own affairs also in this way, for they did not take food with them. In fact, another Evangelist made this clear by saying that, when He spoke to them of the leaven of the Pharisees, they thought that it was because they had brought no bread.[23] Further, when he mentioned that they were hungry, and that they plucked ears of corn and ate them,[24] and when he asserted that He came to the fig-tree because of hunger,[25] by all these references he taught us nothing else than to have contempt for our appetite, and not to think that provision to satisfy it is to be an object of great solicitude. Moreover, look at them in this instance also. They neither brought anything with them, nor, though they had not brought it, did they take thought for it right at the start of the day, but went to buy food only at the time when all would breakfast.

However, we are not like them, for we take thought for this before everything else, from the very moment when we rise from our couch. We summon our cooks and stewards, and very carefully give them directions, and in this way occupy ourselves with other matters only afterwards. We take care of earthly needs before spiritual ones, and regard as necessary things which ought to be considered as superfluous. For

---

22 Ps. 109.7.
23 Cf. Matt. 16.6,7.
24 Cf. Matt. 12.1.
25 Cf. Matt. 21.18.

this reason everything is upside down. The contrary ought to be the case; when we have taken much thought for all our spiritual needs, after providing for them, then we ought to take the others in hand.

Not only is [Christ's] endurance of hardship shown by this text, but also His humility: both through His being weary and sitting by the side of the road and through His being left alone while His disciples went off. Yet it was possible, if He wished, either not to send all of them off, or, when they had gone, to have other servants. He did not, however, desire this, for in this way He was accustoming His disciples to trample on all things as vanity.

Now, someone may say: 'What great thing is it if they were not puffed up, since they were fishermen and tent-makers?' Yes, they were fishermen and tentmakers, but they had advanced straight up to the very highest point of heaven, and were holier than any king, since they had been considered worthy to be associates of the Lord of the world, and to accompany everywhere Him who is so much to be admired. Moreover, you know this, also: When men of low estate receive honors, they are more easily elated to the point of foolishness, since they are inexperienced in such marks of esteem. Therefore, to keep them in their humble state of mind, He taught them to be humble in all things and never to require to be served.

But He Himself, 'wearied as he was from the journey, was sitting at the well.' Do you perceive that His being seated there was because of weariness, because of the heat, because He was waiting for His disciples? He knew, indeed, what was going to happen among the Samaritans, but He did not repair to that spot for that reason; only incidentally. Yet, though He did not go there for that reason, it was not necessary for Him to treat the woman harshly when she came, since she showed herself so very thirsty for knowledge.

The Jews, to be sure, drove Him away even when He

came to them, but the Gentiles drew Him to them even when
He was traveling in another direction. Moreover, the former
envied Him, the latter believed in Him; the former were
angry at Him, the latter wondered at and adored Him.
What, then? Ought He ignore the salvation of so many, and
disdain such sincere desire?

This would surely be unworthy of His mercy; therefore,
He directed with wisdom befitting Himself everything which
took place. He sat down beside the well to rest and refresh
His body. And it was noonday, as the Evangelist showed
when he said: 'It was about the sixth hour, and he was
sitting thus.' Now, what does 'thus' mean? He was sitting,
not upon a seat, he meant, or upon a cushion, but simply
and informally on the ground. 'There came a Samaritan
woman to draw water.'

Do you see how he made it clear that the Samaritan woman
also came there for another purpose, always forestalling,
as he was, the impudent attack of the Jews: that no one
might say that in speaking to Samaritans He was transgressing His own precept bidding [His disciples] not to enter
a Samaritan city.[26] That is also the reason why the Evangelist
stated: 'His disciples had gone away into the town to buy
food,' so that He might mention many reasons to account
for His conversation with her.

Then what did the woman do? Having heard the words:
'Give me to drink,' she very cautiously made these words of
Christ an occasion for beginning to question Him, and said:
'How is it that thou, although thou art a Jew, dost ask
drink of me, who am a Samaritan woman? For Jews do not
associate with Samaritans.' Why did she think He was a
Jew? Perhaps from His dress, or from His speech. And notice,
if you please, how discerning the woman was. For, if it was
necessary for anyone to be careful, it was so for Jesus,
not for her. To be sure, she did not say: 'Samaritans do

26 Cf. Matt. 10.5.

not associate with Jews,' but: 'Jews do not approach Samaritans.' Nevertheless, the woman—even though not guilty herself of any fault—because she thought that the other was leaving Himself open to censure, did not remain silent. Instead, she corrected what, according to her way of thinking, was not in accordance with the Law.

However, someone might be puzzled at this and ask how it was that Jesus asked her for a drink, if the Law did not permit this. And if someone should say that it was because He foreknew that she would not give to Him, then on that very account He ought not to have asked. What, then, can be concluded? That it was now a matter of indifference to Him to cast aside such observances as these. Indeed, He who encouraged the others to break them would much more readily transgress them Himself. For it is not that which goes into the mouth which defiles a man, but that which comes out.[27]

Moreover, the conversation with the woman would be no trivial source of reproach to the Jews, because they frequently were drawn to Him by words and deeds and did not yield themselves, while she—see how she was won over by a simple request! He Himself had not as yet begun this work [of the conversion of souls] nor entered upon its path, but if any at all came to Him, He did not prevent them. And He acted thus, for He merely forbade His disciples to enter a Samaritan city, but did not tell them to reject those who approached them, since this was unworthy of His mercy.

Therefore, He answered the woman and said: 'If thou didst know the gift of God and who it is who says to thee, "Give me to drink," thou, perhaps, wouldst have asked of him, and he would have given thee living water.' First He showed that she deserved to be heard and not to be slighted, and then He revealed Himself to her. And He did so because,

---

27 Cf. Matt. 15.11.

as soon as she had learned who He was, she was going to listen to Him and pay attention to Him—something which could not be said of the Jews. For when they had learned His identity they did not request anything of Him or desire to learn anything worth while, but insulted Him and drove Him away.

On the contrary, when the woman had heard these words, see how fittingly she replied: 'Sir, thou hast nothing to draw with, and the well is deep. Whence then hast thou living water?' He now disabused her of her lowly opinion of Him and of the thought that He was an ordinary man. Not without reason did she here call Him 'Sir,' but intended to show Him great respect in doing so. For it is clear from the words that follow that she said this to show respect. She did not ridicule or make fun, though she was in doubt for the moment. And if she did not comprehend everything immediately, do not be surprised, for Nicodemus did not, either.

What, indeed, did he say? 'How can these things be?' And again: 'How can a man be born when he is old?' And once more: 'Can he enter a second time into his mother's womb and be born again?'

On the contrary, she said more respectfully: 'Sir, thou hast nothing to draw with, and the well is deep. Whence then hast thou living water?' He was saying one thing to her, but she interpreted it otherwise, since she heard nothing more than the words, not yet being capable of grasping lofty teachings. Yet, she could have said impertinently: 'If you had living water, you would not ask a drink of me, but would provide it for yourself first, but as it is you are just boasting.' However, she did not say any of this, but replied to Him with great decorum, both at first and afterwards.

At first she said: 'How is it that thou, although thou art a Jew, dost ask drink of me?' Now, she did not say to Him, as if speaking to a foreigner and an enemy: 'Far be it from me to share with you, an enemy, and one who is hostile to our nation.' And afterwards, also, when she had heard Him making high-sounding statements, such things as are particularly apt to annoy one's enemies, she did not ridicule or disparage Him. What did she say? 'Art thou greater than our father Jacob who gave us the well, and drank from it himself, and his sons, and his flocks?' Do you perceive how she was forcing her way into the noble line of the Jews?

But what she said meant some such thing as this: 'Jacob made use of this water and had nothing more to give.' Now, she said this to show that from the first answer she had grasped a great and lofty idea. For the words, 'He drank from it, himself, and his sons, and his flocks,' are those of one implying no other thing than that she had an idea of the existence of a greater water, but had not found it, and did not clearly know about it.

Indeed, to speak more clearly, what she wished to say is this: 'You cannot say,' she declared, 'that Jacob gave us this well but used another himself. For he himself and his sons drank from it, and they would not have done so if he had another, better, one. You yourself will not be able to give of it, and it is not possible for you to have another one, better than it, unless you declare that you yourself are greater than Jacob. Where, then, will you get the water which you proclaim that you will give to us?'

The Jews, on the other hand, did not speak so kindly to Him, although He discoursed to them also about the same idea, and made mention of such water as this; yet they derived no profit. And when He made mention of Abraham they even tried to stone Him.[28] The woman, however, did not act this way with Him, but with great propriety, in the midst of the heat, and at midday, both spoke and listened to everything with great patience. Further, she did not even think any such thing as the Jews were likely to say: 'He is mad, and out of His mind, and is deceiving me about a

---

28 Cf. John 8.59.

fountain and a well, using big words but producing nothing.'
Moreover, she persisted, and remained with Him until she
found what she sought.

Now, if the woman made such an effort to learn something
worth while and stayed at Christ's side, though she did
not know Him, what pardon shall we receive—we who know
Him, and are not beside a well, nor in a desert, at midday,
with the sun beating down, but in the early morning, under
such a roof as this,[29] enjoying shade and comfort—if we
do not persevere in listening to anything that is said, but
show weariness? However, she was not like that, but heeded
His words to such an extent that she called others also to
hear Him. The Jews, on the contrary, not only did not call
others, but even forbade and prevented those who wished to
approach Him; and therefore they said: 'Has any one of the
rulers believed in him? But this crowd, which does not know
the Law, is accursed.'[30]

Let us, then, imitate the Samaritan woman; let us converse
with Christ. For even now He has taken up His stand in
the midst of us, speaking to us through the Prophets and
the disciples. Therefore, let us listen and obey. How long
shall we live fruitlessly and senselessly? For, not to do what
is pleasing to God is to live fruitlessly—not only fruitlessly
but even harmfully. Indeed, when we have spent to no
profit the time given us, we shall depart this life to pay the
extreme penalty for our ill-timed extravagance. For, if the
man who has received money to traffic with, and then has
squandered it, will be required to give a reckoning by the
person who entrusted him with it, surely he who has spent
such a life without profit will not escape without punishment.

God has not brought us into the present life and breathed
into us a soul only that we may merely make use of this

---

29 The *Homilies* were preached either in the so-called 'Great Church'
with its famous golden ceiling, or in some other church in Antioch.
30 John 7.48,49.

life, but for this reason: that we may conduct all our affairs with an eye to the life to come. Irrational creatures, to be sure, are useful only for the present life, but we possess an immortal soul on this account: that we may do all things with a view to the attainment of that other life. For, if someone inquires about the purpose of horses, and asses, and oxen, and other animals of the kind, we reply that they exist for nothing more than their service in the present life.

But it is not possible to say this of us, for there is a nobler condition in store for us after our departure from this life. And we must do everything so that we may be illustrious there, that we may join in the chorus with the angels, that we may stand near the King forever, through the everlasting ages. It is for this reason, indeed, that the soul is immortal and the body will be immortal: that we may enjoy blessings without end. Moreover, if you cling to the earth, when heaven lies before you, consider how great an insult this is to the Giver. For He holds out to you heavenly blessings, while you, not considering them worth much, choose the earth instead. On this account He has even threatened you with hell, if you scorn His gifts, that you may learn from this how great the blessings are of which you deprive yourself.

However, may we not experience that punishment, but, having made ourselves pleasing to Christ, may we attain to everlasting blessings, by the grace and mercy of our Lord Jesus Christ, with whom glory be to the Father, together with the Holy Spirit, forever and ever. Amen.

Homily 32 (John 4.13-21)

'In answer Jesus said to her, "Everyone who drinks of this water will thirst again. He, however, who drinks of the water that I will give him shall never thirst; but the water that I will give him shall become in him a fountain of water, springing up unto life everlasting." '[1]

Scripture at one time calls the grace of the Spirit fire, at another, water, to show that these appellations are applicable not to His substance but to His work. The Spirit is not made up of different substances, since He is invisible and simple. John the Baptist referred to the one when he said: 'He will baptize you with the Holy Spirit and with fire';[2] and Christ said of the other: 'From within him there shall flow rivers of living water. He said this, however, of the Spirit whom they were to receive.'[3] Thus, also, in speaking to the woman, He called the Spirit water. 'He, however, who drinks of the water that I will give him shall never thirst.'

So, at one time He called the Spirit by the appellation of fire, referring indirectly to the fervor and ardor of grace and its destruction of sin; and at another, by that of water, to illustrate the purification that comes from It and the abundant refreshment for those souls who receive It. Rightly so; for It beautifies the well-disposed soul as a park verdant with all sorts of trees—both fruit-bearing and evergreen— and does not permit it to feel despondency or the wiles of Satan, since It readily quenches all the fiery darts of wickedness.

And do you, pray, reflect on the wisdom of Christ, how He drew the woman upward gradually. He did not say from the outset: 'If thou didst know who it is who says to thee, "Give me to drink," ' but when He had furnished her with a pretext to call Him a Jew and she had brought the charge against Him, He then said this to refute the accusation. Further, when He had said: 'If thou didst know who it is who says to thee. "Give me to drink," thou, perhaps,

1 John 4.13,14.
2 Matt. 3.11.
3 John 7.38,39.

wouldst have asked of him,' and by promising great things had caused her to make mention of the patriarch, He thus caused the woman to understand more clearly.

Then, when she replied: 'Art thou greater than our father Jacob?' He did not say: 'Yes, I am greater,' for He would have seemed merely to be boasting, since there was not yet proof apparent, but He prepared her for this knowledge by what He said. Indeed, He did not simply say: 'I will give you water,' but, having first disposed of Jacob's, He then extolled His own, desiring to show from the nature of the gifts that there also was as much difference between the persons of the givers. And He also wished to show His superiority to the patriarch. 'For, if you wonder at Jacob,' He said, 'because he has given this water, if I give a much better than this, what will you say? You have already acknowledged by anticipation that I am greater than Jacob by the question you asked in replying to Me: "Art thou greater than our father Jacob since you declare that you give a better water?" If you accept [the idea of] that water, you completely acknowledge that I am greater.'

Do you perceive that the woman gave an unprejudiced opinion, forming it, with regard both to the patriarch and to Christ, from their deeds? Not so, however, with the Jews; when they saw Him casting out demons, not only did they not declare that He was greater than the patriarch, but they even called Him a demoniac.[4] The woman was not like that, but formed her opinion on the grounds which Christ wished, namely, from the evidence of His deeds. Now, He Himself also formed a judgment on this basis, when He said: 'If I do not perform the works of my Father, do not believe me. But if I do perform them, and if you are not willing to believe me, believe the works.'[5] And it was in this way that the woman was brought to the faith.

---

4 Cf. Luke 11.15.
5 John 10.37.

Accordingly, when He Himself had heard: 'Art thou greater than our father Jacob?' making no mention of Jacob, He spoke about the water, saying: 'Everyone who drinks of this water will thirst again.' He made the comparison not by disparagement, but by pointing out an obvious superiority. He did not say that this water was of no account, nor that it was ordinary and to be despised, but stated something to which nature bears testimony. 'Everyone who drinks of this water will thirst again. He, however, who drinks of the water that I will give him shall never thirst.' The woman had heard, before this, of 'living water,' but did not understand. Since the term 'living water' also signifies that which is ever flowing and continually gushing forth because its springs are freely open, the woman thought this was meant.

Therefore, to render clearer to her what He had said, and to make evident His own superiority, He added the words: 'He, however, who drinks of the water that I will give him shall never thirst.' By this statement, as I have said, He demonstrated His superiority, and also by the words which follow, for ordinary water has none of these qualities. Now, what are the words which follow? 'It shall become in him a fountain of water, springing up unto life everlasting.' For, just as a man who had a fountain located within him would never be overcome by thirst, so also is this the case with him who possesses this water.

Moreover, the woman at once believed, and appeared wiser than Nicodemus; indeed, not only wiser, but even stronger. For, though he heard countless things of this kind, he neither summoned any other person to Christ, nor did he himself speak freely of Him; while she engaged in apostolic work, spreading the good news to all, and calling them to Jesus, drawing to Him a whole city from outside the faith.

And when Nicodemus had heard, he said: 'How can

these things be?'[6] Even when Christ used the wind as a clear illustration of His words he did not even then accept His explanation. But it was not so with the woman. At first, to be sure, she doubted; then, though she had not received any special preparation before receiving the statement, but merely had it told her as a fact, she at once was sufficiently convinced to accept it. For when Christ had said: 'It shall become in him a fountain of water, springing up unto life everlasting,' the woman said immediately: 'Give me this water, that I may not thirst, or come here to draw.'

Do you perceive how He led her upward, little by little, to the loftiest of His teachings? At first she thought that He was a transgressor of the Law, since He was a Jew; next, after He had answered this charge (for it was essential for His person not to be held in question, since He was going to give her such instruction), when she heard of 'living water' she thought water perceptible to the senses was meant. But later, having learned that He was speaking of spiritual things, she believed that the water was able to dispense with the need of thirst. However, she did not yet know what this water was, for she was still puzzled, thinking that it was superior to things of sense, but not understanding it clearly. And, at this point, since she had a clearer perception than before, though she did not comprehend everything, she said: 'Give me this water that I may not thirst, or come here to draw.'

Now she has placed Him ahead of Jacob. 'For I do not need this well, if I receive that water from you.' Do you see how she esteemed Him as greater than the patriarch? This was the action of a prudent soul. She had shown how great was her opinion of Jacob; she saw that Christ was superior and she was not held back by prejudice. Therefore, the woman was not gullible, on the one hand (since she did not accept His words without question, for how was it that

---

6 John 3.9.

she made inquiry with such precision?), nor was she obdurate and contentious. And she showed this by her request.

He also said to the Jews: 'He who eats my flesh shall not hunger and he who believes in me shall never thirst.'[7] Yet they not only did not believe, but even were scandalized. The woman had no such reaction, but remained and made requests. To the Jews, furthermore, He said: 'He who believes in me shall never thirst.' However, He did not speak thus to the woman, but more obscurely: 'He who drinks of this water shall never thirst.' It was a proclamation of spiritual and not of visible things. Therefore, though uplifting her mind by promises, He still kept to material things in His words, because she was not yet ready for the complete comprehension of spiritual things. Indeed, if He said: 'If you believe in me, you will never thirst,' she would not understand the words, since she did not know who the speaker was nor of what sort of thirst He spoke.

Why, then, did He not do this also in the case of the Jews? Because they had been witnesses of many miracles, while she had seen no miracle, but heard His words for the first time. That is why He finally revealed His power by acting as a seer, but did not give her immediate concrete proof of it. But what did He say? ' "Go, call thy husband and come here." The woman answered and said, "I have no husband." Jesus said to her, "Thou hast said well, I have no husband, for thou hast had five husbands, and he whom thou now hast is not thy husband. In this thou hast spoken truly." '

'The woman said to him, "Sir, I see that thou art a prophet." ' Goodness, what great wisdom the woman showed; with what docility she received the proof! 'How indeed would she not,' do you ask? How, indeed! Tell me, did He not often give proof to the Jews, and greater proof than this one? It is not equally difficult to bring to light a thing

---

7 Cf. John 6.35.

said only in the mind and to reveal a deed done in secret. The former belongs only to God, and no one else knows it except the one who has the thing in his mind; but all who take part in the secret deed know about it.

However, when given proof, the Jews did not act with docility, but when He said: 'Why do you seek to put me to death?'[8] they not only did not express wonder as the woman did, but even abused and insulted Him. Yet they had proof from other signs as well, while she had heard this one thing. Still, not only did they not express wonder, but they even insulted Him, saying: 'Thou hast a devil. Who seeks to put thee to death?'

She, on the contrary, not only did not insult Him, but was amazed and astonished, and suspected that He was a prophet, even though this refutation affected the woman more strongly than the other did them. For this sin belonged to her alone, while the other was shared by many. Now, we do not suffer remorse for things done in common with others as we do for our own misdeeds. Moreover, they thought they would accomplish something great if they should kill Christ, while the deed of the woman was acknowledged by all to be wicked. Nevertheless, the woman did not show resentment, but astonishment and wonder.

Now, in the case of Nathanael, Christ acted in the same way. He did not begin by making the prophecy, and did not at once say: 'I saw thee under the fig-tree.' However, when the other had said: 'Whence knowest thou me?' then He added this.[9] For in the case of both prophecies and miracles He wished the initiative to be taken by the persons themselves who came to Him, so that they might be more effectually won over by the events and He might avoid the appearance of vainglory. Accordingly, this is what He did here also. For, to begin with the charge: 'You have no

8 John 7.20.
9 John 1.48.

husband,' seemed to be futile and unnecessary, while to admonish for all these faults after having received the opportunity from the woman herself was very fitting and rendered her more docile when she heard the admonition.

'How, pray, was it fitting,' you will ask, 'to say, "Go call thy husband"?' The discussion was about a gift, and about grace overcoming human nature. The woman persisted in asking to receive it, and He said: 'Call thy husband,' as if to indicate that he also ought to share in these teachings. The woman, in haste to receive the gift, concealing the disgrace of her deeds and thinking that she was speaking to an ordinary man, said: 'I have no husband.' Upon hearing this, Christ finally introduced the admonition opportunely, stating both facts accurately: He enumerated all the previous husbands and accused her of concealing the current one.

What, then, did the woman do? She did not show resentment, nor leave Him and run away, nor think the whole affair a disgrace; rather, she marveled at Him and persevered the more, for she said: 'I see that thou art a prophet.' Moreover, notice her wisdom. At this point she did not immediately hasten to give way completely to Him, but was circumspect and expressed wonderment. For the words 'I see' mean 'You seem to me to be a prophet.' Next, when she had formed this opinion, she asked Him nothing earthly: not about bodily health, or about possessions, or about wealth, but at once about His teachings. For what did she say? 'Our fathers worshipped on this mountain,' meaning those at the time of Abraham, for they say that he brought his son there—'And how do you say that at Jerusalem is the place where one ought to worship?'

Do you perceive how she had grown more exalted in mind? She who at first was concerned about not being troubled by thirst now even asked questions about religious teachings. How did Christ then respond to this? He did not directly answer the inquiry (for it was not His chief concern merely to reply to what she said, since that was superfluous), but He brought the woman to a still more sublime point. Yet He did not discourse to her about these matters until she had acknowledged that He was a prophet, so that she then would listen to His words even with much confidence. For, since she was persuaded that He was a prophet, she could no longer be in doubt about what He said.

Let us, then, be ashamed and let us now blush. A woman who had had five husbands, and was a Samaritan, manifested such deep interest in doctrine, and neither the time of day, nor her interest in anything else, nor any other thing diverted her from her quest for knowledge of such things. We, on the contrary, not only do not make inquiry about doctrine, but are indifferent and casual about everything. Everything, therefore, is neglected.

Furthermore, tell me who of you, when at home, ever takes the Christian Book in his hands and goes through what is contained therein, and studies Scripture? No one would be able to say he does. However, we shall find that games and dice are in most houses; but never books, except in a few. And the latter have the same attitude as those who do not possess books, since they tie them up and store them away in chests all the time, and their whole interest in them lies in the fineness of the parchment and the beauty of the writing, not in reading them. They have not bought them with a view to obtaining help and profit, but are eager to acquire them to make a display of wealth and ambition, so excessive is their vainglory. Actually, I hear no one priding himself because he knows their contents, but because he possesses one written in gold letters.

Now, what profit is there in this, pray? The Scriptures were not given merely that we might have them in books, but that we might engrave them on our hearts. The very possession of them was of itself, in truth, an object of Jewish ambition, since their laws were set down only in writing;

yet from the very beginning the Law was not given thus to us but was set down in the bodily tablets of the heart. I am saying these things not to proscribe the possessing of books, since, on the contrary, I approve this and desire it very much, but I wish both the letter and the meaning of them to be borne about in our minds, that, upon acquiring the knowledge of these writings, our minds may in this way be purified.

Moreover, if the Devil does not dare to enter into the house where the Gospel lies, much less will he ever seize upon the soul which contains such thoughts as these, and no evil spirit will approach it, nor will the nature of sin come near. Well, then, sanctify your soul, sanctify your body, by having these thoughts always in your heart and on your tongue. For, if foul language is defiling and evokes evil spirits, it is evident that spiritual reading sanctifies the reader and attracts the grace of the Spirit.

The Scriptures are divine incantations. Let us, then, chant them over ourselves and let us derive from them remedies for the passions in our souls. Indeed, if we perceive what it is that is read, we shall listen to it with much eagerness. Continually do I say this, and I shall not cease saying it. For, is it not strange that those who sit in the marketplace tell the names, and races, and cities and talents of charioteers and dancers, nay, even accurately state the good and bad qualities of horses; while those who assemble in this place understand nothing of what is taking place here and even are ignorant of the number of the [sacred] Books.

If, in truth, you indulge in those pursuits for pleasure, I shall show that there is more pleasure here. For, which is more enjoyable, pray, which more wonderful: to see a man striving with a man, or a man wrestling with a devil, a human body locking with a bodiless power and prevailing? Let us, then, look at these contests, for it is praiseworthy and advantageous to imitate these, and it is possible for those who imitate them to be crowned; not so, however, with those other contests, enthusiasm for which brings shame to him who imitates them. You will watch that kind of contest in company with evil spirits—if, indeed, you watch it—while the other you will see in company with angels and the Lord of the angels.

Now, tell me: If it were possible for you, seated in company with rulers and kings, to watch and enjoy the spectacle, would you not think that this was a very great honor? Then, will you not hasten to such a spectacle here, to watch it in company with the King of angels and see the Devil seized from behind and making every effort to escape, but not succeeding? 'But how,' you will say, 'can this take place?' If you have the Book in your hands. In it you will see the contests, and the long races, and the holds of the opponent, and the skill of the just man. And by watching these things you yourself will learn how to wrestle in this way and will be rid of evil spirits.

The pagan performances are really festivals of evil spirits, not human shows. Moreover, if it is not right to enter into a temple of idols, much more is it sinful to go to a festival of Satan. I will not cease saying these things and continually prodding you until I see a change. For, to say these things 'is not irksome to me, but it is necessary for you,'[10] Scripture says. Accordingly, do not feel annoyed at my admonition. If anyone ought to feel annoyed, I ought to, because I speak often and am not listened to; but you ought not, because you are always hearing yet always turning a deaf ear.

However, may you not suffer these reproaches forever, but, having put an end to this shameful conduct, may you be deemed worthy of the spiritual vision and enjoy the glory to come, by the grace and mercy of our Lord Jesus Christ, with whom glory be to the Father, together with the Holy Spirit, forever and ever. Amen.

---

10 Phil. 3.1.

Homily 33 (John 4.21-28)

'Jesus said to her, "Woman, believe me, the hour is coming when neither on this mountain nor in Jerusalem will you worship the Father. You worship what you do not know; we worship what we know, for salvation is from the Jews." '[1]

In all circumstances, beloved, we need faith—faith, the mother of virtues, the medicine of salvation—without it we cannot grasp any teachings on sublime matters. But [those who are without faith] are like people trying to cross the sea without a ship. These are able to swim for a while by using hands and feet, but when they have gone farther out they are soon swamped by the waves. So, also, those who have recourse to their own reasoning before accepting any knowledge are inviting shipwreck, even as Paul says: 'who have made shipwreck of the faith.'[2]

In order that we, too, may not suffer this fate, let us use the sacred anchor by which Christ brought the Samaritan woman into safety. When she said: 'How do you say that at Jerusalem is the place where one ought to worship?' Christ replied: 'Woman, believe me, the hour is coming when neither on this mountain nor in Jerusalem will you worship the Father.' He was revealing a very great teaching to her, one which He had given neither to Nicodemus nor to Nathanael.

She was trying, of course, to show that her doctrines were holier than those of the Jews, and she had been taught this through her ancestors. Christ, however, did not reply directly to this inquiry. At this point it was superfluous to discuss this and show why it was that her fathers worshiped on the mountain, and the Jews, in Jerusalem. Therefore, He was silent on this matter; but, taking away the prestige of both places,

1 John 4.21,22.
2 1 Tim. 1.19.

He set her soul right by pointing out that neither the Jews nor the Samaritans could claim any superiority in comparison with the gift to come, and then He arrived at the difference between them.

Nevertheless, He did show that the Jews were more excellent, though not by giving the preference to one place over the other. He allowed them pre-eminence because of their well-known belief [in God], as if He said: 'There is no need to dispute about a place. But the Jews are indeed superior to the Samaritans because of their manner of worship,' for He declared: 'You worship what you do not know; we worship what we know.'

How, then, did the Samaritans not know what they worshiped? Because they thought that God was confined to a place and divisible; at least it was in that way that they worshiped Him. And it was in this spirit that they sent to the Persians and announced that the God of this place was displeased with them.[3] According to this, their idea of Him was no greater than their conception of their idols. Therefore, they continued to worship both evil spirits and Him, combining things that were altogether incompatible. But the Jews for the most part were free of this taint, and knew that He is God of the universe, even though not all of them [were faithful]. That is why He said: 'You worship what you do not know; we worship what we know.'

Now, do not be surprised that He numbered Himself among the Jews, for He was answering the suspicious inquiry of the woman as to how He was a prophet, though a Jew. And it was for this reason that He used the expression 'we worship.' For it is evident to all universally that He is to be worshiped [and does not offer worship.] To offer worship, in truth, is the part of the creature, while to be worshiped belongs to the Lord of creation. For the moment, however,

3 Cf. 4 Kings 17.26.

He was speaking as a Jew. Therefore, the word 'we' here means 'we, the Jews.'

After praising the Jewish worship, then, He once more caused her to believe Him more readily and persuaded her to pay closer attention to His words, since He placed them above suspicion by showing that it was not by reason of a feeling of kinship toward His own race that He praised the Jewish religion. He also revealed the truth about the place on which the Jews particularly prided themselves and because of which they considered that they had superiority over all men,[4] and He declared their holy rites at an end. Thus, it was very evident in the light of this that He was speaking, not to gain the favor of anyone, but with truth and prophetic power.

Therefore, though He had avoided for the moment discussing the issues which she had mentioned,[5] by saying, 'Woman, believe me,' and so on, He added, 'for salvation is from the Jews.' What He meant is something like this: 'The good things in the world have come from that source (for the knowledge of God and the renouncing of idols took their beginning from there, and also all the other teachings; and even among you the act of worship itself, though not carried out correctly, at least had its beginning from the Jews).' 'Salvation,' then, means either these things or His own coming; indeed, one would not err in calling both of these 'salvation,' since He said it was from the Jews. And Paul also said this by implication in the words, 'From whom is the Christ according to the flesh, who is over all things, God.'[6]

Do you perceive how He was commending the Old Testament and showing that it is the source of blessings and

---

4 I.e., Jerusalem.
5 I.e., that the Samaritans and Jews respectively preferred different places of worship.
6 Rom. 9.5.

not at all contrary to the Law, since, indeed, He said that the foundation of all blessings is from the Jews? However, 'the hour is coming and is now here when the true worshipers will worship the Father. We are superior to you, woman,' He meant, 'in the manner of our worship; this, too, however, will at last come to an end. Not only will the prescriptions regarding the place of worship be changed, but also the manner of worship; and this change is at your doors. Indeed the hour is coming and is now here.'

Now, because the Prophets prophesied about events a long time before they took place, He here said: 'And is now here,' to dispel this notion [with regard to Himself]. 'Do not think,' He meant, 'that this is the kind of prophecy that will be fulfilled after a long time. The arrangements have already been made and the hour is at your doors when the true worshipers will worship the Father in spirit and in truth.'

When He said 'true' He excluded the Jews as well as the Samaritans. For, even if the former were superior to the latter, they were much inferior to future worshipers [under the New Law], as much so, indeed, as figure is inferior to reality. Indeed, He was speaking of the Church, because it itself is the true worship, worship befitting God. This is so for 'The Father seeks such to worship him.' Then, if of old He was seeking such as these, He did not willingly give in to those others in accepting their manner of worship, but merely tolerated it that He might in this way conduct them to the true worship.

Who, therefore, are the true worshipers? They who do not restrict their worship to a place, but serve God in spirit as well, as Paul says: 'Whom I serve in my spirit in the gospel of his Son'; and again: 'I exhort you to present your bodies as a sacrifice, living, pleasing to God—your spiritual service.'[7]

---

7 Rom. 1.9; 12.1.

And when Christ says 'God is spirit,' He means nothing else than that He is incorporeal.

It is necessary, then, for the worship of a spiritual being to be also spiritual and to be offered by that which is spiritual in us, that is, by the soul and with purity of mind. That is why He says: 'They who worship him must worship in spirit and in truth.' For, because both Samaritans and Jews disregarded the soul and took much thought for the body, purifying it in every kind of way, He declared that it is not by purity of body but by the spiritual element in us, that is, by the mind, that the spiritual Deity is worshiped. Accordingly, 'Do not sacrifice sheep and heifers, but offer to God your whole self as a holocaust, for this is to present a living sacrifice. For you must worship in truth; as formerly there were in figure circumcision, holocausts, sacrificial offerings, incense, now these are no longer, but all is worship in truth. Indeed, you must circumcise, not the flesh, but evil thoughts, and crucify self; and remove and sacrifice inordinate desires.'

The woman was bewildered at His words and failed to grasp the sublimity of His meaning. Listen to what she said in her perplexity: 'I know that the Messias is coming (who is called Christ), and when he comes he will tell us all things.'

'Jesus said to her, "I who speak with thee am he." '

What was the source of the Samaritans' expectation of the coming of Christ, since they accepted only Moses? The very writings of Moses. I say this because he revealed the Son at the beginning of them. For the words, 'Let us make mankind in our image and likeness'[8] were spoken with reference to the Son. And He it was who spoke to Abraham in his tent. And Jacob said in prophecy of Him: 'The sceptre shall not depart from Juda nor the staff from between his feet, until he comes to whom it belongs. To him shall be the obedience of nations.'[9] And Moses himself said: 'A

8 Gen. 1.26.
9 Gen. 49.10.

prophet like me will the Lord, your God, raise up from among your own kinsmen; to him you shall listen.'[10] And the references to the serpent, and the rod of Moses, and Isaac, and the Lamb and many others made it possible for those who desired to do so to find prophecies of His coming.

'Well, why,' you will ask, 'did Christ not convince the woman by referring to these? Though He brought up the serpent to Nicodemus and recalled prophecies to Nathanael, why did He say nothing of the kind to her?' Why and wherefore? Because they were men and well versed in Scripture, while she was a poor woman, unlearned, and unfamiliar with it. For this reason He did not start from it in speaking with her, but started with the water, and led her on by a prophecy—and so brought her to mention Christ—and then finally revealed Himself. If He had said this to the woman at the beginning, when she was not looking for it, He would have seemed foolish to her and to be talking nonsense. But now, by gradually leading her to recall the Messias, He revealed Himself opportunely.

Moreover, when the Jews kept saying: 'How long dost thou keep us in suspense? If thou art the Christ, tell us,'[11] He did not give a direct reply, but He told her plainly that He was. The woman was better disposed in mind than the Jews, since they did not question Him to gain knowledge, but always to make a fool of Him. If they really desired to learn, there was sufficient instruction available in His words, in the Scriptures, and in the types and figures. She, on the contrary, said what she did with an unprejudiced mind and an understanding open to conviction, as is clear from her subsequent actions. For she listened, and believed, and converted others besides. And in all this we may perceive the faith and earnestness of the woman.

---

10 Deut. 18.15.
11 John 10.24.

'And at this point his disciples came.' They arrived at a very timely moment, since His teaching was finished. 'And they wondered that He was speaking with a woman. Yet no one said: "What dost thou seek?" or: "Why dost thou speak with her?" ' Now, why did they wonder? At His condescension, His exceeding humility, because, though He was so exalted in dignity, He deigned to converse with such a lowly woman, poverty-stricken and a Samaritan. Yet, though struck with astonishment, they did not inquire the reason of His action, so well trained were they in keeping their place as disciples, and so much did they reverence and respect Him. Even if they did not as yet have the proper esteem of Him, they attended on Him as on one worthy of admiration and paid Him great respect.

Yet, at other times they did appear somewhat forward, as when John leaned on His breast, and when they came to Him and said: 'Who is greatest in the kingdom of heaven?'[12] And as when the sons of Zebedee petitioned that one might sit at His right hand and the other at His left.[13]

Why, then, did they not ask questions on this occasion? Because in all the latter instances they had a compelling reason for the inquiry, since the matter concerned their own interest, while here the affair was not so important to them. And John acted as he did much later, at the very end, when he enjoyed much greater freedom and took courage from the love of Christ, for he was the one, he says, 'whom Jesus loved.'[14] What could equal such a blessed privilege?

However, let us not, beloved, remain content with calling the Apostle blessed, but let us do all our actions in such a way as to become of the blessed ourselves; let us imitate the Evangelist, and let us see what it was that caused Christ's love for him. What, then, was it? He left father, and boat, and net, and followed Jesus. But this he did in common

12 Cf. Matt. 18.1.
13 Cf. Mark 10.35,37.
14 John 13.23.

with his brother and Peter and Andrew, and the other Apostles. What, then, was the excellence in him which attracted greater love? Indeed, he himself says nothing personal of himself except this only: that he was beloved; but he remained silent, out of modesty, on the reasons for which he was loved.

That Christ did in truth love him with a love of predilection was clearly evident to all, yet he is not to be observed [in the Gospels] conversing with Him or questioning Him privately, as Peter frequently did, and also like Philip, Judas, and Thomas, but only when he wished to do a favor for a fellow Apostle at the latter's request. For, when the chief of the Apostles bade him and put pressure on him, it was then he asked the question. These two Apostles, indeed, had great love for one another. And so, for example, we see them going up to the Temple together and addressing the people together.

Yet Peter in every instance was more deeply moved and spoke more ardently than John. And at the end he heard Christ saying: 'Peter, dost thou love me more than these do?'[15] Now, it is very clear that if he had more affection for Him than the others, he was also loved in return. However, in his case this fact is evident from his love for Jesus, while in the case of John it is evident from the affection shown him by Jesus.

What, then, is it that aroused this love of predilection? It seems to me that the man manifested great modesty and gentleness, and therefore on many occasions he appeared retiring and reserved. The example of Moses demonstrates how great a virtue this is, for it made him the kind of man he was and as great as he was. Truly, there is nothing to equal humility. For this reason Christ began the Beatitudes with this virtue. In the manner of one who intends to set in place the foundation stone and firm basis for a very

15 John 21.15.

large building, so He has set humility in first place. Indeed, without it, it is not possible—it is not possible, I repeat—to be saved; but even if one fasts, prays, and gives alms, if he does so with a proud spirit, all these are trifling and foolishly done, since this virtue is not present. Similarly, when it is present, all these actions become desirable and commendable and are done with safety.

Let us, then, act with humility, beloved; let us act with humility. And let us do so because, if we are on our guard, it is very easy to succeed in practising it. What is it, O man, that raises you up to senseless pride? Do you not perceive the vileness of your nature? The weakness of your will? Consider your last end; consider the number of your sins. But perhaps you are proud because of many good deeds? By this very fact, therefore, you will lose all of them. For this reason it is not as necessary for the sinner to strive to act with humility as it is for the upright man. Why in the world is that? Because the former has the power of his conscience spurring him on, while the latter, if he is not very much on his guard, is seized upon and wafted away [by pride], as if carried away by a blast of wind, like the Pharisee.

But you give to the poor? Not, however, what is your own, but the property of the Lord, shared in common with your fellow servants. A man ought to be humble especially on this account: that he foresees his own lot mirrored in the misfortunes of his fellow mortals, and learns his own nature by looking at them. Perhaps we also had the same ancestors. And if wealth has come to us, it is just as likely to leave us again. What, indeed, is wealth at all? Shadow without substance, smoke that vanishes, flower of the field—nay, rather, more worthless than a flower. Why, then, do you boast of grass? Does not wealth belong to thieves, and effeminates, and harlots, and grave-robbers? Do you, then, vaunt yourself on this: that you have such as these as sharers of your wealth?

But you love honor? Nothing is more useful than almsgiving to win a word of praise. For the honor won by wealth and power has been forcibly obtained, and is accompanied by hatred; while the other comes from the free choice and volition of those who pay this honor. Therefore, the latter can never discharge the debt completely. Now, if men hold almsgiving so much in esteem, and pray for every blessing for their benefactors, consider how great a recompense, what sort of repayment these will receive from the mercy of God.

Let us, then, seek this wealth which always remains and never will flee from us, in order that, becoming both great here and resplendent hereafter, we may attain to the everlasting blessings by the mercy of our Lord Jesus Christ, with whom glory be to the Father, together with the Holy Spirit, now and always, and forever and ever. Amen.

Homily 34 (John 4.28-40)

'The woman therefore left her water-jar and went away into the town, and said to the people, "Come and see a man who has told me all that I have ever done. Can he be the Christ?" '[1]

We need much fervor and thoroughly awakened zeal, for without them it is not possible for us to attain to the blessedness promised to us. Now, to show this, Christ said at one time: 'He who does not take up his cross and follow me is not worthy of me.'[2] And again: 'I have come to cast fire upon the earth, and what will I but that it be kindled?'[3] By both these sayings He wished to portray to us a fervent disciple, on fire with zeal and prepared to risk any danger.

Such a one was this woman. In fact, so much was she kindled by His words that she left behind her water-jar and

---

1 John 4.28,29.
2 Matt. 10.38.
3 Luke 12.49.

abandoned the purpose for which she had come, and running into the city drew all the people to Jesus. For she said: 'Come and see a man who has told me all that I have ever done.' Consider her zeal and prudence. She had come to draw water, but when she had attained to the fountain of Truth she then scorned the one perceptible only to bodily sense. This was intended to teach us—if only by a trifling example—when listening to spiritual things to put aside all material things and to make no account of them. For, as far as she could, she herself did as the Apostles had done; nay, with even more alacrity than they, for they left their nets after being called, while she of her own accord, with no summons, left her water-jar and did the work of an evangelist with excited elation as a result of her joy.

She called not one only and then a second, as had Andrew and Philip,[4] but having roused the entire city, even though it included so great a throng, she brought it all to Him. And see how prudently she spoke. She did not say: 'Come and see the Christ,' but she, too, attracted the people with a gradual approach similar to that by which Christ had drawn her on. 'Come and see a man,' she said, 'who has told me all that I have ever done.' She was not ashamed to say: 'who has told me all that I have ever done.' Yet she might have said, using a different approach: 'Come and see a prophet.' However, since her soul had been set on fire with divine fire, she did not take account of earthly considerations, such as glory or shame, but she was in the power of one thing only, namely, the flaming zeal that possessed her.

'Can he be the Christ?' Notice once more the great wisdom of the woman. She neither revealed His identity clearly, nor did she remain silent. She desired, not to persuade them by her own conviction, but to make them share in her opinion

---

4 Cf. John 1.41,45.

of Him by hearing Him themselves, since this would make her words more convincing.

He had not revealed her whole life, but from what He did say she was convinced He knew the rest. Yet, she did not say 'Come and believe,' but 'Come and see,' which was less difficult than the other, and attracted them more strongly. Do you see the wisdom of the woman? Indeed, she knew, she knew clearly that, having once tasted that fountain, they would believe the same truths as she. Still, if she were of the more stupid sort, she would have covered up the reproof given her; instead, she exposed her private life, and brought it into view, so as to attract and win all men [to Christ].

'Meanwhile, his disciples besought him, saying, "Rabbi, eat."' The word 'besought' here means 'urged' in this context. They urged Him because they saw that He was wearied by the journey and by the oppressive heat. Indeed, their insistence about food was the result, not of their being in a hurry, but of their warm affection for their Teacher. What, then, said Christ? 'I have food to eat of which you do not know.' Therefore, they said to one another: 'Has someone brought him something to eat?'

Why, then, do you wonder if the woman, when she had heard the word 'water,' still thought of actual water, inasmuch as even the disciples still had the same reaction as she, in that they did not yet think His words had a spiritual meaning, but were puzzled by them? Yet, once more they showed their customary reverence and respect for their Teacher, conversing with one another, but not venturing to question Him. And they acted in this way on other occasions also, when they desired to ask questions, but did not ask them.

What did Christ say then? 'My food is to do the will of him who sent me, to accomplish his work.' In this place He called the salvation of men 'food' to show how great a desire He has to take care of us. Indeed, our salvation is as much an object of desire to Him as eating is to us. And notice how He frequently did not reveal all the details at once, but first cast the listener into uncertainty, in order that, having begun to inquire into what was meant, then because of being confused and growing weary, the latter might receive with more eagerness the explanation of the difficulty, and might be better disposed to listen attentively.

But why did He not say at once: 'My food is to do the will of my Father'? Though this was not altogether clear in meaning, it was clearer than what preceded. Why, instead, did He first say: 'I have food to eat of which you do not know'? He did so because He wished first to make them more attentive, as I have said, as a result of their perplexity, and to dispose them to listen carefully to His words, by reason of such enigmatic statements.

What, moreover, is the will of His Father? He went on to answer this question and to explain it. 'Do you not say, "There are yet four months, and then comes the harvest"? Well, I say to you, lift up your eyes and behold that the fields are already white for the harvest.' See once again how by references to ordinary things He leads them to the contemplation of the most sublime. By saying 'food' He signified nothing else than the salvation of the men who were going to come to Him. Now, the field and the harvest signify the same thing; namely, the multitude of souls ready to receive their preaching. By 'eyes' He here meant both those of the understanding and those of the body, for as He saw the crowd of Samaritans already on their way and the receptiveness of their dispositions, He said they were fields already white. Just as the ears of corn are ready for harvesting when they are white, so these people also, He meant, were prepared and ready for salvation.

Now, why in the world did He not say in so many words that the people were on the verge of faith and ready to receive the Word, because of having been instructed by the

Prophets, and, in short, that they were showing the results of this already? Why, instead, did He refer to a field and a harvest? What end did these figures of speech accomplish for Him? For He used them, not here only, but also all through the Gospel. And the Prophets similarly have made use of the same device, uttering many metaphorical sayings. What in the world, then, is the reason for this? Indeed, it is not by chance that the grace of the Spirit has dictated these things; but why, pray, and wherefore?

It is with two ends in view; one, so that the teaching may become more emphatic and bring what is said more clearly into focus. For the understanding, by receiving an image illustrative of the ideas, is stimulated more acutely and grasps them better, as if it had seen them in a picture. This is the first end, then; and the second is, so that the matter may be more pleasing and the remembrance of the words more lasting. No statement convinces as well and gets as wide a hearing as the explanation by means of example, and illustration drawn from experience. We may see this principle very wisely put in practice in this parable.

'And he who reaps receives a wage, and gathers fruit unto life everlasting.' The fruit of an earthly harvest, in truth, is of benefit not for life everlasting, but for this temporal life, while spiritual fruit is for the everlasting and immortal life. Do you see how, while the words refer to sensible objects, the significance is spiritual, and by the words themselves He distinguished the things of earth from the heavenly? What He had done in speaking about the water—positing something characteristic of it, 'He who drinks of this water shall never thirst'—this He did here also when He said that this fruit is gathered unto life everlasting, 'so that the sower and the reaper may rejoice together.'

Who is 'the sower' and who, 'the reaper'? The Prophets are the sowers, though they did not themselves reap, but the Apostles did so. They are not on that account deprived of the pleasure accruing from their toils and of the recompense for them, but they join with our pleasure and joy, even if they do not reap with us. The task of harvesting is not such heavy work as the sowing. 'Accordingly, I have preserved you for that task where the toil is less, and the pleasure is greater, instead of for the sowing. For in it much effort and toil are expended. In the harvest, on the contrary, the return is abundant, while the toil is not so great but it is even quite easy.'

In this text, moreover, He wished to intimate the following as well: 'This is the desire of the Prophets, also: that men should come to Me.' And this the Old Law, too, foreshadowed. It was for this reason they sowed: that they might bring forth this fruit. Further, He showed that He Himself had given them also their mission and that the New Testament has great affinity with the Old. In fact, by this parable He brought out all these points at the same time.

He also recalled a proverbial expression in common use, for He said: 'Herein is the proverb true, One sows, another reaps.' People used to say this whenever some expended the toil, while others gathered the fruits, and He declared that this saying is especially true in this case. 'For the Prophets labored, while you gather in the fruits of their toils.' Now, He did not say 'the reward,' for that great toil was not without reward for them, but 'the fruits.' Daniel also did this, for he also recalled a proverb, saying: 'From the wicked shall wickedness come forth.'[5] And David, too, recalled this proverb in his grief.[6]

Accordingly, He was anticipating when He said: 'so that the sower and the reaper may rejoice together.' Since

---

5 1 Kings 24.14.
6 The words assigned to Daniel are in reality David's; cf. note 5, *supra*. The allusion confused with this is found in Dan. 12.10. The Benedictine editor suggests, with reason, that the names Daniel and David have been exchanged here by some mischance, though all the manuscripts agree in the order as given here.

He was going to say that one has sowed while another reaps, in order that no one might think that, as I have said, the Prophets were deprived of their reward, He stated something strange and unusual and not agreeing with the observations of the senses, but chosen from the realm of the spirit. In material affairs, if it should happen that one man sows while another reaps, they do not rejoice together, but the sowers grieve in that they have toiled for others, while the reapers only rejoice. Here, however, it is not so; they who do not reap what they have sown rejoice at the same time with those who gather in the harvest. From this it is plain that they themselves also share the rewards.

'I have sent you to reap that on which you have not labored. Others have labored, and you have entered into their labors.' By these words He was encouraging them still more. Since it seemed to be a very laborious task to go into the whole world and preach, He showed that it was comparatively easy. Actually, it is a very toilsome thing and entails much fatigue, to cast the seeds and lead on a pagan soul to the knowledge of God. Why, then, did He speak as He did? So that, when He sent them to preach, they would not be bewildered, as if being sent on a very difficult mission. 'For that of the Prophets was more laborious,' He said, 'and the actual present bears witness to the truth of my statement that you have come to the easy task. Just as in the harvest, in truth, the fruit is gathered in with ease, and in one moment the threshing-floor is filled with sheaves, not waiting for the changes of the seasons: winter and spring and rain; so it is now also, and the facts shout it aloud.'

Meanwhile, then, while He was saying these things, the Samaritans came out and the 'fruit' was assembled in a dense throng. That is why He said: 'Lift up your eyes and behold that the fields are already white for the harvest.' He said these words and at once the fact was evident, and His words came completely true in the final result, for 'Many of the Samaritans of that town believed in him because of the word of the woman who bore witness, "He told me all that I have ever done." ' They, in truth, saw at once that the woman would not have praised through gratitude one who had accused her of her shortcomings, nor would she have made a show of her private life if she desired to curry favor with another.

Let us, accordingly, imitate the woman ourselves, and let us not cater to human respect with regard to our sins, but let us fear God as we ought, since He both sees what is happening now and punishes hereafter those who do not repent now. At present, however, we are doing the very opposite of this, for we do not fear Him who is going to judge us, while we shudder with fear of those who have no power to harm us and dread disgrace at their hands. Therefore, in the degree in which we have had this fear, in that degree we shall pay the penalty. He who now looks only to human respect and is not ashamed to do any disgraceful deed in the sight of God, if he is unwilling to repent and mend his ways, in that day will be put to shame, not in the presence of one or two only, but with the whole world looking on.

And let the parable of the sheep and the goats[7] teach you that a mighty audience will be seated there to review both good deeds and those that are not so. Likewise, let blessed Paul instruct you, when he says: 'For all of us must be made manifest before the tribunal of Christ, so that each one may receive what he has won through the body, according to his works, whether good or evil.'[8] And again: 'Who will bring to light the things hidden in darkness.'[9] Have you done anything wicked, or thought it, and are you concealing it from man? You are not hiding it from God,

---

7 Cf. Matt. 25.31-46.
8 2 Cor. 5.10.
9 1 Cor. 4.5.

however. But you care nothing for this, since it is the eyes of men that are fearful to you. Well, then, consider that you will be able to manage concealment not even from men in that day. Then all things will be set before our eyes, as in a mirror, so that each one will be self-condemned.

This is also evident from the example of the rich man. And this is so, because the rich man saw standing before his eyes the poor man—I mean Lazarus—who had been despised, and called for the finger at which he had felt disgust to become an assuagement for him then.[10]

Well, then, I beseech you, let each one of us, even if no one sees our deeds, enter into his own conscience, and set up his reason as judge, and bring to light his transgressions. And if he should not wish to become a spectacle in that fearful day, let him apply the remedy of repentance and let him thus heal his wounds. It is possible, it is possible for one replete with countless wounds to go away healed. 'For if you forgive,' He says, 'your offenses will be forgiven, but if you do not forgive, they will not be forgiven.'[11] Indeed, just as the sins forgiven in baptism do not still remain, so these also will vanish, if we wish to repent. Moreover, repentance consists in no longer doing the same things, for he who reverts to the same sins is like a dog returning to his vomit[12] and also like the person who, according to the proverb, cards wool into the fire[13] or draws water into a container full of holes.[14]

We must, then, refrain both in deed and thought from former sins, and while refraining from them we must apply to the wounds remedies which are the opposite to our sins. What sort do I mean? Have you robbed and acted greedily?

10 Cf. Luke 16.19-26.

11 Cf. Matt. 6.14,15.

12 Cf. 2 Peter 2.21,22.

13 I.e., works fruitlessly or in vain. Cf. Plato, *Laws* 6, p. 750. E. L. Leutsch and F. G. Schneidewin, *Paroemiographi Graeci II* (Gottingen 1841) 27.

14 Euripides, *Hecuba* 869. Cf. Leutsch and Schneidewin, *op. cit.* 752.

Refrain from rapacity, and apply almsgiving to the wound. Have you been impure? Refrain from impurity, and apply purity to the sore. Have you spoken evil of your brother and done him harm? Cease from evil-speaking, and apply kindliness.

Let us act in this way regarding each one of our transgressions and not merely treat our sins in a cursory way, for the time of reckoning is close at hand, is close at hand hereafter. That is why Paul also said: 'The Lord is near. Have no anxiety.'[15] But perhaps the opposite ought to be said to us: 'The Lord is near. Be careful.' They who were in the midst of affliction and toils and trials might well hear: 'Have no anxiety'; but those who are living in the midst of rapine and in luxury, and who have a difficult reckoning to give, would with reason hear not the latter, but that other: 'The Lord is near. Be careful.'

Indeed, not much time remains before our consummation, for the world is hastening to its final end. The wars point to this, afflictions, also, and earthquakes, and charity that has grown cool. In truth, just as a body which is breathing its last and is near its end draws to itself countless ills; and as when a house is about to collapse, many things usually fall beforehand from its roof and from its walls; so also the consummation of the world is close at hand at our doors, and that is why numberless ills are ranged on every side. To be sure, if the Lord then was near, He is now much nearer. If, 400 years ago, when he said these words, Paul also called that period the 'fullness of time,'[16] much more should the present be so called.

Perhaps some do not believe for this very reason.[17] Yet they ought rather to believe more firmly on this account.

---

15 Phil. 4.6.
16 Gal. 4.4.
17 I.e., because the 400 years had elapsed, but the end of the world had not yet taken place.

How do you know, my man, that the end is not near and that after a short time those words will not be fulfilled? Indeed, just as we do not say that the end of the year is the last day, but even the last month, though it has thirty days, so also if I call even 400 years the end of so many years I shall not be mistaken—so that he was foretelling the end beginning from his own time.

Let us, then, gird up our loins; let us delight in the fear of God. Let us do so because, otherwise, while we are living in security, and not being very solicitous or watchful, His coming will be suddenly at hand. Christ, to make this clear, said: 'And as it was in the days of Noe, and in the days of Lot, even so will it be at the end of this world.'[18] And Paul also made this clear when he said: 'When they shall say, Peace and security, even then sudden destruction will come upon them, as birth pangs upon her who is with child.'[19]

What is the meaning of 'birth pangs upon her who is with child'? Frequently, pregnant women have suddenly been seized with birth pangs while indulging in recreation, or preparing a meal, or in the bath, or in the marketplace, when they were not at all expecting this eventuality. Therefore, since our situation is something like this, let us be always ready. We shall not be hearing this warning forever; we shall not forever possess the power to heed it. 'For in the underworld who praises Thee?'[20] says Scripture.

Let us, then, repent here that God may be merciful to us in the time to come and we may be able to enjoy pardon in abundance. May we all obtain this by the grace and mercy of our Lord Jesus Christ, to whom be glory and power forever and ever. Amen.

---

18 Cf. Luke 17.26-35; Matt. 24.37.
19 1 Thess. 5.3.
20 Ps. 6.6.

Homily 35 (John 4.40-53)

'When therefore the Samaritans had come to him, they besought him to stay there; and he stayed two days. And far more believed because of his word. And they said to the woman, "We no longer believe because of what thou hast said, for we have heard for ourselves and we know that this is in truth the Saviour of the world, the Christ." Now after two days he departed from that place and went into Galilee.'[1]

Nothing is worse than envy and malice, nothing more destructive than vainglory; it is wont to spoil good things without number. Because of this vice, the Jews, who had more knowledge than the Samaritans and had been brought up on the Prophets, appeared to less advantage here than did the Samaritans. For the latter believed even from the testimony of the woman, and though they had seen no miracle they came to urge Him to stay with them. The Jews, on the contrary, even after witnessing miracles, not only did not keep Him with them, but even drove Him away and made every effort to cast Him out of their country. And even though His very coming took place for their sakes, they drove Him away, while the others kept insisting on His staying with them.

I ask you, then, was it not right for Him to visit those who were urging and begging Him to do so, instead of taking up His abode among those who plotted against Him and tried to drive Him away, and instead of refusing Himself to those who loved Him and wished Him to stay with them? The latter course of action was not in keeping with His loving kindness. And that is why He received the Samaritans kindly and remained with them two days. They, indeed, wished to keep Him always (the Evangelist shows this when he says, 'They besought him to stay there'). However, He did not allow

---

1 John 4.40-44.

this, but remained two days only, and in that time 'far more believed' in Him.

Now, it was not to be expected that they would believe, because of their not having seen any miracle, and also because of their hostile attitude toward the Jews. Nevertheless, since they judged that His words were spoken with truth, these obstacles did not remain in their way, but they conceived an opinion of Him too sublime for these hindrances, and vied with one another in admiring Him more and more. 'They said to the woman, "We no longer believe him because of what thou hast said, for we have heard for ourselves and we know that this is in truth the Saviour of the world, the Christ." '

The pupils had gone further than their instructress. Indeed, they would have been a reproach to the Jews, both because they believed in Him and because they received Him. The Jews, on the contrary, in whose behalf He had engaged in the entire project [of the Incarnation], repeatedly stoned Him, while the others drew Him to themselves, though He did not intend to come to them. And the Jews remained unconverted, even though they had seen miracles, while these, without the aid of miracles, showed great faith in Him. They even emulated one another in this very thing: that is, in believing without the aid of miracles. On the other hand, the Jews did not cease seeking for signs and trying Him out.

Thus, all men everywhere need an open mind, so amenable that, if truth makes an onslaught, she easily prevails over it. And if she should not prevail, this happens, not because of her weakness, but by reason of the perverseness of the mind. Similarly, when the sun reaches clear eyes, it easily gives them light, but if it does not do so, the fault is in their defectiveness, not in its weakness.

Listen, therefore, to what these men said. 'We know that this is in truth the Saviour of the world, the Christ.' Do you perceive that they concluded at once that He was going to

win over the whole world, and had come to accomplish the
salvation of all, that He did not intend to confine His
providence to the Jews, but to sow His word everywhere?
It was not thus, however, with the Jews; while they sought
'to establish their own justice, they have not submitted to
the justice of God.'[2]

The others, on the contrary, confessed that all are subject
to punishment, illustrating that saying of the Apostle: 'All
have sinned and have need of the glory of God. They are
justified freely by his grace.'[3] For by saying that He is the
Saviour of the world they showed that it was perishing,
and not merely that He is a Saviour, but that He is so in
a very great sense. For many have come—both prophets and
angels—to save mankind, but this is the true Saviour, they
said, who brings real salvation, not that which is but temporary.

This is an evidence of genuine faith. I say this because
they are remarkable on two counts: both because they
believed and because they did so without the aid of miracles.
Christ was calling them also blessed when He said, 'Blessed
are they who have not seen, and yet have believed.[4] And
they are remarkable, too, because they believed sincerely.
Though they had heard the woman saying enigmatically,
'Can he be the Christ?' they did not also say: 'We likewise
suspect He is,' or 'We think,' but 'We know.' And not that
only, but 'This is in truth the Saviour of the world.' It was
not, indeed, as one of many saviours that they professed
belief in Christ, but actually as the Saviour.

Yet, whom had they seen saved? They but listened to His
words and then said what they would have said if they had
seen many great wonders. Now, why do the Evangelists not
tell us these words of His and that He spoke in a remarkable

2 Rom. 10.3.
3 Rom. 3.23.
4 John 20.29.

way? In order that you may learn that, though they omit to mention many important details, they have really told the whole story of this episode in telling its result. He persuaded a whole population and an entire city by what He said. But in instances where His listeners were not persuaded by His words, then [the Evangelists] are forced to report these words, lest anyone pass an unfavorable judgment on the preacher because of the lack of discernment on the part of His hearers.

'Now after two days he departed from that place and went into Galilee, for Christ himself bore witness that a prophet received no honor in his own country.' Why does the Evangelist add this statement? Because He did not go into Capharnaum, but into Galilee and from there into Cana. To forestall your asking why He did not remain with His own people, inasmuch as He had stayed with the Samaritans, He states the reason, declaring that they had not accepted Him. That is why He did not go there: that their guilt might not become greater.

And I say this because I think that he here is speaking of Capharnaum as 'His country.' Listen to Christ's own testimony that He had not enjoyed honor there: 'And thou, Capharnaum, shalt thou be exalted to heaven? Thou shalt be thrust down to hell.'[5] But [the Evangelist] calls it 'His own country' in support of the doctrine of the Incarnation, dwelling on the point the more for this reason.

'What is this, then,' you will say; 'do we not see many men admired even by their countrymen?' It is particularly necessary not to judge such matters from rare examples. And if there are some men who are held in honor in their own country, they would be much more so in a strange country, since familiarity breeds contempt.

'When, therefore he had come into Galilee, the Galileans received him, having seen all that he had done in Jerusalem

---

5 Luke 10.15. Cf. Matt. 4.12,13; Christ made Capharnaum His headquarters during His public life.

during the feast, for they also had gone to the feast.' Do you perceive that it is those who were most maligned who were found coming to Him here? For someone had said: 'Can anything good come out of Nazareth?'[6] And another: 'Search and see that out of Galilee arises no prophet.'[7] They said these things to taunt Him, since He seemed to many to be of Nazareth. And they also reproached Him with being a Samaritan; 'Thou art a Samaritan and hast a devil,'[8] they said. 'But see,' the Evangelist is saying, 'both Samaritans and Galileans believe, to the shame of the Jews. And the Samaritans are found to be better even than the Galileans, for the former received Him by reason of the woman's words, while the latter did so on seeing the miracles which He had worked.

'Jesus came again therefore to Cana of Galilee where he had made the water wine.' The Evangelist recalls the miracle to his audience, to add still further to the praise of the Samaritans. For while the Galileans received Him by reason of the miracles which had taken place both there and in Jerusalem, the Samaritans accepted Him, not stimulated by this help, but merely as a result of His teaching.

Furthermore, he said only that He came there, but did not add the reason why He came. He did, indeed, go into Galilee because of the envy of the Jews, but why to Cana? On the former occasion He was invited to a wedding, but why did He go there now, and wherefore? It seems to me that it was to make stronger by His presence the faith begotten by the miracle, and to attract them more strongly to Him by coming without invitation, since He was leaving His own country and giving the preference to them.

'And there was a certain royal official whose son was lying sick at Capharnaum. When he heard that Jesus had

6 John 1.46.
7 John 7.52.
8 John 8.48.

come from Judea into Galilee, he went to him and besought him to come down and heal his son.' Either he was actually of royal lineage or he was called royal because there was some other dignity of his office to which the title was attached. Some think, then, that he is the one found in Matthew,[9] but the latter appears to be another person, not only by reason of his rank, but also because of his faith. Even when Christ wished to come to his house, he thought it not fitting for Him to come, while this man entreated Him to come to his house, even though He had manifested no desire to do so. Further, the other said: 'I am not worthy that thou shouldst come under my roof,' while this one pressed Him, saying: 'Come down before my child dies.' Also, in the passage in Matthew, after having come down from the mountain, He entered Capharnaum, while in this one, He was coming from Samaria, and not going to Capharnaum, but to Cana, when this man met Him. Too, the servant of the former lay sick of paralysis, while the son of this man was afflicted with fever.

'He went to him and besought him to heal his son, for he was at the point of death.' What, then, did Christ say? 'Unless you see signs and wonders, you do not believe.' Yet, to come and beseech Him was an evidence of faith; and afterwards the Evangelist also bears witness to this, when he declares that when Jesus had said to him, 'Go thy way, thy son lives,' he believed His word and departed. Why, then, did He make this rejoinder here? He said this either out of admiration for the Samaritans because they had believed without miracles, or to upbraid Capharnaum, whence this man came, and which was deemed His own city.

Besides, when another man, in St. Luke's gospel, said: 'I do believe; help my unbelief,'[10] He spoke in similar vein,

9 Matt. 8.5-13.
10 This is found, not in Luke, but in Mark 9.23. Since the manuscripts seem to be in agreement in reading 'Luke,' this is probably a lapse of memory on the part of St. John Chrysostom.

so that, even if this ruler believed, he did not do so fully or soundly. And this he made evident by seeking to learn at what hour the fever left him, for he wished to discover whether this happened of itself or at the command of Christ. When, therefore, he knew that it was 'yesterday at the seventh hour, . . . he himself believed, and his whole household.' Do you perceive that he believed at the time when his servants spoke, but not when Christ did? Well, then, He was rebuking him for the disposition in which he had come and made his request. Since he was so disposed, He drew him even more strongly to the faith, because before the miracle his faith was not very deep.

Now, even though he came and entreated Christ, that fact was not at all remarkable. Fathers are eager, because of their great love, not only to approach physicians in whom they have confidence, but also to address those in whom they have none, wishing to leave nothing untried. Besides, there is the fact that he approached Him only incidentally: when He came into Galilee, then he went to see Him; because, if his faith in Him had truly been very strong, he would not have hesitated to go into Judea, since his son was on the point of dying. And if he had been afraid to do so, not even this was excusable.

See, indeed, how even his words betray the weakness of the man. After Christ's rebuke of his attitude, he ought to have been entertaining great hopes of Him, even if he had not done so before, yet listen to the way in which he still was clinging to an earthly outlook. He said: 'Come down before my child dies,' just as if He were unable to raise him up after death, and as if He did not know what the condition of the child was. That is why He rebuked him and pricked his conscience, to show that miracles take place first and foremost for the sake of the soul. He was ministering here to the father, who was ill no less than his child, ill as regards his state of mind. He did so to persuade us to give

Him our attention, not by reason of His miracles, but for His teaching. Miracles, in truth, are not for those who believe, but for unbelievers and those whose faith is somewhat sluggish.

At that moment, then, the ruler did not pay very close attention to His words, because of his anguish, except only to those about his child. He later would recall what had been said and gain the greatest profit from it; and this, accordingly, did eventuate. But why is it that in the case of the centurion He promised to come without being asked to do so, while here He did not go even when requested? Because in the former instance faith was perfect. He promised to go for this reason: that we might learn of the good dispositions of the man; while in the other instance we might discover that this man was imperfect.

Therefore, since he persisted in urging Him by saying: 'Come down,' and did not yet realize that He could heal even when absent, He showed that He had this ability, in order that, from Jesus' not coming, he might learn what the centurion knew by intuitive knowledge. Accordingly, when He said: "Unless you see signs and wonders, you do not believe,' He meant this: 'You have faith that is by no means what it should be, and you are still disposed to believe as if you were listening to a prophet.' To make Himself known, therefore, and to show that it was necessary to believe in Him without miracles, He said what He had said also to Philip: 'Do you believe that I am in the Father, and the Father in me? Otherwise believe because of the works.'[11]

'But even as he was now going down, his servants met him, saying that his son lived. He asked of them therefore the hour in which he had got better. And they told him, "Yesterday, at the seventh hour, the fever left him." The father knew then that it was at that very hour in which Jesus had said to him, "Thy son lives." And he himself believed, and his

11 John 14.11.

whole household.' Do you perceive how evident the miracle was? The child was freed from danger not in an ordinary way or by chance, but suddenly, so that what happened no longer appeared to be an effect of nature, but of the power of Christ. Indeed, just when the child was at the very gates of death, as his father made clear when he said: 'Come down before my child dies,' he was suddenly freed from his disease, and this excited even the servants. For they met him not only, perhaps, to bring him word, but also with the thought that the coming of Jesus was now unnecessary. They knew, of course, that he had gone to Him, and therefore met him on the same road.

But the man, once his fear had been laid aside, finally began to penetrate to the faith, and desired to prove that the cure did take place because of his journey. In consequence, he tried to make it clear that he had not undertaken the journey unnecessarily. Therefore, he carefully ascertained all the details. 'And he himself believed, and his whole household.' And they did so, for the evidence was after this incontestable. Though they had not been present, nor had they heard Christ speak, nor did they know the time, upon learning from their master that this was the time they held the evidence of His power incontestable, and for this reason they themselves also believed in Him.

What, then, do we learn from these things? Not to wait for miracles or to seek guarantees of the power of God. Even now I see many who, on becoming more prayerful at the time when their child is ailing or their wife sick, enjoy some alleviation of their trouble. But they must, even when not obtaining this petition, nevertheless continue giving thanks and glorifying God. This is the part of faithful servants, this the part of those who are prayerful and love God as they ought: to fly to Him not only when in consolation, but also in desolation. And I say this because these are alike the works of the providence of God. 'For whom the Lord loves he chastises, and he scourges every son whom he receives.'[12]

But when a person serves Him only in time of consolation, he does not give proof of much love, nor does he love Christ purely. And why do I speak merely of health, or abundance of means, or poverty, or disease? Even if you hear gehenna[13] mentioned, or any other dreadful thing, not even then ought you to cease from giving praise to the Lord, but you ought to suffer and endure all things out of love for Him. This is the part of faithful servants and of a steadfast soul. And he who is disposed to live in this fashion will both easily bear with present things, and obtain the blessings of the life to come, and also enjoy great familiarity with God. May we all obtain this boon, by the grace and mercy of our Lord Jesus Christ, to whom be glory forever and ever. Amen.

Homily 36 (John 4.54-5.6)

'This was a second sign that Jesus worked when coming from Judea into Galilee. After this there was a feast of the Jews, and Jesus went up to Jerusalem.'[1]

Just as in working gold mines an expert in metallurgy would not allow even the smallest vein to be passed by, since it could be productive of great wealth, so also in the sacred Scriptures we may not overlook one jot or flourish without loss, but must examine everything closely. For all are uttered by the Holy Spirit and there is nothing unimportant in them.

Take note, for instance, of what the Evangelist says here: 'This was a second sign that Jesus worked when coming from Judea into Galilee.' He did not add the word 'second' undesignedly, but was still extolling the remarkable faith of

---

12 Heb. 12.6.
13 Cf. above, Homily 5 n. 5.

---

1 John 4.54; 5.1.

the Samaritans, showing that, though even a second miracle had taken place, those who witnessed it by no means attained to the sublime faith of the Samaritans who had seen none.

'After this there was a feast of the Jews.' What feast? It seems to me it was that of Pentecost.[2] 'And Jesus went up to Jerusalem.' He frequently visited the city during the feasts, partly that He might appear to be celebrating the feast with them, partly that He might attract to Himself the untutored multitude. For it was especially in those days that those who were more simple-hearted would be assembled in a group.

'Now there is at Jerusalem, by the Sheepgate, a pool called in Hebrew Bethsaida, having five porticoes. In these were lying a great multitude of the sick, blind, lame, and those with shrivelled limbs, waiting for the moving of the water.' What manner of healing is this? What mystery is being intimated to us? For these details have not been written without design or by chance. On the contrary, they give promise of the future to us in figure and type, so that the very unusual events to come later might not impair the strength of the faith of most of us, by happening without previous preparation. What, then, is it that this event foreshadows? He was on the point of giving baptism, which has much power and is a very great gift, baptism which cleanses of all sin and brings men to life, when they have been dead. These effects were foreshadowed as if in figure by the pool and by many of the other details of the event.

Now, in the beginning He gave water to purify from bodily stains and also to cleanse those who are not defiled, but seem to be, like those tainted by caring for the dead, by leprosy, or by any similar cause. Indeed, one may see in the Old Testament[3] many things occurring through the agency of water, precisely for the sake of foreshadowing this [sacra-

---

2 The note on John 5.1 in the Confraternity edition suggests that it was the Passover.
3 Cf. for example, Num. 19.11-22; Lev. 14.2-57.

ment]. However, let us now return to the passage under discussion.

First, then, as I have just said, He caused bodily stains to be removed by water and, after them, bodily infirmities. For, since God wished to lead us closer to the gift of baptism, He no longer purified of stains merely, but also healed diseases [by means of water]. Indeed, the figures which were nearer in time to the reality, both in the case of baptism and in that of the Passion, and in that of others, too, were clearer than figures which were more ancient. Just as the bodyguards who are near the King are more illustrious that those who are at a distance, so it is with figures.

Now, an angel came down and stirred the water, and put the power of healing in it, in order that the Jews might learn that the Lord of angels is much more able to heal the diseases of the soul. However, just as here it was not merely the nature of the water that healed (if it were, surely this healing would have occurred every time), but water supplemented by the power of the angel, so in our case: it is not merely the water that acts, but, when it has received the grace of the Spirit, then it frees us from every sin.

Around this pool 'were lying a great multitude of the sick, blind, lame, and those with shrivelled limbs, waiting for the moving of the water.' At that time, however, sickness was an impediment to him who wished to be healed; now, on the contrary, each one is capable of approaching of himself. It is not an angel who now stirs the water, but the Lord of the angels who does everything. And it is not possible for the sick man to say: 'I have no one'; he cannot say: 'While I am coming to go down, another steps down before me.' But, even if the whole world should come, grace is not used up, nor is the power diminished; it remains the same, now, still what it was before. And just as sunbeams give light every day and do not dwindle in size, nor does their light become less because of its lavish spending, so it is much more true that the power of the Spirit is not lessened by the number of those who receive its benefit.

Moreover, this [miraculous healing] took place in order that those who learned that it was possible to heal diseases of the body by water, and who had been schooled in this knowledge for a long time, might readily believe that it is possible for water also to cure diseases of the soul. But why in the world did Jesus, passing by all the rest, go to one who had been infirm for thirty-eight years? And why did He ask: 'Dost thou want to get well?' It was not that He might get this information (that was unnecessary), but that He might show the perseverance of such a person as this, and that we might learn that it was because of his perseverance that He passed by the rest and came to this man.

What, then, did the sick man say? 'He answered him, "Sir, I have no one to put me into the pool when the water is stirred; for while I am coming, another steps down before me." ' It was for this reason He had asked: 'Dost thou want to get well?' namely, to elicit this information for our benefit. However, He did not say to him: 'Dost thou want Me to heal thee?' for the man did not yet attribute greatness to Him, but: 'Dost thou want to get well?'

The patience of the paralytic is striking: he stayed there and did not give up for thirty-eight years, each year thinking he would be rid of his affliction. For, if the past years had not succeeded in bringing him away from the place, were not the future ones[4] capable of doing so unless he had been patient? And think, I ask you, how likely it was that the other sick persons there also were carefully watching, for it was not known at what time the water was to be troubled. The lame and the maimed, of course, were able to be on watch, but how did the blind perceive it? Perhaps they became aware of it from the noise that accompanied it.

Let us, then, be ashamed; let us be ashamed, beloved,

---

4 I.e., the hopelessness, as it appeared, of his future.

and let us bewail our great sluggishness. He spent thirty-eight years lying there, and did not obtain what he wished, yet did not give up. Besides, he had failed to obtain help, not through his own carelessness, but because he was pushed aside by others and given harsh treatment; yet, even though treated this way, he did not lose heart.

On the contrary, if we persist for ten days earnestly praying for some favor and do not obtain it, we hesitate to expend the same effort in future. We do persevere, to be sure, for just as much time in human affairs—doing military service, engaging in strenuous labor, and doing menial work—often losing at the end the very thing we hoped to gain. But we cannot endure, on the other hand, persevering in the service of our Lord with the necessary effort, though it is altogether possible to obtain from Him a return much greater than our works (for 'Hope does not disappoint,'[5] Scripture says).

How much punishment do not our actions deserve? Even if it were not possible to obtain any return, ought we not to consider it worth any number of favors even to enjoy the privilege of conversing with Him unceasingly? But prayer without ceasing is hard to practice? And which practice of virtue is not hard, I ask?

'That very point,' you will say, 'is itself very puzzling to us; namely, that pleasure inevitably accompanies evil-doing, while hardship is the companion of virtue.' And many, I think, seek the answer to this question. What in the world is the reason for this, then?

In the beginning, God gave us a life free from cares and exempt from toil. We did not rightly make use of the gift, but perverted our leisure and lost paradise. Therefore, He made our life thereafter a toilsome one, as if speaking to the human race and saying: 'In the beginning I granted you a life of ease, but you became worse because of your leisure;

5 Rom. 5.5.

therefore, I have enjoined toils and sweat upon you for the future.'

But, since not even that toil held us in check, He once more laid down a law, this one with many precepts, as if placing bits and reins on a horse that is hard to tame, as horse-breakers do to check its prancing. That is why our life is toilsome, because not to toil was likely to spoil us. Our nature does not allow us to be idle; when we are idle it is easily inclined to evil. Let us suppose that neither the temperate man nor he who successfully practices other virtues needs to work, but accomplishes all he does with ease: how would we still use our freedom from toil? Would it not be in foolish pursuits and proud boasting?

'But why,' you will say, 'does great pleasure accompany evil-doing, while much toil and sweat are associated with virtue?' Well, what sort of thanks would you have had or for what would you receive a reward, if the activity were not toilsome? And I say this because at present I can point to many who by nature hate intercourse with women and avoid association with them as if it were loathesome. Shall we, then, call these men chaste, or shall we pay them honor, pray tell, and celebrate their praise? By no means. Chastity is self-control and overcoming the pleasurable desires that beset us. And in warfare, also, it is when the contest is severe that the trophies are more celebrated, not when no one offers any opposition.

Likewise, many are easy-going by nature; shall we call them meek? By no means. That is the reason why even Christ, in speaking of the three classes of eunuchs, passes over two without praise, but one He introduces into His kingdom.[6]

'But what need is there of evil?' you will say. And I say this, also. What, then, was responsible for evil? What else but laziness, the laziness of the will.

'But there ought to have been good people only,' you will

---

6 Cf. Matt. 19.12.

say. What is characteristic of a good person? To live soberly and to be watchful, or to sleep and snore?

'But why,' you will say, 'is it not considered virtue when a man lives virtuously, but does not have to exert any effort to do so?' Now you are talking to me like cattle, like gourmands who consider their belly their god. Indeed, to prove that these words come from laziness, answer me this question. Suppose there are a king and a general. Then, while the king is sunk in drunken sleep, the general by working hard has set up trophies of victory. To whom will you attribute the victory? And who has obtained pleasure as the fruit of these deeds?

Do you perceive that the soul derives more satisfaction from those things for the sake of which it has expended toil? In the desire, therefore, to attract the soul to virtue God has made effort essential to its practice. Accordingly, we admire virtue, even if we do not practice it, while we condemn vice, even though it be very pleasurable.

But, if you say: 'Why do we not admire those who are virtuous by nature more than those who are so because they will to be?' it is because it is right to esteem the man who expends effort more than the one who does not.

'But why,' you will ask, 'are we now toiling?' Because you did not maintain an attitude of detachment with regard to not working hard. Rather, if the matter be closely studied, there is yet another way by which laziness has been active in corrupting us and causing us much trouble.

Now, if you please, suppose that we lock up a man, merely feeding him and keeping him sated with food, but not permitting him to walk or requiring him to work. Suppose we let him enjoy table and couch and continually live luxuriously. What, indeed, would be more wretched than this life? However, you will say: 'It is one thing to work, and another to toil.' Yet, in the beginning it was possible to work without toil.

'That was possible?' you will say.

Yes, it was, and God desired this, but you did not allow it. It was for this reason that He set you to work the garden of paradise, stipulating that you must work, but not mixing toil with the work. If man had toiled from the beginning, He would not have inflicted toil as a punishment afterward. It is indeed possible both to work and at the same time not to labor hard, as is the case with the angels. To prove that they work, listen to what Scripture says, 'You mighty in strength, who execute His word.'[7] At present, to be sure, our lack of strength makes for great toil, but at that time this was not yet so. 'For he who has entered into his rest, has also rested from his own works,' Scripture says, 'even as God did from his,'[8] not meaning idleness here, but cessation from toil. God still works even now, as Christ says: 'My Father works even until now, and I work.'[9]

Therefore, I beseech you, putting aside all arguments belittling labor, strive earnestly for virtue. The pleasure derived from vice is short-lived, while the pain of punishment is everlasting; contrariwise, the joy derived from virtue is timeless, while the toil it entails is but temporary. Besides, the latter, even before the reward is attained, encourages him who practices it, nourishing him with hope; but the former, even before the punishment is inflicted, chastises him who practices it, troubling his conscience, and frightening it, and rendering it in a condition to be suspicious of everything. Yet, are not these afflictions worse than any toils or any sweats?

But, if this were not so and sensual pleasure were present, what more worthless than that pleasure? As soon as it appears it flies away, withering and escaping before being caught, whether you speak of pleasure of the body, or that of luxury,

7 Ps. 102.20.
8 Heb. 4.10.
9 John 5.17.

or of wealth; they do not cease, indeed, to decay day by day. And since, in addition, there is in store [for this pleasure] both punishment and torture, what could be more wretched than those who embrace it?

Therefore, since we know these truths, let us endure all things for the sake of virtue. Thus we shall enjoy the true pleasure by the grace and mercy of our Lord Jesus Christ, with whom glory be to the Father, together with the Holy Spirit, forever and ever. Amen.

Homily 37 (John 5.7-13)

'Jesus said to him, "Dost thou want to get well?" The sick man answered him, "Yes, Lord, but I have no one to put me into the pool when the water is stirred." '[1]

Great is the profit to be derived from the sacred Scriptures and their assistance is sufficient for every need. Paul was pointing this out when he said: 'Whatever things have been written have been written for our instruction, upon whom the final age of the world has come, that through the patience and the consolation afforded by the Scriptures we may have hope.'[2] The divine words, indeed, are a treasury containing every sort of remedy, so that, whether one needs to put down senseless pride, or to quench the fire of concupiscence, or to trample on the love of riches, or to despise pain, or to cultivate cheerfulness and acquire patience—in them one may find in abundance the means to do so.

Truly, who of those struggling for a long time with poverty, or overcome with a serious malady, will not receive great consolation on reading the brief text quoted at the start? This paralytic, after waiting for thirty-eight years, and each year seeing others cured, while he himself was still burdened

1 John 5.7.
2 Rom. 15.4; 1 Cor. 10.11.

with his malady, did not, even so, lose heart and give up. Yet, not only the cheerlessness of the past, but also the hopelessness of the future, was enough to try his patience.

Listen, indeed, to what he said, and learn the magnitude of his misfortune. When Christ said: 'Dost thou want to get well?' he answered: 'I do, Lord, but I have no one to put me into the pool when the water is stirred.' What could be more pitiable than these words, what more pathetic than his plight? Do you perceive that his spirit had been chastened by his long illness? Do you see that all spleen had been checked? He did not utter any blasphemy, as we hear many doing in the midst of troubles. He did not curse the day he was born; he did not rant at his questioner, nor did he say: 'It is to ridicule and make fun of my condition that you ask whether I want to get well.' But, gently and very mildly: 'I do, Lord.'

Yet, he did not know who his questioner was or that He was going to heal him. Nevertheless, he stated everything with mildness, and made no importunate demand, as if he were speaking to a physician and desired only to make his affliction known. Perhaps he thought that Christ would be of service to him in putting him into the water, and he wished, by means of these words, to lead Him to do so.

Then what did Christ reply? Showing by His words that He was able to do all things, He said: 'Rise, take up thy pallet and walk.' Some conclude because of this that this man is the one also found in Matthew,[3] but it is clear for many reasons that he is not.

In the first place, it is evident from his lack of helpers. The man in Matthew, on the contrary, had a number of men taking care of him and carrying him, but this man had no one, and for that reason he said: 'I have no one.' In the second place, it is also evident from the reply he gave. The other said nothing, but this man explained all the circum-

---

3 Cf. Matt. 9.1-8; Mark 2.3-12; Luke 5.18-26.

stances of his plight. And there is a third indication from the time of the year and the day. This man was cured during a festival on the Sabbath; the other, on another day. There is a difference, too, in the place where each cure occurred: the one was healed in a house; the other, beside the pool.

The manner of healing also was different. In the other instance He said [at once]: 'Son thy sins are forgiven thee,'[4] while here He first restored the body and then cared for the soul. In the other, there was, to be sure, forgiveness of sins, for He said: 'Thy sins are forgiven thee,' but here there was also an admonition and a threat, cautioning him for the future, for He said: 'Sin no more, lest something worse befall thee.' The indictments made by the Jews also were different, for here they brought forward the charge of work on the Sabbath, while there they accused Him of blasphemy.

Now, I beseech you, reflect on the surpassing wisdom of God. He did not raise up the invalid at once, but first won his regard by His questioning, to prepare the way for the faith that was to follow. Not only did He raise him up, but He also bade him take up his pallet, so that the miracle which had taken place was believed, and no one thought the incident an illusion or a deceit. For he would not have been able to carry his pallet if his limbs had not been made very strong and steady.

Now, Christ often acted in this way to confute in superabundant measure those whose aim was to treat Him impudently. For instance, in the case of the loaves, so that no one might say that the people had merely had their fill and that the miracle was only fancied, He contrived that many fragments of the loaves were left over.[5] Also, in the case of the man cleansed of leprosy, He said: 'Go, show thyself to the priest,'[6] at the same time both giving the most certain

---

4 Matt. 9.2.
5 Cf. John 6.12,13.
6 Matt. 8.4.

proof of his being cleansed and stopping up the impudent mouths of those who were saying that He was acting as a law-giver in opposition to God. In the miracle of the wine he acted similarly, for He not merely produced the wine, but also had it brought to the chief steward,[7] so that, by acknowledging that he knew nothing of what had taken place, the latter would furnish to the miracle testimony that was above reproach. Indeed, that is why the Evangelist said that the chief steward did not know whence it was, namely, to stress the reliability of his testimony.

And elsewhere, when He had raised up the dead girl to life, He said: 'Give her something to eat,'[8] to provide this as a proof that she had certainly been raised from the dead. By all these means He gave convincing evidence for the benefit of even the undiscerning that He was not a deceiver or a conjurer, but had come for the salvation of all mankind.

Now, why did He not require faith of this man as He did in the case of the blind men, when He said: 'Do you believe that I can do this to you?'[9] Because this man did not yet know clearly who He was. It was not before His miracles, but after them, that He appeared to seek this prerequisite [of faith]. Indeed, it is with reason that those who had witnessed His power heard this question, while they who had not yet learned His identity, but were going to become aware of it from His miracles, were required to have faith only after they had witnessed them. Therefore, it is not at the beginning of His miracles that Matthew refers to Christ as making this stipulation, but only to the two blind men, at the time when He had worked many miracles.

Observe, then, the faith of the paralytic here. When he had heard the words: 'Take up thy pallet and walk,' he did not laugh Him to scorn, or say: 'What in the world is this?

7 Cf. John 2.8.
8 Luke 8.55.
9 Matt. 9.28.

An angel comes down and stirs the water, and heals one man only. Do you who are but a man think you can accomplish more than angels by means of a mere word of command? This is conceit, and boastful pride, and ridiculous.' On the contrary, he said none of these things, nor did he even think them, but as soon as he heard Him he rose up, and on becoming well did not fail to obey the command He had given him: 'Rise, take up thy pallet and walk.'

This, to be sure, was certainly wonderful, but what took place afterwards was still more so. To believe in the beginning, when no one was objecting, was surely not as remarkable as it was afterwards, when the Jews were in a rage and besetting him on every side, censuring and importuning him. Though they said: 'Thou art not allowed to take up thy pallet,' he not only took no notice of their rage, but also proclaimed his benefactor with much courage in the midst of the assemblage, and put a stop to the shameless talk. This, I for my part declare was very courageous. For, when the Jews were conspiring against him and saying to him censoriously and impudently: 'It is the Sabbath; thou are not allowed to take up thy pallet,' listen to what he replied.

'He who made me well said to me, "Take up thy pallet and walk." ' By this he was as much as saying: 'You are insane and out of your wits if you bid me, when I have been cured in this way of a long and difficult illness, not to think well of the Healer and not to obey everything He may command.' Yet, if he wished to be ignoble, he could have spoken in quite a different vein; for example: 'I did not do this of my own accord, but because someone else told me to. If this is blameworthy, charge it to the one who gave the order, and I will put down my couch;' and he would have concealed the cure. In this event he would have acted in this way because he knew very well that they were irked not so much because He broke the Sabbath as that He cured the sick.

Actually, however, he did not conceal this, nor did he

speak in this way, and he did not plead any excuse, but acknowledged his benefactor and proclaimed him in a loud voice. This is, in truth, what the paralytic did, but notice how wickedly the others acted. They did not say: 'Who made thee well?' They were silent on this point, but brought to the front, with much ado, his seeming transgression. ' "Who is the man who said to thee, 'Take up thy pallet and walk'?" But the man who had been healed did not know who it was, for Jesus had slipped away, since there was a crowd in the place.'

Now, why was it that Jesus slipped away? In the first place, in order that with Him out of the way the testimony might be above suspicion, for the one who had experienced the return to health was a trustworthy witness of this benefaction. It was, besides, that He might not cause their ill-feeling to flare up more strongly, for He knew that the mere sight of the object of their envy kindles no small spark in the envious. For this reason, by going out of the way, He permitted them to discuss His deed on its own merits, so that it might be no longer He that spoke about Himself, but those who had been healed, and even His accusers themselves as well. And I say this because these unwittingly testified to the miracle, since they did not say: 'Why did you order this to take place on the Sabbath?' but: 'Why do you do these things on the Sabbath?' It was not because of His transgression that they were indignant; they were envious because He restored the paralytic.

Yet, as far as regards the amount of human work involved, what the paralytic did was more truly work, while the healing was accomplished by word and speech. Here, therefore, He caused the Sabbath to be broken by the agency of another, while elsewhere He did this by His own agency, when He mixed clay and spread it over the eyes [of the blind man.][10] And this He did, not transgressing the Law, but transcending

10 Cf. John 9.6.

it. Now, more of this later, for when accused by them with regard to the Sabbath He did not everywhere defend Himself in the same way, and we must examine into this with care.

For the present, let us see how great an evil envy is and how it blinds the eyes of the soul to the detriment of the salvation of the one caught in its toils. For, just as madmen often thrust their swords against themselves, so also the envious, since they have one thing only in view, namely, the destruction of him who is the object of their envy, pay no heed to their own salvation.

They are worse than wild beasts, even. The latter are either in need of food or have been antagonized by us when they make an attack on us, while envious men, when they have even been the object of benefaction, have frequently treated their benefactors like wrong-doers. Accordingly, they are more dangerous than wild beasts and like demons—perhaps even worse than these—because, though demons have implacable enmity toward us, they do not exercise their wiles on their own kindred. Therefore, it was by this fact that Christ silenced the Jews when they said that He cast out the demon by Beelzebub.[11]

The envious, however, have neither shown respect for those who share their nature nor spared themselves. They punish their own souls instead of the objects of their envy, foolishly and vainly filling them with every kind of confusion and unhappiness. Why, O man, do you grieve at the good fortune of your neighbor? We ought to grieve at the misfortunes which cause us to suffer, not because we see others blessed with good fortune.

This sin, therefore, has been shorn of all excuse. The impure man has concupiscence to offer as excuse; the thief, his poverty; the murderer, his anger—fruitless and unreasonable excuses, to be sure; nevertheless they have these excuses to

11 Cf. Luke 11.14-23.

offer. But what sort of excuse will you give, I ask you? None at all, surely, but only that of the utmost degree of wickedness. For if, though we are told to love our enemies, we hate the very ones who love us, what penalty shall we pay?

Now, if they who love those who love them are no better than the heathen,[12] what pardon, what consolation shall he have who abuses those who have done him no wrong? Listen to what Paul says: 'If I deliver my body to be burned, yet do not have charity, it profits me nothing.'[13] Now, it is altogether plain that where envy and slander are, there charity has been destroyed. This passion is worse than that of fornication and adultery. The latter is confined to the one guilty of it, but the despotism of envy has upset whole churches and laid waste the whole world. It is the mother of murder: because of it Cain killed his brother; because of it Esau condemned Jacob to death; because of it his brothers [plotted to kill] Joseph;[14] because of it the Devil [seeks to] destroy all men.

Moreover, though at present you do not actually commit murder, you do many things more serious than murder when you pray for your brother to act in an unseemly fashion, placing snares for him on all sides, hindering his efforts to acquire virtue, grieving because he is pleasing to the Lord of the world. Surely, you are striving not against him, but against Him whom he worships; you are insulting Him by preferring your own honor to His. Accordingly, what you consider to be a trivial fault is the most serious of all; in fact, worse than the rest. For, even if you give alms, even if you keep vigil, even if you fast, you have become the worst of all sinners if you envy your brother.

The following illustrates the point. Once, a certain Cor-

---

12 Cf. Matt. 5.46,47.
13 1 Cor. 13.3.
14 Cf. Gen. 4.4-9; 27.41,42; 37.11-20.

inthian committed fornication; he was accused, however, and quickly made amends.[15] Cain envied Abel, but he was never cured of it, and though even God frequently reproached him with his ulcerous fault, he writhed and seethed the more and was driven to commit murder. Thus, this passion is more serious than that, and is not readily amenable to cure unless we are watchful.

Well, then, let us ever pull it up by the roots, keeping in mind that just as we aim a blow at God when we are consumed with envy at the good fortune of others, so we are pleasing to Him when we rejoice with them, and we make ourselves sharers in the blessings which lie in store for the upright man. That is why Paul also exhorts us: 'Rejoice with those who rejoice; weep with those who weep,'[16] that we may enjoy great profit as the fruit of both.

Keeping in mind, then, that when we rejoice with the toiler, even if we do not toil, we become sharers in his crown, let us cast aside all envy and plant charity in our own souls, so that, by applauding the efforts of those of our brethren who act laudably, we may obtain blessings both now and in future, by the grace and mercy of our Lord Jesus Christ, through whom and with whom glory be to the Father, together with the Holy Spirit, now and always, forever and ever. Amen.

Homily 38 (John 5.14-21)

'Afterwards Jesus found him in the temple, and said to him, "Behold, thou art cured. Sin no more, lest something worse befall thee." '[1]

Sin is a terrible thing, terrible and destructive of the soul;

---

15 1 Cor. 5.1-6; cf. Homily 38.
16 Rom. 12.15.

---

1 John 5.14.

frequently, this evil becomes so superabundant that it passes the bounds of the soul and seizes upon the body. Now, even though our soul be afflicted with many ills, we are untroubled, whereas, if our body receives even a small injury, we exert every effort to free it from its indisposition, because we can perceive this with our senses. For this reason God often punishes the body because of offenses committed by the soul, so that by the chastisement of the inferior part the superior part may obtain a cure.

It was thus that Paul restored to rectitude the immoral man in Corinth, checking the disease of his soul by the 'destruction of the flesh.'[2] And I say this because, having introduced the knife into bodily desire, he checked the evil in this way, like a good physician who cauterizes dropsy or spleen externally when they do not respond to internal remedies. This is what Christ did in the case of the paralytic. Notice how He Himself, to make this clear, said: 'Behold, thou art cured. Sin no more, lest something worse befall thee.'

What, then, do we learn from this? In the first place, that the disease developed in him as a result of sin; second, that the doctrine of hell is to be believed; third, that long and unending punishment is an actuality. Where, then, are they who say: 'Do I suffer punishment that is eternal, when I have committed murder in one hour merely, or have committed adultery in a short period of time?' Yes, for see that he also had not sinned for as many years as he suffered punishment, yet he spent a man's whole lifetime in the duration of his punishment. In truth, sins are judged, not according to the time it took to commit them, but according to the very nature of the offenses.

Besides this, we may also see that even if we have paid a severe penalty for former sins, if we then fall again into the same ones we shall in turn endure far more severe pains, and very rightly so. For he who has not become

2 1 Cor. 5.5.

better by reason of his punishment is afterwards subjected
to more severe chastisement, on the ground that he is
callous and contemptuous. Punishment was sufficient of itself
to check and make wiser the man who had fallen once; but
when, not made wiser by the punishment endured, he
dares to do the same things again, such a man would rightly
pay the penalty, since he himself has called it down upon
himself. Moreover, if even here we are chastised more severely
when we fall again into the same sins after being punished,
if we do not endure any punishment at all after committing
sins, ought we not to be very much afraid and tremble at
this, inasmuch as we are going to endure unending sufferings
[hereafter]?

'But why,' you will ask, 'are not all punished in this way?
We see many evil-doers thriving and healthy and enjoying
great prosperity.' Let us not, however, take courage at
this; rather, let us weep especially for them, because their
not having anything to suffer here is a guarantee of greater
punishment in the next world. Paul, to show this, said: 'But
when we are judged, we are being chastised by the Lord
that we may not be condemned with this world.'[3] Afflictions
here are a form of reproof, while those in the other world
are a form of punishment.

'What, then,' you will say, 'do all illnesses come in punishment for sin?' No, not all, but many do; some spring from
laxity. I say this because gluttony and drunkenness and sloth
give rise to sicknesses of this kind.

Accordingly, we must be watchful for one thing only:
that we bear every blow with gratitude. At times, the blow
comes to chastise sin, as in the Book of Kings we see a man
seized with a foot disease for this reason.[4] On the other hand,
the blow may be inflicted to increase righteousness still further, as God says to Job: 'Do you think that I have had

---

3 1 Cor. 11.32.
4 Cf. 3 Kings 15.23.

dealings with you for any other reason than 'that thou mayest be justified'?[5]

But why is it that in the case of these paralytics Christ drew attention to their sins? For He certainly did say to the one in Matthew: 'Take courage, son; thy sins are forgiven thee,'[6] and to this one: 'Behold, thou art cured. Sin no more.' Now, I know that there are some who slander this paralytic and say that he was an accuser of Christ, and that it was for this reason that he heard these words. In that case, what shall we say about the one in Matthew who actually heard the same thing? For He said to him also: 'Thy sins are forgiven thee.' From this fact it is clear that the other one did not hear this said for this reason, either.

Indeed, we may learn this still more clearly from the context. 'Afterwards Jesus found him in the temple,' it says. This is evidence of very great piety, for he did not withdraw to forums and clubs or give himself to luxury and licence, but stayed in the Temple, even though he expected to undergo such an attack and to be driven from there by all. None of these considerations, however, persuaded him to stay away from the Temple. When Christ, then, had found him, even after his conversation with the Jews, He hinted at no such thing [as that he had been His accuser]. If He had desired to make this charge, He would have said to him: 'Are you doing the same things again, and have you become no better because of your cure?' However, He said nothing of this, but only reassured him with regard to the future.

Why in the world is it, then, that, though He cured both the lame and the maimed, He said nothing like this? It seems to me that, while the diseases of the paralytics were the result of sin, those of the others came from physical weakness. Or, if this is not the case, He may have spoken

5 Cf. Job 40.3.
6 Matt. 9.2.

to the others through these and by means of the words addressed to the paralytics. Further, since this disease is more severe than the others, in His words to its victims He was also instructing the less severely afflicted. Just as when He had cured another person He bade him to give glory to God, not enjoining this upon him alone, but also on all in his person, so, too, in what He said to these paralytics He was giving the same encouragement and advice through them to all the rest of these afflicted persons.

Besides, we may add that He saw in his soul great patience, and so gave an admonition to him as to one able to profit by the warning, holding him in check both by the benefit he had received and by the fear of possible future evils with regard to his health. And note His modest way of speaking; He did not say: 'Behold, I have made you well,' but: 'Thou art cured. Sin no more.' Once more, He did not say: 'That I may not punish thee,' but: 'Lest something worse befall thee,' making both statements in an impersonal way, and also showing that the restoration of health came to the man by a gratuitous grace rather than by his just deserts. He did not declare that because he had paid the penalty deserved he was freed from punishment, but that he was made whole out of merciful love. If this were not truly so, He would have said: 'Behold, thou hast suffered sufficient punishment for thy sins; be careful in future.' Actually, however, He did not speak in this way. How did He speak? 'Behold, thou art cured. Sin no more.'

Now, let us frequently address these words to ourselves, also, and if we are set free after having been punished, let each one say this to himself: 'Behold, thou art cured. Sin no more.' And if we do not suffer punishment, though we continue in the same [evil] conduct, let us repeat that warning of the Apostle: 'The goodness of God leads us to repentance, but according to our hardness and unrepentant heart, we treasure up wrath to ourselves.'[7]

---

7 Cf. Rom. 2.4,5.

Further, it was not alone by repairing the body but also by another means that He furnished him a strong proof of His own divinity. For by saying 'Sin no more' He showed that He knew all the offenses he had previously committed, and therefore that He deserved to be trusted with regard to the future.

Accordingly, 'The man went away and told the Jews that it was Jesus who had healed him.' Notice that he persevered in the same good dispositions. He did not say: 'He is the one who said, "Take up thy pallet." ' Indeed, when they kept bringing forward continually the ostensible charge,[8] he repeatedly came to His defense by once more acknowledging Him as his healer and striving eagerly to attract and win over the others to Him. He was not so unfeeling as to betray his benefactor, after such a favor and encouraging advice, and to say what he did with malicious intent. Even if he were a beast, or some inhuman and stony-hearted monster, the favor done him, and his fear, were sufficient to hold him in check.

Indeed, with the threat still ringing in his ears, he would have been afraid that something worse might befall him, since he had received very great proofs of the power of his restorer. Rather, if he had wished to slander Him, keeping silence about his restoration to health, he would have spoken of the transgression of the Law and accused Him. This, however, is not so; it is not so. On the contrary, his words reveal great courage and honesty, and proclaim his benefactor no less than those of the blind man did. What did the latter say? 'He made clay and anointed my eyes.'[9] So this man also said: 'It is Jesus who healed me.'

'And this is why the Jews kept persecuting Jesus and sought to kill him, because he was doing these things on the Sabbath.' Then what did Christ say? 'My Father works

---

8 I.e., that He had broken the Sabbath.
9 John 9.11.

even till now, and I work.' When He needed to make a defense of His disciples, He cited the example of David, their fellow servant, saying: 'Have you not read what David did when he was hungry?'[10] But when He had to defend Himself, He took refuge in His Father, showing the equality of dignity of both, not only by speaking of the Father in a personal way, but also by saying that He does the same works as He.

And why did He not refer to the events that took place around Jericho?[11] He desired to lead them up from the earth, that they might no longer regard Him as a mere Man, but as God, and as having the right to make laws. If He were not truly the Son of God and of the same substance as He, the defense was out of proportion to the accusation. For, if a subordinate official who had changed a royal law, upon being charged with this, should then make this sort of defense and say that he made the change because the king could even nullify the law, he would not be able to escape punishment, but would thus incur a still more serious charge.

In this instance, on the contrary, since there is equality of rank, He has therefore elaborated the details of His defense with complete security. 'For of the same charges of which you acquit God you also acquit Me,' He says. That is why He began by saying, 'My Father,' in order to persuade even the recalcitrant to concede the same attributes to Him out of reverence for His clearly proven Sonship.

But if someone should say: 'How does the Father "work," since He ceased from all His works on the seventh day?' let him study the way in which He works. What, then, is the manner of His work? He plans for, He sustains, everything that exists. When you see the sun rising, then, and the

---

10 Matt. 12.3.
11 Jericho was captured on the seventh day by express command of God; cf. Jos. 6.4,15.

moon going through its phases; and streams and fountains and rivers and rains; and the course of nature in seeds, in our bodies, and in those of irrational animals; and all the other things of which the whole universe consists, learn the unceasing work of the Father. 'He makes his sun to rise on the good and the evil,' He says, 'and sends rain on the just and the unjust'; and again: 'If God so clothes the grass of the field, which today is alive and tomorrow is thrown into the oven'; and also speaking of the birds: 'Your heavenly Father feeds them.'[12]

To resume, in the account in Matthew[13] He accomplished everything He did on the Sabbath by His words only, and did nothing in action. Moreover, He refuted the charges [of breaking the Sabbath] by referring to what was done in the Temple,[14] and by mentioning what the Jews themselves were in the habit of doing.[15] But in our text He ordered actual work to be done, namely, the taking up of the pallet. It was, of course, a work which accomplished nothing of importance to the miracle, but had one function only. By showing a clear instance of the Sabbath being broken He led the discussion up to the more important issue, since He wished, rather, to strike them with awe at the dignity of the Father and to conduct them to something still more sublime.

Therefore, when there was a discussion regarding the Sabbath, He made His defense neither as Man alone, nor as God alone, but now as one, again as the other. He wished the two truths to be believed: both the condescension of the Incarnation and the dignity of His Godhead. It is for this reason that in the present instance He made His defense

---

12 Matt. 5.45; 6.30; 6.26.

13 I.e., in the discussion on the breaking of the Sabbath found in Matt. 12.

14 I.e., by David when he 'entered the house of God and ate the loaves of proposition'; cf. Matt. 12.4.

15 I.e., rescuing an animal from a pit on the Sabbath; cf. Matt. 12.11.

as God. If He were to speak to them always from a human point of view only, they would have persisted in the same lowly opinion of Him. Therefore, in order to prevent this from happening, He brought His Father into the discussion.

Now, even the very universe works on the Sabbath. The sun moves in its course, rivers flow, fountains gush forth, and women bear children. However, that you may learn that He is not a creature, He did not say: 'Yes, I work because the universe works.' But what did He say? 'Yes, I work because My Father works.'

'This, then, is why the Jews were seeking the more to put him to death; because he was not only breaking the Sabbath, but was also calling God his own Father, making himself equal to God.' However, He did not stop at merely declaring this, for He proved it, not by His words only, but more especially by His deeds. And why did He do this? Because they could pick His words apart and accuse Him of boasting, but when they saw the truth attested by His deeds, and the power revealed by His works, they could say nothing against Him in future.

However, those who do not wish to accept these proofs with good dispositions say that Christ did not mean that He was equal to God, but that the Jews deduced this. Come, then, let us return to the words recorded above. Tell me, I ask: Did the Jews persecute Him or did they not? It is quite clear that they did persecute Him. And did they persecute Him for this reason or for some other? It is acknowledged that it was for this reason. Therefore, did He break the Sabbath or did He not break it? No one could deny this, also. Did He say that God is His Father, or did He not say it? He certainly said it. Well, then, the conclusion which follows on this series is valid. Just as the fact that He said that God is His Father, and the fact that He broke the Sabbath, and the fact that He was persecuted by the Jews for that reason—and still more because of calling

God His Father—are not products of false suspicion, but are actual reality, so also His making Himself equal to God was a statement of the same tenor.[16]

Now, this is more clearly to be seen from the words quoted above. The statement, 'My Father works, and I work,' is that of One showing that He is equal to God. Indeed, He indicated that there was no difference between Them. He did not say: 'He works and I work under Him'; but: 'Just as He works, so do I also.' And He showed that Their equality is complete. Now, if He Himself did not wish to convey this, but the Jews foolishly conceived the notion that He did, He would not have allowed their minds to remain in error, but would have corrected this.

The Evangelist also would not have kept silence about this, but would have said openly that the Jews did conceive this suspicion, but that He Himself did not make Himself equal to God—the very procedure which he adopted elsewhere when he saw that what was said meant one thing but was interpreted to mean another.

For example, Christ said: 'Destroy this temple, and in three days I will raise it up,' speaking about His body. The Jews, however, not understanding this, and thinking He was speaking about the Jewish Temple, said: 'Forty-six years has this temple been in building, and wilt thou raise it up in three days?' Therefore, since He Himself was saying one thing, and they were interpreting it as something else— He was speaking of His body, while they thought this was being said of their own Temple—the Evangelist, to explain this or, rather, to correct their wrong idea, added the words: 'But he was speaking of the temple of his body.'[17]

Thus, in this context also, if Christ did not make Himself equal to God and did not wish to give this impression, but the Jews had acquired the incorrect idea that He did, the

16 Literally, 'with the same meaning.'
17 Cf. John 2.19-22.

Evangelist would have corrected their false idea here, also, and would have said: 'The Jews thought that He made Himself equal to God, but He did not mean that equality.'

Now, it is not this Evangelist alone who does this—and he not here only—but elsewhere another Evangelist also may be found so doing. When Christ had given warning to the disciples in the words: 'Take heed and beware of the leaven of the Pharisees and Sadducees, they began to argue among themselves, saying, "We have brought no bread." '[18] He meant one thing, calling that teaching 'leaven,' while the disciples interpreted it as something else, thinking that He was talking about food. This idea, not the Evangelist any more, but Christ Himself, corrected in the following words: 'Why do you not understand that it was not of bread I said to you, "Beware?" ' In our text, however, no such comment is found.

Still, you will say: 'It was to correct that very idea[19] that Christ added: "The Son can do nothing of himself." ' In reality, He did quite the contrary, my friend, for He was not destroying, but strengthening, the concept of His equality when He said this. However, pay attention carefully, because the inquiry is no trifling one. The expression 'of himself' occurs frequently in Scripture, both with reference to Him and to the Holy Spirit. We must study the force of the expression, that we may not fall into very serious errors. If one takes it from the context in this way, interpreting it in its literal meaning, see what astonishing conclusion will follow. For, of course, He did not mean that there are some things, on the one hand, which He could do of Himself, while there are others which He could not, but He said in general: 'The Son can do nothing of himself.'

Let us, then, ask our opponent: 'Can the Son, then, do nothing of Himself, I ask you?' And if he replies that He

18 Cf. Matt. 16.6-12.
19 I.e., of His equality to the Father.

can do nothing at all of Himself, we shall answer that He has, nonetheless, done the greatest of good things 'of Himself.' And Paul cries this out: 'Who, though he was by nature God, did not consider being equal to God a thing to be clung to, but emptied himself, taking the nature of a slave.'[20] Again, Christ Himself says elsewhere: 'I have the power to lay down my life, and I have the power to take it up again and no one takes it from me; I lay it down of myself.'[21] Do you see that He has power over life and death and carries out such a great plan 'of Himself'?

But why do I confine my remarks to Christ? Though nothing could be more ineffectual than we are, actually we do many things of ourselves, both when we choose evil of ourselves and when we go in quest of virtue of ourselves. And if it is not of ourselves that we do so, and if we have not the power, we shall not fall into hell, either, when we sin, nor shall we obtain the kingdom of heaven when we act virtuously.

Therefore, 'He can do nothing of himself' means nothing else than that He can do nothing in opposition to His Father, nothing different, nothing foreign, an attribute especially belonging to one who is giving proof of equality and of complete agreement as well. But why did He not say 'He does nothing in opposition' instead of 'He cannot'? It was in order that He might show from this once more that His equality is undeviating and complete. This statement does not imply any weakness in Him, but testifies to His great power. Besides, Paul says elsewhere of the Father: 'That by two unchangeable things, in which it is impossible for God to deceive'; and again: 'If we disown him, he remains faithful, for he cannot disown himself.'[22] Now this word

20 Phil. 2.6.
21 John 10.18.
22 Heb. 6.18; 2 Tim. 2.12,13.

'cannot' is not, of course, indicative of weakness but of strength; indeed, ineffable strength.

What He means, accordingly, is this: that His nature is incompatible with all such things. Just as when we ourselves, too, say that God cannot commit sin we are not accusing Him of weakness, but are bearing witness to His ineffable power, so also when He Himself says: 'I can do nothing of myself' His meaning is as follows: 'It is impossible and inconceivable for Me to do anything in contradiction to My Father.'

Now, in order that you may learn that this is His meaning, let us pass on to what follows and see which opinion Christ approves: our words or yours. On the one hand, you maintain that that statement of His detracts from His power and the autonomy proper to Him, and shows His strength to be weak; on the other hand, I say that this statement proves His equality and that it is undeviating and results from identity of purpose and power and strength.

Let us, then, ask Christ, and let us see by means of His subsequent words whether He interprets His statement according to your idea or ours. What, therefore, did He say? 'Whatever the Father does, this the Son also does in like manner.' Do you see how He has pulled your interpretation up by the roots and has confirmed ours? For, if He does nothing of Himself, the Father also will not be doing anything of Himself, that is, if Christ does everything 'in like manner' to Him.

Indeed, if this is not so, another strange conclusion will also follow. He did not say that He did what He had seen the Father doing, but that He does nothing except 'what He sees the Father doing,' making His statement include all time, while according to you He will be always learning to do the same things [as the Father]. Do you perceive how sublime the thought is, while the humility of His words forces even the most shameless to flee, even though unwilling to do so, from the interpretation that is both degrading and most unbecoming His dignity?

In truth, who is so wretched and unhappy as to say that the Son learns each day what He must do? And how, in that case, would it be true to say: 'Thou art the same, and Thy years have no end' and also: 'All things were made through him, and without him was made nothing,'[23] if, that is, He Himself sees and imitates the things which the Father does? Do you perceive that the proof of His autonomy is demonstrated both by the above-mentioned statements and by the words which follow them?

And if He introduces some statements somewhat more lowly in tone, do not wonder at it. Since they kept persecuting Him, when they heard sublime doctrine, and thought He was inimical to God, having descended from the sublime for a little while, by His words only, He once more conducted His discourse to more lofty heights, then again to lower levels, thus varying His teaching, so that it would be acceptable even to the perverse.

Please notice. Having said: 'My Father works and I work,' and having revealed that He is equal to God, He once more said: 'The Son can do nothing of himself, but only what he sees the Father doing.' Then, again rising to the sublime: 'For whatever he does, this the Son does also in like manner.' Once more to the lower level: 'The Father loves the Son, and shows him all that he himself does. And greater works than these he will show him.'

Once again, do you perceive how great His humility is? Of course, you do. Indeed, I shall now repeat what I just now stated and will not cease saying: when He said something humble and lowly in tenor, He thus expressed it to an exaggerated degree, in order that the humble tone of His words might persuade even the perverse to receive the ideas with a docile attitude. If this be not the case, consider

---

23 Ps. 101.28; John 1.3.

how strange the statement is if interpreted by the letter of the words.

When He says: 'And greater works than these he will show him,' He will be found [apparently] not yet to have learned many things, an assertion which can be made not even of the Apostles. For, once they had received the grace of the Spirit, they immediately both knew everything and could do everything that they needed to know and to do. He, on the contrary [if we interpret His words literally], will be found not yet in possession of much knowledge that He needed to have. Now, what could be stranger than this?

What, then, do His words mean? He spoke in this way because He had cured the paralytic and was going to raise the dead also, as much as saying: 'Do you marvel because I have cured a paralytic? You will see greater marvels than this.' He did not, however, actually say this, but continued in a somewhat more humble strain in order that He might calm their anger. And that you may be convinced that the expression, 'He will show,' is not used in the literal sense, listen to the words with which He continues. 'For as the Father raises the dead and gives them life,' He says, 'even so the Son also gives life to whom he will.'

The words 'to whom he will,' to be sure, seem contradictory to 'He can do nothing of himself.' For, if it is to whom He wills that He gives life, He can do it of Himself (the word 'will' implies that power); but if 'He can do nothing of himself,' He no longer gives life 'to whom he will.' In reality, the words 'as the Father raises' show the complete identity of His power with that of the Father, while the words 'to whom he will' show the equality of His will. Do you perceive that the words 'He can do nothing of himself' do not minimize the extent of His power, but demonstrate the complete identity of His power and will [with those of the Father]? Similarly, consider also the words 'He will show him,' for elsewhere He said likewise: 'I will raise him up on the last day.'[24] And again, to show that He does not receive power from outside Himself when He does this, He said: 'I am the resurrection and the life.'[25]

Further, that you might not say that, though He raises the dead 'whom he will' and 'gives life to whom he will,' He did not do the rest as He willed, He refuted every argument of the kind by anticipation when He said: 'Whatever he does, this the Son also does in like manner.' By this He made it clear that He both does all that the Father does, and also does it in the manner in which the Father does it. Whether you mention resurrection from the dead, or creation of bodies, or forgiveness of sins, or anything else whatsoever, He does it in the same way as His Father.

However, men who are unmindful of their own salvation pay attention to none of these truths, so great an evil is the ambition to hold first place. This has spawned heresies; it has confirmed the heathen in their impiety. For, while God has willed that His invisible world be known through this created universe,[26] they disdain these things and, scornfully refusing to submit to this schooling, have carved another road for themselves. Therefore, they have strayed from the right one. That is why the Jews also did not believe, since they received glory from one another and did not seek the glory which comes from God.

On the contrary, beloved, let us flee this disease with all zeal and earnestness. Even if we have innumerable virtues, the plague of vainglory is capable of destroying them all. If, then, we desire praises let us seek those which come from God. The praise that comes from men, of whatever sort it may be, perishes as soon as it appears. Even if it does not perish, it has brought no profit to us, and frequently is the product of a warped judgment.

---

24 John 6.40.
25 John 11.25.
26 Cf. Rom. 1.20.

Indeed, what wonderful advantage has that worldly glory which youthful dancers, and corrupt women, and misers, and robbers enjoy? He who is praised by God is praised, not in the company of these, but with those well-known saints— I mean the Prophets, the Apostles—who have lived an angelic life. If we desire to attract crowds and to be the object of all eyes, let us assess this on its own merits and we shall discover that it is worth nothing.

In short, if you love the crowd, attract to yourself the throng of the angels and become hostile to demons and you will give no weight to human opinions. On the contrary, you will then trample the glitter of this world as slime and mud, and you will then perceive clearly that nothing so defiles the soul as the love of glory. It is not possible, truly it is not possible, for him who loves glory not to live a life of torture, just as it is not possible for him who tramples on it to fail to trample many more vices at the same time. The man who conquers it will also vanquish envy and avarice and all grave sinful maladies.

'But how shall we conquer it?' you say. If we look to the glory from heaven, of which this is seeking to deprive us. That glory accompanies us to the life to come, and even in this life, and frees us from all the carnal servitude to which we are now enslaved most wretchedly, if we are giving ourselves over wholly to the world and its affairs. Whether you go to the market-place, or enter your home; whether you are on the roads, or go to lodgings, or inns, or shops, or a ship, or an island, or the royal palace, or the law court or the senate, everywhere you will observe preoccupation with present affairs and the things of this life, and each man greatly concerned about these. Whether going away or returning; undertaking journeys or staying at home; whether sailing the sea or tilling the soil; whether in the fields or in the cities—all, in a word, are busy with temporal affairs.

What hope of salvation, then, will there be for us if,

while dwelling on God's earth, we do not think of the things of God, but, though bidden to be strangers to the things of this life, are actually strangers to the things of heaven, and citizens of this world? What could be worse than this stupidity if, though hearing every day about the judgment and the kingdom, we imitate those living in the time of Noe, and the people in Sodom, waiting to learn everything by experience? Yet it was for this reason that all those events were preserved in writing, that if one should be incredulous with regard to things to come he might receive, from things that have already occurred, a clear assurance of the future.

Reflecting on these truths, then, both past and future, let us obtain at least some relief from this slavery and consider our souls also of some account, that we may attain to both present and future blessings by the grace and mercy of our Lord Jesus Christ, to whom be glory and power forever and ever. Amen.

Homily 39 (John 5.22-30)

'For neither does the Father judge any man, but all judgment he has given to the Son, that all men may honor the Son even as they honor the Father.'[1]

We need to show great earnestness in all our affairs, beloved. And I say this because we shall give a reckoning, and we shall render a strict accounting both of our words and of our deeds. Our affairs are not restricted to the present life, but still another state of life will receive us on leaving here, and we shall stand before a fearful tribunal. 'All of us,' says Paul, 'must take our stand before the tribunal of Christ, so that each one may receive what he has won through the body, according to his works, whether good or evil.'[2]

---

1 John 5.22-23
2 Cf. 2 Cor. 5.10.

Let us, then, always be mindful of this tribunal, and thus we shall be able to persevere unceasingly in virtue. He who has ruled that day out of his mind is borne to destruction, like a horse that has snapped off his bridle, for Scripture says: 'His ways are filthy at all times'; and to assign a cause for this it adds: 'Thy judgments are far from his sight.'[3] So he who unceasingly keeps the fear of judgment in mind will comport himself as he ought.

'Remember thy last end,' says Scripture, 'and thou shalt never sin.'[4] He who now forgives our sins will sit in judgment then; He who has died for our sake will again appear to judge the universe. 'The second time he will appear with no part in sin to those who wait for him unto salvation.'[5] That is why He said in our context: 'My Father does not judge any man, but all judgment he has given to the Son, that all men may honor the Son even as they honor the Father.'

'Well, then,' you ask, 'shall we address Him also as Father?' Perish the thought! He has said 'the Son' in order that we may honor Him in the same way as the Father, while He continues to be the Son. He who calls Him Father has no longer honored the Son as the Father, but has mixed everything up.

To continue: since men are not won over as effectively by mild words as by being reproved, for that reason He spoke as frighteningly as He did, so that fear at least might draw His listener to honor Him. Now, when He said 'All [judgment]' He meant this: that He has power both to punish and to give honor, and to do each as He wills. And He used the expression 'he has given' that you might not conceive the suspicion that He is unbegotten and think that there are two Fathers. Everything that the Father is, the Son is

3 Cf. Ps. 9.27.
4 Eccli. 7.40.
5 Heb. 9.28.

also, though He has been begotten and remains in the condition of Son.

And that you may know that the expression 'He has given' is equivalent to 'He has begotten,' listen to this being made clear from another place.[6] 'For as the Father has life in himself, even so he has given to the Son also to have life in himself.' What then? Did he beget Him first, and then give Him life? For he who gives, gives to a person who exists. Was He, then, begotten without life? Not even demons, however, would conceive this idea, for besides its impiety it is also very foolish. Therefore, just as 'He has given life' means 'He has begotten Him who is Life,' so also 'He has given judgment' means 'He has begotten Him who will be Judge.'

Now, in order that you may not think, on hearing that He has the Father as cause, that He is different in some way in substance and inferior in dignity, He Himself comes to judge you, proving His equality to the Father also from that circumstance. Indeed, He who has power to punish and to honor whom He wills has the same powers as the Father. Besides, if this be not so, but He received His dignity after being begotten, what has happened so that He was afterwards given this honor? By what sort of promotion did He come to the point that He was chosen and received this rank? Do you not blush to be applying these human and cheap ideas to the pure nature that admits of no addition?

'Why, then,' you say, 'did He speak in this way?' In order to make what He said more readily believed and to prepare the way for sublime words to come. It was for this reason that He mingled the latter with the other type, and these with those. Moreover, see how He did it, for it is good at this point to review this from the beginning.[7]

He had said: 'My Father works and I work,' showing by

---

6 Cf. John 5.26.
7 Cf. John 5.17-23.

this His equality and Their equal rank. 'And they were seeking to put him to death.' What did He do next? He softened His words, but kept the same ideas, speaking as follows: 'The Son can do nothing of himself.' Then, once again He raised His discourse to the sublime: 'For whatever he does, this the Son also does in like manner.' Next, once more to a lower level: 'For the Father loves the Son and shows him all that he himself does. And greater works than these he will show him.' Then, again to the more sublime: 'For as the Father raises the dead and gives them life, even so the Son also gives life to whom he will.' And after this, again to the lowly, but also, nonetheless, sublime: 'For neither does the Father judge any man, but all judgment he has given to the Son.' Next, to the more sublime: 'That all men may honor the Son even as they honor the Father.'

Do you perceive how He varied His discourse, weaving together both lofty and lowly phrases and sentences, so that what He said might be readily accepted by those who were then present, and those to come afterwards might not be misled, since in truth they would receive from the lofty expressions the correct idea regarding the rest. Indeed, if this be not so, and His words were not spoken as condescending to His listeners, why were the sublime ones added? When the man who has a right to say great things of himself says something of little account and humble, he has the obvious appearance of doing this with some wise end in view. On the other hand, if the man who ought to speak in moderate terms of himself should say something great, what does he accomplish by saying things that are above and beyond his nature? This no longer seems a part of some plan, but an evidence of extreme impiety.

And so we have a correct explanation, and one worthy of God, for His speaking with humble words: namely, His condescension and His teaching us to act with moderation; also, the salvation He planned to come to us by this means.

This He Himself made clear when He said in another place: 'I say these things that you may be saved.'[8] Since, forsaking His own testimony, He had taken refuge in the testimony of John [the Baptist], a course of action which was unworthy of His greatness, He explained such depreciation of His words by saying: 'I say these things that you may be saved.'

But you who say that He has not the same might and power as He has, who begot Him, what would you say if you should hear Him uttering words by which He shows that His power and might and glory are equal to the Father's?[9] And why does He claim the same honor if He is very much inferior, as you say? Yet He did not stop here, when He had spoken in this way, but even went on to say: 'He who does not honor the Son does not honor the Father who sent him.' Do you perceive how the honor of the Son is bound up with the honor of the Father?

'And what of this?' someone will say. 'For it is possible to see this also in the case of the Apostles. "For he who receives you receives me," ' Christ says.[10] But there He spoke in this way because He was treating as His own the interests of His slaves who belong to Him, while here He spoke thus because there is identity of His substance and glory [with the Father's]. Besides, in the case of the Apostles He did not say: 'that they may honor you,' but with reason He said: 'He who does not honor the Son does not honor the Father.'

And I say this because, if, when there are two kings, one should be insulted, the other also would share the insult, especially if the one insulted were his son. Indeed, he is also insulted if even a soldier is maltreated; not, of course, in the same way, but as if through an intermediary. Here, on the contrary, the dishonor is not of this sort, but as if done

8 Cf. John 5.34.
9 Cf. John 5.23.
10 Matt. 10.40.

to Himself. That is why He said by anticipation: 'That they may honor the Son even as they honor the Father,' so that when He said: 'He who does not honor the Son does not honor the Father,' you might realize that Their honor is the same. For it is not merely 'he who does not honor,' but 'he who does not honor in the way which I have mentioned,' He says, that 'does not honor the Father.'

'And how,' you will say, 'can He who sends and He who is sent be of the same substance?' You are once again confining the discussion within human limits and are not keeping in mind that all these things were said for no other reason than that we might know of that First Cause, and that we might not fall into the error of Sabellius;[11] and that the fallacy of the Jews might be corrected in this way, so that He might not be thought by them to be an enemy of God. I say this because they kept saying: 'This man is not of God; this man has not come from God.'[12] In order to dispel this erroneous idea He placed before them not so much the lofty ideas of Himself as the humble ones. It was on this account that He frequently said, here, there, and everywhere, that He had been 'sent'; not that you might think that this way of speaking was a kind of depreciation of Himself, but in order to put a stop to their remarks.

That is why also He frequently took refuge in the Father, putting aside, for the time being, even His own autonomy. If He had made all His statements in accordance with His proper dignity, they would not have accepted His words, seeing that because of even a few such statements they persecuted Him and often stoned Him. If on the other hand, with their attitude in mind, He had uttered only statements of humble tenor, many would afterwards have suffered harm. He therefore mingled and blended His teaching. Employing this strategy, as I have said, He put a stop to the remarks of

11 I.e., that there is but one Person in God; cf. *Catholic Encyclopedia, s.v.*
12 Cf. John 9.16.

His opponents by His statements of humble tenor. And by those couched in accordance with His proper dignity, He dispelled from the right-minded the inferior conception of Him resulting from His other words, and showed that it was not at all worthy of Him.

'Now, being "sent" implies change in place and God is everywhere present. Why, therefore, did He say He was sent?' He was using somewhat material terms to make clear His identity with the Father; similarly, He also used this approach in the words which follow, with the same purpose in mind. 'Amen, amen, I say to you,' He says, 'he who hears my word and believes him who sent me, has life everlasting.' Do you perceive how He repeatedly set forth the same idea to cure that mistaken notion? And do you see how in this text and in what follows—both by instilling fear and by announcing a reward—He sought to destroy the envy felt toward Him? And do you see that in this text He once again displayed much condescension in His words?

He did not say: 'He who hears My word and believes in Me.' They surely would have thought that this was conceit and exaggerated boastfulness in speech. If, indeed, after so long a time and after witnessing numberless miracles, they had in fact conceived this mistaken notion of Him, they would have done so the more if He spoke in this way. As a matter of fact, they did say to Him on such an occasion: 'Abraham is dead, and the prophets, and how dost thou say, "If anyone keep my word he will never taste death?" '[13] Therefore, that they might not become as savage as beasts here, also, see what He said: 'He who hears my word, and believes him who sent me, has life everlasting.'

Now, this in no small way made His words readily acceptable—I mean when they learned that they who hear Him believe in the Father—for when they had accepted this willingly they would accept the rest more easily. So that, by

13 John 8.52.

making a statement of humble tenor, He both contributed to and paved the way for the more sublime.

When He had said 'has life everlasting,' He added 'and does not come to judgment, but has passed from death to life.' He made His words readily acceptable by these two things: by saying that it is the Father who is believed and by declaring that the believer will enjoy many rewards. And the words 'does not come to judgment' mean 'is not punished.' This 'death' He mentioned is not that experienced on earth, but that in eternity, just as, similarly, that 'life' is eternal life.

'Amen, amen, I say to you, the hour is coming, and now is here, when the dead shall hear the voice of the Son of Man,[14] and those who hear shall live.' In making the statement He was also offering them the evidence of His deeds. Since He had said: 'As the Father raises the dead and gives them life, so also the Son gives life to whom he will,' in order that this might not seem to be conceit and boasting, He now offered the evidence also of His deeds, saying: 'The hour is coming.' Then, in order that you might not conceive the idea that the time of waiting would be long, He added: 'And now is here, when the dead shall hear the voice of the Son of God, and those who hear shall live.'

Do you perceive here His autonomy and His ineffable power? 'For just as it will be in the resurrection, so it is now,' He says. And this is so because at that time, when we hear the word of command, we shall arise. 'With the cry of command of God the dead will arise,' Scripture says.[15] Now, 'Whence is it clear,' someone will perhaps ask, 'that these statements are not empty boasting?' From the words that He added: 'and now is here.' If He had made the announcement only for the times to come, they would have looked

---

14 Unanimously elsewhere: 'Son of God,' as St. John Chrysostom himself has it also a few lines below.
15 Cf. 1 Thess. 4.16.

upon the statement with suspicion. But, as it is, He gave them proof. 'For while I am dwelling with you,' He said, 'this will take place.' If He did not have the power, He would not have made the announcement for that time so as not to incur more ridicule by reason of the promise. Besides, He added a statement that explained His words still further, saying: 'For as the Father has life in himself, even so he has given to the Son also to have life in himself.'

Do you perceive how Their equality is shown and that They differ in one respect only, namely, that one is the Father, while the other is the Son? The expression 'he has given' implies this distinction only, and shows that all the other attributes are equal and without difference. From this it is clear that He does everything with as much authority and power as the Father and is not endowed with power from some outside source, for He has life as the Father has.

Accordingly, that is why He has immediately added once more what follows: that we might understand that point from this context, also. What, then, follows? 'He has granted him power also to render judgment.' Now, why did He repeatedly turn the discussion to resurrection and judgment?[16] 'For as the Father raises the dead and gives them life, even so the Son also gives life to whom he will'; and again: 'The Father does not judge any man, but all judgment he has given to the Son'; and once more: 'As the Father has life in himself, even so he has given to the Son also to have life in himself'; and again: 'Those who hear the voice of the Son of God shall live'; and in this place, once again: 'He has granted him power also to render judgment.' Why, therefore, did He continually turn the discussion to these matters—I mean 'judgment' and 'life' and 'resurrection'? Because these are the things best calculated to influence even the stubborn listener. For, if a man believes that he will rise again and will give an accounting for his sins to Him, even if he sees

---

16 For the following, cf. John 5.21,22,26,27.

no other sign, if he has accepted this truth, he will put forth every effort to render the Judge propitious to him.

'Because he is Son of Man, do not wonder at this.' Paul of Samosata,[17] indeed, does not say it this way, but how does he say it? 'He has granted him power to render judgment, because he is Son of Man.'[18] However, when read in this way, it has no logical sequence. He did not receive the power to judge for the reason that He is Son of Man (because what would prevent all men from being judges?), but because He is Son of that ineffable being; He is for that reason Judge. Well, then, it must be read as follows: 'Because he is Son of Man, do not wonder at this.' Since what was said seemed to His listeners to be contradictory and they thought it meant nothing more than a mere man, while what was said actually was greater than belonged to man—nay, rather, greater than belonged to angels—and belonged to God alone, to do away with this contradiction He added: 'Do not wonder because he is Son of Man, for the hour is coming in which those who are in the tombs shall hear his voice, and they who have done good shall come forth unto resurrection of judgment.'

Now, why did He not say: 'Do not wonder because He is Son of Man, since He is also Son of God,' but instead recalled the resurrection? He did indeed mention this above, when He said: 'They shall hear the voice of the Son of God.' But if He here refrained from mentioning it,[19] do not be surprised. By mentioning the work that is proper to God he made it possible for His hearers to reason from this that He also was God and Son of God. If He stated this truth repeatedly it would then have become objectionable to them, whereas He made the teaching less offensive when it

17 Cf. above, Homily 4 n. 5.
18 This is the accepted punctuation and phrasing today, not the one advocated by St. John Chrysostom in the following passage.
19 Cf. John 5.29.

was proved by a logical conclusion drawn from His miracles.

I say this because, when those who make syllogisms have undeniably proved the question at issue by laying down the premises, they themselves often do not add the conclusion. But when they have by this means made the listener more kindly disposed, in order to make the victory more brilliant they contrive that that opponent himself should pronounce the conclusion. Thus, those of the opposition who are present will be persuaded to agree with them rather than to approve the argument of their own side.

Therefore, when He predicted the resurrection of Lazarus,[20] He refrained from mentioning judgment, for it was not on this account that He raised Lazarus from the dead. But in speaking of the general resurrection He also added this: 'They who have done good shall come forth unto resurrection of life; but they who have done evil unto resurrection of judgment.' Thus John, too, urged his hearers on by recalling the judgment and that 'He who is unbelieving towards the Son shall not see life, but the wrath of God rests upon him.'[21] So also, Christ Himself said to Nicodemus: 'He who believes in the Son is not judged; but he who does not believe is already judged.'[22]

Thus, here likewise He has made mention of both judgment and punishment for evil deeds. For, since He had said above: 'He who hears my word and believes him who sent me is not judged,' in order that no one might think that faith alone is sufficient for salvation, He also mentioned the works of man's life, saying, 'They who have done good, unto resurrection of life; and they who have done evil, unto resurrection of judgment.'

Since, therefore, He had said that the whole world would give an account to Him and would rise at His voice, a novel

20 Cf. John 5.25.
21 John 3.36.
22 John 3.18.

and paradoxical idea even yet—one which at present is still incredible to many even of those who seem to be of the faith, and at the time was not credible to the Jews—listen to the way in which He set it forth, condescending to the weakness of His hearers. 'Of myself I can do nothing. As I hear I judge; and my judgment is just because I seek not my own will, but the will of him who sent me.'

Yet, He had just now given no small proof of the resurrection when He had cured the paralytic. Moreover, He had not discoursed about the resurrection until He had done something not very unlike the resurrection. And at that time He had hinted at the judgment, after the cure of the body, when He said: 'Behold, thou art cured. Sin no more, lest something worse befall thee.' And He went on to predict the resurrection of Lazarus and that of the world.

Now, when He had foretold these two resurrections: that of Lazarus, which was to come very soon, and that of the world, which would take place a long time afterwards, He gave a guarantee of the former by the cure of the paralytic, and of its close proximity in time by saying: 'The hour is coming, and now is here.' And He gave a guarantee of the latter by the resurrection of Lazarus, bringing to light things that had not yet taken place by means of events that had already occurred. It is possible to see Him doing this on very many occasions, when He has made two, or even three, prophecies and has always given assurance of things to be by those that have already taken place.

Still, notwithstanding the fact that He had said and done such great things, He did not consider this enough for them, because they were as yet somewhat weak. But by the words which He added He forestalled their contentiousness by saying: 'Of myself I can do nothing. As I hear, I judge; and my judgment is just because I seek not my own will, but the will of him who sent me.' Now, He seemed to be saying something strange and different from the Prophets (for they

used to say that it is God who judges the whole earth, that
is, the human race. This David said, proclaiming it many
times: 'He judges the peoples with equity,' and 'God is a
righteous judge; strong and patient,'[23] as did all the Prophets
and Moses). But Christ said: 'The Father does not judge any
man, but judgment he has given to the Son,' and this was
sufficient to upset any Jew who then heard Him, and to dispose him to suspect once more that He was an enemy of God.
Hence, He here condescended very low in His words, and
as much as their weakness required, so as to tear up this
destructive suspicion by the roots, and said: 'Of myself I
can do nothing,' that is: 'You will see Me doing or hear
Me saying nothing strange, nothing different, nothing that
is contrary to the Father's will.'

Now, as He had said previously that He is the Son of
Man and had gone on to show that they mistakenly supposed
that He was human only, so He here also added something.[24]
Therefore, just as when He said above: 'We speak of what
we have heard, and we bear witness to what we have seen,'
and as when John [the Evangelist] said: 'He bears witness to
that which he has seen, and his witness no one receives,'[25]
reference was being made in both instances to the accuracy
of His knowledge and not merely to hearing and seeing—
so here also, when He mentioned hearing, He meant nothing else than that it is impossible for Him to will anything
else than what the Father wills.

However, He did not say this explicitly (for they would
not have accepted it if they heard it at that time openly
expressed). How did He say it? Humbly and very humanly:
'As I hear, I judge.' Again, when He here said this, He did
not mean instruction (He did not say, 'As I am taught,' but
'As I hear'); nor did He say it as if He needed to listen

---

23 Ps. 95.10; Ps. 7.12.
24 I.e., 'As I hear I judge.'
25 John 3.11, 32.

(for not only was He without need of instruction but also without need of hearing); but He spoke in this way to make clear the agreement and identity of His will [with the Father's]. What He meant is this: 'I judge as if it were the Father Himself who is judging.'

Then He added: 'And I know that my judgment is just because I seek not my own will, but the will of him who sent me.' What is it You are saying? Do You have a will other than the Father's? Yet, elsewhere You have said: 'Even as thou and I are one.'[26] And again, speaking with regard to harmony of will: 'Grant them that they also may be one in us,' that is, in their belief in us. Do you perceive that words which seem to be especially humble are the very ones that have sublime meaning concealed in them? What He implied is some such truth as this: not that the Father wills one thing and He another, but, 'Just as an individual soul has one will, so My will and the Father's are one.'[27]

Now, do not wonder if He has spoken of so close a union. I say this because Paul used this illustration with regard to the Spirit when he said: 'For who among men knows the things of a man, save the spirit of a man which is in him? Even so, the things of God no one knows but the Spirit of God.'[28] Christ was saying nothing else than this: 'I will nothing exclusively, apart from the Father, but if He wills anything, this I also will; and if I will anything, this He also wills. Therefore, just as no one could find fault with the Father when He acts as Julge, so also no one could find fault with Me, for the decision of each of Us proceeds from the same opinion.'

If He discoursed on these matters in a somewhat human fashion, do not be surprised. They still considered Him as merely man. Therefore, it is very necessary in such instances

26 Cf. John 17.23,21.
27 I.e., in complete agreement.
28 1 Cor. 2.11.

not only to search out the meaning of what is said, but also
to take into consideration the suspicious attitude of His
hearers and to hear His words as addressed to that suspicion.
Otherwise, many strange conclusions will follow. For example,
notice that He said: 'I seek not my own will.'

'Is His will, then, different from and also very inferior
[to the Father's]; nay, not merely inferior, but even ineffectual? Because, if it was capable of effecting salvation
and conformed to that of the Father why did You not seek
it? Men, indeed, might rightly speak in this fashion, since
they have many desires contrary to what God wills, but why
do You say this, if You are like the Father in all respects?
One would say that this is the statement not even of a man
who is mortified and practicing perfection. But, if Paul
has so conformed himself to the will of God as to say: "It
is now no longer I that live, but Christ lives in me,"[29] how
could the Lord of all say: "I seek not my own will but the
will of him who sent me," as if that will were different? What
is it, then, that He means?'

He is speaking in human language and addressing Himself
to the suspicious attitude of His listeners. Inasmuch as, beginning from the former discussion, He had uttered His words,
now in divine fashion, again in human fashion, He once
again repeated this same procedure and said, human-wise:
'My judgment is just.' And how is this evident? 'Because
I seek not my own will, but the will of him that sent me.'
Now just as, among men, when a man is free of self-seeking
he could not be justly accused of having given a judgment
that is contrary to what is right, so you will not now be able
to find fault with Me in this way. To be sure, a man who
desires to secure his own interests might perhaps be suspected
by many of corrupting justice for this end; but what reason
would the man who is not looking out for his own interests
have for not judging with justice? Apply this reasoning, then,

29 Gal. 2.20.

to Me. If I had said that I was not sent by the Father and had not referred to Him the renown accruing from what has been done, perhaps some of you would suspect that, because I desired to make myself renowned, I did not tell the truth. If, on the contrary, I refer and attribute to another what has taken place, why or whence would you be able to hold My words in suspicion?'

Do you perceive to what point He has brought the discussion, and on what grounds He has said that His judgment is just, namely, for a reason which even an ordinary man might have employed in his own defense? Do you perceive how clearly what I have often said is illustrated? And what is it that I have said? That the excessive humility of His words is of itself convincing in a particular manner to the intelligent, persuading them, when they have received His words, not to interpret them readily in a lowly sense, but to prepare to ascend to the sublimity of the thought. And it even easily raises up by degrees those disposed to cling to earth.

Therefore, being mindful of these things, I beseech you, let us not merely skim over His words, but search out all their meaning carefully, and let us consider in every instance the reason for what is said. And let us not think that our ignorance and simplicity suffice as excuse for us. For He bade us not merely to be 'simple,' but also 'wise.'[30] Let us, then, exercise prudence, together with simplicity, both in matters of doctrine and in the right conduct of life. Let us pass judgment on ourselves here that we may not then be condemned with this world, and act towards our fellow slaves as we wish our Lord to act toward us. 'Forgive us our debts as we also forgive our debtors,' [we say].[31]

Now, I know that the soul, when injured, does not easily endure it, but if we are mindful that, when we do bear it, we are doing a favor, not to the offender, but to ourselves,

30 Cf. Matt. 10.16.
31 Matt. 6.12.

we shall quickly forego the poisonous malice of our anger. I say this, because the man who did not forgive his debtor ten denarii did not injure his fellow slave but made himself liable to the debt of ten thousand talents of which he had formerly been absolved.[32] Therefore, when we do not forgive others, we do not forgive ourselves.

Let us not, then, merely say to God: 'Do not remember our sins,' but let all of us address to ourselves the words: 'Let us not remember the offenses of our fellow slaves committed against us.' And we should do this because you pass judgment on your sins and then God follows; you write the law about forgiveness and punishment, and proclaim the sentence for such things. You are, therefore, responsible for God's remembering or not remembering them. That is why Paul bids us to forgive, 'if anyone has a grievance against any other,'[33] and not merely to forgive, but in such a way that no trace remains.

Besides, Christ not only has not brought our sins to light, but has not even reminded us that we ourselves have transgressed or said: 'You have committed such or such sins.' On the contrary, He has both forgiven and wiped out the record, and has not kept an account of our sins, as Paul has also made clear.[34] Let us also do this, and let us erase everything from our minds. Of course, if something good be done by the offender, let us keep a record of this only, but if he has done something annoying and painful to us, let us cast it aside and erase it so that no trace remains. If nothing good has come to us from him, a still greater reward will in turn redound to us if we yield place to him, and more credit will be ours.

Others, to be sure, blot out their sins by night watches, and sleeping on the ground, and innumerable penances, while

32 Cf. Matt. 18.28-35.
33 Col. 3.13.
34 Cf. Col. 2.14.

you have it in your power to make all your sins disappear by an easier way; I mean by not remembering the evil done to you. Why, then, by thrusting the sword against yourself like madmen and lunatics, do you cast yourself out of the life to come, when it is within your power to do all in such a way as to obtain possession of it?

If the present life is so desirable, what could one say of that life from which grief and pain and mourning have fled? There, death is not to be feared, nor need we anticipate any end of those blessings. Blessed and thrice blessed, and that many times over, are they who are enjoying that blessed lot; but wretched and thrice wretched, and that many times over, are they who have deprived themselves of that state of blessedness.

'But what can we do,' you say, 'to obtain the enjoyment of that life?' Listen to the Judge Himself conversing with a certain young man on this subject. When the latter asked: 'What shall I do to obtain eternal life?'[35] Christ, after mentioning to him the other commandments, ended with the love of his neighbor. And perhaps some of my listeners, like that rich young man, will say: 'We also have kept these, for we have not stolen, we have not committed murder, we have not committed adultery.' However, you will not be able to say this, also: that you have loved your neighbor as you ought. For, if a man has been envious, or has spoken slander, or has not helped one who wronged him, or has not shared his possessions, he has not loved his neighbor.

Moreover, Christ not only enjoined this, but also something else. And what was that? 'Sell what thou hast,' He said, 'and give to the poor, and come, follow me,' meaning by 'following Him' that we should imitate Him in our deeds. What, then, do we learn from this? In the first place, that it is not possible for one who has not dispossessed himself of all to attain to the highest degree of that place of blessedness.

---

35 Matt. 19.16.

For, after he had said, 'I have done all,' Christ replied, as if there was something of considerable importance lacking to complete perfection: 'If thou wilt be perfect, sell what thou hast, and give to the poor, and come, follow me.'

First, then, it is possible to learn this lesson; and second, that He was reproaching that young man himself with making a vain display. For, if a man is living amid such abundance and neglecting the others who are in want, how could he be loving his neighbor? Well, then, he did not speak the truth in saying that he had kept that commandment.

Let us, however, keep both this one and the rest as well; let us strive to pour out our possessions and to purchase heaven. If a man frequently expends his whole fortune for the sake of worldly honor, an honor which will remain in this world, and does not even last a long time (for many have been stripped of this position even long before death, and frequently some have been penalized on its account, even to losing life itself; yet, though they know these things, they spend everything to secure it)—if, then, they perform such feats for the sake of worldly honor, what could be more wretched than we, if we put forth not even a slight effort to obtain that honor which will endure and cannot be taken away, and do not share those things which we shall lose after a little while, even while we are here? Therefore, what kind of madness is it—while it is possible to give up willingly, and so to take with us, those things of which we shall perforce be deprived—not to be willing to do so?

However, if someone were being led to death and then it was proposed to set him free in exchange for all his wealth, we should regard the deed even as a favor. But now, while it is possible for us who are being conducted on the road to hell to be set free by giving up half our possessions, we choose both to suffer punishment and rashly to keep the possessions that are not ours, and thus to lose what is truly ours. What defense, therefore, shall we have? What pardon shall we deserve, if, when so easy a road to life has been laid open to us, we are carried headlong down the precipice, as we walk the profitless way and deprive ourselves of everything both here and hereafter, though it is possible for us to enjoy the fruit of both with freedom?

However, if we have not done so before, let us at least now return and, coming back to ourselves, let us dispense this world's goods as we ought, in order that we may readily receive those of the world to come, by the grace and mercy of our Lord Jesus Christ, with whom glory be to the Father, together with the Holy Spirit, forever and ever. Amen.

Homily 40 (John 5.31-38)

'If I bear witness concerning myself, my witness is not true. There is another who bears witness concerning me, and I know that his witness is true.'[1]

If a person, even though inexperienced in mining, should undertake to dig a mine, he would not produce gold, but by his confused and disorderly efforts he would engage in the work fruitlessly and even harmfully. So those who do not know the sequence of holy Scripture and do not examine into its distinctive forms and laws, but merely peruse all of it in the same way, mix gold with earth and will by no means discover the treasure lying hidden within it.

I am saying this here because the text lying before us at present holds much gold, not readily apparent, but shrouded in much obscurity from on high. Therefore, we must arrive at its true sense by digging and purifying. Who would not be at once perturbed on hearing Christ saying: 'If I bear witness concerning myself, my witness is not true'? And I say this because He clearly bore witness to Himself on many occasions. For example, in conversing with the Samaritan

1 John 5.31-32.

woman He said: 'I who speak with thee am he'; similarly, to the blind man: 'He it is who speaks with thee'; also to the Jews, in reproof: 'You say, Thou blasphemest, because I said, I am the Son of God.'[2] And elsewhere, too, in many instances He did this. Therefore, if all these statements are lies, what hope of salvation have we in store? And where shall we discover the truth, when the Truth Itself says: 'My witness is not true.'

Moreover, not only does this statement seem to be contradictory, but another one, likewise, not less than this. Further on, He says: 'Even if I bear witness to myself, my witness is true.'[3] Which one, therefore, I ask, shall I accept? And which shall I consider a lie? If we excerpt them merely in their literal sense, without having sought to learn the person to whom they were spoken, or the reason, or anything else of that nature, both will be false. If His witness is not true, not even this statement itself is true; not the second one only, but the first as well.

What, then, is the meaning? We need much watchfulness, or, rather, God's grace in abundance, lest we go no further than the bare words. It is in this way that the heretics go astray, because they seek to know neither the point of view of the speaker nor the attitude of his hearers. Accordingly, if we do not add this information and other items as well, such as times and places and opinion of the listeners, many ridiculous conclusions will follow.

What, then, is the meaning here? The Jews were going to taunt Him as follows: 'If thou bearest witness to thyself, thy witness is not true.'[4] For this reason He made the above statement in anticipation of this, as if to say: 'You will certainly say, "We do not believe you." For among men no one who bears witness to himself is ever considered trust-

---

2 John 4.26; 9.37; 10.36.
3 John 8.14.
4 John 8.13.

worthy.' Therefore, the words 'is not true' must not be read in their literal sense, but in the light of the suspicious attitude of the listeners; that is: 'is not true in your eyes.' He did not, then, say these words with His own proper dignity in view, but in consideration of their suspicious attitude. So, when He said: 'My witness is not true,' He was reproving their attitude and the charge that they would level against Him.

On the other hand, when He said: 'Even if I bear witness to myself, my witness is true,' He was pointing out the very core of the matter, namely that, as God He must be regarded as worthy of belief, even when speaking of Himself. But when He had mentioned raising the dead, and judgment, and said that he who believes Him does not come to judgment, but passes to life; and that He will sit in judgment to require all accounts; and that He has the same authority and power as the Father—since He was going to ratify all these things presently in another way, of necessity He gave prime importance to their objection.

'I have said,' He declared, ' "As the Father raises the dead and gives them life, even so the Son also gives life to whom he will." I have said: "The Father judges no man, but all judgment he has given to the Son." I have said: "The Son must be honored as the Father." I have said: "He who does not honor the Son does not honor the Father." I have said: "He who hears my words and believes them will not see death, but has passed from death to life." I have said that My voice will raise the dead, both those now dead and those to die hereafter. I have said that I will demand from all an accounting for their sins, that I will judge with justice and will reward the upright.'

Since, therefore, all these statements were merely enumerated—and certainly they were remarkable ones—and no proof of them had as yet been clearly explained to [the Jews], but only rather subtly implied, He gave their objection prior consideration, intending to proceed thence to the true meaning of His words. He was implying some such thing as the following, even if not actually in these words: 'But perhaps you will say, "Though You make all these statements, You are not a reliable authority when bearing witness of Yourself." '

First, then, having put a check on their contentiousness by this setting forth of what they were going to say, and having furnished an important proof of His power by showing that He knew the secret thoughts of their minds, then, having disposed of their objection, He gave other clear and unanswerable proofs, citing three witnesses to corroborate His words; namely, the deeds He performed, the witness of the Father, and the message of John. And He placed the least of these first, that of John. For, when He had said: 'There is another who bears witness concerning me, and I know that his witness is true,' He added: 'You have sent to John, and he has borne witness to the truth.'

'Yet, if Your witness is not true, how can You say: "I know that John's witness is true" and "He has borne witness to the truth"?' Do you perceive how clear it is from this text that the words 'My witness is not true' were said in answer to their suspicion?

'What, then, if John bore witness in order to curry favor?' you will say. In order that they might not say this, notice how He disposed of this suspicion, too. He did not say: 'John has borne witness to Me,' but first He said: 'You have sent to John—and you would not have sent to him, if you did not consider him trustworthy.' More than this: they did not send to him to inquire about Christ, but about himself. And if they considered that he was to be believed in matters pertaining to himself, much more would they think this in those pertaining to another. We are, to be sure, so constituted by nature that all say that they do not believe men when they are speaking about themselves as they do those speaking of others. Yet [the Jews] considered this man so trustworthy that they did not need any other witness even in regard to matters pertaining to himself.

For, those who were sent did not say: 'What hast thou to say of Christ?'—but: 'Who art thou? What hast thou to say of thyself?'[5] So wonderful did they consider the man. All this He was implying by saying: 'You have sent to John.' That is also why the Evangelist did not merely state that they sent to him, but was specific about who were sent, namely, that they were priests and some of the Pharisees, not chance messengers, or outcasts, or people susceptible of being misled and deceived, but those who were capable of grasping accurately what was said by him.

'I however do not receive the witness of man.' 'Why then, did You refer to that of John?' Surely, his witness was not that of a mere man, for he said: 'He who sent me to baptize with water said to me.' Consequently, the witness of John was the witness of God, for he said what he did on learning it from Him.

However, that they might not say: 'Whence is it evident that he learned it from God?' and that they might not become concerned about this, He refuted them more than sufficiently, still speaking in answer to their suspicious thoughts. It was not really likely that many knew these facts, but until then they were giving ear to John, as to one speaking on his own authority. That is why He said: 'I do not receive the witness of man.'

'But if You did not intend to receive the witness of man, and to be fortified by it, why did You refer to his witness?' That they might not say this, listen to how He refuted this objection by the conclusion of the sentence. When He had said: 'I do not receive the witness of man,' He added: 'but I say these things that you may be saved.' What He meant is something like this: 'I do not need the witness of man,

5 John 1.22.

since I am God, but, inasmuch as you pay more attention to John, and consider him most reliable of all, and run to him as to a Prophet (He said this because the entire city flocked to the Jordan), while you do not believe in Me even when I work miracles, for this reason I am reminding you of that witness of his.'

'He was the lamp, burning and shining; and you desired to rejoice for a while in his light.' Now, that they might not say: 'What if he did speak, but we did not receive his words?' He indicated that they also approved what he said. And this is evident because it was not chance messengers whom they sent, but priests and Pharisees. Thus, they admired the man and they then had no objection to offer to his words. But the expression 'for a while' is used by One who is pointing out their fickleness and that they quickly were estranged from him.

'The witness, however, that I have is greater than that of John. For, if you were willing to accept the faith in accordance with the logical sequence of things, I should have brought you to it from My works. Since you are not willing, I am bringing you to John, not as if I were in need of his witness, but because I am doing everything toward this end: that you may be saved. In truth, I have a greater witness than that of John; namely, that of My works. I am concerned not only that I may be acceptable to you through trustworthy evidence, but also that I may be so through persons well known to you and admired by you.'

And so, as He chided them by saying: 'You desired to rejoice for a while in his light,' and showed that that enthusiasm of theirs was but passing and unstable, by calling John a 'light' He was pointing out that he did not have the light of himself, but from the grace of the Spirit: He did not yet state the real point of difference between Himself and John, namely, that He is the Sun of Justice. Merely hinting at it for the moment, He rebuked them firmly and showed that the same state of mind as that by which they had scorned him made them unable to believe in Christ. And this is true, because they admired the object of their admiration[6] 'for a while' only, since, if they had not done this, he would quickly have brought them to Jesus.

Having shown, then, that they were altogether undeserving of pardon, He went on to say: 'The witness, however, that I have is greater than that of John.' What is this? That of His works. 'For the works which the Father has given me to accomplish,' He said, 'these very works bear witness to me, that the Father has sent me.' Here He was reminding them of the paralytic who had been cured, and of many other things besides. Now, one of them might perhaps have said that His words, on the one hand, were empty show and designed to win the friendship of John (though, to be sure, it would not be logical for them to say this of John, a man capable of precise discernment, and for this reason admired by them); however, His deeds could no longer be regarded with suspicion even by utter madmen. For this reason He cited this second witness, saying: 'The works which the Father has given to me to accomplish, these very works that I do bear witness to me, that the Father has sent me.'

And here He also refuted the charge of breaking the Sabbath. They had asked: 'How can He be from God when He does not keep the Sabbath?' Because of this He said: [works] 'which the Father has given me.' Yet He acted independently, but in order to make it superabundantly evident that He did nothing in opposition to His Father, He therefore considerably belittled Himself.

You will ask why He did not say: 'The works which the Father has given me bear witness that I am equal to the Father'? Both facts could, in truth, be learned from His works: that He does nothing in opposition and that He is

6 I.e., John the Baptist.

equal to Him who begot Him. And elsewhere, to show this, He said: 'If you do not believe me, believe my works, that you may know and may believe that I am in the Father and the Father in me.'[7] By these words He was bearing witness to Himself in both things, then; namely, that He is equal to the Father and that He does nothing in opposition to Him. Why, therefore, did He not say so, but ignored the greater thing, and stated the other?

Because it was this for which He was striving first. Even if it was much less to believe that He came from God than to believe that He is equal to Him—for Prophets also had said the former, while they had not yet stated the latter— He Himself put much effort into achieving the lesser end, knowing that, when it had been accepted, the other also would finally be readily received. And while making no mention of the greater testimony, He set forth the lesser effect in order that by this means they might accept the other, also.

After accomplishing this, He added: 'The Father himself, who sent me, has borne witness to me.' How did He bear witness to Him? At the Jordan, when He said: 'This is my beloved Son, in whom I am well pleased. Hear ye him.'[8] However, this also needed explanation. The testimony of John, on the contrary, was unquestionable, for they themselves had sent to him and could not deny it. And so with the witness of His miracles, for they had seen what had happened and heard of it from the one restored to health, and they had believed and therefore were making accusation[9] against Him. Last of all, it remained to give proof of the Father's testimony. Then, with a view to bringing this about, He added: 'But you have never heard his voice.'

Then how does Moses say: 'God was speaking and Moses

7 John 10.38.
8 Matt. 3.17.
9 That He was breaking the Sabbath.

was answering'?[10] And how does David say: 'He heard a
tongue which he did not know'?[11] And Moses again: 'Did
a people ever hear the voice of God?'[12]

'You have never seen his face.' Yet Isaias, and Jeremias,
and Ezechiel, and many others besides, say that they have
seen Him. What is it, therefore, that Christ meant here?
He was introducing them to a philosophic teaching, showing
gradually that with regard to God there is neither voice nor
outward appearance, but He is superior to such forms and
sounds. Just as by saying: 'You have never heard his voice,'
He did not mean that He does utter sound, but is not heard,
so by saying: 'You have never seen his face,' He did not
mean that He has outward form, but cannot be seen. He
meant that neither of these things exists with regard to God.
Indeed, in order that they might not say: 'You are making
a display of knowledge in vain, since God spoke only to
Moses' (and they actually did say: 'We know that God spoke
to Moses; but as for this man, we do not know where he
is from'),[13] for this reason He spoke in this way, to show
that with regard to God there is neither voice nor outward
appearance.

'What do I mean by this?' He said. 'Not only have you
never heard His voice or seen His face, but you cannot
even assert the thing in which you glory most of all, and with
regard to which you are all especially inflated with pride,
namely, that you have received His commandments and
possess them.' Therefore, to make this also plain, He added:
'And you have not his word abiding in you,' that is, the
commandments, the precepts, the Law, the Prophets. 'Even
if God has given these precepts, they are not in you, since
you do not believe in Me. If the Scriptures say repeatedly
that it is necessary to believe in Me, and you do not believe,

10 Exod. 19.19.
11 Ps. 80.6.
12 Deut. 4.33.
13 John 9.29.

it is evident that His word has departed from you.' Therefore, He added again: 'since you do not believe him whom he has sent.'

Next, in order that they might not say: 'How, then, if we have not heard His voice, has He borne witness to You?' He said: 'Search the Scriptures, because it is they that bear witness to me,'[14] showing that the Father has borne witness by them. Now, the Father did indeed bear witness to Him at the Jordan and on the Mount. However, Christ did not invoke as evidence the words heard on those occasions. In truth, perhaps they would have been incredulous even of that authority, for they had not heard the one Voice, namely, that on the Mount, while they did not pay attention to the other which they did hear.

Therefore, He sent them to the Scriptures, to show that the witness of the Father is taken from there. First, however, He disillusioned them of the prerogatives on which they prided themselves of old: specifically, that they had either seen God or heard His voice. Since it was probable that they would not believe His word and would get a mental picture of what took place on Mount Sinai, after He had first corrected their erroneous idea in regard to these matters and had shown that these events happened by a kind of condescension, He then sent them to the witness of the Scriptures.

Well, then, when we also fight and take up arms against the heretics, let us gain our strength likewise from that source. For, 'All Scripture is inspired by God,' Paul says, 'and useful for teaching, for reproving, for correcting, for instructing in justice; that the man of God may be perfect, equipped for

14 John 5.39. The Greek 'ereunâte' may be equally well translated: 'You search,' as in the Confraternity New Testament, or by the imperative: 'Search,' as in the Challoner-Douay-Rheims version. That St. John Chrysostom was interpreting it in the latter sense becomes clear from Homily 41 (p. 415). Other writers of the early tradition and older English versions accept the imperative; the consensus of present scholarly opinion favors the indicative.

every good work.'[15] Not that he may have some good works
but not others, for such a man is not perfect.

Of what use is it, I ask you, if a man prays assiduously
but does not give alms generously; or if, though he does give
alms generously, he is greedy or violent; or if, though he is
not greedy or violent, he acts in this way to gain men's notice
and win the approval of those who witness it; or if, though he
gives alms with all exactness and as God wills, he is therefore puffed up and proud; or if, though he is humble and
given to fasts, he is avaricious and engrossed in business and
attached to earthly interests, introducing the mother of evils
into his soul? For avarice is the root of all evils.

Let us, then, dread it; let us flee from this sin. It has
ravaged the world, it has thrown all into confusion, it has
seduced us from Christ's most blessed servitude. 'You cannot
serve God and Mammon,' He says,[16] for the latter gives
commands the opposite of those of Christ. He says: 'Give
to the needy.' But the other: 'Plunder from those in need.'
Christ says: 'Pardon those who plot against and wrong you.'
He, on the contrary: 'Lay snares for those who have done
you no wrong.' Christ says: 'Be merciful and kind.' He, contrariwise: 'Be cruel and heartless and think that the tears
of the poor are of no account,' so that in that day he may
make the judge severe to us.

Then all our deeds will be set before our eyes, while both
those whom we have wronged and those whom we have
stripped of their possessions deprive us of all defense. If
Lazarus, who had not been wronged by Dives, except that
he had not enjoyed a share of the latter's possessions, stood
forth at that tribunal as his stern accuser and prevented him
from obtaining any pardon,[17] what defense, I ask you, will
they have who, in addition to not sharing their own fortune,

---

15 2 Tim. 3.16,17.
16 Luke 16.13.
17 Cf. Luke 16.19-26.

both take the possessions of others and upset the homes of orphans? If they who did not give nourishment to Christ when He was hungry[18] have drawn so much fiery punishment on their heads, what consolation will they enjoy who seize unlawfully upon what does not belong to them, conjuring up numberless law-suits, and unjustly attributing to themselves the possessions of all men?

Let us, then, cast from us this desire. We shall cast it from us if we reflect on those before us who have done wrong, who have been avaricious and have perished. Do not others enjoy the fruit of their wealth and labors, while they are languishing in punishment and torture and unendurable evil fortune? How is it not, then, utter madness to toil and spend ourselves in order that, even while living, we may be worn out by our labors and that, when dead, we may undergo unspeakable punishment and torture? On the contrary, it is possible for us even here to live in happiness (for nothing causes so much pleasure as almsgiving and a clear conscience), and, on departing to the next world, to be freed from all sufferings and to attain to numberless blessings.

Just as evil-doing usually punishes those who share in it, even before [they reach] hell, so also virtue causes those who practice it to enjoy happiness here, even before [they come to] the Kingdom, and makes them dwell amid hopes of good things to come and uninterrupted pleasure. Therefore, let us apply ourselves to good works in order that we may attain to this, both here and in the life to come. Thus, indeed, we shall obtain our future crown. May we all secure it by the grace and mercy of our Lord Jesus Christ, through whom and with whom glory be to the Father, together with the Holy Spirit, now and always, and forever and ever. Amen.

---

18 Cf. Matt. 25.41,42.

Homily 41 (John 5.39-47)

'Search the Scriptures, because in them you think that you have life everlasting. And it is they that bear witness to me, yet you are not willing to come to me that you may have life everlasting.'[1]

Let us take much thought, beloved, of spiritual things; let us not think that it is sufficient for our salvation just to skim over them superficially. If in worldly matters a man will be able to produce nothing worth while if He deals with them only perfunctorily and casually, much more will this be so in spiritual matters, because these require even more painstaking care.

That is why Christ, in sending the Jews to the Scriptures, sent them, not merely to read them, but carefully to search and ponder them. And so He did not say, 'Read the Scriptures,' but 'Search the Scriptures.' Indeed, it was because the texts concerning Him require much careful study (since He was foreshadowed in earlier times according to the needs of the people of that period) that He now bade them to dig out the meaning of the Scriptures with precision so as to be able to discover what lies hidden in their depths. Their meaning is not expressed superficially or set forth in their literal sense, but, like a treasure, lies buried at a great depth. And he who seeks for hidden things will not be able to find the object of his search if he does not seek carefully and painstakingly.

For this reason, when He had said: 'Search the Scriptures,' He added: 'for in them you think that you have life everlasting.' He did not say 'You have' but 'You think,' to show that they derived no significant and real profit if they thought that they would obtain salvation by the mere reading, while they were actually without faith. What He meant, then, is something like this: 'Do you not marvel at the Scriptures?

---

1 Cf. John 5.39,40.

Do you not think that they are sources of all life? From them even I Myself am now deriving support. For it is they that bear witness to Me, yet you are not willing to come to Me that you may have life everlasting.' With reason, then, did He say 'You think,' because they did not wish to believe, but boasted of the mere reading alone.

Next, that they might not suspect Him of vainglory because of His great solicitude, and think that He was seeking His own interest in wishing them to believe in Him (for He had reminded them of the words of John and the testimony of God, and His own works, and had said it all to attract them to Himself, and had also promised them life everlasting), since, then, it was likely that many would conceive the idea that He said these things out of love for fame, see what He added: 'I do not receive glory from men,' that is, I do not need it. 'My nature is not such,' He means, 'as to need glory from men. For, if the sun does not receive any additional light from the light of a lamp, I am much further removed from needing glory from men.'

'But why,' you will ask, 'do You say these things, if You do not need it?' 'That you may have salvation.' This, to be sure, He had said before, and here He also was implying it in the words: 'that you may have life.' But here He also added another reason. What is this? 'But I know that you have not the love of God in you.'

They frequently persecuted Him because He made Himself equal to God, as if they really loved God, and He knew that they would not believe in Him now. Hence, in order that no one might say: 'Why, then, do you speak thus?' He declared that He spoke in this way: 'That I may reprove you because it is not for the love of God that you persecute Me. I say this because He Himself also bears witness to Me both by works and by the Scriptures. Therefore, just as, before this, you drove Me away, thinking that I was an enemy of God, so now, from the time I have pointed out these facts to you, you ought to hasten to Me if you really love God, but you do not love Him. Accordingly, that is why I have spoken thus: to show that you are exceedingly conceited, since you vainly rant on and cover up your own envy.'

He drew these conclusions not from this evidence only, but also from future events, for He said: 'I came in the name of my Father, and you did not receive me. If another come in his own name, him you will receive.' Do you perceive that He said He had been 'sent,' and that judgment had been received from the Father, and that He did nothing without Him in order that He might forestall every pretext they might allege for their senseless attitude?

But who is it that He said would come in his own name? He was alluding to Antichrist here, and gave irrefutable proof of their want of sense. If you persecute Me on the ground that you love God, much more ought you to do so in regard to Antichrist. He, indeed, will say no such thing as that he has been sent by the Father, or has come in accordance with His will. He will say everything quite the opposite, despotically seizing upon things that do not belong to him, and declaring that he himself is God over all things, even as Paul says: "Above all that is called God, or that is worshipped, and gives himself out as if he were God."[2] For this is to come in his own name. It is not thus with Me, however, but I have come in the name of My Father.'

Accordingly, the fact that they did not receive Him who said that He had been sent by God was sufficient to show that they did not love God. But now, in addition, He pointed out their utter shamelessness also from the opposite fact, that they would receive Antichrist. Inasmuch as they did not receive the One who said that He was sent by God, but were going to worship one who did not know Him and who would boastfully declare that he was God over all things, it is clear that their persecution stemmed from envy and

---

2 2 Thess. 2.4.

from hatred of God. That is why, then, He assigned two reasons for His assertions: 'that you may be saved' and 'that you may have life.' The former, to be sure, was in a more ordinary vein, but, since they would scoff at Him, He added the other more striking one, to point out that, even if they who heard Him were not won over, God would accomplish His designs without exception.

Paul, to be sure, in speaking of Antichrist said by way of prophecy: 'God will send them a misleading influence, that all may be judged who have not believed the truth, but have preferred wickedness.'[3] Christ did not say 'He will come,' but 'If he come,' out of consideration for his hearers. And since their wrong-doing had not yet been completely carried out, for this reason He Himself refrained from speaking of the reason for his coming. Paul, on the contrary, disclosed it clearly to those who were able to comprehend. And I say this because it is he who deprives them of all excuse.

In the next place, Christ assigned the cause of their unbelief by adding the words: 'How can you believe who receive glory from one another, and do not seek the glory which is from the only God? He was once again pointing out by this assertion also that they were not seeking the things of God, but that by pretending to do so they wished to cover up their own secret feeling. And this is so, because they were so far from acting as they did for the sake of His glory that they actually preferred glory from men to that coming from God. How, then, would they be likely to display such indignation in defense of what they despised so much that they chose to have human glory instead of it?

To resume. Having stated that they did not have the love of God, and having proved this in turn by reference to the incidents which had taken place in His regard, and those which would transpire with regard to Antichrist, and having clearly proved that they were without any excuse,

---

3 2 Thess. 2.11,12.

He concluded His words to them as follows, by adducing Moses, also, as their accuser, as He said: 'Do not think that I shall accuse you to the Father. There is one who accuses you, Moses, in whom you hope. For if you believed Moses you would believe me also, for he wrote of me. But if you do not believe his writings, how will you believe my words?'

What He meant is something like this: 'It is not I, but he who is insulted by what is done against Me, for you have disbelieved Moses rather than Me.' See how He has deprived them of all excuse on every side. 'You said that out of love for God you were persecuting Me,' He declares; 'I have proved that you did this out of hatred for Him. You said that I was breaking the Sabbath and transgressing the Law; I have freed Myself of this accusation, also. You strongly asserted that you were professing faith in Moses by what you dared to do against Me; once more I am showing that this course of action most especially does not profess belief in Moses. Indeed, I am so far from having come in opposition to the Law that he who will be your accuser is none other than he who has given you the Law.' Therefore, just as He had said, regarding the Scriptures: 'In them you think that you have life everlasting,' so also He declared with regard to Moses: 'In whom you hoped,' worsting them on all sides by their own words.

'But what proof is there,' they will ask, 'that Moses will be our accuser and that You are not just talking boastfully? What in truth have you in common with Moses? You have broken the Sabbath which he decreed for us to keep; how, then, will he accuse us? And where is the proof that we shall also believe in another who will come in his own name? You are making all these statements without documentation.'

Yet, He has support for all these statements from above. For, when He affirms: 'I have come from God as evidenced by My works, by the words of John, and by the testimony of the Father,' it is very clear that Moses will be their accuser.

What did the latter say? Was it not that, if someone should come, performing wonders, and leading them to God, and foretelling the future with truth, they must listen to Him with complete docility?[4] Did not Christ do all these things, then? He did indeed perform miracles. He did attract all men to God, and did bring His prophecies to fulfillment. Where is the proof, however, that they will believe in another? From the fact that they hated Christ, for it is very clear that they who spurn Him who comes by the will of God will also receive him who comes in opposition to God.

But, if He now appealed to the testimony of Moses, though He had just previously been saying: 'I do not receive the witness of man,' do not be surprised, for He was referring them not to Moses actually but to the writings of God. Besides, since the Scriptures inspired less fear in them, He led the discussion to the person [who inscribed them], mentioning the very Law-giver as their accuser, thereby both rendering their fear much more awe-inspiring and refuting each of the statements made by them.

Notice how He did it. They said that they were persecuting Him out of love for God; He pointed out that they really did this because of hatred for God. They said that they adhered to Moses; He pointed out that they acted in this way because they did not believe Moses. If they were zealous for the observance of the Law, they ought to have received Him who was the fulfillment of it; if they loved God, they ought to have believed Him who was drawing them to Him; if they believed Moses, they ought to have worshiped Him who was foretold by him. 'If indeed, even before My coming Moses was not believed, it is only to be expected that I who am foretold by him would be rejected by you.'

Accordingly, just as He had shown that even those who admired John were showing contempt for John in what they did against Him, so He showed that those who thought they

---

4 Cf. Deut. 18.15-22; 13.1.

believed Moses did not believe him. He repeatedly turned back on their own heads all the evidence which they thought they were citing in support of their position. Truly, 'I am so far removed from leading you away from the law,' He says, 'that I even summon the law-giver himself as your accuser.'

Moreover, though He did assert the fact that the Scriptures bear witness to Him, He did not go on to tell the places where the testimony is given, because He wished to inspire in them deeper awe and to impel them to search out the texts, and to force them to inquire into their meaning. If He had given the information at once, and not in answer to their questions, they would have rejected His testimony; but now, if they were paying attention to His words, they ought to have asked for this information first of all, and to have learned the answer from Him. Indeed, that is why He multiplied more abundantly, not only His proofs, but also both penalties and threats, to see whether even by this means He might persuade them through fear inspired by what He said. But they, even so, remained silent. Such, indeed, is the habit of evil-doing; whatever one may say or do, it is not changed, but persists in keeping its own poison.

Therefore, it is necessary for us to cast all evil from our souls and never to engage in deceit. 'For God sends crooked ways to the perverse,'[5] Scripture says; and: 'The Holy Spirit of discipline will flee from the deceitful, and will withdraw himself from thoughts that are without understanding.'[6] Indeed, nothing makes men so stupid as does habitual evil-doing. When a man is deceitful, when he is unjust, when he is churlish (and these, to be sure, are different forms of evil-doing), when, without having been wronged in any way himself, he inflicts pain, when he connives at trickery—how will he not be exhibiting signs of utter stupidity?

On the other hand, nothing makes men so wise as a

---

5 Cf. Prov. 21.8.
6 Wisd. 1.5.

virtuous life. It renders them affable and just, merciful, kindly, gentle, refined; it frequently engenders all the other good qualities as well. Virtuous living is really the source and root of wisdom, just as all wickedness has its source in folly. I say this because the braggart and the slave of passion are taken captive by these vices as a result of a lack of wisdom. For this reason the Prophet has said: 'There is no health in my flesh. My sores are foul and festering because of my folly,'[7] to indicate that all sin takes its beginning from a lack of wisdom; just as the virtuous man who fears God is wisest of all. That is why a certain wise man also says: 'The fear of the Lord is the beginning of wisdom.'[8] If, then, to fear God is to have wisdom, and the evil-doer does not possess this fear, he is really bereft of wisdom; and he who is bereft of wisdom is truly the most foolish of all.

Yet, many stand in awe of evil-doers because they can inflict injury and do harm, not realizing that they ought to consider them most wretched of all men because, when they think that they are harming others, they are turning the sword against themselves. This, to be sure, is a mark of utter madness: when a man in striking himself does not realize that he is doing so, but thinks he is injuring another man in murdering himself. That is why Paul also, because he knew that in striking at others we destroy ourselves, said: 'Why not rather suffer wrong? Why not rather be defrauded?'[9] Not suffering wrong consists in not doing wrong, just as not to be ill treated consists in not doing evil to others— even if this statement seems a riddle to many and to those who do not desire to be wise.

Therefore, since we know these truths, let us not pity and weep for those who suffer wrong and receive injury, but for those who do these deeds. For they suffer wrong most of all

7 Ps. 37.4,6.
8 Prov. 1.7.
9 1 Cor. 6.7.

who make God their enemy, opening the mouths of count-less accusers, gaining a reputation for wickedness in the present life, and preparing for themselves severe punishment in the life to come. In like manner, they who suffer wrong and nobly bear all injuries have God pitying them, and also all men sympathizing with them, and praising them and ap-proving them. Such as these will enjoy, even in the present life, much honorable repute, since they are giving an out-standing example of wisdom; and in the life to come they will share in the everlasting blessings. May we all obtain these by the grace and mercy of our Lord Jesus Christ, with whom glory be to the Father, together with the Holy Spirit, now and always, and forever and ever. Amen.

Homily 42 (John 6.1-15)

'After this Jesus went away to the other side of the sea of Galilee, which is that of Tiberias. And there followed him a great crowd because they were witnessing the signs he worked on those who were sick. Jesus therefore went up the mountain, and was sitting there with his disciples. Now the Passover, the feast of the Jews, was near.'[1]

Let us not take issue with wicked men, beloved, but let us learn to give way to their evil designs, when such conduct does not work any harm to our virtue. In this way their ag-gressiveness is altogether checked. Just as when javelins strike against a taut and hard surface they are very forcefully directed back again at those who have shot them, but when the furious speed of the shot meets with no resistance it is quickly exhausted and spent, so it is with aggressively wicked men. When we contend with them they become more aggressive, but when we are calm and withdraw we easily cause the tension of their fury to relax entirely.

1 John 6.1-4.

It was for this reason that, when Christ learned that the Pharisees had heard that He was making more disciples and baptizing more than John, He went to Galilee, by His departure quenching the fire of their envy and calming the indignation which was likely to have been engendered by these reports. Moreover, in going away once more into Galilee He did not visit the same places, for He did not go into Cana, but to the other side of the sea. Therefore, great crowds followed Him to witness the signs He worked.[2]

What sort of signs were these? Why did he not mention them and specify what kind they were? Because this Evangelist sought to devote most of his book to discussions and discourses. Notice, indeed, how in one entire year, or, rather, how even here at the feast of the Pasch, he gave us no more information, with regard to signs, than that He cured one paralytic and the ruler's son. He did not try to give an account of all the miracles, since in any case he could not, but only of a few of the many great ones.

'And there followed him a great crowd, because they were witnessing the signs he worked.' Their following Him was not an indication of a very stable mental attitude. Though they had enjoyed the benefit of such sound teaching, they were led on rather by signs, a fact which was indicative of a somewhat coarse mind. 'Signs,' Scripture says, 'are intended not to believers but to unbelievers.'[3] However, that crowd which is mentioned in Matthew was not like this one. Listen to what it was like: 'All were astonished at his teaching, for he was teaching them as one having authority.'[4]

Why was it that on this occasion He went to the mountain and sat there with His disciples? Because of the miracle that

---

2 The Evangelist mentioned that these miracles were worked 'on those who were sick,' but did not go into further detail. However, he gave a detailed account of the miracle of the loaves because it provided a basis for the discourse on the Eucharist to follow.
3 1 Cor. 14.22.
4 Matt. 7.28,29.

was going to take place. Moreover, the fact that only His disciples went up is an indictment of the crowd because they did not follow Him. However, He did not do this—namely, go to the mountain—only for the reason I have mentioned, but also to teach us always to shun applause and escape from the midst of the tumult of praise, for solitude is a necessity for the pursuit of wisdom. Frequently, He Himself went to the mountain alone and spent the night and prayed, to teach us that it is necessary for the man who is to approach very close to God to get away from all noisy confusion and to seek out both a time and a place free from disturbance.

'Now the Passover, the feast of the Jews, was near.' 'How is it, then, that He did not go to the festival,' you will ask; 'when all were making their way to Jerusalem, why did He Himself go to Galilee? And why did He not go alone, but take His disciples with Him; and why did He go from there to Capharnaum?' Because in future He would be gradually breaking away from the Law, taking occasion from the perversity of the Jews.

And raising His eyes, He saw a great crowd. Here He shows that He never sat down with His disciples without a purpose, but perhaps to explain something to them, or to teach them, or to attract them to Himself. From this fact, and especially in this instance, we can learn His devotion to them and both the humility and the condescension of His manner toward them. They were sitting down with Him, probably looking at one another. Then, looking up, He saw the crowd coming toward Him.

The other Evangelists say that the disciples came to Him to ask questions and to beseech Him not to send them away fasting,[5] while this Evangelist asserts that Philip was questioned by Christ. It seems to me that both accounts are true, but that the incidents did not take place at the same time, but those [recounted by the other Evangelists] took place before

---

5 Cf. Matt. 14.13-21; Mark 6.31-44; Luke 9.10-17.

these [recounted by John], so that those are one thing, these another.

Why, then, did He question Philip? He knew those of His disciples who most needed instruction. For he is the one who later said: 'Show us the Father and it is enough for us.'[6] That is why He began to condition him from the start. For, if the miracle merely took place, its miraculous character would not appear so great, but now He first forced him to acknowledge that there was a scarcity, in order that, knowing in what a plight he was, he might thus learn more clearly the magnitude of the miraculous event that was to take place.

Now, notice what He says: 'Whence have we enough bread that these may eat?' That is how He spoke also to Moses in the Old Testament, for He did not work the sign until He had asked him: 'What is that in your hand?'[7] Since strange events which happen suddenly tend to make us forgetful of what went before, He first bound him by his acknowledgment of the present state of things, so that, when the wonderful event took place, he would not be able then to cast aside the memory of what he had acknowledged, and might thus learn by comparison the greatness of the miracle. This, accordingly, takes place also in the text we are now considering. And when he was asked, Philip answered: 'Two hundred denarii worth of bread is not enough that each one may receive a little. But he had said this to try him, for he himself knew what he would do.' What does 'to try him' mean? Surely, He was not ignorant of what he would say? We cannot, of course, say this.

What, then, is the meaning of the expression? We can learn this from the Old Testament. There, also, the following is found: 'After these events God put Abraham to a test.

6 John 14.8.
7 Exod. 4.2. When Moses replied: 'A staff,' God then changed it into a serpent.

He said to him: "Take your only son Isaac whom you love." [8] Now, the meaning here does not appear to be that He was waiting to ascertain the outcome of the trial: whether Abraham would comply or not (for how would He 'who knows all things before they come to pass'[9] be obliged to do so?). But both statements were made from a human point of view. Just as when Scripture says: 'He searches the hearts of men,'[10] it does not mean a search proceeding from ignorance of them, but that He has complete knowledge of them, so also when the statement is made that He 'tried' him, nothing else is meant than that He understood him completely.

Yet, it would be possible to make another interpretation and say that He was thus adding to Philip's merit, just as He did to Abraham in his day, for He was now bringing him also by such questioning to a clear realization of the miracle. Accordingly, that is why the Evangelist, to guard against anyone's dwelling on the weaker interpretation of the words and conceiving the suspicion that there was something strange in what was said, added: 'For he himself knew what he would do.'

Besides, we must take note of that characteristic way in which the Evangelist very zealously corrected at once any evil suspicion that might arise. Just as, in this context, in order that his hearers might not entertain some such suspicion he immediately added the correction of it in the words: 'For he himself knew what he would do,' so also when he mentioned in another place that the Jews were persecuting Him, 'not only because he was breaking the Sabbath, but was also calling God his own Father, making himself equal to God,' if the declaration made by Christ Himself were not confirmed in fact, he would have added an explanation of this sort in that case, also. If, in regard to what He Himself

---

8 Gen. 22.1,2.
9 Dan. 13.42.
10 Rom. 8.27.

said, the Evangelist sees to it that no one is misled, much rather would he have done so with regard to what others said about Him, unless he saw that it was the correct opinion of Him which prevailed. However, he did not explain away anything, since he knew that the interpretation was correct and the conclusion inescapable. Therefore, when he had said: 'Making himself equal to God,' he did not employ any such explanation, since what was said was not an erroneous idea of theirs, but His own statement confirmed by the facts.

When Philip, then, had been questioned, 'Andrew, the brother of Simon Peter, said to him, "There is a young boy here who has five barley loaves and two fishes; but what are these among so many?"' Now, Andrew had a more exalted point of view than Philip, but he did not altogether outstrip him. And I think that he did not say this merely casually, but because he had heard of the miracles worked by the Prophets, and how Eliseus performed the miracle of the loaves.[11] Therefore, that is why he ascended to a certain sublimity of thought, but was not strong enough to reach to the very peak. Let us learn from this, we who are given to delicate living, what food those wonderful and great men used to eat, and let us notice and imitate the frugality of their table, with respect both to the quantity and the quality of the things brought to it.

His concluding words, to be sure, betray a great weakness, for, after having said: 'He has five barley loaves,' he added, 'but what are these among so many?' Indeed, he thought that the Wonder-worker would make little from little and more from more, but this was not the case. Actually, it was easy alike for Him to cause the substance of the loaves to spring from more and from fewer. He did not need the material substance of the bread; however, He made use of the creature itself so that what He made miraculously

11 Cf. 4 Kings 4.42-44.

might not seem to be alien to His wisdom as those afflicted with the disease of Marcion[12] lyingly have asserted.

Therefore, when both disciples had given up the hope of a miracle, He then performed one, for in this way they derived greater benefit from it, since they had first acknowledged the difficulty of the deed, so that, when it took place, they might learn the power of God. Indeed, inasmuch as the miracle which was about to take place was one which had been performed also by Prophets, even though not in the same way, and since He was also going to perform it after having given thanks, in order to prevent His audience from suspecting some imperfection on His part, see how and in what way He lifted their thoughts on high by every detail and showed the difference.

He performed the miracle when the loaves were not yet in sight in order that you may learn that things that do not exist, as well as those that do, are subject to Him, as Paul says: 'He who calls things that are not as though they were.'[13] Indeed, He bade them at once to recline, as though the table were prepared and ready. Thus, by this means also He aroused the interest of His disciples. And because they had derived benefit from His questioning, they at once obeyed and did not become perturbed or say: 'What in the world is this? How is it that you give the order to recline, when there is nothing in evidence in our midst?' Thus, even before seeing the miracle, they began to believe, who in the beginning were so lacking in faith as to say: 'Whence shall we buy bread?' In fact, they began even eagerly to make the crowd recline.

But why is it that He did not pray when He was about to cure the paralytic, or to raise the dead, or to calm the sea,

---

12 For a detailed treatment of his life and heretical teachings, cf. art. 'Marcionites,' *Catholic Encyclopedia.*
13 Rom. 4.17.

while here in the miracle of the loaves He did so? It was to show that those who are beginning to partake of food ought to give thanks to God. Besides, He did it particularly in the case of a lesser miracle that you may learn that it was not out of necessity that He did so. If He needed to pray beforehand, He would have done so much more in the case of the greater miracles. But, since He performed these without having recourse to prayer, it is very clear that He prayed before this miracle in condescension to our lowliness.

Besides, there was a large crowd present and they had to be persuaded that He had come by the will of God. Wherefore, whenever He performed a miracle apart from the multitude, He did not make such an open display of prayer, but when He performed one in the presence of many people, so that they might believe that He was not an enemy of God or hostile to the Father, He dispelled that suspicion by giving thanks.

'And He distributed them to those reclining, and they were filled.' Do you perceive how much difference there is between servant and master? The former, since they were in possession of a limited amount of grace, in that measure were workers of miracles, while God, who acts with unlimited power, does all His works with complete freedom. 'And he said to his disciples, "Gather the fragments that are left over." They therefore gathered them up, and they filled twelve baskets.' This was not an empty display of power, but was intended that the miracle might not be thought an illusion; and that is also why, in miraculously producing the loaves, He started with substantial material.

Why did He not give the loaves to the crowds to carry off, but only to the disciples? It was because He wished particularly to instruct those who were going to be teachers of the world. The people, indeed, would as yet derive no great benefit from His miracles; they forgot them almost at once, and would ask for another miracle, while the disciples, on the contrary, would obtain no merely transitory profit from them. Then, too, what took place was a reproach, and not merely a coincidental one, to Judas, since he carried a basket. And that these details were intended for their instruction is plain from what was said later, when He recalled them to them in the words: 'Do you not yet understand how many baskets you took up?'[14] It was for the same reason that the baskets of remnants were equal in number to the disciples.[15] Later, when they had been instructed, there were not so many, but seven baskets only.[16]

I marvel not only at the large number of the loaves that He brought into being, but also, besides the large number, at the exactness of the size of the surplus, since He brought it about that neither too much nor too little remained, but just as much as He willed, foreseeing how much they would use up, something which was an indication of ineffable power. The fragments, therefore, confirmed the miracle, testifying to it on both counts, namely, that what had happened was not an illusion and that it was with these miraculous loaves that they had been fed.

The multiplication of the fishes also was effected at that time by means of material fishes, while after the Resurrection it no longer was achieved by means of material substance. Why was that? It was that you might learn also that in the instance we are discussing it was not because He needed to do so that He made use of matter, nor because He had to have elementary materials as a basis of the miracle, but so that He might stop up the mouths of the heretics.

'The people said, This is indeed the Prophet.' Oh, the overmastering power of gluttony! He had performed innumerable miracles more wonderful than these, but in none of them had they made this acknowledgment except in the

14 Matt. 16.9.
15 I.e., of course, twelve.
16 Cf. Matt. 15.37.

one where they had been filled. However, is it not clear from this declaration that they were awaiting a chosen Prophet? I say this because others were saying: 'Art thou the Prophet?'[17] And now these: 'This is the Prophet.'

'So when Jesus perceived that they would come to take him by force and make him king, he fled again to the mountain.' Alas, how great is the tyranny of gluttony; how great the fickleness of their minds! No longer were they concerned about the breaking of the Sabbath, no longer were they consumed with zeal for the honor of God, but everything was cast to one side since their bellies had been filled. And so He was a prophet in their midst and they were going to choose Him king, but Christ fled. Why was that? To teach us to despise worldly honors and to show that He was in need of nothing belonging to earth. He who had chosen for Himself everything lowly—mother, home, city, rearing, and clothing—was not going to make a display of Himself afterwards by worldly means.

The heavenly possessions which He had were indeed both illustrious and great: angels and a star, the Father giving testimony, the Spirit bearing witness, and Prophets heralding from afar; while His earthly possessions were all lowly, that by this means also His power might appear to greater advantage. He came, to be sure, to teach us to despise the things of this world and never to admire or be struck with wonderment at the glittering attractions of this life, but to scorn all these and to desire those of the life to come. He who makes much of the things of this world will not hold in esteem those of heaven. That is why He said to Pilate: 'My kingdom is not from here,'[18] so that He might not afterwards seem to have been employing mere human fear and power to persuade him. How is it, then, that the Prophet said: 'Behold thy king comes to thee, meek and seated upon

17 To John the Baptist; cf. John 1.21.
18 John 18.36.

a beast of burden'?[19] It was because he meant that other kingdom, the one in heaven; not this one on earth. And that is also the reason why Christ said on another occasion: 'I do not receive glory from men.'[20]

Let us learn, then, beloved, to despise the honor that comes from men, and not to desire it. We have been marked out for the greatest honor, compared to which that honor is actually insult and ridicule and caricature. Therefore, just as the wealth of this world, compared to that, is poverty, and this life, without that, is death ('Leave the dead,' Christ says, 'to bury their own dead'),[21] so also this glory, compared to that, is but shame and ridicule. Let us not, then, pursue it. If, indeed, those who give it are of less worth than shadows and dreams, how much more so is the glory itself. The glory that comes from men is 'as the flower of the field.'[22] And what could be more perishable that the flower of the field?

Even if such glory were lasting, what power would it have to be of assistance to the soul? None at all; on the contrary, it even does it the greatest harm, since it creates slaves who are in a worse state than those bought with silver, slaves not under one master only, but slaves who are subject to two or three thousands of masters, all enjoining different commands. How much better it is to be free than to be enslaved, free from the slavery of men, but subject to the mastery of God?

If, notwithstanding, you wish to love glory, do so, but let it be immortal glory that you love. And it is better worth your efforts, for its theater is more brilliant and its prize, greater. These spectators here bid you to go to expense to please them, while Christ is just the opposite. He gives you a hundredfold in return for what is given by you, and gives

---

19 Zach. 9.9.
20 John 5.41.
21 Matt. 8.22.
22 Isa. 40.6.

eternal life besides. Which is better, then: to be esteemed on earth or in heaven, by men or by God? For punishment or for reward? To be crowned for one day or for endless ages?

Give to the needy, but not to a dancer, in order that you may not lose his soul together with your money. You are indeed responsible for his damnation because of your ill-advised sponsorship. If dancers in theaters knew that their efforts would go unrewarded they would long ago have ceased from putting on these shows, but, when they see you applauding, attending, spending, expending all your wealth on them, even if they do not wish to continue, they are constrained to do so by the desire for the recompense. If, on the contrary, they knew that no one would praise their efforts, they would quickly desist from their labors because of the lack of remuneration, but, when they see the show watched with admiration by many, the praise of others becomes an attraction for them.

Let us, then, refrain from this profitless expenditure; let us learn for what and when we ought to dispense our wealth. Let us not incur the anger of God by reason of the two extremes: both if we amass wealth from a source whence we ought not, and if we spend it lavishly for what we ought not. Indeed, how much wrath would you not deserve if, while giving to a harlot, you ignore a poor man? Even if you are dispensing the fruits of honest toil, would it not be blameworthy to furnish the means of paying for evil, and to show esteem for things which deserve only punishment? If ever you support licentiousness by stripping orphans and dealing unjustly with widows, think what sort of punishment by fire is in store for those who dare to do these deeds. Listen to what Paul says: 'Not only do they do these things, but they applaud others doing them.'[23]

Perhaps we are finding fault too severely with you, but,

_____
23 Rom. 1.32.

even if we do not find fault, punishment for their deeds awaits those who sin without making amends. What help, therefore, would it be for me to speak pleasant words to those who are going to be punished for their deeds?

Do you applaud the dancer, do you praise him, and admire him? Well, then, you have become worse than he. Poverty, to be sure, provides an excuse for him, even if it is an unreasonable one, but you are deprived even of this pretext. And if I ask him: 'Why in the world have you overlooked other occupations to pursue this impure and coarse one?' he will reply that in it it is possible for one to gain much profit with little expenditure of toil. And if I ask you: 'Why in the world do you hold in esteem a man who lives in licentiousness and spends his life for the destruction of many men?' you will not be able to take refuge in the same defense, but must bend your head low and blush for shame.

Now, if you have nothing to say, when we ask you for an accounting, when that dreadful and inevitable judgment comes where we shall give the reckoning of our thoughts and deeds and all things, how shall we stand? With what kind of eyes shall we look at the Judge? What shall we say? What defense shall we offer? What sort of good or bad excuse shall we make? That of the money we spent? That of the pleasure we enjoyed? Or that of the destruction of others whom we caused to perish by the art of that actor? We shall be able to say nothing, but will have to endure a punishment that has no end and knows no bounds.

In order that this may not happen, let us provide for everything now in this life so that, after departing from it with good hope, we may attain to everlasting blessedness. May we all obtain this by the grace and mercy of our Lord Jesus Christ, through whom and with whom glory be to the Father, together with the Holy Spirit, now and always, and forever and ever. Amen.

Homily 43 (John 6.16-25)

'Now when evening had come, his disciples went down to the sea. And getting into a boat, they went across the sea to Capharnaum. And it was already dark, but Jesus had not come to them. Now the sea was rising, because a strong wind was blowing.'[1]

It was not only when Christ was present bodily with His disciples, but also when He was away from them, that He took thought for their well-being. In fact, because He is both powerful and wise, He brings about one and the same effect by completely opposite means. Notice, for example, what He did in this instance. He sent away His disciples and went up to the mountain.

When evening had come, the disciples, who had been left behind by their Master, went down to the sea and waited for Him until sunset, thinking that He would come to them. But as evening came on, they could no longer restrain themselves from going in search of Him, so great was the love of Him that possessed them. Indeed, they did not say: 'It is already evening and night has overtaken us; where shall we go now? The place is dangerous; the time is perilous.' But, on fire with longing for Him, they embarked in their boat. It is not, therefore, merely casually that the Evangelist mentions the time, but to show by this their burning love of Him.

Why, then, did He send them off and depart from them? Further, why did He appear again, alone, walking on the sea? It was to teach them by the former what it is to be left by Him, and to make their longing for Him greater, and by the latter to show His power once more. Just as, with regard to His teaching, they did not listen to everything in the presence of the crowd, so also with regard to His

---

1 John 6.16-18.

miracles: they did not witness all of them in the company of the multitude. Indeed, it was necessary for those who were going to be entrusted with the spiritual leadership of the world to have something more than the rest. 'But what sort of miracles did they see when by themselves?' you will ask. The transfiguration on the mountain,[2] this miracle on the sea, the many remarkable ones which took place after the Resurrection.[3] And judging from these, I think there were others besides.

Now, they went toward Capharnaum, without any definite knowledge, but expecting to find Him there, or even in the middle of the voyage. At least John implies this by the words: 'And it was already dark, but Jesus had not come to them. Now the sea was rising because a strong wind was blowing.' What, then, did they do? They became alarmed; and there were many and varied causes which made them become so. They were perturbed because of the time, of course, for it was dark; and because of the storm, for the sea was rising; and because of the place, for they were not near land, but 'they had rowed some twenty-five stadia'; and, finally, because of the unexpectedness of it all, for 'they beheld him walking upon the sea.' When they grew very much alarmed, He said to them: 'It is I, do not be afraid.'

Why, then, did He appear? To show that it was He who controlled the storm. The Evangelist certainly implies this in the words: 'They desired to take him; and immediately the boat was at the land.' He made the journey not only safe, but even prosperous. But He did not show Himself to the people, as He walked upon the sea, for the miracle was too great for their imperfect understanding. Indeed, He was not seen doing this for long even by the disciples, but, as soon as He had been seen, He withdrew from them.

It seems to me that this miracle is different from the one

2 Cf. Matt. 17.1-8; Mark 9.1-7; Luke 9.28-36.
3 Cf., especially, John 20-21; Luke 24.

in Matthew.[4] There is evidence on many counts that it is different. For He frequently performed the same miracles so as to bring it about, not so much that the witnesses of them might become used to them, but that they might accept them with stronger faith.

'It is I; do not be afraid.' By these words He dispelled the fear from their souls. But in the other instance His words did not have this effect. That is why Peter then said: 'Lord, if it is thou, bid me come to thee.'[5] Why is it, then, that in the latter instance they did not at once accept the fact [that it was Christ], while in the other they believed it? Because on that occasion the storm continued rocking their boat, while in this one, at the sound of His voice, there came a calm. Or, if this is not the case, the other explanation which I have just now mentioned holds good; namely, that by performing the same miracles He caused those which occurred later in time to be more readily believed because of the previous ones.

Why did He not enter the boat? It was because He wished to make the miracle greater, and at the same time to reveal His Godhead more clearly to them, and to prove that, at the time when He gave thanks, He did so, not because He was in need of assistance, but to condescend to their lowliness. He permitted the storm to take place that they might continue to seek Him out, and He stopped it again suddenly that they might learn His power; He did not get into the boat in order to make the miracle still greater.

'The next day, the crowd which had remained, upon observing that there had been but one boat at that place, the one into which his disciples had entered, and that Jesus had not gone into it with them,' themselves embarked in other boats which had come from Tiberias. Now, why did John give such precise details? Why did he not simply say that

---

4 Cf. Matt. 14.22-33.
5 Matt. 14.28.

the crowd departed and crossed over on the following day? He wished to teach us something more. What is this? That Christ permitted the people, also—even though not so manifestly—to have at least an inward suspicion of what had happened. For he says: 'They observed that there had been but one boat at that place, and that Jesus had not gone into it,' and embarking in the boats from Tiberias, 'they came to Capharnaum seeking Jesus.'

What, indeed, was there for them to think but that He had come by walking over the sea? It was not possible to say that He crossed on another boat, since there was one boat, he declares, the one on which His disciples crossed. Nevertheless, though they had come to Him after such a wonderful occurrence, they did not ask Him how He crossed or how He came to be there, nor did they seek to learn about such a great miracle. Moreover, what was it that they said? 'Rabbi, when didst thou come here?' were their words, unless someone may say that in this place 'when' is used by them in the sense of 'how.'[6]

It is worth while here also to take note of their fickleness of character. The very ones who had been saying: 'This is the Prophet,' and who had been striving to take Him by force and make Him king, now when they had found Him had no such course of action in mind. On the contrary, discarding the memory of the miracle, as I, for my part, think, they finished up by no longer admiring Him for what had taken place previously. Therefore, the reason why they were seeking Him was because they desired once more to share in His table as they had before.

Now, the Jews also had crossed the Red Sea, under the leadership of Moses,[7] but there is a great difference here. Moses accomplished everything by praying, and in the manner of a servant, whereas while Christ acted altogether by His

6 John 6.25.
7 Cf. Exod. 14.19-22.

own power. And in the episode of the Red Sea the water gave way by means of the wind which then was blowing, so as to make a passage on dry land, while in this episode a greater wonder took place. Though the sea kept its own nature, even so it carried the Lord on its surface, to bear out that Scriptural text which says: 'Who walketh upon the sea as on a pavement.'[8]

It was with reason, to be sure, that He performed the miracle of the loaves at the time when He was about to enter into Capharnaum, that harsh and obdurate city, since He wished to soften the obduracy of its inhabitants, not only by miracles worked within its borders, but also by those performed outside. Indeed, what stony heart could resist being softened when such great crowds, showing great enthusiasm, should come into that city? However, they were not thus affected, but merely desired bodily nourishment once more, and for that reason they were upbraided by Jesus.

Therefore, beloved, since we know this, let us give thanks to God, both for material things and much more for spiritual ones. Not only does He Himself will that we do so, but also it is for the sake of the latter that He gives the former, encouraging and instructing the less perfect by this means, since they still cling to this world. But if, when they have received material blessings they become attached to them, they are reproved and rebuked. Indeed, when in the case of the paralytic He willed to give a spiritual gift first, the by-standers objected, for when He said: 'Thy sins are forgiven thee,' they said: 'This man blasphemes.'[9]

Let us not, then, I beseech you, have any such sentiments, but let us consider spiritual things of more account. Why? Because, if spiritual blessings are present, no injury results from the lack of material ones, whereas, if the former are not present, what hope will remain for us then? And what

8 Job 9.8.
9 Matt. 9.3,4.

consolation? Therefore, we must continually beseech God for these and urgently ask for them.

In fact, Christ also taught us to make such petitions. And if we consult that prayer[10] we shall find nothing material in it; all is spiritual. Even that small section itself that refers to things of sense becomes spiritual by its mode of expression. For, to counsel us to seek for nothing more than bread for present needs, that is, 'daily bread,' could only proceed from a spiritual attitude, the disposition of the truly wise. Notice, too, the petitions that precede this one. 'Hallowed be thy name. Thy kingdom come. Thy will be done on earth as it is in heaven.'[11] Then, after mentioning that material need, He quickly turns away from it again and once more returns to spiritual things. 'Forgive us our debts,' He says, 'as we also forgive our debtors.'[12] He placed in the prayer, not power to rule, not wealth, not fame, not might, but everything calculated to aid the soul; nothing earthly, but everything heavenly.

Well, then, if we are bidden to refrain from the things of this present life, how wretched and miserable would we not be if we should ask of God those things which He has directed us to dispose of, if we possess them, in order to free us from anxiety about them? Things in behalf of which He has enjoined us to put forth no effort; rather, neither to possess nor to desire them? Certainly, this is to babble petitions in vain. And that is why, even though we pray, we accomplish nothing.

How is it, then, you will ask, that the wicked grow wealthy? And how is it that the unjust, the impure, the dishonest prosper? Not with God's help; perish the thought! Yet, how does God permit it? Just as He permitted the rich man in his day to go his way, deferring him to a greater

10 The Lord's Prayer; cf. Matt. 6.11; Luke 11.3.
11 Matt. 6.9,10.
12 Matt. 6.12.

punishment. Therefore, listen also to what He says to him: 'Son, thou hast received good things, and Lazarus evil things; but now he is comforted whereas thou art tormented.'[13]

Accordingly, in order that we, too, may not hear these words, as we foolishly and vainly live in luxury and pile up many sins for ourselves, let us choose for ourselves the true wealth and the correct philosophy of life so as to obtain the blessings promised. May we all share in these by the grace and mercy of our Lord Jesus Christ, through whom and with whom glory be to the Father, together with the Holy Spirit, now and always, and forever and ever. Amen.

Homily 44 (John 6.26-27)

'Jesus answered them and said, "Amen, I say to you, you seek me, not because you have seen signs, but because you have eaten of the loaves and have been filled. Labor not for the food that perishes, but for that which endures unto life everlasting." '[1]

Kindness and gentleness are not helpful on all occasions, but there is a time when the teacher has need of greater severity. When the pupil is lazy and phlegmatic, it is necessary to use a goad to prod such great sluggishness. This even the Son of God has done time and again, and especially in today's text.

When the people came and found Jesus and fawned on Him, saying: 'Rabbi, when didst thou come here?' to show that He was not seeking human honor, but looked to one thing only—their salvation—He answered them reprovingly. By this He desired not only to correct them but also to expose

---

13 Luke 16.25.

1 John 6.26,27.

and bring to light the attitude they had. What, indeed, did He say? 'Amen, amen I say to you,' with emphasis and assurance, 'You seek me, not because you have seen signs, but because you have eaten of the loaves and have been filled.' By His words He attacked and reproved them, not, however, sharply and too strongly, but acting with great restraint.

Moreover, He did not say: 'O you gourmandizers and gluttons, I have worked such great miracles, and you have not followed after Me, nor have you marveled at what happened.' On the contrary, He spoke gently and kindly: 'You seek me, not because you have seen signs, but because you have eaten of the loaves and have been filled,' referring not only to past events but also to the present miracle. By His words to them He was all but saying this: 'It is not the miracle of the loaves that has struck you with wonder, but the being filled.'

And they immediately proved that He was not merely surmising when He made these remarks. That was indeed the reason why they came once again: with the hope of enjoying the same benefits as before. And that is also why they said: 'Our fathers ate the manna in the desert,' to bring Him back again to the consideration of bodily nourishment, a procedure which was surely reprehensible and extremely blameworthy.

However, He Himself did not stop with reproaches, but even gave them additional instruction: 'Do not labor for the food that perishes, but for that which endures unto life everlasting, which the Son of Man will give you. For upon him the Father, God himself, has set his seal.' And what He means is some such thing as this: 'Do not consider this bodily nourishment of value, but only that spiritual food.'

However, since some who wish to live without working misapply this statement by saying that Christ was renouncing manual labor, it is timely to speak also against them. They are slandering the whole of Christianity, so to speak, and laying it open to be ridiculed for laziness. But first we ought to quote the words of Paul. And what does he say? 'Remember the Lord who said: "It is more blessed to give than to receive." '[2] Yet, from what source would he who possessed nothing be able to give?

How is it, then, that Jesus said to Martha: 'Thou art anxious and troubled about many things; and yet only one thing is needful. Mary has chosen the best part'?[3] And again: 'Do not be anxious about tomorrow'?[4] It is indeed necessary to explain all these texts now, not only in order that we may cause those who are lazy to cease to be so—if they should be open to persuasion—but also that we may prove that no statements made by God contradict one another.

The Apostle says in another place: 'We exhort you to make progress and to strive to live peacefully, minding your own affairs, so that you may walk becomingly towards outsiders.'[5] And again: 'He who was wont to steal, let him steal no longer; but rather let him labor, working with his hands, that he may have something to share with him who suffers need.'[6] Here, indeed, Paul not merely has bidden us to work, but to labor so industriously that we have something from our efforts to share with another. Elsewhere, too, the same sacred writer says: 'These hands of mine have provided for my needs and those of my companions.'[7] And writing to the Corinthians he said: 'What then is my reward? That preaching the gospel, I deliver the gospel without charge.'[8] And when he was in that city: 'He stayed with Aquila and Priscilla and he set to work; for they were tent-makers by

2 Acts 20.35.
3 Luke 10.41,42.
4 Matt. 6.34.
5 1 Thess. 4.10,11.
6 Eph. 4.28.
7 Acts 20.34.
8 1 Cor. 9.18.

trade.'[9] Moreover, these quotations seem to contradict those others still more strongly if interpreted according to the letter. We must, therefore, produce the answer at last.

What, then, should we say in reply? It is that 'not to be anxious' is not the same as 'not to work,' but it means not to be solicitous for tomorrow's refreshment, but to consider that this anxiety is unnecessary. It is possible both for one who works not to be hoarding for tomorrow and for one who works not to be solicitous. Solicitude, indeed, is not the same thing as work. One does not labor as if setting store by the work, but in order to share with him who suffers need.

And what was said to Martha did not refer to work and daily labor, but to the necessity of knowing the time for it and of not spending the time, intended for listening to Him, on more material occupations. Well, then, He did not say these things to encourage her to idleness, but to compel her to listen to Him. 'I have come,' He meant to say, 'to teach you the things necessary for salvation, and are you busying yourself about a meal? Do you wish to make Me welcome and to prepare a lavish table? Prepare another kind of refreshment by making yourself an attentive and enthusiastic listener and imitating the loving attention of your sister.' It was not, then, to forbid hospitality that He spoke as He did to her; perish the thought! How, indeed, could He do so? But it was to show that one must not be preoccupied with other things when it is the time to listen to Him.

Further, the words: 'Do not labor for the food that perishes' do not imply that one ought to be idle. I say this because this very conduct is most especially 'food that perishes' ('for idleness hath taught much evil').[10] On the contrary, these words imply that one ought to work and to share. This is really the food that does not perish. And if some lazy fellow

---

9 Acts 18.2.
10 Eccli. 33.29.

should glut himself and exert every effort for nourishment, he is working for 'the food that perishes'; whereas, if a worker should feed Christ, and give Him drink, and clothe Him, no one would be so dull and ignorant as to say that such a one is laboring for food that perishes, since in return for this there is the promise of the Kingdom to come and of the well-known rewards.[11] This food, indeed, endures forever.

But since at that time, on the contrary, they made no account of the faith, and did not make it their business to learn who it was that was working these miracles, and with what power, but wished for only one thing—namely, to glut themselves without doing any work—with good reason did He call such nourishment as this 'food that perishes.' 'I nourished your bodies,' He said, 'in order that because of this you might seek for the other kind of nourishment, that which endures, that which nourishes your souls, but you once again are in pursuit of earthly food. That is why you do not realize that I am leading you, not to this imperfect food, but to that which gives life, not merely for time but for eternity; that which nourishes, not the body, but the soul.'

Next, since He had in this way taken merit to Himself by saying that He Himself would give this food, so that what was said might not once more give offense to them, to make His words credible He attributed to the Father the responsibility for the gift. After saying: 'which the Son of Man will give you,' He added: 'For upon him God the Father has set his seal'; that is: 'He has sent Him for this purpose: to provide this nourishment for you.'

The text, however, is open to another interpretation, for Christ says elsewhere: 'He who listens to my words, the Father has set his seal on him because God is true';[12] that

---

11 Cf. Matt. 25.34-40.
12 Cf. John 3.33. The actual reading, however, is: 'He who receives his witness has set his seal on this, that God is true.'

is: 'has given unqualified approval to Him.' It seems to me that here, also, the text implies this. For the words, 'The Father has set his seal,' mean nothing else than 'has given approval to,' 'has made known by His testimony.' Of course, He also revealed Himself, but since He was discoursing to the Jews He brought to their notice this testimony of the Father.

Let us learn, then, beloved, to ask the Father for what it is fitting to seek from Him. Then, those things, I mean the things of this life, whatever their condition, will bring no harm. On the one hand, if we are rich, we shall enjoy luxury here only, and if, on the contrary, we fall into poverty, we shall feel no frightful suffering. Neither the bright side of this present life nor the dark one has the power to fix us in a condition of unhappiness or happiness; both are equally to be despised, and pass away very speedily. Therefore, they are with good reason called 'a road,' since they are transitory and do not usually remain for long. In the future life, on the contrary, both states endure forever: that of punishment and that of the Kingdom. Let us, then, make vigorous efforts with regard to these, so as to avoid the one and obtain the other. What advantage, indeed, is there in living in luxury here? Today it is, and tomorrow it does not exist; today a bright flower, and tomorrow dust scattered far and wide; today a blazing fire, and tomorrow burned-out ashes.

The things of the spirit, however, are not like this, but they keep shining and blooming forever, and become each day more radiant. That wealth will never perish, never passes away, never comes to an end, never brings on worry and envy and accusation, does not utterly destroy the body, does not corrupt the soul, does not cause jealousy, does not heap up envy—but all these things accompany the wealth of this world. That other glory does not puff up foolishly, does not cause to become inflamed, never ceases, and does not grow dim. The rest and enjoyment of heaven continue forever and are always the same, since they are perpetually unchanged and immortal, for it is not possible to find their limit or end.

Let us desire this life, I beseech you. If we truly desire it, we shall make no account of present things, but shall despise and scorn them all. Even if someone bids us to enter into the court of the king, we shall prefer not to do so, since we have hope of that other Kingdom. Although nothing seems to be a happier lot than the former, even this is little and worthless and of no account to those possessed by the desire for heaven. In truth, nothing which has an end is to be much sought for; all that comes to an end—and is today while tomorrow it does not exist—even if it be very important, seems actually to be very little and despicable.

Let us not, then, cleave to fleeting things or to those that are passing and transient, but to those that are lasting and immutable, in order that we may be able in fact to obtain them, by the grace and mercy of our Lord Jesus Christ, through whom and with whom, glory be to the Father, together with the Holy Spirit, now and always, and forever and ever. Amen.

Homily 45 (John 6.28-40)

'They said therefore to him, "What are we to do in order that we may perform the works of God?" In answer Jesus said to them, "This is the work of God, that you believe in him whom he has sent. They said therefore to him, what sign, then, dost thou, that we may see and believe thee? What work dost thou perform?" '[1]

There is nothing worse than gluttony, nothing more degrading. It makes the mind dull; it renders the soul carnal;

---

[1] John 6.28-31.

it blinds [its victims] and does not permit them to see. See how this actually happened in the case of the Jews. Since they sought greedily to eat to satiety, and were altogether given to the things of this world, and did not have a spiritual outlook, Christ attempted to rouse them by numerous words which were at once goading and indulgent. However, not even thus were they converted, but still continued in their worldly attitude.

Consider, for example, the present text. He had said to them: 'You seek me, not because you have seen signs, but because you have eaten of the loaves and have been filled.' He began the attack by this charge. He then showed what sort of food they ought to seek by the words: 'Do not labor for the food that perishes.' He set the reward before them in the words: 'but for that which endures unto life everlasting.' Next, He answered what might have been their objection by declaring that He was sent by the Father. What, therefore, did they reply? Just as if they had heard nothing, they said: 'What are we to do in order that we may perform the works of God?' They said this, not in order to get the information and act on it (what follows proves this), but to cause Him once more to provide food, desiring to prevail on Him to satisfy their hunger again.

What reply did Christ make? 'This is the work of God, that you believe in him whom he has sent.' And they said: 'What sign dost thou, that we may see and believe thee? Our fathers ate the manna in the desert.' There is nothing more dull, nothing more stupid than they. Though there was a sign still before their eyes, as if there were none, they kept saying: 'What sign dost thou?' And as they spoke, they did not even permit Him to decide the very choice of a sign, but thought they would place Him under the necessity of performing no other miracle than one similar to that which had taken place in the case of their ancestors. Hence, they said: 'Our fathers ate the manna in the desert,' thinking by this to provoke Him to perform some such miracle as this, which, of course, could provide bodily food for them.

Otherwise, why was it that they recalled no other miracles of olden times—though many, to be sure, had then taken place, both in Egypt, and at the [Red] Sea, and in the desert[2] —but only that of the manna? Was it not because they had their heart very much set upon it by reason of being enslaved to their appetite? And how is it that you who, when you saw the miracle, said He was a prophet and tried to make Him king, now have become ungrateful and unmindful, as if none had taken place, and are demanding a sign, uttering speech suited to parasites and famished dogs? And is the manna admirable to you now because your soul is hungry?

Notice their hypocrisy. They did not say: 'Moses performed this miracle; what sign dost thou?' because they thought they would disconcert Him. But, for the moment they addressed Him with great respect, in the expectation of receiving food. Besides, they did not say: 'God did this; what sign dost thou?' in order that they might not seem to be making Him equal to God. On the other hand, they did not mention Moses, lest they might seem to belittle Him, so they steered a middle course and said: 'Our fathers ate manna in the desert.'

Now, He could have declared: 'I have just now performed a greater wonder than Moses, since I did not need a rod, nor did I have need of prayer, but accomplished everything of Myself, and if you even make mention of the manna, see, I also have furnished bread for you.' However, it was not now the time for these words; His efforts were centered on a single object, namely, to bring them to spiritual food. And see His boundless wisdom in the way in which He replied: 'Moses did not give you the bread from heaven, but my Father gives you the true bread from heaven.'

2 Cf., for example, Exod. 7-11.

Why is it, then, that He did not say: 'Moses did not give it, but I did'? Why, on the contrary, did He put God in place of Moses, and in place of the manna, Himself? Because the imperfection of His listeners was great; this is clear from what follows. And I say this because not even when He had spoken in this way did He check them by this means, though, to be sure, He had begun by saying: 'You seek me, not because you have seen signs, but because you have eaten of the loaves and have been filled.' Since they were actually seeking for this [corporeal food], He also corrected them in what follows; yet not even then did they give up.

Further, when He promised the Samaritan woman to give 'the water' He made no mention of His Father, but He spoke somewhat after this manner: 'If you knew who it is who says to thee, Give me to drink, thou wouldst have asked of him, and he would have given thee living water.'[3] And again: 'The water that I will give,' and He did not refer to the Father. But here He did make mention of the Father, that you may learn what was the quality of the faith of the Samaritan woman and what the imperfection of the Jews.

Surely, the manna was not from heaven; how is it, then, that He said 'from heaven'? Just as Scripture says: 'The birds of heaven,' and again: 'And the Lord thundered from heaven.'[4] And He calls that bread 'true,' not because the miracle in the case of the manna was false, but because it was figure, not the reality. But in mentioning Moses He did not put Himself in his place, for they did not yet think Him greater than Moses, but still had a higher opinion of the latter. That is why, when He said: 'Moses did not give,' He did not add: 'I am giving,' but said that, instead of Himself, the Father was giving.

But when they had heard, they said again: 'Give us this

3 John 4.10,14.
4 Ps. 8.9; 17.14.

bread to eat.' They still thought it was something material; they still expected to satisfy bodily hunger, and therefore they were thronging about Him still more insistently. What did Christ then reply? To uplift them by degrees He added: 'The bread of God is that which comes down from heaven and gives life to the world'; not to the Jews only, but to the whole world, He declared. Therefore, He did not merely say 'food,' but 'life,' so that He made it clear that it was another and a different life, since they were all dead.[5]

They still inclined to earthly things and said: 'Give us this bread.' And reproving them because, as long as they had the idea that His table was a material one they flocked to Him, but when they learned that it was spiritual they did so no longer, He said once more: 'I am the bread of life. He who comes to me shall not hunger, and he who believes in me shall never thirst. But I have told you that you have seen me and you do not believe me.'

Previous to this, John also spoke in this way by anticipation in the words: 'He speaks what he knows and he bears witness to that which he has seen, and his witness no one receives.' And once again, Christ said: 'We speak what we know, and we bear witness to what we have seen, and our witness you do not receive.'[6] He did this to warn them, and to show that the fact itself did not disturb Him and that He was not seeking for fame, but that He was not ignorant of the unspoken thoughts of their minds, neither those then present nor those of the future.

'I am the bread of life.' He was now about to plunge them into the revelation of the mysteries. So first He spoke of His Godhead in the words: 'I am the bread of life.' He was not saying this of His body (for with reference to His body He said at the end: 'The bread that I will give is my

---

5 I.e., because they lacked sanctifying grace.
6 Cf. John 3.32,11.

flesh'),[7] but for the moment [by 'the bread of life'] He meant His Godhead. This is so because the Godhead is 'bread' through God the Word, just as this bread likewise becomes bread from heaven because of the Spirit coming upon it. And in this place He did not make use of witnesses to support His words, as He had done in the previous gathering, for He had the very miracle of the loaves itself as evidence, and an audience who pretended for the time to believe in Him. On the other occasion they were raising objections and finding fault; that is why here He even revealed Himself as God.

Now, as long as these men were in expectation of enjoying bodily refreshment, they persevered and were not disturbed at His words until they afterwards gave up this hope. However, not even then did Christ keep silence; He even said many things in reproof. And they who, when they were eating, kept saying He was a Prophet now took offense and said He was only the son of the carpenter; not, however, when they were eating the loaves, for then they kept saying: 'This is the Prophet,' and they desired to make Him king. Ostensibly, then, they were provoked because He said He had come down from heaven; actually, this did not cause their annoyance, but the fact that they were disappointed of the hope of enjoying food for their bodies. Besides, if they really were provoked, they should have made inquiry and sought to learn how He was the bread of life, how He had come down from heaven; as a matter of fact, they did not do this, but murmured. And it is clear from this that it was not this statement that offended them.

Now, when He said: 'My Father gives you bread,' they did not say: 'Ask Him to give.' What was it they said? 'Give us this bread.' Yet, He did not say: 'I give,' but 'My Father gives.' Because of their excessive desire for food, they deemed Him capable of dispensing it. Well, then, if they deemed

---

7 John 6.52.

Him capable of giving it, how is it that they would afterwards take offense when they heard Him say: 'My Father gives'? What, therefore, is the reason? Because they heard that it was not possible to eat they once more were incredulous and actually alleged, as pretext of their unbelief, that His statement was above His dignity. That is why He said: 'You have seen me and you do not believe,' referring partly to His miracles and partly to the testimony of the Scriptures. 'It is they,' He said, 'that bear witness to me'; and 'I have come in the name of my Father, and you do not receive me'; and 'How can you believe who receive glory from one another?'[8]

'All that the Father gives to me shall come to me, and him who comes to me I will not cast out.' Do you perceive how He was doing everything for the sake of their salvation? Accordingly, that is why He also continued His remarks, so that He might not seem to be meddlesome and to be making these statements capriciously. But what is it that He says? 'All that the Father gives to me shall come to me . . . and I will raise him up on the last day.'

Why did He make mention of the general resurrection— in which even the impious shall share—as if it were a special prerogative of those who believe in Him? Because He was not merely referring to resurrection, but to such a resurrection as the following. When he said previously: 'I will not cast him out' and 'I should lose nothing of it,' He was then speaking of the resurrection. For, in the resurrection some are cast out, as we may learn from the words: 'Away with him, and cast him forth into the darkness outside.'[9] And some are lost, as He makes clear in the words, 'Rather be afraid of him who is able to destroy both soul and body in hell.'[10] So that the words: 'I give everlasting life' mean

8 John 5.40,43,44.
9 Matt. 22.13.
10 Matt. 10.29.

this: 'They who have done evil shall come forth unto resurrection of judgment, but they who have done good unto resurrection of life.'[11] Here, then, He was referring to this resurrection: that of the good.

Now, what did He wish to show by the words: 'All that the Father gives to me shall come to me'? He was upbraiding their unbelief and showing that he who does not believe in Him is transgressing against the will of the Father. He did not say this in so many words, but did so by implication. Moreover, you will notice that He did this on many occasions, since He wished to show that those who do not believe have offended not only Him but also His Father. If this is His will, and He has come for this reason, namely, that He may save the whole world, those who do not believe are offending against His will. Therefore, He meant: 'When My Father directs anyone, there is nothing preventing him from coming to Me.' And He went on to say this, also: 'No one can come to me unless the Father draw him.' Paul also said that He Himself will deliver them to the Father: 'When he delivers the kingdom to God the Father.'[12] Accordingly, just as the Father, in giving, does not first deprive Himself when so doing, so also the Son, in delivering us, is not casting us off from Himself in doing this. But He is said to be 'delivering' us because we have access [to the Father] through Him.

Further, the words 'by him' are also said in regard to the Father, just as when Scripture says: 'By him, you have been called into fellowship with his Son'[13] that is, by the will of the Father. And once more: 'Blessed art thou, Simon Bar-Jona, for flesh and blood has not revealed this to thee.'[14] In our present text He is all but implying something like

11 John 5.29.
12 1 Cor. 15.24.
13 1 Cor. 1.9.
14 Matt. 16.17.

this: 'Faith in Me is not a thing of chance, but needs assistance from on high.' Moreover, this is the point He was
making in the entire discourse. He was showing that faith
itself requires a truly virtuous soul and one that is drawn by
God.

However, perhaps someone will say: 'If all that the Father
gives comes to You, and those whom He draws, and if no
one can come to You except it be given him from above,
those are free from all blame and accusation to whom the
Father does not give [this grace].' These are foolish words
and mere pretense. We also need our own free will, since
to learn and to believe are matters of choice. Indeed, the
words, 'What my Father gives,' here mean nothing else than
that to believe in Me is not a matter of chance or of human
reasoning, but requires both revelation from above and a
soul well disposed to receive the revelation. And the words,
'He who comes to me will be saved,' mean 'will enjoy much
care.' 'I have come in behalf of them,' He meant, 'and
have taken on flesh and put on the form of a slave.' Then
He added: 'I have come down, not to do my own will, but
the will of him who sent me.'

What is it that You are saying? Is Your will one thing
and His another? In order that no one might conceive this
suspicion, He cleared it up by adding the words: 'This is
the will of him who sent me, that whoever beholds the Son,
and believes in him, shall have everlasting life.' Is not this,
then, Your will? And how is it that You said elsewhere: 'I
have come to cast fire upon the earth, and what will I but
that it be kindled'?[15] Now, if You desire this, it is very
clear that there is but one will, for elsewhere You say: 'As
the Father raises the dead and gives them life, even so the
Son also gives life to whom he will.'[16] What, then, is the will
of the Father? Is it not that not even one of these may be

---

15 Luke 12.49.
16 John 5.21.

lost? And further, do not You Yourself desire this? Well, then, that is not one thing and this, another.

Elsewhere, He also proved His equality to the Father, making it still more certain by saying: 'The Father and I will come and make our abode with him.'[17] Accordingly, what He meant is this: 'I have come to do nothing else but what the Father wills, since I do not have any will of My own, contrary to the will of the Father, for everything that is the Father's is Mine, and Mine is His.' If, then, the wishes of the Father and of the Son are mutually shared, with good reason did He say: 'Not to do my own will.'

However, He did not speak so openly here, but kept this for the end. For the moment, as I have said, He concealed and spoke guardedly of the sublime, and wished to indicate that if He had said: 'This is My will,' they would have ridiculed Him. He declared, then: 'I am co-operating with Him in accomplishing His will,' because He wished to impress them the more strongly, as if He said: 'What do you think? That by your unbelief you are rousing Me to anger? You are, in fact, angering My Father.'

'Now this is the will of him who sent me, that I should lose nothing of what he has given me.' Here He made it clear that He did not need their service, nor did He come for His own advantage, but for their salvation; not for the sake of any honor to be gained from them. And He had also said this in the previous gathering: 'I do not receive glory from men'; and again: 'I say these things that you may be saved.'[18] Everywhere, indeed, He strove to show that He had come for their salvation. He also declared that He was seeking the Father's glory, so that He would seem altogether above reproach. And that He did speak in this way for this reason, He made still more clear in words that follow later: 'If anyone seeks his own will, he seeks his own

17 John 14.23.
18 John 5.41,34.

glory. But he who seeks the glory of the one who sent him is truthful, and there is no injustice in him.'[19]

'This is the will of my Father, that whoever beholds the Son and believes in him shall have everlasting life, and I will raise him up on the last day.' Why is it that He everywhere stressed the resurrection? It was in order that they might not think that the providence of God governs only present events, and that, even if they should not prosper here, they might not on that account be disheartened, but might center their hopes on the future; also, in order that they might not despise Him because of their escaping punishment in the present, but might look to another life.

However, even if they derived no profit from His speaking continually of the resurrection, let us strive to profit thereby. If we get the desire to become rich, to take possession of things unlawfully, or to do anything wrong, let us at once call to mind that day, and let us picture to ourselves the judgment, and that way of thinking will check the unruly impulse more effectively than any bridle. Let us say both to others and to ourselves as well: 'There is a resurrection, and a fearful judgment awaits us.' If we see someone puffed up and aglow because of temporal prosperity, let us say the same thing to him, to warn him that all this remains in this world. On the other hand, if we see another person downcast and afflicted with misfortune, let us address the same words to him, also, to remind him that his ill fortune will have an end. And if we see someone who is lazy and slothful, let us chant the same theme to him, to admonish him that he must render an accounting for laziness. This sentence is more potent than any remedy to cure the disease of our soul.   And I say this because there is a resurrection and the resurrection is at the door, not far distant or far away in time. 'For yet a little while,' says Paul, 'and he

19 John 7.18.

who is to come will come, and will not delay.'[20] And again: 'All of us must be made manifest before the tribunal of Christ,'[21] that is, both wicked and just—the former, that they may be put shame before all men; the latter, on the contrary, that they may be made more resplendent before all. Just as judges in this life both punish the wicked and honor the just publicly, so it will be in the next world, so that the former will have greater shame, while the latter have more brilliant glory.

Let us, then, picture these things to ourselves daily. If we ponder these things unceasingly, no temporal and perishable concerns will have power to captivate us. 'For the things that are seen are temporal, but the things that are not seen are eternal.'[22] Let us, therefore, repeat unceasingly both ourselves and to one another: 'There is a resurrection, and a judgment, and an accounting to be rendered of our deeds.' And let those who believe in fate but say this, and they will at once be rid of the corrupting influence of this plague. If there is a resurrection and a judgment, there is no such thing as fate, even if some contend and endlessly put forth vigorous arguments that there is. However, I am ashamed to be instructing Christians about the resurrection. He who needs to learn that there is a resurrection, and has not convinced himself thoroughly that things do not happen by blind force or at random or by chance, could not be a Christian.

Therefore, I beg and beseech, let us purify ourselves of all wickedness, and let us perform all our actions so as to obtain pardon and excuse in that day. But someone will perhaps ask: 'When will the end be? When will the resurrection take place? See how much time has passed and no

<hr/>

20 Heb. 10.37.
21 2 Cor. 5.10.
22 2 Cor. 4.18.

such thing has happened.' It will, however, take place, believe me. And I say this because those who were living before the flood were saying such things as these and ridiculing Noe, but the flood came and overwhelmed all these unbelievers, and spared only the believer.[23] And those at the time of Lot did not expect that divinely sent blow until those thunderbolts and the lightning descended and consumed them all.[24] Now, neither in their case nor in that of those in the time of Noe was there preparation for what was about to happen, but, while they were all feasting and drinking to the point of intoxication, then those insufferable ills came upon them.

So also will the resurrection take place, not exacting vengeance after preliminary warning, but while we are in the midst of good fortune. That is why Paul also says: 'When they shall say: Peace and security, even then sudden destruction will come upon them, as birth pangs upon her who is with child, and they will not escape.'[25] And God has ordained it thus in order that we may be always ready, and that we may not be overconfident, even in the very time of security. But what is it you say? You do not expect that resurrection and judgment will take place? Even demons acknowledge this fact, and do you not confess it? For, 'Hast thou come here,' they say, 'to torment us before the time?'[26] And as they say that torture will take place, they also know the judgment and accounting and punishment.

Let us not, then, provoke the anger of God by disbelieving in the teaching of the resurrection in addition to boldly doing evil deeds, for, just as Christ has created a precedent for us in other respects, so also in this. I say this because it is for this reason that He is called the 'first-born from the

---

23 Cf. Gen. 7.5-24.
24 Cf. Gen. 19.23-25.
25 1 Thess. 5.3.
26 Matt. 8.29.

dead.'[27] If there were no resurrection, how could He be first-born, if there were none of the dead to follow Him? If there be no resurrection, how will the justice of God be preserved, since so many of the wicked prosper, and so many of the just are afflicted and pass their lives in distress? How, indeed, will each of these receive his just deserts if there be no resurrection? None of those who live uprightly fail to believe in the resurrection, but every day they pray for that day as they say the sacred words: 'Thy kingdom come.'[28]

Who are they, therefore, who do not believe in the resurrection? Those who tread unholy ways and live an impure life, as the Prophet says: 'His ways are always filthy; thy judgments are far from his mind.'[29] Indeed, it is not possible, it is not possible, I repeat, for a man to lead a pure life if he does not believe in the resurrection, since those who are conscious of no evil-doing on their part both say, and desire, and believe that they will receive a reward for this.

Let us, then, not provoke Him to anger, but let us listen to Him saying: 'Be afraid of him who is able to destroy both soul and body in hell,'[30] in order that we may become better because of our fear, and, being free from this destruction, may be deemed worthy of the kingdom of heaven. May we all obtain this by the grace and mercy of our Lord Jesus Christ, through whom and with whom glory be to the Father, together with the adorable and all-holy and life-giving Spirit, now and always, and forever and ever. Amen.

27 Col. 1.18.
28 Matt. 6.10.
29 Ps. 9.26.
30 Matt. 10.28.

Homily 46 (John 6.41-53)

'The Jews therefore murmured about him because he had said: I am the bread that has come down from heaven. And they kept saying: "Is this not the son of Joseph, whose father and mother we know? How, then, does he say: I have come down from heaven?" '[1]

'Their god is the belly, their glory is in their shame,'[2] said Paul, writing to the Philippians about certain men. Now, it is clear from what had gone before that the Jews were just like these men, and this is likewise clear from the words they addressed to Christ as they approached Him. When, indeed, He gave them bread and satisfied their hunger, they kept calling Him a prophet and sought to make Him king. But when He taught them about their spiritual food, about life everlasting, when He led them away from things of sense, when He spoke to them of the resurrection, and elevated their thoughts, when, in short, they ought most of all to have admired Him, then they murmured and went away.

Now, if He was in truth the Prophet, as they had just said: 'This is indeed he about whom Moses said, "The Lord thy God will raise up to thee a prophet of thy brethren like unto me: him shalt thou hear," '[3] they ought to have listened to Him when He said: 'I have come down from heaven.' On the contrary, they did not listen to Him, but murmured. Of course, they still held Him in awe because of the recent miracle of the loaves. That is why they did not oppose Him openly, but by murmuring they showed that they resented it, because He did not give them the table which they desired. And as they murmured, they kept saying: 'Is this not the son of Joseph?'

From this it is clear that they did not yet know His mar-

---

1 John 6.41,42.
2 Phil. 3.19.
3 Deut. 18.15.

velous and strange generation. That is why they still called Him the son of Joseph. Yet, He did not reprove them or say to them: 'I am not the son of Joseph.' This was not, to be sure, because He was the son of Joseph, but because they were not yet able to hear of His wonderful Incarnation. And if they were not ready for a clear revelation of His birth according to the flesh, much more was that the case with that ineffable one from above. If He did not reveal the humble one, much less would He have treated of the other. And though it scandalized them very much to think that He was of a lowly and ordinary father, He nevertheless did not reveal His true parentage, in order that, in removing one scandal, He might not cause another.

What, then, did He reply when they murmured? 'No one can come to me unless the Father who sent me draw him.' The Manichaeans pounce on this and say that no action lies within our power,[4] though the statement actually proves conclusively that we are in possession of free will. 'If a man has the power to come to Him,' they say, 'what need has he of being drawn?' In reality, Christ's words do not dispense with free will, but underline our need for assistance [in exercising our free will], because He here was pointing out that it is not anyone who happens to do so that comes to Him, but that it is a person enjoying the benefit of much assistance who comes.

In the next place, He also pointed out the manner by which He draws him. In order that they might not suspect of God some purely material operation, He added: 'Not that anyone has seen the Father except him who is from God, he has seen the Father.'

'How, then, does He draw him?' you will ask. The Prophet

---

4 The heresy of the Manichaeans came to the zenith of its power in the Eastern Roman Empire during the period when St. John was preaching these Homilies. For a detailed treatment, cf. art. 'Manichaeism,' in *Catholic Encyclopedia*.

foretold this of old, prophesying in the words: 'They all shall be taught of God.' Do you see the high dignity of faith? And do you see how he predicted that they were going to learn, not from men, nor through a man, but through God Himself? Indeed, that is why He despatched them to the Prophets, namely, to corroborate His words.

'But,' you say, 'if he says, "They all shall be taught of God," how is it that not all men are believers?" Because his words were spoken of the majority of men. Besides, even apart from this, the prophecy refers not to all men in general, but to all who will to be taught. For, as a teacher, He is at the disposal of all men, ready to give them His teachings, pouring out His teaching in abundance unto all.

'And I will raise him up on the last day.' In this text the Son has no inconsiderable dignity, for if, to be sure, the Father draws men, the Son it is who raises them up, not, of course, separating His works from those of the Father (for how could that be?), but showing that Their power is the same. Therefore, just as in the place where He said: 'And the Father, who has sent me, bears witness to me,' in order that none might contend against His words, He thereupon referred them to the Scriptures; so also in this text, in order that they might not conceive the same suspicion, He referred them to the Prophets, to whom He repeatedly turned to prove that He was not in opposition to the Father.

'But,' you will say, 'what of those before this time? Were they not "taught of God"? Then, what is better here?' The fact is that, before this, people learned the things of God through men, while now they learn them through the only-begotten Son of God and through the Holy Spirit. Next He added: 'Not that anyone has seen the Father except him who is from God,' not saying this here in the sense of causality, but of the mode of His existence. Because, if He had said it in the sense of causality, we are all, likewise, 'from God.' Where then would be the superiority and pre-eminence of the Son? 'But why,' you will say, 'did He not make it clearer?' Because of their weakness. If they were scandalized to such a degree when He said: 'I have come down from heaven,' what scandal would they not have taken if He added this?

He called Himself 'living bread' because He welds together for us this life and the life to come. Therefore, He added: 'If anyone eat of this bread he shall live forever.' Surely, 'bread' here means the teachings of salvation, and faith in Him, or else His Body, for both strengthen the soul. Yet, when He said elsewhere: 'If anyone hear my word, he will not taste death,'[5] they were scandalized, while here they did not have any such reaction, perhaps because they still were in awe of Him on account of the loaves He had [miraculously] brought into being.

Moreover, notice what a distinction He made between the living bread and the manna, by telling them the kind of effect that each of these foods produces. To show that the manna had no unusual effect He added: 'Your fathers ate the manna in the desert and have died.' Next, He placed before them very convincing evidence that they themselves were deemed worthy of much greater blessings than their fathers, by referring indirectly to those well-known and wonderful men who lived at the time of Moses. Therefore, when He had said that they who had eaten the manna had died, He added: 'If anyone eat of this bread, he will live forever.' And He did not use the words 'in the desert' without design, but to imply that the manna was not provided for a long period of time and did not accompany them into the Promised Land.

This Bread, however, is not such. 'And the bread that I will give is my flesh that I will give for the life of the world.' With good reason at this point someone might inquire in perplexity whether that was a good time for Him to say these

5 John 8.52.

words, which were not then constructive or profitable, but rather were even injurious to what had already been built up. 'From this time,' Scripture says, 'many of his disciples turned back, saying, "This is a hard saying. Who can listen to it?" ' It seems that these teachings ought to have been given to the disciples alone, as Matthew[6] has said: 'He explained privately to them.'

What reply, then, shall we make to this objection? That even now these teachings were both very profitable and very necessary. Since they were urgently asking for food, but bodily food—and in recalling to Him the nourishment provided for their forefathers were stressing the greatness of the manna—in order to prove that all this was type and figure, while the reality thus foreshadowed was actually present, He made mention of spiritual nourishment.

'But,' you will say, 'He ought to have said: "Your fathers ate the manna in the desert, and I have provided bread for you." ' However, there was a great difference between the two. The latter, indeed, seemed inferior to the former, because this was brought from above, while the other, the miracle of the loaves, took place on earth. Therefore, since they were seeking for food brought down from heaven, for this reason He kept saying repeatedly: 'I have come down from heaven.'

Now, if someone should inquire: 'Why in the world did He shroud the explanation in mystery?' we should say this in reply to him: It was just the right time for such words, for the obscurity of the meaning of what is said always attracts the attention of the listener and makes him listen more carefully.

They ought not, therefore, to have been scandalized, but they should have asked questions and made inquiries. Instead, they went away. If, indeed, they thought He was a prophet, they ought to have believed His words. The scandal, then, consisted in their perversity, not in the doubtful meaning

---

6 Actually, Mark 4.34; but cf. Matt. 13.36.

of His words. And notice, too, how He had gradually bound His disciples to Himself, for it was they who said: 'Thou hast words of life; where else shall we go?' This was notwithstanding the fact the He here represented Himself as the giver, not His Father: 'The bread that I will give is my flesh.' However, the crowd did not react as His disciples did, but quite the contrary: 'This is a hard saying.' And they therefore went away.

Yet, the teaching was not strange and new. John, in truth, had implied it when he addressed Him as 'Lamb.' 'Even so, they did not know,' you will say. I am fully aware they did not, but even the disciples did not completely understand. If they did not know anything clearly about the resurrection, and for that reason were ignorant of the meaning of the words: 'Destroy this temple, and in three days I will raise it up,'[7] much more would they not understand the words said here, for the former were less obscure than these. They did, indeed, know that Prophets had raised people from the dead, even if the Scriptures did not say this clearly, but no Scripture had ever said that someone ate flesh. Nevertheless, they believed and followed Him and confessed that He had the words of eternal life. It is the part of a disciple not to inquire impertinently into the teachings of his master, but to listen and believe and await the proper time for explanation .

'Why is it, then,' you will say, 'that the contrary also happened and [the others] turned back and went away?' This was because of their perversity. When the question 'how' comes in, unbelief also accompanies it. Nicodemus likewise was disturbed in this way when he said: 'How can a man enter into his mother's womb?'[8] And these men were similarly perturbed when they said: 'How can this man give us his flesh to eat?' Now, if you really are looking for the

7 John 2.19.
8 Cf. John 3.4.

'how,' why did you not say this in the case of the loaves: 'How has He multiplied the five into so many?' Because then they were concerned only with being filled, not with witnessing the miracle. 'But on that occasion,' you will say, 'experience taught them.' Well, then, as a result of that, these words also ought to have been readily accepted. It was for this reason that He first worked that wonder, so that, having been instructed by it, they might no longer fail to believe what was said afterwards.

At that time, then, they actually derived no profit from His words, but we have enjoyed the benefit of the very realities. Therefore, we must learn the wondrousness of the mystery, what it is, why it was given, and what is the benefit to be derived from it. 'We are one body,' Scripture says, 'and members made from his flesh and from his bones.'[9] Let the initiated attend studiously to these words.

Therefore, in order that we may become of His Body, not in desire only, but also in very fact, let us become commingled with that Body. This, in truth, takes place by means of the food which He has given us as a gift, because He desired to prove the love which He has for us. It is for this reason that He has shared Himself with us and has brought His Body down to our level, namely, that we might be one with Him as the body is joined with the head. This, in truth, is characteristic of those who greatly love. Job, indeed, was implying this when he said of his servants—by whom he was loved with such an excess of love—that they desired to cleave to his flesh. In giving expression to the great love which they possessed, they said: 'Who will give us of his flesh that we may be filled?'[10] Moreover, Christ has done even this to spur us on to greater love. And to show the love He has for us He has made it possible for those who desire, not merely to look upon Him, but even to touch Him and to consume

9 Eph. 5.30.
10 Job 31.31.

Him and to fix their teeth in His Flesh and to be commingled with Him; in short, to fulfill all their love. Let us,
then, come back from that table like lions breathing out
fire, thus becoming terrifying to the Devil, and remaining
mindful of our Head and of the love which He has shown
for us.

'Parents, it is true, often entrust their children to others to
be fed, but I do not do so,' He says; 'I nourish Mine on My
own flesh. I give Myself to you, since I desire all of you to
be of noble birth, and I hold out to you fair hopes for the
future. He who gives Himself to you here will do so much
more in the life to come. I wished to become your brother.
When for your sake I had assumed flesh and blood, I gave
back again to you the very Flesh and Blood through which
I had become your kinsman.' This Blood makes the seal of
our King bright in us; it produces an inconceivable beauty;
it does not permit the nobility of the soul to become corrupt,
since it refreshes and nourishes it without ceasing.

The blood which we receive by way of food is not immediately a source of nourishment, but goes through some
other stage first; this is not so with this Blood, for it at once
refreshes the soul and instils a certain great power in it.
This Blood, when worthily received, drives away demons
and puts them at a distance from us, and even summons to
us angels and the Lord of angels. Where they see the Blood
of the Lord, demons flee, while angels gather. This Blood,
poured out in abundance, has washed the whole world
clean. The blessed Paul has uttered many truths about this
Blood in the Epistle to the Hebrews.[11] This Blood has purified the sanctuary and the Holy of Holies.

Now, if its type had so much power, both in the Temple
of the Hebrews and in the midst of the Egyptians, when
sprinkled on the doorposts,[12] much more power does the

11 Cf. Heb. 9.
12 Cf. Exod. 12.7,13.

reality have. In its types this Blood sanctified the golden altar; without it, the High Priest did not dare to enter the sanctuary. This Blood has ordained priests; in its types it has washed away sins. And if it had such great power in its types, if death shuddered so much at the figure, how would it not be in terror of the reality itself, pray tell? This Blood is the salvation of our souls; by it the soul is cleansed; by it, beautified; by it, inflamed. It makes our intellect brighter than fire; it renders our soul more radiant than gold. This Blood has been poured forth and has opened the way to heaven.

Awe-inspiring, in truth, are the mysteries of the Church; awesome, in truth, her altar. A fountain sprang up out of paradise, sending forth sensible streams; a fountain arises from this table, sending forth spiritual streams.[13] Beside this fountain there have grown, not willows without fruit, but trees reaching to heaven itself, with fruit ever in season and incorrupt. If someone is intensely hot, let him come to this fountain and cool down the feverish heat. It dispels parching heat and gently cools all things that are very hot; not those inflamed by the sun's heat, but those set on fire by burning arrows. It does so because it takes it beginning from above, and has its source from there, and from there it is fed. Many are the streams of this fountain, streams which the Paraclete sends forth; and the Son becomes its Custodian, not keeping its channel open with a mattock, but making our hearts receptive.

This fountain is a fountain of light, shedding abundant rays of truth. And beside it the Powers from on high have taken their stand, gazing on the beauty of its streams, since they perceive more clearly than we the power of what lies before us and its unapproachable flashing rays. Just as if one were to put one's hand or tongue into molten gold—if that were possible—he would at once make the object golden,

13 Cf. Gen. 2.10; Apoc. 22.1,2.

the mystery lying before us here affects the soul, but much more so. The stream gushes up more vigorously than fire; it does not burn, however, but only cleanses what it touches.

This Blood was formerly foreshadowed continually in altars, in sacrifices of the Law. This is the price of the world; by it Christ purchased the Church; by it He adorned her entirely. Just as a man in buying slaves gives gold and, if he desires to beautify them, does this with gold, so also Christ has both purchased us with His Blood and adorned us with His Blood. Those who share in this Blood have taken their stand with angels, and archangels, and the Powers from on high, clad in the royal livery of Christ and grasping spiritual weapons. But I have not yet mentioned anything great, for they are wearing the King Himself.

However, since it is a great and wonderful thing, if you approach with purity you come unto salvation, but if with conscious unworthiness, unto punishment and dishonor. 'For he that eats and drinks the Lord unworthily,' Scripture says, 'eats and drinks judgment to himself.'[14] If, then, those who defile the royal purple are punished in the same way as those who have rent it, why is it unfitting that those who receive the [sacred] Body with unworthy dispositions have in store for them the same punishment as those who pierced it through with nails? Indeed, see how Paul has described the fearful punishment in the words: 'A man making void the law of Moses dies without any mercy on the word of two or three witnesses; how much worse punishments do you think he deserves who has trodden under foot the Son of God, and has regarded as unclean the blood of the covenant through which he was sanctified.'[15]

Let us who enjoy such blessings, beloved, take heed to ourselves, and when we are tempted to utter a sinful word, or when we find ourselves being carried away by anger or

---

14 1 Cor. 11.29.
15 Heb. 10.28,29.

some other such passion, let us reflect on what privileges we have been granted, what Spirit it is whose presence we enjoy, and this thought will check in us the unruly passions. How long, in truth, shall we be attached to present things? How long shall we remain asleep? How long shall we not take thought for our own salvation? Let us remember what privileges God has bestowed on us, let us give thanks, let us glorify Him, not only by faith, but also by our very works, in order that we may obtain blessings also in the world to come, by the grace and mercy of our Lord Jesus Christ with whom glory be to the Father, together with the Holy Spirit, now and always, and forever and ever. Amen.

Homily 47 (John 6.54-72)

'Jesus therefore said to them: Amen, amen, I say to you, unless you eat the flesh of the Son of Man, and drink his blood, you shall not have life in you. He who eats my flesh and drinks my blood has life in himself.'[1]

When we discuss spiritual things, let there be nothing worldly in our souls, nothing of earth. On the contrary, let all such things depart from us, let them be banished, and let us become engrossed only in hearing the word of God. If every disturbing element is repressed upon a king's visiting a city, much more ought we to listen with great docility and with much reverence when the Spirit speaks to us. I say this because today's text merits reverential awe. And now, listen to me as I explain how.

'Amen, I say to you,' He says, 'unless you eat my flesh, and drink my blood, you shall not have life in you.' Since they had said previously that this was impossible, He now pointed out that it not only was not impossible, but that it was even very necessary. Therefore He added: 'He who

---

1 John 6.54-55.

eats my flesh and drinks my blood has life everlasting and I will raise him up on the last day.' Since He had said: 'If anyone eat of this bread, he will not die forever,' and they were likely to object to this, as they also would do in the words which I quoted previously: 'Abraham is dead, and the prophets, and how canst thou say, "He will never taste death"?'[2] He went on to mention the resurrection, to forestall their objection and to make it clear that death is not final. And He continually directed the discussion to the subject of the mysteries to show that the matter is essential, and that it is altogether necessary for them to take place.

'For my flesh is food indeed, and my blood is drink indeed.' What does this mean? Either He desired to say this: 'This is indeed food since it saves the soul,' or to give them assurance with regard to His words, so that they would not think that what was said was a riddle or a parable, but would know that it was necessary actually to eat His Body.

Next, He declared: 'He who eats my flesh abides in me.' He said this to show that he who eats His flesh becomes closely united with Him. But the words that follow seem to be disconnected unless we study their meaning. For what connection is there, you will say, after declaring: 'He who eats my flesh abides in me,' to add: 'As the living Father has sent me, and as I live because of the Father'? Actually, the statement follows very logically. Since He kept mentioning eternal life repeatedly, He added the words 'abides in me' to confirm that idea. 'For if a man abides in me, and I am alive, it is evident that he also will be alive.'

He then said: 'As the living Father has sent me.' Now this is a comparison and a simile. What He meant is some such thing as this: 'I live in the same manner as the Father does.' But, that you might not think that He is unbegotten, He at once added the words: 'because of the Father,' not, however, to indicate that He has need of any vivifying source

---

2 John 8.52.

for His life. Before this, indeed, He had said, to refute this: 'For as the Father has life in himself, even so he has given to the Son also to have life in himself.'[3] Now, if He needs a vivifying source, it follows that the Father has not 'given' in the way mentioned, and the statement is false; for, if He has 'given' as described, He will afterwards need no one else to support Him.

What, then, does 'because of the Father' mean? Here He was merely hinting at the cause. He meant something like this: 'As the Father is living, so do I also live. So, he who eats Me shall also live because of me.' Here He meant not merely life, but the blessed life. The context makes it clear that He was speaking not merely of life, but of that glorious and ineffable one, for all are alive, even unbelievers and the uninitiated, who do not eat of that Flesh. Do you see that the discussion was not about this life, but about that other? It meant something like this: 'He who eats my flesh will not perish when he dies, nor will he be punished.' However He was not speaking of the general resurrection, for all men alike will rise, but of that of the elect, the glorious one, which brings with it a reward.

'This is the bread that has come down from heaven; not as your fathers ate the manna, and died. He who eats this bread shall live forever.' He kept returning continually to the same topic, so as to impress it on the minds of His listeners and also to instill belief in the doctrine of the resurrection and in that of everlasting life (since instruction on these matters was fundamental). That is why He added mention of the resurrection when He said 'life everlasting.'[4] At the same time, also, He did so to point out that this 'life' is not the present one, but that after the resurrection. 'Now, whence is this proved,' you ask? From the Scriptures, for He sent them to consult them on all occasions, bidding them

---

3 John 5.26.
4 Cf. John 6.55,56.

to get this knowledge from them. And when He said: 'gives life to the world' He was even inciting them to emulation, so that, because of the unrest awakened in them at the thought of others enjoying the gift, they would not remain without it.

He also recalled the manna to them repeatedly, both to point out the difference [between it and that other Bread] and to spur them on to faith. For, if it was possible to support their ancestors' life for forty years without food and drink, and all that goes with them, much more would this be possible now when He had come to accomplish greater things. Besides, if when those were merely figures, men gathered without sweat or toil what was bestowed, now when it was very different it would seem much more possible both not to die and to enjoy the true life.

He did well to remind them often of 'life,' since all men have a desire for it, and nothing is as sweet as not to die. Further, even in the Old Testament this promise occurs: length of life, and many days; now, however, it is not merely length of life, but life without end. At the same time He desired also to show that He was now revoking the punishment resulting from sin, destroying that well-known sentence of death and substituting for former blessings, not merely life, but everlasting life.

'These things he said when teaching in the synagogue at Capharnaum,' the town where most of His miracles took place, so that He should have obtained a most attentive hearing. And why did He teach in the synagogue and in the Temple? He wished, on the one hand, to catch the crowd, and He desired also to show that He was not in opposition to His Father.

'Many of his disciples, when they heard this, said, "This is a hard saying," ' What is the meaning of 'hard'—harsh, toilsome, annoying? He was saying no such thing, for He was not discoursing of mundane matters, but of doctrine, discussing from every angle faith in Himself. What, then, is the meaning of the words: 'It is a hard saying'? Because He proclaimed life and resurrection? Because He said He had come down from heaven? Or because it is not possible for him to be saved who does not eat His flesh? Are these sayings hard, I ask you? Who would say so? What, then, does 'hard' mean? Hard to understand, too great for their weakness, causing great fear. They thought He was making exaggerated claims in excess of His own dignity and beyond His power. That is why they said: 'Who can listen to it?' perhaps making excuse for themselves, since they were about to go away.

'But Jesus, knowing in himself that his disciples were murmuring at this,' then said (for it is a proof of His divinity that He can bring to light unspoken thoughts): 'Does this scandalize you? What then if you should see the Son of Man ascending where he was before?' He had done this also in the case of Nathanael, when He said: 'Because I said to thee that I saw thee under the fig tree, thou dost believe. Greater things than these shalt thou see.' And also in the case of Nicodemus: 'No one has ascended into heaven except the Son of Man who is in heaven.'[5]

What, then, was He but adding difficulties to difficulties? By no means. Perish the thought! But He desired to attract them by the greatness of His teachings and by their fullness. If He had said merely: 'I have come down from heaven,' and had added nothing more, He would have given greater offense. But, since He had said: 'My body is the life of the world,' and, 'As the living Father has sent me and as I live because of the Father,' when He also said: 'I have come down from heaven,' He dispelled any difficulty. If a man should say but one great thing of himself he could be suspected of lying, but if he enumerates such great things one after the other, he removes suspicion. Well, then, it was not

---

5 John 1.50; 3.13.

with desire to increase the scandal that He said this, but to dispel it. Anyone who thought He was the son of Joseph would not have accepted His words, while anyone who was convinced that He had come down from heaven and would ascend there would more readily give credence to His words.

Besides this, He added still another explanation in the words: 'It is the Spirit that gives life; the flesh profits nothing.' What He meant is something like this: 'What is said of Me must be heard with the spiritual faculties, for he who hears it merely carnally gains nothing and derives no useful profit.' It was merely earthly to inquire how He had come down from heaven, and to think that He was the son of Joseph, and to say: 'How can he give us his flesh to eat?' All these are earthly reflections on matters which ought to be thought of in a mystical and spiritual sense.

But you will say: 'How could those men understand what in the world was meant by eating flesh?' Even so, they ought to have awaited the opportune time to acquire this understanding; they ought to have asked questions without growing weary of doing so. 'The words that I have spoken to you are spirit and life;' that is, are divine and spiritual, with no carnal or natural application. They are both free from the necessity of all such and independent of the laws that govern things of earth, and have another, and different, sense. Therefore, just as He here said 'the spirit' instead of 'listening with the spiritual faculties,' so when He said 'flesh' He did not mean 'earthly things' but 'listening to Him with an earthly view,' at the same time telling them by implication that they always had earthly desires, when they ought to have been seeking spiritual things. For if a person listens with an earthly view, he gains no profit.

What, then? Is not His flesh, flesh? Of course, it is. How, then, could He say: 'The flesh profits nothing'? He was not speaking of His own flesh—perish the thought!—but of those who hear His words with an earthly mind. And what is meant by understanding them 'carnally'? It is to look merely at the literal sense and not to penetrate the meaning more deeply. This is indeed 'carnally,' for one ought not to come to a conclusion in this way from what lies before his eyes, but must penetrate beneath all mysteries with inward eyes. This, in truth, is 'spiritually.' If, therefore, he who does not eat His flesh and drink His blood has not life in him, how does the flesh profit nothing, since, without it, it is not possible to live? Do you perceive that the words 'The flesh profits nothing' are not said of His flesh, but of listening to Him carnally?

'But there are some among you who do not believe.' Once more, according to His custom, He gave additional weight to His words, both by foretelling the future and by showing that He was speaking, not out of a desire for their esteem but out of concern for them. And by saying 'some,' He was excepting His disciples. Now, from the beginning He had been saying: 'You have seen me and you do not believe,' and here: 'There are some among you who do not believe.' He knew from the beginning who did not believe and who would betray him. And He said: 'This is why I have said, "No one can come to me unless he is enabled to do so by my Father in heaven." '

Here the Evangelist is implying to us the permissive will and long-suffering of divine Providence. The words 'from the beginning' are not used merely casually, but that you may learn of His previous foreknowledge, that He knew His betrayer even before these words, and not simply after they had murmured or after they were scandalized, but even before this, which was a proof of His divinity.

He then added the words, 'unless he is enabled to do so by my Father in heaven,' to persuade them to consider God, not Joseph, as His Father, and to point out that faith in Him is not a matter of chance. He as much as says this:

'Those who do not believe do not disturb, or vex, or astonish Me; I knew this of old, before they existed; I knew whom my Father "has enabled" [to come to Me].' And when you hear 'has enabled' do not think that the grace has been merely allotted by chance, but believe this: that he who makes himself worthy to receive it is the one who receives it.

'From this time many of his disciples turned back and no longer went about with him.' The Evangelist did well to say, not 'went away,' but 'turned back,' thus making it clear that when they cut themselves off from Him they were cutting short their growth in virtue and that they lost the faith which they once had possessed. The twelve, however, did not act thus. Therefore, He said to them: 'Do you also wish to go away?' to show once again that He did not need their ministry and worship, and to point out that it was not for this reason that He led them about with Him. For, how could one who said these words to them be in need of them?

But why did He not praise them? Why did He not show admiration of them? In the first place to preserve His dignity as teacher, and, then, to show that it was a necessity for them to be drawn to Him in this way. If He praised them, they would have reacted in human fashion and concluded they were doing Him a favor, but by showing that He did not need their company He held them to Him the more firmly. And notice how prudently He spoke. He did not say: 'Go away,' since that would have been the command of one who was driving them away, but asked a question: 'Do you also wish to go away?' These were the words of one avoiding all force and compulsion and not wishing anyone to be bound to Him by a feeling of shame, but, rather, by a feeling of gratitude.

Besides, by not upbraiding them openly, but gently appealing to them, He showed how we ought to act in such circumstances. However, we manifest quite the contrary reaction

—and understandably so, since we do everything through a desire for our own glory. Therefore, we think that our prestige suffers loss if our following drops away from us. But He did not practice wiles on His followers as we do, nor did He drive them off from Him, but merely asked them a question. It was not, I repeat, the action of one who scorned them, but of one who did not wish to hold them by force and compulsion. In this way it was the same whether they remained or went away.

What did Peter then say? 'To whom shall we go? Thou hast the words of everlasting life, and we have come to believe and to know that thou art the Christ, the Son of the living God.' Do you perceive that it was not really His words that were offensive but the inattentiveness and apathy and ignorance of [many of] His hearers? I say this because, even if He had said nothing, they would have been scandalized and would not have ceased to be so, since their thoughts were always centered on bodily nourishment and attached to things of earth. Moreover, those who were with the Twelve also heard Him; nevertheless, they showed a feeling just the opposite of theirs when they said: 'To whom shall we go?' These words were indicative of a great and tender love, for they showed that their Master was dearer to them than all else—father and mother and all the rest—and that, if they departed from Him, they had nowhere to go for refuge.

Next, lest Peter might seem to have said the words: 'To whom shall we go?' because they had no other refuge, he at once added: 'Thou hast words of everlasting life.' Some, to be sure, had listened to Him carnally, and with human reasonings, but these heard Him spiritually and entrusted all His teaching to faith. That is why Christ said: 'The words that I have spoken to you are spirit'; that is: 'Do not conceive the notion that My doctrine is subject to the sequence of events and the necessity of human things. Spiritual things are not of this kind and are not constrained to be enslaved by the laws of earth. Paul also makes this clear when he says: 'Do not say in thy heart, Who shall ascend into heaven? (that is, to bring down Christ); or, Who shall descend into the abyss? (that is, to bring up Christ from the dead).'[6]

'Thou hast words of everlasting life.' They had already accepted the resurrection and all that will be appointed therein. And see how this lover of his brethren, this warm-hearted friend, spoke out in the name of the whole group, for he did not say: 'I know' but 'We know.' And more than this, notice how he came near using the very words of the Master, not the same ones as the Jews. They had said: 'This is the son of Joseph,' while he said: 'Thou art the Christ, the Son of the living God,' and 'Thou hast words of everlasting life,' perhaps because he had often heard Him saying: 'He who believes in me has everlasting life.'[7] Indeed, by recalling His very words he showed that he cherished all that Christ said.

What did Christ do then? He did not praise Peter; He did not show admiration, though He did this on other occasions. On the contrary, what did He say this time? 'Have I not chosen you, the Twelve? Yet one of you is a devil.' Because Peter had said: 'We have come to believe,' Christ excluded Judas from the group. Elsewhere, in truth, he said nothing about the disciples, but when Christ said: 'Who do you say that I am?' he said: 'Thou art the Christ, the Son of the living God.'[8] On this occasion, however, when he said: 'We have come to believe,' Christ with reason did not allow Judas to be included in the group. He did this to check the wickedness of the traitor from the very start, though He knew that He would effect nothing, yet doing what He could.

Furthermore, see His wisdom: He neither disclosed the

6 Rom. 10.6,7.
7 John 6.47.
8 Matt. 16.15.

traitor's identity nor did He permit him to remain altogether concealed: the former, in order that he might not act brazenly and become more obstinate; the latter, in order that, thinking he was unobserved, he might not continue his daring behavior without fear. And that is why, as the discussion progressed, He accused him more openly. At first He merely included him with the rest when He said: 'There are some among you who do not believe.' (And the Evangelist makes it clear that He included the traitor, also, in this, by saying: 'For he knew from the beginning who they were who did not believe, and who it was who should betray him.') But since he persisted, He added a stronger charge: 'One of you is a devil,' yet made the fear common to all of them, wishing to protect him.

At this point it is worth while to study why it was that the disciples now said nothing, while later they feared, and doubted, and looked at one another, inquiring: 'Is it I, Lord?'[9] And Peter made a sign to John to find out the traitor and to inquire of the Master who he was. What, then, is the explanation? Peter had not yet heard: 'Get behind me, Satan;'[10] therefore, he had no fear.

But when he had been rebuked—even though he spoke out of deep feeling, Christ did not praise him, but he even heard 'Satan'—when after this experience, he heard the words: 'One of you will betray me,' with reason did he then finally fear. However, Christ did not now say: 'One of you will betray me,' but spoke in a different way: 'One of you is a devil.' That is why they did not understand what was meant, but thought they were merely being reproved for their sinfulness.

Why, then, did He say: 'Have I not chosen you, the Twelve? Yet one of you is a devil'? To show that His teaching was not in any way colored by flattery. Since they alone re-

---

9 Matt. 26.22.
10 Matt. 16.23.

mained after all had left Him, and they were acknowledging through Peter that He was the Christ, in order that they might not think that on this account He was going to cater to them, He did away with the possibility of their entertaining this notion. What He meant is something like this: 'Nothing keeps Me from reproving the wicked; do not think that because you have remained with Me I shall feel compelled to cater to you, or that because you have followed Me I shall not find fault with you if you do wrong. Indeed, a thing that ordinarily holds more weight than this with a teacher does not prevail over Me. The disciple who stays with his teacher does give proof of his love, but if he who has been chosen by the teacher deserts him, he gives the teacher a reputation for foolishness in the eyes of the unwise. However, not even this prevents Me from giving reproofs.'

This charge, to be sure, the heathen even now cast at Christ, bitterly and foolishly. God is not wont to make men good by compulsion and force, and His election and choice are not coercive of those called, but, rather, persuasive. And that you may learn that the vocation does not coerce, consider how many of those called have been lost. It is plain from this that salvation and damnation lie in our will.

Therefore, when we hear these things, let us learn always to be careful and vigilant. If he who was classed among that saintly company, who had enjoyed so great a gift, who had worked miracles (for he, also, along with the rest, was one of those sent to raise the dead and to heal lepers), when he had become infected with the dread evil of greed, even betrayed his own Master, and neither his good works helped him, nor his gifts, nor his being with Him, nor his healing, nor the washing of his feet, nor partaking at His table, nor his custody of the purse, but these things became even causes of punishment for him—let us also fear that we may ever imitate Judas by avarice.

You do not betray Christ? When you neglect a poor man

wasted with hunger, or perishing with cold, you are liable to the same punishment as Judas. And when we partake of the mysteries unworthily we are lost in the same way as those who kill Christ. When we rob, when we despoil those weaker than we, we shall draw upon ourselves the greatest punishment, and very rightly so. How long, indeed, will the love of present things, vain and foolish as they are, hold us thus captive? Wealth is among the vain things in which there is no profit. How long shall we be attached to trifles? How long shall we not look to heaven, not live soberly, not have our fill of these earthly and passing things?

Do we not learn their worthlessness by experience? Let us consider those who have been wealthy before us. Are not all those things a dream? Are they not a shadow and a flower? Are they not a stream that flows by? Are they not a tale and a story? A certain man was rich, and where now is his wealth? It has perished and vanished, but the sins he committed remain, and the punishment of his sins. Nay, rather, if there were no punishment and no kingdom to come, it would still be a necessity for those who have a race and family like ours to be treated with respect, for those who have feelings like ours to awaken our pity. As it is, we feed dogs, and many of us feed asses and bears, and different wild beasts, while we neglect a man who is wasted with hunger. In truth, a different species is dearer to us than our own, and we esteem our own race less than creatures which are not of it and are not related to us.

'But,' you object, 'is it not a good thing to build fine houses, and to have many slaves, and to recline and look up at a golden roof?' In all truth, it is a vain and foolish thing. There are other dwellings much more splendid and grand than these; you must gladden your eyes with such as those, for no one will hinder you. Do you wish to see a most beautiful ceiling? As evening descends, look at the sky adorned with stars. 'But that is not my ceiling,' you will say. But it is yours, much more than that other. And I say this because it has been made for you and is yours in common with your brothers, while the other is not yours, but belongs to your heirs after your death. Besides, the one can be of the greatest assistance by drawing you to the Creator by its beauty, while the other will be of the greatest harm to you by becoming your most powerful accuser on the day of judgment, since it itself has been covered with gold, while Christ has not had even the necessary clothing.

Accordingly, let us not engage in such foolishness; let us not pursue fleeting things, while we flee from those that remain steadfast; let us not give up our salvation, but cleave to the hope to come: the aged, on the one hand, since they know clearly that little time of life remains to us; the young, on the other hand, because they are undoubtedly convinced that not much is left. 'That day is to come as a thief in the night.'[11] Therefore, since we know these truths, let those of us who are women encourage their husbands, and let men exhort their wives. Let us teach younger men and maidens, and let us all instruct one another to despise the things of this life and long for those of the next, that we may be able to obtain them by the grace and mercy of our Lord Jesus Christ, through whom and with whom glory be to the Father, together with the Holy Spirit, now and always, and forever and ever. Amen.

---

11 1 Thess. 5.2.

THE FATHERS OF THE CHURCH SERIES

(A series of approximately 100 volumes when completed)

486

488

VOL. 18: ST. AUGUSTINE (1953)
LETTERS 83-130 (vol. 2), (trans. by Sr. Wilfrid Parsons)

VOL. 19: EUSEBIUS PAMPHILI (1953)
ECCLESIASTICAL HISTORY, Bks. 1-5 (trans. by Deferrari)

VOL. 20: ST. AUGUSTINE (1953)
LETTERS 131-164 (vol. 3), (trans. by Sr. Wilfrid Parsons)

VOL. 21: ST. AUGUSTINE (1953)
CONFESSIONS (trans. by Bourke)

VOL. 22: ST. GREGORY OF NAZIANZEN and ST. AMBROSE (1953)
FUNERAL ORATIONS (trans. by McCauley, Sullivan, McGuire, Deferrari)

VOL. 23: CLEMENT OF ALEXANDRIA (1954)
CHRIST, THE EDUCATOR (trans. by Wood)

VOL. 24: ST. AUGUSTINE (1954)
CITY OF GOD, Bks. XVII-XXII (trans. by Walsh and Honan)

VOL. 25: ST. HILARY OF POITIERS (1954)
THE TRINITY (trans. by McKenna)

VOL. 26: ST. AMBROSE (1954)
LETTERS 1-91 (trans. by Sr. M. Melchior Beyenka)

VOL. 27: ST. AUGUSTINE (1955)—Treatises on Marriage and Other Subjects:
THE GOOD OF MARRIAGE (trans. by Wilcox)
ADULTEROUS MARRIAGES (trans. by Huegelmeyer)
HOLY VIRGINITY (trans. by McQuade)
FAITH AND WORKS, THE CREED, IN ANSWER TO THE JEWS (trans. by Sr. Marie Liguori Ewald)
FAITH AND THE CREED (trans. by Russell)
THE CARE TO BE TAKEN FOR THE DEAD (trans. by Lacy)
THE DIVINATION OF DEMONS (trans. by Brown)

VOL. 28: ST. BASIL (1955)
LETTERS 186-368 (vol. 2), (trans. by Sr. Agnes Clare Way)

490

BR
60
F3 C4
v.1

Chrysotomus, Joannes, Saint,
    Patriarch of Constantinople,
    d. 407.
    Commentary on Saint John the
apostle and evalgelist, homilies 1-47.

BR60 F3 C4
+Commentary on Sa+Chrysotomus, Joa

0 00 02 0025833 3
MIDDLEBURY COLLEGE